Quick Tax Facts—2004 Tax Act Changes in Context

10-Year Tax Forecast

The chart below provides important amounts and percentages for 2002 through 2011. Changes made by the Working Families Tax Relief Act of 2004 are indicated in the shaded portion of the chart. See the Explanations in CCH's *Working Families Tax Relief Act of 2004: Law, Explanation and Analysis* for complete discussions of the changes.

		2002	2003	2004	2005	2006	2007	2008	2009	2010	2011
EXPANSION OF 10% BRACKET											
Taxable income limit—joint filers		$12,000	$14,000	$14,000*	$14,000*	$14,000*	$14,000*	$14,000*	$14,000*	$14,000*	No 10% bracket
Taxable income limit—single filers		$6,000	$7,000	$7,000*	$7,000*	$7,000*	$7,000*	$7,000*	$7,000*	$7,000*	No 10% bracket
MARRIAGE PENALTY RELIEF											
Basic standard deduction for joint filers—Percentage of single filer amount	Did not apply		200%	200%	200%	200%	200%	200%	200%	200%	ply
15% bracket size for joint filers—Percentage of 15% bracket size for single filers	Did not apply		200%	200%	200%	200%	200%	200%	200%	200%	ply
CHILD TAX CREDIT											
Amount per child		$600	$1,000	$1,000	$1,000	$1,000	$1,000	$1,000	$1,000	$1,000	$500
AMT EXEMPTION											
Joint filers		$49,000	$58,000	$58,000	$58,000	$45,000	$45,000	$45,000	$45,000	$45,000	,000
Single filers		$35,750	$40,250	$40,250	$40,250	$33,750	$33,750	$33,750	$33,750	$33,750	3,750

*before adjustment for inflation

Quick Tax Facts—2004 Tax Act Changes in Context

Extended Provisions

The chart below highlights some of the key expired provisions that were extended by the Working Families Tax Relief Act of 2004. See the Explanations in CCH's *Working Families Tax Relief Act of 2004: Law, Explanation and Analysis* for complete discussions of all of the extended provisions.

Extended Provision	Was Scheduled to Expire On	Now Extended Through	Reported On
Research credit	6/30/04	12/31/05	Form 6765
Work opportunity credit	12/31/03	12/31/05	Forms 5884, 8850
Welfare-to-work credit	12/31/03	12/31/05	Forms 8861, 8850
Expensing of environmental remediation costs	12/31/03	12/31/05	Taxpayer's income tax return
Renewable electricity production credit	12/31/03	12/31/05	Form 8835
Repeal of credit phaseout for qualified electric vehicles	12/31/03	12/31/05	Form 8834
Repeal of deduction phaseout for qualified clean-fuel vehicles	12/31/03	12/31/05	Taxpayer's income tax return
Donations of qualified computers, enhanced deduction	12/31/03	12/31/05	Form 8283
Teacher's classroom expenses, above-the-line deduction	12/31/03	12/31/05	Form 1040 or 1040A
Offset of personal credits against regular tax and AMT	12/31/03	12/31/05	Form 1040, 1040A, 6251
Availability of Archer medical savings accounts (MSAs)	12/31/03	12/31/05	Forms 1099-MSA, 5498-MSA, 8853
Tax incentives for investment in District of Columbia	12/31/03	12/31/05	Forms 8859, 8844
NY Liberty Bonds, authority to issue	12/31/04	12/31/09	Form 8038
NY Liberty Advance Refunding Bonds, authority to issue	12/31/04	12/31/05	Form 8038, 8038-G, 8038-GC

TAX LEGISLATION 2004

Working Families Tax Relief Act of 2004

Law, Explanation and Analysis

CCH Editorial Staff Publication

CCH INCORPORATED
Chicago

A WoltersKluwer Company

This publication is designed to provide accurate and authoritative information in regard to the subject matter covered. It is sold with the understanding that the publisher is not engaged in rendering legal, accounting, or other professional service. If legal advice or other expert assistance is required, the services of a competent professional person should be sought.

ISBN 0-8080-1205-3

©2004, **CCH** INCORPORATED

4025 W. Peterson Ave.
Chicago, IL 60646-6085
1 800 248 3248
http://tax.cchgroup.com

Working Families Tax Relief Act of 2004

Something for Everyone

Two weeks before its scheduled adjournment for the November 2004 election, Congress, with bi-partisan support, approved a $146 billion tax package of "middle-class" tax benefits. After months of political wrangling, the Working Families Tax Relief Act of 2004 sailed through Congress on September 23, 2004, with a 339-65 vote in the House and a 92-3 vote in the Senate, after a compromise was reached to drop revenue offsets to help pay for these provisions. As we go to press, President Bush has indicated that he will sign the bill into law.

The bill contains something for everyone. Although its primary focus was relief for married taxpayers with children, the extension of the increased alternative minimum tax exclusion is the most costly provision included in the legislation for the period to which it applies. Several business tax provisions that had generally expired at the end of 2003 were retroactively extended through 2005, and tax provisions needing technical corrections were addressed. Some of these, such as the provisions relating to qualified dividends, are substantive in nature.

The Act extends through 2010 several individual tax cuts originally scheduled to expire at the end of 2004:

- $1,000 child tax credit,

- elimination of the marriage penalty in the standard deduction and the 15-percent tax bracket, and

- the expansion of the 10-percent income tax bracket.

These provisions remain subject to the automatic sunset provision contained in the Economic Growth and Tax Relief Reconciliation Act of 2001 (P.L. 107-16). Absent future legislation to make them permanent, these provisions will disappear at the end of 2010 or will revert to pre-2001 Act law.

The 15-percent refundability percentage for the child tax credit was also accelerated one year to 2004. In addition, a new uniform definition of child under several tax provisions was enacted, and the definition of earned income was expanded to include combat pay for purposes of the refundable child tax credit and earned income credit. Alternative minimum tax relief that had originally been enacted as part of the 2003 Act was extended for one year through 2005.

Several business incentives, some of which have application to individuals, that had for the most part expired in 2003 were retroactively extended generally through 2005. These include:

- research credit,

- work opportunity tax credit and welfare-to-work tax credit,

- repeal of the credit phaseout for electric vehicles and the deduction phaseout for clean-fuel vehicles,

- above-the-line deduction for a teacher's classroom expenses,

- charitable contributions of computer technology and equipment used for educational purposes and of scientific property used for research,

- credit for electricity from renewable resources,

- expensing of environmental remediation costs,

- tax incentives for investment in the District of Columbia, and

- New York Liberty Zone Bond incentives (issuing authority extended through 2009).

About This Work and CCH

CCH's *Working Families Tax Relief Act of 2004: Law, Explanation and Analysis* provides readers with a single integrated reference tool covering all aspects of the Working Families Tax Relief Act of 2004.

Along with the relevant Internal Revenue Code provisions, as amended by the Act, and supporting committee reports, CCH editors, together with several leading tax practitioners and commentators, have put together the most timely and complete practical analysis of the new law. Tax professionals looking for the Conference Report, including the related bill text, can find it in a separate CCH publication. Other books and tax services relating to the new legislation can be found at our website http://tax.cchgroup.com.

As always, CCH remains dedicated to responding to the needs of tax professionals in helping them quickly understand and work with these new laws as they take effect.

Mark A. Luscombe
Principal Analyst
CCH Tax and Accounting

September 2004

Outside Contributors

Sidney Kess
New York, New York

Vincent J. O'Brien
Vincent J. O'Brien, CPA, PC
Lynbrook, New York

Barbara J. Raasch
Ernst & Young LLP
New York, New York

Michael Schlesinger
Schlesinger & Sussman
New York, New York

Arthur M. Seltzer
Brown Smith Wallace LLC
St. Louis, Missouri

Prof. Joseph W. Walloch
University of California Riverside
Riverside, California

Gail T. Winawer
American Express Tax & Business Services, Inc.
New York, New York

CCH Tax and Accounting Publishing

EDITORIAL STAFF

¶ 1
Features of This Book

This publication is your complete guide to the Working Families Tax Relief Act of 2004 (H.R. 1308). The core portion of this publication contains the CCH Explanations and Analysis of the Act. The CCH Explanations outline all of the law changes and what they mean for you and your clients. The explanations feature practical guidance, examples, planning opportunities and strategies, as well as pitfalls to be avoided as a result of the law changes. Insights supplied by expert tax practitioners are highlighted throughout our analysis.

The law text and committee reports are reproduced following the analysis. Any new or amended Internal Revenue Code sections appear here, with changes highlighted in italics. You will also see the law text for portions of the Act that did not amend the tax code. The legislative history of each provision follows the law text. Relevant portions of the House Committee Report, Senate Committee Report, or Joint Committee Explanation make up the legislative history for each law change.

The book contains numerous other features designed to help you locate and understand the changes enacted in the 2004 Act. These features include cross references to related materials, detailed effective dates, and numerous finding tables and indexes. A more detailed description of these features appears below.

CCH EXPLANATIONS

CCH Explanations are designed to give you a complete, accessible understanding of the new law. Explanations are arranged by subject for ease of use. There are three main finding devices you can use to locate explanations on a given topic. These are:

- A detailed table of contents at the beginning of the publication listing all of the CCH Explanations on the new law;
- A table of contents preceding each chapter; and
- An extensive topical index covering all subjects under the 2004 Act.

Each CCH Explanation contains special features to aid in your complete understanding of the new law. These include:

- A background or prior law discussion that puts the law changes into perspective;
- Practitioner commentary incorporated throughout the explanations, identifying planning opportunities and strategies, as well as pitfalls to avoid;
- Editorial aids—examples, cautions, planning notes, elections, comments, compliance tips, and key rates and figures—that highlight the impact of the new law;
- Charts and examples illustrating the ramifications of specific law changes;
- Boldface captions at the end of each explanation identifying the Code sections added, amended or repealed, as well as the Act sections containing the changes;
- Cross references to the law and committee report paragraphs related to the explanation;
- A line highlighting the effective date of each law change, marked by a star symbol;

- References at the end of the discussion to related information in the Standard Federal Tax Reporter, Federal Tax Service and Federal Tax Guide.

The CCH Explanations begin at ¶105.

AMENDED CODE PROVISIONS

Changes to the Internal Revenue Code made by the Working Families Tax Relief Act of 2004 appear under the heading "Code Sections Added, Amended or Repealed." *Any changed or added law text is set out in italics.* Deleted Code text, or the Code provision prior to amendment, appears in the Amendment Notes following each reconstructed Code provision. An effective date for each Code change is also provided.

The amendment notes contain cross references to the corresponding Committee Reports and the CCH Explanations that discuss the new law. *The text of the Code begins at ¶5001.*

NON-CODE PROVISIONS

Sections of the Working Families Tax Relief Act of 2004 that do not amend the Internal Revenue Code appear in full text following "Code Sections Added, Amended or Repealed." Some of these "non-code" provisions amend prior tax acts, such as the Jobs and Growth Tax Relief Reconciliation Act of 2003 (P.L. 108-27) and the Economic Growth and Tax Relief Reconciliation Act of 2001 (P.L. 107-16). *The text of these provisions appears in Act Section order beginning at ¶7005.*

COMMITTEE REPORTS

Committee Reports explain the intent of Congress in enacting the provisions in the 2004 Act. Included in this publication is the Conference Committee Report accompanying H.R. 1308 (H.R. Conf. Rep. No. 108-696), which was filed on September 23, 2004. At the end of each section of Committee Report text, you will find references to the corresponding explanation and Code provisions. *These Committee Reports appear in Act Section order beginning at ¶10,001.*

EFFECTIVE DATES

A table listing the major effective dates provides you with a reference bridge between Code Sections and Act Sections and indicates the retroactive or prospective nature of the laws explained. *This effective date table begins at ¶20,001.*

SPECIAL FINDING DEVICES

Other special tables and finding devices in this book include:

- A table cross-referencing Code Sections to the CCH Explanations (*see ¶25,001*);

- A table showing all Code Sections added, amended or repealed (*see ¶25,005*);

- A table showing provisions of other acts that were amended (*see ¶25,010*);

- A table of Act Sections not amending the Internal Revenue Code (*see ¶25,015*);

- A table of Act Sections amending Code Sections (*see ¶25,020*);

- An explanation of the sunset provision contained in the 2004 Act (*see ¶29,001*); and

- A listing of clerical amendments to the Internal Revenue Code (*see ¶30,050*).

¶11

¶ 2
Table of Contents

¶ 3
Detailed Table of Contents

CHAPTER 1. INDIVIDUALS

CHAPTER 2. BUSINESS AND GOVERNMENT EXTENSIONS

CHAPTER 3. TECHNICAL CORRECTIONS

Chapter 1

Individuals

ACCELERATED TAX CUTS

¶ 105

Child Tax Credit Increased

Background

Taxpayers who have a qualifying child are eligible for the child tax credit under Code Sec. 24. A qualifying child must be the taxpayer's child, stepchild, sibling, step-sibling or a descendent of any of these, or an eligible foster child, who is under age 17 at the close of the calendar year. In addition, the child must be a U.S. citizen or resident alien, and qualify to be claimed as a dependent by the taxpayer. Prior to passage of the Jobs and Growth Tax Relief Reconciliation Act of 2003 (JGTRRA) (P.L. 108-27), the credit was scheduled to be $600 per qualifying child for 2003 and 2004, $700 for 2005 through 2008, $800 for 2009 and $1,000 for 2010. JGTRRA increased the child tax credit from $600 to $1,000 per qualifying child, effective for tax years 2003 and 2004. In 2003, the increase in the child tax credit was paid in advance, using the taxpayer's 2002 tax return as a basis for information. The child tax credit was scheduled to revert to the levels provided under the Economic Growth Tax Relief Reconciliation Act of 2001 (EGTRRA) (P.L. 107-16), decreasing to $700 per qualifying child for tax years 2005 through 2008, then rising to $800 for tax year 2009, and to $1,000 for tax year 2010. These amounts sunset for tax years beginning after Decem-

Background

ber 31, 2010; therefore, in tax year 2011 and thereafter, without legislative intervention, the child tax credit will return to $500 per qualifying child.

Working Families Tax Act Impact

Child credit amount increased for 2005 through 2009.—The new law increases the amount of the child credit to $1,000 for tax years 2005 through 2009 (Code Sec. 24(a), as amended by the Working Families Tax Relief Act of 2004). Thus, taxpayers who have one or more qualifying children under age 17 at the close of the calendar year may be entitled to a child tax credit of $1,000 per child for tax years through 2010.

Comment: The child tax credit amount had been increased to $1,000 by the Job and Growth Tax Relief Act for 2003 and 2004. Without the extension, the child tax credit amount would have reverted back to $700 for 2005 through 2008, increasing to $800 for 2009 and not reaching $1,000 until 2010.

Compliance Tip: Taxpayers must file either Form 1040 or Form 1040A to claim the child tax credit. The credit will be limited if the taxpayer's modified adjusted gross income exceeds a certain threshold amount ($75,000 for single taxpayers and $110,000 for joint filers). Taxpayers can generally use the worksheet provided in the instructions to these forms, but may be required to use the worksheet provided in IRS Publication 972 if their modified adjusted gross income exceeds the threshold amounts.

Caution Note: The $1,000 child credit amount is not adjusted annually for inflation.

Caution Note: The Conference Committee Report states that the provision generally applies to tax years beginning after December 31, 2004, which reflects the fact that the change made by Act Sec. 101(a) will not impact taxpayers until tax year 2005. This effective date is different from the effective date provided in Act Sec. 101(e) as noted below.

PRACTICAL ANALYSIS. Sidney Kess, New York, CCH consulting editor, author and lecturer, observes that Congress has done the right thing for over 25 million taxpayers who have claimed the child credit. The child credit is finally going to be $1,000 through 2010. Under the Economic Growth and Tax Relief Reconciliation Act of 2001 (EGTRRA), it was scheduled to increase gradually to $1,000 in 2010. It was raised to $1,000 in 2003 and 2004 in the Jobs and Growth Tax Relief Reconciliation Act of 2003 (JGTRRA) and was scheduled to go down to $700 in 2005. What a difference an election can make in the way tax legislation is enacted!

Couples going through a divorce should realize that the agreement as to which parent is entitled to claim the dependency exemption is more important than ever before since the credit is raised to $1,000 through 2010. The parent who is entitled to claim the dependency exemption is the one who may be eligible to claim the child tax credit.

For further information on this subject, consult any of the following CCH reporter explanations:

- Standard Federal Tax Reporter, 2004FED ¶3770.01
- Federal Tax Service, FTS § A:19.202
- Federal Tax Guide, 2004FTG ¶2222

¶105

★ *Effective date.* The provision applies to tax years beginning after December 31, 2003 (Act Sec. 101(e) of the Working Families Tax Relief Act of 2004).

EGTRRA sunset provision. The amendments made by Title I of the 2004 Working Families Tax Act are subject to the sunset provision found in Title IX of the Economic Growth and Tax Relief Reconciliation Act of 2001 (P.L. 107-16). These 2004 amendments are subject to the EGTRRA sunset provision to the same extent and in the same manner as the provision of EGTRRA to which the amendment relates (Act Sec. 105). See ¶ 29,001 for the CCH Explanation of the sunset provision.

Act Sec. 101(a) of the Working Families Tax Relief Act of 2004, amending Code Sec. 24(a); Act Sec. 101(e); Act Sec. 105. Law at ¶ 5020. Committee Report at ¶ 10,010.

¶ 110

Marriage Penalty Relief in Standard Deduction

Background

A marriage penalty exists when the tax on the combined income of a married couple exceeds the sum of the taxes that would be imposed if each spouse filed a separate return as a single person. This situation exists most often when both spouses have income. If one spouse does not work or has a small amount of income a marriage bonus may occur—that is, the couple pays less tax by filing a joint return than they would have if each spouse filed his or her own return. Although many factors can contribute to a marriage penalty, the two most significant are the disparity in the size of a married and single person's standard deduction and the income levels at which the various tax brackets are applied. Parity with respect to the first factor would require the standard deduction of a married couple to be twice as large as that of a single person. Parity with respect to the tax bracket factor would require the tax brackets of a married person to be applied to an amount of taxable income that is twice the amount of taxable income to which the same tax brackets of a single person apply.

The Economic Growth and Tax Relief Reconciliation Act of 2001 (EGTRRA) (P.L. 107-16) included provisions that addressed these two issues. First, EGTRRA included a provision to increase the size of a joint filer's 15-percent tax bracket over four years beginning in 2005 to an amount equal to twice the size of a single person's 15-percent tax bracket. EGTRRA also included a provision to increase the size of the standard deduction for joint filers to twice the size (i.e., 200 percent) of the standard deduction for a single filer. The standard deduction for joint filers was scheduled to increase beginning in 2005, with a phase-in completed in 2009. The phase-in percentages were 174 percent for 2005, 184 percent for 2006, 187 percent for 2007, 190 percent for 2008, and 200 percent for 2009 and 2010. The EGTRRA sunset provision, however, will reinstate prior law after 2010.

The Jobs and Growth Tax Relief Reconciliation Act of 2003 (JGTRRA) (P.L. 108-27) accelerated the phase-in of the increased standard deduction, providing that the standard deduction amount of a married taxpayer filing jointly (and surviving spouses) is twice the amount of the standard deduction amount of a single filer for tax years beginning in 2003 and 2004. In later tax years, the standard deduction of married taxpayers was to be based on the same applicable percentages that were scheduled to go into effect under the Economic Growth and Tax Relief Reconciliation Act of 2001 (EGTRRA) (P.L. 107-16).

Working Families Tax Act Impact

Marriage penalty relief in standard deduction extended.—The new law increases the basic standard deduction amount for joint returns to twice the basic standard deduction amount for single returns for tax years 2005 through 2008 (Code Sec. 63(c)(2), as amended by the Working Families Tax Relief Act of 2004). Thus, the basic standard deduction for joint returns is twice the basic standard deduction for single returns for tax years through 2010.

> **Comment:** The Economic Growth Tax Relief Reconciliation Act of 2001 (P.L. 107-16) had provided phase-in percentages beginning in 2005 for the marriage penalty benefit (doubling the amount of the standard deduction given to single taxpayers), scheduled for full phase-in for 2009 and 2010. The benefit was then accelerated by the Jobs and Growth Tax Relief Reconciliation Act of 2003 (P.L. 108-27) for 2003 and 2004 only.

> **Comment:** Prior to enactment of the new law, the standard deduction for married taxpayers filing joint returns would have been only 174 percent of the standard deduction amount for unmarried taxpayers for 2005 (or $8,700, which is 174% of $5,000), the standard deduction amount for unmarried taxpayers as projected by CCH. Under the new law, the 2005 projected standard deduction for married taxpayers filing joint returns is $10,000—twice the $5,000 standard deduction for single filers.

> **Key Rates and Figures:** The 2005 basic standard deduction amounts as projected by CCH under the new law are: $10,000 for married taxpayers filing joint returns and surviving spouses, $7,300 for head of household filers, and $5,000 for unmarried taxpayers and married taxpayers filing separate returns.

> **Planning Note:** A married taxpayer who itemizes deductions will not benefit from the increased standard deduction. However, as a result of the increase, fewer married taxpayers will need to itemize since their standard deduction could exceed their itemized deductions.

> **Caution Note:** The Conference Committee Report states that the extension of the marriage penalty relief in the standard deduction is effective for tax years beginning after December 31, 2004, which reflects the fact that the change made by Act Sec. 101(b) will not impact taxpayers until tax year 2005. This effective date is different from the effective date provided in Act Sec. 101(e) as noted below.

PRACTICAL ANALYSIS. Sidney Kess, New York, CCH consulting editor, author and lecturer, points out that for the past two presidential campaigns, eliminating the marriage penalty had been a major issue. With the enactment of the Economic Growth and Tax Relief Reconciliation Act of 2001 (EGTRRA), the hypocrisy of the legislators was obvious. Marriage penalty relief was scheduled to begin in the year 2005. And then it was scheduled to be phased in when it would be fully effective in 2009 and later. The Jobs and Growth Tax Relief Reconciliation Act of 2003 (JGTRRA) phased in the benefit to 2003 and 2004. Now, Congress has effectively given relief through 2010.

It is important to note that the increase in the standard deduction for a married couple 65 or older for 2004 will result in a deduction of $11,600 ($9,700 plus the additional age deduction of $1,900). Many seniors do not have itemized deductions exceeding this amount.

It is important to note that the increase in the standard deduction does not benefit married taxpayers claiming itemized deductions.

¶110

For further information on this subject, consult any of the following CCH reporter explanations:

- Standard Federal Tax Reporter, 2004FED ¶ 6023.01
- Federal Tax Service, FTS § A:12.61[2]
- Federal Tax Guide, 2004FTG ¶ 6020

★ *Effective date.* The provision applies to tax years beginning after December 31, 2003 (Act Sec. 101(e) of the Working Families Tax Relief Act of 2004).

EGTRRA sunset provision. The amendments made by Title I of the 2004 Working Families Tax Act are subject to the sunset provision found in Title IX of the Economic Growth and Tax Relief Reconciliation Act of 2001 (P.L. 107-16). These 2004 amendments are subject to the EGTRRA sunset provision to the same extent and in the same manner as the provision of EGTRRA to which the amendment relates (Act Sec. 105 of the 2004 Working Families Tax Relief Act). See ¶ 29,001 for the CCH Explanation of the sunset provision.

Act Sec. 101(b)(1) of the Working Families Tax Relief Act of 2004, amending Code Sec. 63(c)(2); Act Sec. 101(b)(2)(A), amending Code Sec. 63(c)(4); Act Sec. 101(b)(2)(B), striking Code Sec. 63(c)(7); Act Sec. 101(e); Act Sec. 105. Law at ¶ 5100. Committee Report at ¶ 10,020.

¶ 115

Marriage Penalty Relief in 15-Percent Bracket

Background

A marriage penalty exists when the tax on the combined income of a married couple exceeds the sum of the taxes that would be imposed if each spouse filed a separate return as a single person. This situation exists most often when both spouses have income. If one spouse does not work or has a small amount of income, a marriage bonus may occur—that is, the couple pays less tax by filing a joint return than they would have if each spouse filed his or her own return. Although many factors can contribute to a marriage penalty, the two most significant are the disparity in the size of a married and single person's standard deduction and the income levels at which the various tax brackets are applied. Parity with respect to these two factors would require the standard deduction of a married couple to be twice as large as that of a single person and the tax brackets of a married person to be applied to an amount of taxable income that is twice the amount of taxable income to which the same tax brackets of a single person apply.

The Economic Growth and Tax Relief Reconciliation Act of 2001 (EGTRRA) (P.L. 107-16) included provisions that addressed these two issues. First, EGTRRA included a provision to increase the size of the standard deduction for joint filers to twice the size (i.e., 200 percent) of the standard deduction for a single filer. Under EGTRRA, the standard deduction of joint filers was scheduled to increase beginning in 2005, with the phase-in period completed in 2009. EGTRRA also provided a phased-in increase in the top end of the 15-percent tax bracket for married taxpayers filing jointly. The phase-in period, which was scheduled to start in 2005 and be completed in 2008, would have caused the amount of taxable income that falls within a joint filer's 15-percent tax bracket to gradually reach twice the amount (i.e., 200 percent) of the taxable income that falls within the 15-percent tax bracket of a single filer. For 2005, the applicable percentage was scheduled to be 180; for 2006, the applicable percentage was scheduled to be 187; and for 2007, the applicable percentage was scheduled to be 193. The marriage penalty relief was to be fully phased in at 200 percent for 2008 through 2010.

Background

The Jobs and Growth Tax Relief Reconciliation Act of 2003 (JGTRRA) (P.L. 108-27) increased the size of a joint filer's 15-percent tax bracket to twice the size of a single person's tax bracket for 2003 and 2004. Beginning in 2005, the size of a joint filer's 15-percent tax bracket was to be determined in accordance with the phase-in schedule enacted by EGTRRA (P.L. 107-16), as amended by JGTRRA (P.L. 108-27).

Working Families Tax Act Impact

Elimination of marriage penalty in 15-percent bracket.—The new law increases the size of the 15-percent rate bracket for joint returns to twice the size of the corresponding rate bracket for single returns for tax years 2005 through 2007 (Code Sec. 1(f)(8), as amended by the Working Families Tax Relief Act of 2004). Thus, the size of the 15-percent rate bracket for joint returns is twice the size of the corresponding rate bracket for single returns for tax years 2005 through 2010.

> **Comment:** The 2004 Working Families Tax Act also increases the standard deduction amount for joint returns to twice the standard deduction amount for single returns for tax years 2005 through 2008. See ¶110.

The following 2005 CCH-projected rate schedules are for taxpayers who are married filing jointly. The first schedule is projected by CCH under the new law. The second schedule was projected by CCH under prior law.

Married Filing Jointly Tax Brackets

2005 With New Law		2005 Without New Law	
2005 Taxable Income	*Tax Rate*	*2005 Taxable Income*	*Tax Rate*
$0—$14,600	10%	$0—$12,000	10%
$14,601—$59,400	15%	$12,001—$53,450	15%
$59,401—$119,950	25%	$53,451—$119,950	25%
$119,951—$182,800	28%	$119,951—$182,800	28%
$182,801—$326,450	33%	$182,801—$326,450	33%
Over $326,450	35%	Over $326,450	35%

> **Caution Note:** The Conference Committee Report states that the extension of the marriage penalty relief in the 15-percent bracket is effective for tax years beginning after December 31, 2004, which reflects the fact that the change made by Act Sec. 101(c) will not impact taxpayers until tax year 2005. This effective date is different from the effective date provided in Act Sec. 101(e) as noted below.

For further information on this subject, consult any of the following CCH reporter explanations:

- Standard Federal Tax Reporter, 2004FED ¶3270.01
- Federal Tax Service, FTS § A:1.42
- Federal Tax Guide, 2004FTG ¶1010

★ *Effective date.* The provision applies to tax years beginning after December 31, 2003 (Act Sec. 101(e) of the Working Families Tax Act of 2004).

EGTRRA sunset provision. The amendments made by Title I of the 2004 Working Families Tax Act are subject to the sunset provision found in Title IX of the Economic Growth and Tax Relief Reconciliation Act of 2001 (P.L. 107-16). These 2004 amend-

¶115

ments are subject to the EGTRRA sunset provision to the same extent and in the same manner as the provision of EGTRRA to which the amendment relates (Act Sec. 105 of the 2004 Working Families Tax Act). See ¶29,001 for the CCH Explanation of the sunset provision.

Act Sec. 101(c) of the Working Families Tax Relief Act of 2004, amending Code Sec. 1(f)(8); Act Sec. 101(e); Act Sec. 105. Law at ¶5005. Committee Report at ¶10,030.

¶120

10-Percent Tax Bracket Increase Extended

Background

The 10-percent tax bracket for individuals was added by the Economic Growth and Tax Relief Reconciliation Act of 2001 (EGTRRA) (P.L. 107-16), beginning in tax years after 2000. Under EGTRRA, the 10-percent bracket applied to: (1) the first $6,000 of taxable income for unmarried taxpayers and married taxpayers filing separately, (2) the first $10,000 of taxable income of head-of-household filers, and (3) the first $12,000 of taxable income of married taxpayers filing joint returns, for tax years 2001 through 2007. In tax years beginning in 2008 through 2010, the 10-percent bracket was scheduled to increase so that it would apply to: (1) the first $7,000 of taxable income for unmarried individuals and married taxpayers filing separate returns and (2) the first $14,000 of taxable income of married individuals filing joint returns.

The Jobs and Growth Tax Relief Reconciliation Act (JGTRRA) (P.L. 108-27) temporarily extended the increase in the 10-percent bracket scheduled for 2008, 2009, and 2010 under EGTRRA to also apply for tax years 2003 and 2004. Thus, for 2003, 2004, 2008, 2009, and 2010, the 10-percent tax bracket applied to the first $7,000 of taxable income for unmarried individuals and married taxpayers filing separate returns, and to the first $14,000 in taxable income of married individuals filing joint returns. JGTRRA provided for inflation adjustments in tax year 2004 and in tax years beginning after 2008. In the absence of congressional intervention, the 10-percent bracket would have returned to the schedule previously established under EGTRRA. Accordingly, it would have been applicable to the first $6,000 of taxable income for unmarried individuals and married taxpayers filing separate returns and to the first $12,000 for married taxpayers filing joint returns for tax years 2005 through 2007.

Working Families Tax Act Impact

10-percent individual tax bracket increase further extended.—The new law makes the expansion of the 10-percent bracket (also referred to as the initial bracket) applicable to tax years 2005 through 2007 (Code Sec. 1(i)(1)(B), as amended by the Working Families Tax Relief Act of 2004). Thus, for tax years through 2010, the 10-percent bracket applies to the first $7,000 of taxable income for unmarried individuals and married individuals filing separately and to the first $14,000 of taxable income of married individuals filing joint returns. The expansion of the 10-percent bracket has no effect on head-of-household filers. Taxable income subject to the 10-percent bracket for these taxpayers remains $10,000.

Comment: JGTRRA had temporarily applied the expanded 10-percent bracket for tax years 2003 and 2004. In tax years beginning after 2004, the taxable income levels for the 10-percent bracket would have reverted to the levels allowed under EGTRRA (i.e., $6,000 of taxable income for unmarried individuals and married individuals filing separate returns and $12,000 of taxable income for married taxpayers filing joint returns).

Comment: The 10-percent bracket will be adjusted for inflation in tax years beginning after 2003. JGTRRA had provided that the 10-percent bracket would be adjusted for inflation only in tax years 2004, 2009, and 2010.

Key Rates and Figures: For 2004, the 10-percent bracket applies to the first $7,150 of taxable income for unmarried taxpayers and married individuals filing separate returns and to the first $14,300 of taxable income of married taxpayers filing joint returns. For 2005, the top of the 10-percent bracket income level is projected by CCH to be $7,300 for unmarried individuals and married individuals filing separate returns and $14,600 for married taxpayers filing joint returns.

Caution Note: The Conference Committee Report states that the extension of the 10-percent bracket is effective for tax years beginning after December 31, 2004, which reflects the fact that the change made by Act Sec. 101(d) will not impact taxpayers until tax year 2005. This effective date is different from the effective date provided in Act Sec. 101(e) as noted below.

Caution Note: The sunset provision under EGTRRA continues to apply, therefore the 10-percent bracket does not apply to tax years after 2010.

PRACTICAL ANALYSIS. Sidney Kess, New York, CCH consulting editor, author and lecturer, points out that with the extension of the size of the 10-percent bracket for 2005 through 2010 at $7,000 for single individuals, more wealthy individuals might consider shifting income to children age 14 or older. In addition to a standard deduction of $4,850, the first $7,000 will be taxed only at the 10-percent rate, which may be substantially lower than the parent's rate.

For further information on this subject, consult any of the following CCH reporter explanations:

- Standard Federal Tax Reporter, 2004FED ¶3270.01
- Federal Tax Service, FTS § A:1.42
- Federal Tax Guide, 2004FTG ¶1010

★ *Effective date.* The provision applies to tax years beginning after December 31, 2003 (Act Sec. 101(e) of the Working Families Tax Relief Act of 2004).

EGTRRA sunset provision. The amendments made by Title I of the 2004 Working Families Tax Act are subject to the sunset provision found in Title IX of the Economic Growth and Tax Relief Reconciliation Act of 2001 (P.L. 107-16). These 2004 amendments are subject to the EGTRRA sunset provision to the same extent and in the same manner as the provision of EGTRRA to which the amendment relates (Act Sec. 105). See ¶29,001 for the CCH Explanation of the sunset provision.

Act Sec. 101(d) of the Working Families Tax Relief Act of 2004, amending Code Sec. 1(i)(1)(B) and (C); Act Sec. 101(e); Act Sec. 105. Law at ¶5005. Committee Report at ¶10,040.

<h1 style="text-align:center">¶125</h1>

Accelerated Increase of Child Tax Credit Refund

Background _____

The child tax credit is refundable for 2004 to the extent of 10 percent of the taxpayer's taxable earned income (which is taken into account in determining taxable income) in excess of $10,750 (indexed for inflation). For 2005 and thereafter, the

Background _____

percentage is increased to 15 percent. Families who have three or more children are allowed a refundable credit for the amount by which the taxpayer's social security taxes exceed the taxpayer's earned income credit, if that amount is greater than the refundable credit based on the taxpayer's taxable earned income in excess of $10,750. Note that the refundable portion of the child tax credit does not constitute income and is not treated as resources for purposes of determining eligibility or the amount or nature of benefits or assistance under any Federal program or any State or local program financed with Federal funds. For tax years beginning after December 31, 2010, the sunset provision of the Economic Growth and Tax Relief Reconciliation Act of 2001 applies to the 15-percent rule for allowing refundable child tax credits.

_____

Working Families Tax Act Impact

Lower-income families may take bigger child tax credit refund faster.—The increase in refundability of the child tax credit for lower income families, from 10 percent to 15 percent of the taxpayer's earned income in excess of $10,750 (with indexing), is accelerated to the beginning of 2004 (Code Sec. 24(d)(1)(B)(i), as amended by the Working Families Tax Relief Act of 2004).

PRACTICAL ANALYSIS. Gail T. Winawer of American Express Tax & Business Services, Inc., New York, New York, notes that the 2004 tax credit of $1,000 per child for 2004 will remain at $1,000 for 2005 through 2010. The credit is allowed to offset both the regular tax and alternative minimum tax (AMT). The AGI phaseout thresholds will stay at current levels as well, with no inflation adjustment. The credit is reduced by $50 for each $1,000 ($20,000 per child) of AGI above the phaseout base for each filing status. The 2005 to 2008 tax credit had been scheduled to go down to $700 per child, or $14,000 of AGI, and the AMT exemption was going to revert back to the amounts allowed for 2000. Obtaining the credit for both 2004 and 2005 would have required planning for the timing of bonuses and other possible income shifting. Since the credit will remain the same for quite a few years, planning is simplified and made more certain.

For parents who are divorced or legally separated, the parent who qualifies for the exemption for a dependent child is also entitled to the tax credit for that child. Because the credit amount will remain constant through 2010, divorced parents will find it easier to allocate the exemption between them.

The refundable portion of the child credit has been significantly increased by raising the refund from 10 to 15 percent of the taxpayer's earned income. A taxpayer with earned income as low as $17,417 could be eligible for a full refund of the child tax credit for one child.

Example. Sue has one child. Her earned income is $17,500 and her AGI is $25,000. Her child tax credit is $1,000. The refundable portion is calculated as 15 percent of earned income of $17,500 minus $10,750 (the inflation-adjusted threshold amount), or $1,012.50. Her potential refund of $1,000 must be reduced by her regular and alternative minimum taxes less the credit for child care, the credit for the elderly and the education credits. Assuming Sue has a regular tax of $950 and a child care credit of $700, she would be entitled to a refund of $750 ($1,000 − ($950 − $700)).

For further information on this subject, consult any of the following CCH reporter explanations:

- Standard Federal Tax Reporter, 2004FED ¶3770.01
- Federal Tax Service, FTS § A:19.202[2]
- Federal Tax Guide, 2004FTG ¶2222

★ *Effective date.* The provision is effective for tax years beginning after December 31, 2003 (Act Sec. 102 of the Working Families Tax Relief Act of 2004).

EGTRRA sunset provision. The amendments made by Title I of the 2004 Working Families Act are subject to the sunset provision found in Title IX of the Economic Growth and Tax Relief Reconciliation Act of 2001 (P.L. 107-16). These 2004 amendments are subject to the EGTRRA sunset provision to the same extent and in the same manner as the provision of EGTRRA to which the amendment relates (Act Sec. 105). See ¶29,001 for the CCH Explanation of the sunset provision.

Act Sec. 102(a) of the Working Families Tax Relief Act of 2004, amending Code Sec. 24(d)(1)(B)(i); Act Sec. 102(b); Act Sec. 105. Law at ¶5020. Committee Report at ¶10,050.

ALTERNATIVE MINIMUM TAX

¶130

One-Year Extension of Minimum Tax Relief for Individuals

Background

Individuals are subject to an alternative minimum tax (AMT) that is payable in addition to all other tax liabilities, to the extent that the tentative minimum tax exceeds the amount of regular tax owed (Code Sec. 55). An individual's tentative minimum tax generally is an amount equal to the sum of: (1) 26 percent of the first $175,000 ($87,500 for a married taxpayer filing a separate return) of alternative minimum taxable income (AMTI) in excess of an exemption amount, and (2) 28 percent of the remaining AMTI (Code Sec. 56(b)(1)(A)(i)). Alternative minimum taxable income is the individual's taxable income adjusted by specified preferences (Code Sec. 57(a)) and adjustments (Code Sec. 56(a)).

A specified amount of AMTI is exempt from the 26-percent and 28-percent AMT rates. The exemption amount varies according to the taxpayer's filing status and the amounts have changed over the past few years. The AMT exemption amounts for tax years beginning in 2000 for individual taxpayers were: (1) $45,000 for joint filers and surviving spouses; (2) $33,750 for single taxpayers who were not surviving spouses; and (3) $22,500 for married taxpayers filing separately (Code Sec. 55(d)(1), prior to amendment by the Economic Growth and Tax Relief Reconciliation Act of 2001 (P.L. 107-16)). The AMT exemption amount was $22,500 in the case of an estate or trust.

There has been much commentary over the years concerning the need for the reform or elimination of the AMT. The AMT regime, as originally enacted, primarily targeted higher-income taxpayers who could take advantage of certain tax incentives and preferences to substantially reduce or eliminate their regular income tax liabilities. The use of the AMT was seen as a means of maintaining a degree of tax equity between wealthy taxpayers and their lower-income counterparts. The present-law structure of the individual AMT expands the scope of the provisions to taxpayers who were not intended to be alternative minimum tax taxpayers. The number of individual taxpayers affected by the AMT will continue to grow due to the lack of indexing of the minimum tax exemption amounts. Congress sought to ameliorate this

Background _____

problem by temporarily increasing the AMT exemption amount for individuals for 2001 through 2004 tax years (Code Sec. 55(b)(1), prior to amendment by Act Sec. 103 of the Working Families Tax Relief Act of 2004).

The AMT exemption amounts for individuals were temporarily increased for tax years beginning in 2001 through 2004. The increased exemption amounts that applied for 2001 and 2002 tax years were: (1) $49,000 in the case of married individuals filing a joint return and surviving spouses; (2) $35,750 in the case of other unmarried individuals; and (3) $24,500 in the case of married individuals filing a separate return (Code Sec. 55(d)(1), as amended by the Economic Growth and Tax Relief Reconciliation Act of 2001 (P.L. 107-16)).

The increased exemption amounts for 2003 and 2004 tax years are: (1) $58,000 in the case of married individuals filing a joint return and surviving spouses; (2) $40,250 in the case of other unmarried individuals; and (3) $29,000 in the case of married individuals filing a separate return (Code Sec. 55(d)(1), as amended by the Jobs and Growth Tax Relief Reconciliation Act of 2003 (P.L. 108-27)).

The exemption amounts are phased out by an amount equal to 25 percent of the amount by which the individual's alternative minimum taxable income exceeds: (1) $150,000 in the case of married individuals filing a joint return and surviving spouses, (2) $112,500 in the case of other unmarried individuals, and (3) $75,000 in the case of married individuals filing a separate return or an estate or a trust (Code Sec. 55(d)(3)). The exemption amounts, threshold phase-out amounts, and rate brackets are not indexed for inflation.

_____

Working Families Tax Act Impact

Extension of individuals' AMT relief.—Increased alternative minimum tax (AMT) exemption amounts now apply to individuals for tax years beginning in 2005 (Code Sec. 55(d)(1), as amended by the Working Families Tax Relief Act of 2004). The increased AMT exemption amounts for individuals are the same as those that applied for 2003 and 2004 tax years. Thus, for tax years beginning in 2003, 2004 or 2005, the AMT exemption amount for an individual taxpayer is $58,000 in the case of a joint return filer or a surviving spouse. The AMT exemption amount for a tax year beginning in 2003, 2004 or 2005 is $40,250 for an individual who is not married and who is not a surviving spouse. The AMT exemption amount for a tax year beginning in 2003, 2004 or 2005 is $29,000 for an individual who is married but files a separate return.

The AMT exemption amount was, and still is, $22,500 in the case of an estate or trust.

> **Caution Note:** Absent another legislative extension of this increased AMT exemption, the alternative minimum tax exemption amount for an individual is scheduled to revert to amounts that applied in the 2000 tax year. Thus, the AMT exemption would revert for tax years beginning after 2005 to $45,000 in the case of a joint return filer or a surviving spouse, $33,750 for an individual who is not married and who is not a surviving spouse, and $22,500 for a married taxpayer who files a separate return.

> **Comment:** Although the AMT exemption amount has increased for the 2005 tax year for individuals, the base amounts for the exemption phase-out computations remain the same. Thus, the increased 2005 tax year exemption amounts are still reduced by 25 percent for each $1 of AMTI in excess of: (1) $150,000, in the case of joint return filers and surviving spouses; (2) $112,500, in the case of

single taxpayers; and (3) $75,000, in the case of married taxpayers filing separate returns and estates and trusts (Code Sec. 55(d)(3)). Consequently, the lack of a corresponding increase to the phase-out levels means the overall benefit of the increased exemption amounts is somewhat offset for those that exceed the phase-out thresholds.

PRACTICAL ANALYSIS. Professor Joseph W. Walloch, CPA, MBT, of the University of California Riverside, states that it is "good news" that the 2005 alternative minimum tax exemption levels have been increased to save millions of additional taxpayers from being ensnared by the AMT in 2005. However, the "bad news" is that this is a temporary "band aid" approach. The AMT exemption levels are scheduled to revert to lower levels in 2006 and future years. Unfortunately, a proposed inflation indexing feature for future AMT exemptions was NOT included in the final law.

PRACTICAL ANALYSIS. Barbara Raasch of Ernst & Young, New York, New York, reports that the good news is that about eight million people who would otherwise have had to deal with the complicated rules associated with AMT and see their federal tax burdens increase as a result of the AMT in 2005 don't have to—for 2005 anyway. The bad news is that this provision only extends AMT relief for these folks for one year, and it cost over $23 billion to do so.

About three million taxpayers still will be subject to AMT for 2004 and 2005. Under current tax laws, that number is expected to grow steadily until 2010 when 90 percent of taxpayers with incomes between $100,000 and $500,000 and 33 percent of all taxpayers are expected to become AMT taxpayers.

Therefore, it is prudent to consider whether AMT may become a way of life for you within the next year or so before making any major changes, including buying a new home, making investment decisions and even getting married or having more children. All these items may cause you to join the ranks of the AMT taxpayer this year, or in future years.

So, before you buy that new home in a high-tax state, make sure you understand how much those real estate taxes and any additional state and local income taxes will actually cost you. In addition, before just using your home equity line of credit for personal expenditures, determine whether you may be better off selling investments to fund the purchase and borrowing to buy those taxable securities back. Of course you'll need to be mindful of waiting 30 days if the sale results in a loss. If the sale results in a gain, that may not be so bad if you believe capital gains taxes are also likely to be higher in the future.

If you expect to be an AMT taxpayer, avoid purchasing private activity bonds and tax-exempt bond funds that are not designed to avoid interest income subject to AMT. In addition, currently you may find your after tax rate of return higher if you invest in taxable money market funds rather than tax-exempt money market funds. Typically, AMT taxpayers will receive a higher after-tax rate of return from municipal bonds (that are not private activity bonds issues after August 7, 1986) rather than comparable taxable bonds when the term to maturity is more than five years.

¶130

For further information on this subject, consult any of the following CCH reporter explanations:

- Standard Federal Tax Reporter, 2004FED ¶5101.01
- Federal Tax Service, FTS § A:22.180
- Federal Tax Guide, 2004FTG ¶1320

★ *Effective date.* The provision applies to tax years beginning after December 31, 2004 (Act Sec. 103(b) of the Working Families Tax Relief Act of 2004).

EGTRRA sunset provision. The amendments made by Title I of the 2004 Working Families Tax Act are subject to the sunset provision found in Title IX of the Economic Growth and Tax Relief Reconciliation Act of 2001 (P.L. 107-16). These 2004 amendments are subject to the EGTRRA sunset provision to the same extent and in the same manner as the provision of EGTRRA to which the amendment relates (Act Sec. 105). See ¶29,001 for the CCH Explanation of the sunset provision.

Act Sec. 103(a) of the Working Families Tax Relief Act of 2004, amending Code Sec. 55(d)(1)(A) and (B); Act Sec. 103(b); Act Sec. 105. Law at ¶5085. Committee Report at ¶10,060.

¶135

Extension of Personal Credits Offset Against Regular and Alternative Minimum Tax Liability

Background

The nonrefundable personal tax credits available to taxpayers include the dependent care credit, the credit for the elderly and disabled, the adoption credit, part of the child tax credit, the credit for interest on certain home mortgages, the education credits, the savers' credit, and the District of Columbia homebuyer's credit. Whether the total amount of all credits a taxpayer qualifies for will, in fact, provide the taxpayer with that same amount of tax relief is dependent on the application of the tax liability limitation rule governing personal nonrefundable credits.

The general tax limitation rule applicable to nonrefundable personal tax credits states that the aggregate amount of nonrefundable personal credits may not exceed the excess of a taxpayer's regular tax liability for the tax year over the taxpayer's tentative minimum tax liability (Code Sec. 26(a)(1)). The personal nonrefundable credits can only offset regular tax liability to the extent that the regular tax exceeds the tentative minimum tax.

Alternative rules and tax rates are used to calculate a taxpayer's tentative minimum tax liability. Some common alternative minimum tax (AMT) provisions affecting broad categories of taxpayers include the disallowance of personal and dependent exemptions, as well as the disallowance of itemized deductions for taxes and miscellaneous deductions. If the tentative minimum tax exceeds the regular tax, the taxpayer pays the difference, known as AMT, in addition to the regular tax.

The Tax Relief Extension Act of 1999 (P.L. 106-170) added Code Sec. 26(a)(2), thereby modifying the general tax liability limitation rule. For tax years 2000 and 2001 taxpayers could use personal nonrefundable credits to offset their total regular tax and their AMT, however, the regular tax liability had to first be reduced by any foreign tax credit (Code Sec. 26(a)(2) and Code Sec. 904(h)). The ability to offset nonrefundable personal credits against both regular tax and AMT liabilities was extended to tax years 2002 and 2003 by the Job Creation and Worker Assistance Act of 2002 (P.L. 107-147).

Background ──────────────────────────────────────

The Economic Growth and Tax Relief Reconciliation Act of 2001 (P.L. 107-16) specifically provides that the adoption credit, the nonrefundable portion of the child credit, and the savers' credit are allowed to the full extent of the taxpayer's regular tax and AMT through December 31, 2010 (except the savers' credit, which expires in 2006). The more restrictive general tax liability limitation rule, which provides that personal nonrefundable credits can offset regular tax liability only to the extent the regular tax exceeds the tentative minimum tax, is effective again in 2004 and thereafter, as to all other nonrefundable personal credits (Code Sec. 26(a)(1)).

───

Working Families Tax Act Impact

Offsets against regular tax and AMT allowed in 2004 and 2005.—For tax years beginning in 2004 and 2005, all nonrefundable personal credits may be offset against both regular tax and AMT (Code Sec. 26(a)(2), as amended by the Working Families Tax Relief Act of 2004). The regular tax, however, must first be reduced by the amount of any applicable foreign tax credit (Code Sec. 904(h), as amended by the 2004 Working Families Tax Act).

> **Comment:** The more restrictive general tax liability limitation rule, which provides that personal nonrefundable credits (other than the adoption credit, the nonrefundable portion of the child credit, and the savers' credit) can only offset regular tax liability to the extent the regular tax exceeds the tentative minimum tax, does not become effective again until after 2005.

The adoption credit, the nonrefundable portion of the child credit, and the savers' credit may continue to be offset against both regular tax and AMT. However, for tax years beginning in 2004 and 2005 the tax liability limitation rule applicable to these three credits is contained in Code Sec. 26(a)(2), as amended by the 2004 Working Families Tax Act. The Economic Growth and Tax Relief Reconciliation Act of 2001 (P.L. 107-16) amendments adding Code Sec. 23(b)(4), Code Sec. 24(b)(3) and Code Sec. 25B(g) are suspended during 2004 and 2005. These amendments will allow the adoption credit, the nonrefundable portion of the child credit, and the savers' credit to be offset against both regular tax and AMT in tax years beginning after 2005 and through December 31, 2010 (except the savers' credit, which expires in 2006).

> **Example 1:** Laura and David are married and have one of their three children attending college in 2004. Their regular tax liability before credits is $5,200 and their tentative minimum tax liability before credits is $4,100. They are eligible for an education credit totaling $1,500. Since the regular tax is higher than the tentative minimum tax, no AMT is triggered. The $5,200 regular tax is reduced by the $1,500 education credit, resulting in a net tax of $3,700.

> **Comment:** Absent the new provision, the taxpayers would have first deducted the $1,500 education credit from the $5,200 regular tax liability, and then compared the remaining regular tax of $3,700 to the $4,100 tentative minimum tax. Since the regular tax is less than the tentative minimum tax, this would trigger AMT in the amount of the difference, $400 ($4,100 minus $3,700). The taxpayer's total liability would have been $4,100 ($3,700 regular tax and $400 AMT).

> **Example 2:** Assume the same facts as in Example 1, except that Laura and David have a regular tax liability before credits of $0. Without the new provision, the taxpayers would get no tax benefit from the education credit. The education credit would not offset the AMT and the taxpayer's net tax liability would be $4,100. Because the offset against both regular tax and AMT has been extended

to tax years 2004 and 2005, the taxpayers can reduce their $4,100 AMT liability by the $1,500 credit, resulting in a net tax liability of $2,600 for 2004.

> **Compliance Tip:** The 2003 version of Form 1040 had the AMT line (42) immediately following the regular tax line (41) to reflect the offset of credits against both regular tax and AMT in 2003. The foreign tax credit is listed as the first credit (line 44) since it must be offset against regular tax before offsetting the other nonrefundable personal credits against regular tax and AMT. The foreign tax credit is limited to the lesser of the foreign taxes paid or the regular tax liability for income generated from sources outside the U.S. and is computed on Form 1116, Foreign Tax Credit, Part III, Figuring the Credit. The amount from line 21 of Form 1116 is carried to line 44 on Form 1040, thereby limiting the foreign tax credit to offset against regular tax only. Presumably the 2004 and 2005 Forms 1040 and 1116 will retain the same structure as to these items.

PRACTICAL ANALYSIS. Professor Joseph W. Walloch, CPA, MBT, of the University of California Riverside, indicates that this retroactive change provides that all nonrefundable personal credits are allowed in full for both regular tax and the alternative minimum tax for both 2004 and 2005.

Comment. **Only three nonrefundable personal credits—the adoption credit, child credit and credit for savers—will be allowed for AMT for 2006 and beyond in the absence of further "extender" legislation.**

For further information on this subject, consult any of the following CCH reporter explanations:

- Standard Federal Tax Reporter, 2004FED ¶3851.01 and ¶27,901.01
- Federal Tax Service, FTS § A:22.163
- Federal Tax Guide, 2004FTG ¶1320

★ *Effective date.* The provision applies to tax years beginning after December 31, 2003 (Act Sec. 312(c) of the Working Families Tax Relief Act of 2004).

Act Sec. 312(a) of the Working Families Tax Relief Act of 2004, amending Code Sec. 26(a)(2); Act Sec. 312(b)(1), amending Code Sec. 904(h); Act Sec. 312(b)(2); Act Sec. 312(c). Law at ¶5030, ¶5285 and ¶7020. Committee Report at ¶10,320.

SAMPLE TAXPAYER SCENARIOS

¶ 140

Taxpayer Impact

Effect on individuals.—The following scenarios illustrate the impact of the extension of the child tax credit increase, the marriage penalty relief, the 10-percent bracket increase, the alternative minimum tax (AMT) exemption amount extension and the extension of the allowance of nonrefundable credits for the AMT on hypothetical individual taxpayers in 2005. The Working Families Tax Relief Act of 2004 is a tax act that will probably be less noted for the fact that it passed than it would have been had it not passed. With a few notable exceptions, the Act primarily preserves existing tax benefits for future years. By continuing several popular tax cuts that benefit a wide range of taxpayers, taxpayers should primarily notice in 2005 that little has changed from 2004. By retroactively extending a large group of expired provisions, taxpayers will primarily notice that 2004 has not changed much from 2003.

This tax law continues a trend of recent tax laws in providing tax relief for a broad range of taxpayers rather than the very targeted tax relief typical of tax legislation of the 1990s. This legislation also continues the recent trend of providing the most tax relief to those that pay the most tax. The child tax credit extension will help a broad range of taxpayers. The acceleration of the refundability portion will particularly help low-income taxpayers. Since the phaseout range of the child tax credit increases as the child tax credit increases, however, the biggest beneficiaries of the increase in the child tax credit are joint filers with adjusted gross incomes in excess of $123,000 and single filers with adjusted gross incomes in excess of $88,000, who otherwise might not have qualified for a full or even a partial credit.

The expansion of the 10-percent tax bracket provides no assistance to joint filers with taxable income under $12,000 or to single filers with taxable income under $6,000, but is helpful to everyone else up the income stream.

The marriage penalty relief provisions obviously help only joint filers. The standard deduction relief helps only taxpayers who do not itemize, who tend to be moderate-income taxpayers. The 15 percent bracket relief helps only joint filers with taxable income of at least $53,450.

The extension of the AMT exemption increase will benefit joint filers with alternative minimum taxable income (AMTI) income above $45,000 and single filers with AMTI above $33,750. Because the AMT exemption increase was extended only for one year while the other tax cuts were extended for several years, this legislation will actually result in additional taxpayers being caught by the AMT after 2005. The extension of the provision allowing nonrefundable credits to qualify for AMT purposes will benefit all taxpayers who are in an AMT situation or whose credits might otherwise put them into an AMT situation. The extension of the AMT exemption amount will significantly reduce the number of taxpayers subject to the AMT in 2005. Even for 2004 and 2005, however, because there was no inflation adjustment to the AMT exemption amount that was also available in 2003, some additional taxpayers will be placed into an AMT situation simply due to cost-of-living adjustments to the regular tax brackets.

As the following scenarios illustrate, the largest tax savings, both in dollar and percentage terms, go to the taxpayers with children, married taxpayers, and higher income taxpayers subject to the AMT. Every scenario illustrated, however, shows that the taxpayer will receive a tax benefit from this legislation.

Single individual, age 65, $30,000 of AGI including $3,000 in dividend income.

2005	Present Law	New Leg.	Savings	% of AGI
Adjusted Gross Income	$30,000	30,000		
Std. Deduction	6,250	6,250		
Personal Exemptions	3,200	3,200		
Taxable Income	$20,550	$20,550		
Tax	$2,483	$2,418		
Tax after credits	$2,483	$2,418	($65)	0.22%

$65 of tax savings due to increase in 10% tax bracket

¶140

Head of household—one child under age 17, $30,000 of earned income.

2005	Present Law	New Leg.	Savings	% of AGI
Adjusted Gross Income	$30,000	$30,000		
Std. Deduction	7,300	7,300		
Personal Exemptions	6,400	6,400		
Taxable Income	$16,300	$16,300		
Tax	$1,945	$1,923	($22)	
Child Tax Credit	(700)	(1,000)	(300)	
Earned Income Credit	(164)	(164)		
Tax Due	$1,081	$759	($322)	1.07%

$22 of tax savings due to increase in 10% tax bracket
$300 of tax savings due to increase in child credit

$322 Total savings

Married couple—two children under age 17, $50,000 of income

2005	Present Law	New Leg.	Savings	% of AGI
Adjusted Gross Income	$50,000	$50,000		
Std. Deduction	8,700	10,000		
Personal Exemptions	12,800	12,800		
Taxable Income	$28,500	$27,200		
Tax	$3,675	$3,350	($325)	
Child Tax Credit	(1,400)	(2,000)	(600)	
Tax after credits	$2,275	$1,350	($925)	1.85%

$195 of savings is due to increase in the standard deduction
$130 of tax savings due to increase in 10% tax bracket
$600 of tax savings due to increase in child credit

$925 Total savings

Single taxpayer—no children, $50,000 of income

2005	Present Law	New Leg.	Savings	% of AGI
Adjusted Gross Income	$50,000	$50,000		
Std. Deduction	5,000	5,000		
Personal Exemptions	3,200	3,200		
Taxable Income	$41,800	$41,800		
Tax	$7,180	$7,115	($65)	0.13%

$65 of tax savings due to increase in 10% tax bracket

Married couple—two children under age 17, $100,000 of income, $15,000 of itemized deductions. $5,000 of dividends

2005	Present Law	New Leg.	Savings	% of AGI
Adjusted Gross Income	$100,000	$100,000		
Itemized Deduction	15,000	15,000		
Personal Exemptions	12,800	12,800		
Taxable Income	$72,200	$72,200		
Tax	$11,605	$10,880	($725)	
Child Tax Credit	(1,400)	(2,000)	(600)	
Tax after credits	$10,205	$8,880	($1,325)	1.33%

$130 of tax savings due to increase in 10% tax bracket
$595 of savings is due to increase in the 15% tax bracket
$600 of tax savings due to increase in child credit

$1,325 Total savings

Single individual—no children, $100,000 of income, $15,000 of itemized deductions. $3,000 of dividends

2005	Present Law	New Leg.	Savings	% of AGI
Adjusted Gross Income	$100,000	$100,000		
Itemized Deduction	15,000	15,000		
Personal Exemptions	3,200	3,200		
Taxable Income	$81,800	$81,800		
Tax	$17,086	$17,021	($65)	0.07%

$65 of tax savings due to increase in 10% tax bracket

Married couple with two children under age 17, $300,000 of income, $10,000 of dividend income and $50,000 of itemized deductions.

2005	Present Law	New Leg.	Savings	% of AGI
Adjusted Gross Income	$300,000	$300,000		
Itemized Deduction (partially phased out)	45,378	45,378		
Personal Exemptions (partially phased out)	4,352	4,352		
Taxable Income	$250,270	$250,270		
Tax	$62,106	$61,381	($725)	
Child Tax Credit	(0)	(0)	(0)	
Tax after credits	$62,106	$61,381	($725)	0.24%

$130 of tax savings due to increase in 10% tax bracket
$595 of savings is due to increase in the 15% tax bracket

$725 Total savings

AMT Scenarios

Married couple—$80,000 of income and one child who is a freshman in college. They pay $3,000 in tuition expense.

2005	Present Law	New Leg.	Savings	% of AGI
Adjusted Gross Income	$80,000	$80,000		
Std. Deduction	8,700	10,000		
Personal Exemptions	9,600	9,600		
Taxable Income	$61,700	$60,400		
Tax	9,480	8,430	(1,050)	
Education Credit	(380)	(1,500)	(1,120)	
Tax after credits	$9,100	$6,930	($2,170)	2.71%

$130 of tax savings due to increase in 10% tax bracket

$595 of savings is due to increase in the 15% tax bracket

$325 of savings is due to increase in standard deduction

$1,120 of savings is due to increase in alternative minimum tax exemption amount

$2,170 Total savings

Married couple—two children under age 17, $100,000 of income, $15,000 of itemized deductions. Itemized deductions included $4,500 in state income taxes, $2,500 in property taxes $3,000 of home equity loan interest expense, and $5,000 in mortgage interest expense and charitable contributions. They incurred $6,000 in child care expenses.

2005	Present Law	New Leg.	Savings	% of AGI
Adjusted Gross Income	$100,000	$100,000		
Itemized Deduction	15,000	15,000		
Personal Exemptions	12,800	12,800		
Taxable Income	$72,200	$72,200		
Tax	12,105	11,380	(725)	
Alternative Minimum Tax	895		(895)	
Child Care Credit		(1,200)	(1,200)	
Child Tax Credit	(1,400)	(2,000)	(600)	
Tax after credits	$11,600	$8,180	($3,420)	3.42%

$130 of tax savings due to increase in 10% tax bracket

$595 of savings is due to increase in the 15% tax bracket

$2,095 of savings is due to increase in alternative minimum tax exemption amount

$600 of tax savings due to increase in child credit

$3,420 Total savings

UNIFORM DEFINITION OF CHILD

¶ 145

Uniform Definition of a Qualifying Child

Background

Child-related tax benefits affect millions of individual tax returns. The existence of a qualifying child can determine whether a taxpayer is entitled to a dependency exemption; whether the taxpayer qualifies as a head of household; and whether the taxpayer can claim the child credit, the earned income credit, and the dependent care credit. Each of these tax items has its own independent definition of a qualifying child, and these varying definitions add to the complexity of the tax code. Factors relevant to the definitions of a qualifying child include the child's age, the child's relationship to the taxpayer, the child's income, the child's residence and who maintains it, and the level of support provided by the taxpayer. A taxpayer must determine eligibility for each of these benefits separately, and an individual who qualifies the taxpayer for benefits under one provision does not necessarily qualify the taxpayer for benefits under another provision.

The dependency exemption is one of the most significant tax items affected by the definition of a qualifying child because each exemption reduces taxable income by the annual exemption amount (although these exemptions are phased out for higher-income taxpayers). A taxpayer can claim a dependency exemption for a dependent who meets the five following tests: (1) a relationship test, (2) a support test, (3) a gross income test, (4) a citizenship test and (5) a return test (Code Sec. 151(c)).

Relationship/household test. A dependent must be a relative of the taxpayer or a member of the taxpayer's household (Code Sec. 152(a)). Persons qualifying as relatives are the taxpayer's children and their descendants; the taxpayer's step-children; the taxpayer's siblings (including half-brothers and half-sisters) and their children; the taxpayer's parents, and their ancestors and siblings; the taxpayer's step-parents and step-siblings; and the taxpayer's son-in-law, daughter-in-law, father-in-law, mother-in-law, brother-in-law and sister-in-law (Code Sec. 152(a)).

For purposes of the relationship test, the taxpayer's children include children who have been legally adopted by the taxpayer under applicable state law, and children who are members of the taxpayer's household after being placed there by an authorized placement agency for legal adoption. A foster child is not the taxpayer's child unless the child and the taxpayer shared a principal place of abode, the child was a member of the taxpayer's household, and the child was cared for as the taxpayer's own (Code Sec. 152(b)(2); Reg. § 1.152-2(c)(4)).

Persons who are not related to the taxpayer can be dependents if they were members of a household during the entire tax year (except for permissible temporary absences) that was occupied and maintained by the taxpayer, that household was their principal place of abode, they were not married to the taxpayer during the tax year, and their relationship with the taxpayer did not violate local law (Code Sec. 152(a)(9) and (b)(5); Reg. § 1.152-1(b)).

Support test. The taxpayer must provide over half of the dependent's total support (Code Sec. 152(a)). Alimony payments are not treated as payments for support (Code Sec. 152(b)(4)), and support provided to a child by a parent's spouse is treated as provided by the parent (Code Sec. 152(e)(5)). If the dependent is the taxpayer's child or step-child and is a student, amounts received as scholarships are disregarded (Code Sec. 152(d)).

Background

There are two significant modifications of the support test. First, if no one person provides at least half of the dependent's support, the persons who provide at least 10 percent of the dependent's support can enter into a multiple support agreement that allows only one of them to claim the dependent's exemption (Code Sec. 152(c)). Second, if the dependent is the child of taxpayers who are (or are treated as) divorced or separated, and the parents jointly or singly have custody of the child for at least six months of the year and provide at least half of the child's support, the dependency exemption is presumed to belong to the parent who has custody for the greater part of the year. The noncustodial parent cannot claim the exemption, regardless of how much of the child's support was provided by each parent, unless the custodial parent releases the dependency exemption. For this purpose, the taxpayer's children include the taxpayer's step-children, as well as the persons defined as the taxpayer's children for purposes of the relationship test. This exception to the support test does not apply if the child is the subject of a multiple support agreement (Code Sec. 152(e)(3)).

Gross income test. The dependent's gross income must be less than the exemption amount (which is $3,100 for 2004). This test does not apply to the taxpayer's children who are under the age of 19, or who are full-time students under the age of 24 (Code Sec. 151(c)). For this purpose, a taxpayer's children include the taxpayer's step-children, as well as the persons defined as the taxpayer's children for purposes of the relationship test (Code Sec. 152(d)(1)). The gross income test does not take into consideration amounts received by a permanently and totally disabled dependent for services rendered at a sheltered workshop, if the availability of medical care is the principal reason for the dependent's presence there and the income arises solely from activities at the workshop that are incidental to the medical care (Code Sec. 151(c)(5)).

Citizenship test. The dependent must be a U.S. citizen or national, or a resident of the United States, Canada or Mexico for some part of the year. However, this test does not apply to the taxpayer's legally adopted child if, for the taxpayer's tax year, the child's principal place of abode is the home of the taxpayer, the child is a member of the taxpayer's household, and the taxpayer is a citizen or national of the United States (Code Sec. 152(b)(3)).

Return test. An individual will not qualify as a dependent if he or she files a joint return with a spouse (Code Sec. 151(c)(2)).

Missing children. A kidnapped child who qualified as the taxpayer's dependent during the portion of the year prior to the kidnapping, and who is presumed by law enforcement authorities to have been kidnapped by someone who is not a member of the family of the child or the taxpayer, continues to be treated as the taxpayer's dependent until the year following the year in which the child would have reached age 18 or, if earlier, is determined to be dead (Code Sec. 151(c)(6)).

Other tax items. The definitions of a taxpayer's child and a taxpayer's dependent are also relevant for many other deductions, credits and tax benefits.

Working Families Tax Act Impact

Dependents are redefined; definition of taxpayer's child is made uniform.— The statutory definition of a dependent has been rewritten to categorize each dependent as a qualifying child or a qualifying relative (Code Sec. 152(a), as amended by the Working Families Tax Relief Act of 2004). For a qualifying child, the existing gross income test is eliminated, and the existing support test is redefined. For qualifying relatives, most of the existing tests for dependents continue to apply. Other tax items that reference a taxpayer's child or dependent are amended to reflect these new definitions.

Compliance Tip: Dependency exemptions are still subject to the existing compliance rules. Thus, to claim a dependency exemption, the taxpayer's return must include the dependent's taxpayer identification number (TIN), which is usually the dependent's social security number (Code Sec. 151(e)).

General rules. Several new provisions are applicable to all dependents, whether they are qualifying children or qualifying relatives.

Uniform definition of a child. A taxpayer's children include the taxpayer's natural children, step-children, adopted children and eligible foster children. A taxpayer's *adopted child* is a child who has been legally adopted by the taxpayer, or a child who has been lawfully placed with the taxpayer for legal adoption by the taxpayer. A taxpayer's *eligible foster child* is a child who has been placed with the taxpayer by an authorized agency or by a judgment, decree or other order of any court of competent jurisdiction (Code Sec. 152(f)(1), as amended by the 2004 Working Families Tax Act).

Student. As under current law, a student is an individual who, during five calendar months of the calendar year in which the taxpayer's tax year begins, is a full-time student at an educational organization, or is pursuing a full-time course of instructional on-farm training (Code Sec. 152(f)(2), as amended by the 2004 Working Families Tax Act).

Citizenship test. The citizenship test is unchanged. Thus, a dependent generally must be a U.S. citizen or national, or a resident of the United States, Canada or Mexico for some part of the year. This test does not apply to a taxpayer's adopted child (as defined above) if the taxpayer is a U.S. citizen or national and if, for the taxpayer's tax year, the child had the same place of abode as the taxpayer and was a member of the taxpayer's household (Code Sec. 152(b)(3)(B), as amended by the 2004 Working Families Tax Act).

Return test. As under current law, an individual will not qualify as a dependent if he or she files a joint return in any tax year that begins in the same calendar year as the tax year for which the taxpayer claimed the dependency exemption (Code Sec. 152(b)(2), as amended by the 2004 Working Families Tax Act).

Dependent's dependents. A person claimed as a dependent cannot claim any dependents during any tax year that begins in the same calendar year as the tax year for which the person was claimed as a dependent (Code Sec. 152(b)(1), as amended by the 2004 Working Families Tax Act).

Example: Grace and her son George are fiscal year taxpayers. Grace's fiscal year begins on March 1, and George's fiscal year begins on November 1. If Grace claims George as a dependent on her return for her fiscal year beginning on March 1, 2005, George cannot claim any dependents on his return for his fiscal year beginning on November 1, 2005.

Qualifying child. A qualifying child for purposes of the dependency exemption must satisfy tests relating to relationship, age, abode, and support (Code Sec. 152(c)(1), as amended by the 2004 Working Families Tax Act). For qualifying children, the gross income test under current law is eliminated, and the support test is redefined.

Relationship test. A qualifying child must be the taxpayer's child or a descendant of the taxpayer's child (i.e., grandchild); or the taxpayer's sibling (including half-brothers and half-sisters) or step-sibling or a descendant of the taxpayer's sibling or step-sibling (Code Sec. 152(c)(2), as amended by the 2004 Working Families Tax Act).

Example: Mariella's household includes her natural son, her son's son (Mariella's grandson), her sister, her nephew, her step-brother, and her step-brother's daughter. All of these people satisfy the relationship test with respect to Mariella.

Age test. As of the close of the calendar year in which the taxpayer's tax year begins, a qualifying child must not have attained the age of 19, or must be a student who has not attained the age of 24. This age test does not apply to a child who is permanently and totally disabled at any time during the calendar year (Code Sec. 152(c)(3), as amended by the 2004 Working Families Tax Act).

Comment: A child who is not a "qualifying child" because she does not meet one of the tests, such as the age test, may still qualify as a dependent under the "qualifying relative" test, below.

Abode test. A qualifying child must have the same principal place of abode as the taxpayer for more than half of the taxpayer's tax year (Code Sec. 152(c)(1)(B), as amended by the 2004 Working Families Tax Act). If a taxpayer's child is presumed by law enforcement authorities to have been kidnapped by someone who is not a member of the family of the child or the taxpayer, and the child shared the same principal place of abode as the taxpayer for more than half of the portion of the tax year preceding the kidnapping, the child satisfies the abode test for all tax years ending during the period in which the child is missing. A missing child ceases to satisfy the abode test in the taxpayer's first tax year beginning after the calendar year in which the child is determined to be dead or, if earlier, in which the child would have attained the age of 18. These rules for missing children also apply for purposes of determining the child tax credit (see ¶160), the earned income credit (see ¶165), and the taxpayer's eligibility for head-of-household filing status (see ¶150) (Code Sec. 152(f)(6), as amended by the 2004 Working Families Tax Act).

Support test. A qualifying child must not have provided more than one-half of his or her own support during the calendar year in which the taxpayer's tax year begins (Code Sec. 152(c)(1)(D), as amended by the 2004 Working Families Tax Act). If the child is the taxpayer's child and is a full-time student, amounts received as scholarships are not considered support (Code Sec. 152(f)(5), as amended by the 2004 Working Families Tax Act).

Example: Jasmine receives one-third of her support from her father, and two-thirds of her support from her aunt. Jasmine now satisfies the support test with respect to her father, because Jasmine provides less than one-half of her own support. Under prior law, she did not satisfy the support test with respect to her father because he did not provide more than one-half of her support.

Tie-breaker rules. A child cannot be claimed as a dependent on more than one tax return for any calendar year, even though the child satisfies the qualifying child tests for two or more taxpayers. Tie-breaker rules determine who may claim the dependency exemption.

Caution Note: The tie-breaker rules are relevant only when one child is treated as a qualifying child for more than one tax return. Thus, the tie-breaker rules apply only if the child satisfies the relationship test with respect to two or more taxpayers, and more than one of them actually claims the child's dependency exemption.

If none of the taxpayers is the child's parent, the child is a qualifying child for the taxpayer with the highest adjusted gross income. If only one of the taxpayers is the child's parent, the child is a qualifying child for that parent. If two of the taxpayers are the child's parents and they do not file a joint return together, the child is a qualifying child for the parent with whom the child resided for the longest period during the year; if the child spent equal amounts of time residing with each parent, the child is a qualifying child for the parent with the highest adjusted gross income (Code Sec. 152(c)(4), as amended by the 2004 Working Families Tax Act).

Comment: These same tie-breaker rules have been used since 2002 for determining a qualifying child for purposes of the earned income credit.

Planning Note: A child can continue to be treated as a dependent of both parents for purposes of the deduction for the child's medical expenses (Code Sec. 213(d)(5)), the exclusion from the parent's gross income for qualified fringe benefits used by the child (Code Sec. 132(h)(2)(B)), and the exclusion from the parent's income for qualified health insurance payments for the child's medical expenses (Code Sec. 105(b)) (Code Sec. 152(f)(7), as amended by the 2004 Working Families Tax Act).

Qualifying relative. A qualifying relative must satisfy tests relating to relationship, gross income, and support (Code Sec. 152(d)(1), as amended by the 2004 Working Families Tax Act). The rules for qualifying relatives generally absorb the relationship, support, and gross income tests under current law.

Not a qualifying child. In the only new dependency test applicable to qualifying relatives, a qualifying relative cannot be a qualifying child for the taxpayer or for any other taxpayer for any tax year beginning in the calendar year in which the taxpayer's tax year begins (Code Sec. 152(d)(1)(D), as amended by the 2004 Working Families Tax Act).

Relationship test. As under current law, persons qualifying as relatives are the taxpayer's children and their descendants; the taxpayer's siblings (including half-brothers and half-sisters) and their children; the taxpayer's parents, and their ancestors and siblings; the taxpayer's step-parents and step-siblings; and the taxpayer's son-in-law, daughter-in-law, father-in-law, mother-in-law, brother-in-law and sister-in-law (Code Sec. 152(d)(2), as amended by the 2004 Working Families Tax Act).

Qualifying relatives also include individuals, other than the taxpayer's spouse, who had the same abode as the taxpayer and were members of the taxpayer's household during the taxpayer's tax year (Code Sec. 152(d)(2)(H)), as amended by the 2004 Working Families Tax Act). An individual is not a member of the taxpayer's household if, at any time during the taxpayer's tax year, the relationship between the individual and the taxpayer violated local law (Code Sec. 152(f)(3), as amended by the 2004 Working Families Tax Act).

Comment: Although these dependents are called "qualifying relatives," this last category includes persons who have no family relationship to the taxpayer.

Support test. As under current law, the taxpayer must provide more than one-half of a qualifying relative's support during the calendar year in which the taxpayer's tax year begins (Code Sec. 152(d)(1)(C), as amended by the 2004 Working Families Tax Act). Also as under current law, alimony payments are not treated as payments for support and, in the case of remarriage, a child's support that is provided by a parent's spouse is treated as provided by the parent (Code Sec. 152(d)(5), as amended by the 2004 Working Families Tax Act). If the child is the taxpayer's child and is a full-time student, amounts received as scholarships are not considered support (Code Sec. 152(f)(5), as amended by the 2004 Working Families Tax Act).

The existing exception to the support test for multiple support agreements also continues to apply. Thus, if two or more persons provide a total of over one-half of the dependent's support, but no one person provides at least one-half of the dependent's support, the taxpayer is treated as providing more than half of the dependent's

¶145

support if the other persons who provided at least 10 percent of the dependent's support waive the dependency exemption by filing a written declaration with the IRS (Code Sec. 152(d)(3), as amended by the 2004 Working Families Tax Act).

The second existing exception to the support test for children of divorced parents also still applies if the parents are divorced, separated, or live apart at all times during the last six months of the calendar year; they jointly or singly have custody of the child for at least six months of the year; and they jointly or singly provide at least half of the child's support. However, the exception no longer presumes that the custodial parent is entitled to the child's dependency exemption; instead, it spells out the tests that must be satisfied before the noncustodial parent can claim the exemption. The child is treated as the qualifying child or qualifying relative of the noncustodial parent only if the parents' divorce or separation instrument provides that the noncustodial parent is entitled to the dependency exemption, or the custodial parent provides the IRS with a signed, written declaration waiving the child's dependency exemption. If the parents' divorce or separation instrument was executed before 1985, the noncustodial parent must also provide at least $600 in support during the calendar year. To be a custodial parent, the parent and the child must have shared the same principal place of abode for the greater portion of the tax year. As under current law, this exception does not apply if the child is the subject of a multiple support agreement (Code Sec. 152(e), as amended by the 2004 Working Families Tax Act).

Gross income test. As under current law, a qualifying relative's gross income for the calendar year in which the taxpayer's tax year begins must be less than the exemption amount (which is $3,100 for 2004) (Code Sec. 152(d)(1)(B), as amended by the 2004 Working Families Tax Act). Also as under current law, if a dependent is permanently and totally disabled at any time during the tax year, the dependent's gross income does not include income attributable to services performed at a sheltered workshop, if the availability of medical care at the workshop is the principal reason for the dependent's presence there, and the income arises from activities that are incident to the medical care (Code Sec. 152(d)(4), as amended by the 2004 Working Families Tax Act).

Comment: The existing exception from the gross income test for the taxpayer's children who are under age 19 (or are students under age 24) is removed, because the gross income test no longer applies to a qualifying child.

Missing children. If a taxpayer's child is presumed by law enforcement authorities to have been kidnapped by someone who is not a member of the family of the child or the taxpayer, and the child was a qualifying relative (rather than a qualifying child) for the taxpayer for the portion of the tax year preceding the kidnapping, the child continues to be a qualifying relative for the taxpayer for all tax years ending during the period in which the child is missing. A missing child ceases to be a qualifying child in the taxpayer's first tax year beginning after the calendar year in which the child is determined to be dead or, if earlier, in which the child would have attained the age of 18. These rules for missing children also apply for purposes of determining the child tax credit (see ¶160), the earned income credit (see ¶165), and the taxpayer's qualification for head-of-household filing status (see ¶150) (Code Sec. 152(f)(6), as amended by the 2004 Working Families Tax Act).

Uniform definition of child. As discussed above, under existing law, a child was generally defined as the taxpayer's child or step-child (Code Sec. 151(c)). The Act expands this definition to include children, step-children, adopted children and eligible foster children (Code Sec. 152(f)(1), as amended by the 2004 Working Families Tax Act). This expansion of the definition of the taxpayer's child also applies to the following:

(1) The rules that make payments to the taxpayer's child ineligible for the dependent care credit (Code Sec. 21(e)(6)(B), as amended by the 2004 Working Families Tax Relief Act), and excludable employer-paid dependent care (Code Sec. 129(c)(2), as amended by the 2004 Working Families Tax Relief Act).

(2) The exclusion from the early distribution penalty for individual retirement plan distributions used to pay the higher education expenses of the taxpayer's child (Code Sec. 72(t)(7)(a)(iii), as amended by the 2004 Working Families Tax Act).

(3) The treatment of an employee's child as the employee for purposes of the exclusion for qualified fringe benefits (Code Sec. 132(h)(2)(B), as amended by the 2004 Working Families Tax Act).

(4) The tests for a married taxpayer to be treated as unmarried (Code Sec. 7703(b)(1), as amended by the 2004 Working Families Tax Act).

Non-uniform definition of dependent. As discussed above, under the new definition of a dependent, a dependent cannot file a joint return or claim dependency exemptions, and a dependent who is a qualifying relative cannot have income in excess of the annual exemption amount. However, these restrictions do not apply to persons classified as dependents for several other tax purposes. Thus, if a person would qualify as a dependent but for filing a joint return, claiming dependency exemptions, or having gross income in excess of the exemption amount, the person is nonetheless treated as a dependent for the following purposes:

(1) The taxpayer's head-of-household filing status (Code Sec. 2(a)(1)(B)(i), as amended by the 2004 Working Families Tax Act) (see ¶150).

(2) The exception from the early distribution penalty for qualified retirement plans distributions used to pay health insurance premiums for an unemployed taxpayer's dependents (Code Sec. 72(t)(2)(D)(i)(III), as amended by the 2004 Working Families Tax Act).

(3) The description of full-time students whose residency will not prevent a rental unit from qualifying for the low-income housing credit (Code Sec. 42(i)(3)(D)(ii)(I), as amended by the 2004 Working Families Tax Act).

(4) The exclusion from income of amounts received under accident and health insurance plans (Code Sec. 105(b) and (c)(1), as amended by the 2004 Working Families Tax Act), and qualified group legal services plans (Code Sec. 120(d)(4), as amended by the 2004 Working Families Tax Act).

(5) The definition of a highly compensated participant for purposes of cafeteria plans (Code Sec. 125(e)(1)(D), as amended by the 2004 Working Families Tax Act).

(6) The exception from the rules that allow certain amounts paid to maintain a student in the taxpayer's home to qualify as deductible charitable contributions (Code Sec. 170(g)(1), as amended by the 2004 Working Families Tax Act).

(7) The deduction for medical expenses incurred by the taxpayer's dependent (Code Sec. 213(a), as amended by the 2004 Working Families Tax Act).

(8) The exclusion for distributions from an Archer medical savings account (MSA) that are used to pay a dependent's medical expenses (Code Sec. 220(d)(2)(A), as amended by the 2004 Working Families Tax Act).

(9) The rules governing the deduction for qualified student loan interest (Code Sec. 221(d)(4), as amended by the 2004 Working Families Tax Act).

(10) The treatment of educational and medical indebtedness in calculating the value of a decedent's qualified family-owned business interests for purposes

of the estate tax (Code Sec. 2057(d)(2)(B), as amended by the 2004 Working Families Tax Act).

PRACTICAL ANALYSIS. Vincent O'Brien, President of Vincent J. O'Brien, CPA, PC, Lynbrook, New York, observes that while the new law rearranges many definitions related to several tax areas, the results of applying the new definitions will be the same as under prior law for many taxpayers.

Dependency Exemption. Prior to the new law, a taxpayer was generally eligible for the dependency exemption for any individual who met five tests (i.e., the relationship or member-of-household test, the support test, the gross income or child-under-certain-age test, the citizenship or residency test, and the restriction-on-filing-a-joint-return test).

Under the new law, dependents have been divided into two groups: qualifying child and qualifying relative.

Qualifying Relative. To be a qualifying relative, the individual must meet the same five tests as existed under the prior law. The category of qualifying relative includes anyone who meets the five tests but does not meet the definition of a qualifying child (discussed next). This is broader than it sounds. It includes a child of the taxpayer who does not meet the definition of a qualifying child (due to the age limits); it also includes an individual who is a member of the taxpayer's household for the entire year (other than the taxpayer's spouse).

Qualifying Child. To be a qualifying child, the child must meet five conditions that are different from the five tests for a qualifying relative:

(1) *Relationship.* The child must be the taxpayer's son, daughter, stepson, stepdaughter, eligible foster child or decedent of such a child, or the taxpayer's brother, sister, stepbrother, stepsister or any decedent of any such relative.

(2) *Age.* The child must be under the age of 19 (or under the age of 24 and a full-time student).

(3) *Citizenship/Residency.* The child must be a citizen or resident of the United States, or a resident of Canada or Mexico.

(4) *Principal Residence.* The child must have the same principal place of abode as the taxpayer for more than half of the year.

(5) *Not Self-Supporting.* The child must not have provided over half of his or her own support.

Comment. These conditions may achieve different results for some taxpayers. Notice that the support test no longer applies to a qualifying child. (It still applies for qualifying relatives.) Therefore, if the taxpayer shares a principal place of abode with the child for more than half of the year, the taxpayer is eligible to claim the child as a dependent, even if the taxpayer does not provide more than half of the child's support.

Breaking Ties. For situations where more than one taxpayer may be otherwise eligible to claim a qualifying child as a dependent, the new law provides three tiebreakers. First, if the child is the son or daughter of one taxpayer, that taxpayer will be entitled to the exemption, even if another taxpayer who is not the child's parent would be otherwise qualified to claim the exemption.

Second, if two parents of the same child file separately, the parent with whom the child resides for the longest period of time during the year will be eligible to claim the child. (If this rule does not break the tie, then the parent with the highest adjusted gross income will be eligible.) Third, if the parents of the child do not claim the child, then the otherwise eligible taxpayer with the highest adjusted gross income will be eligible to claim the child as a dependent.

Comment. Taxpayers with income above prescribed thresholds are subject to a phaseout of the benefit of the dependency exemption (and child credit, if applicable). Thus, the taxpayer with the higher adjusted gross income may not necessarily be able to benefit from the exemption that he or she is entitled to claim.

Example. Jane is a widow. She and her infant son, Sam, live with Jane's mother, Ellen. Sam is a U.S. citizen and has no income. Ellen provides more than half of Sam's support. Jane, who is 28, has earned income of more than the dependent exemption amount; thus, she is ineligible to be claimed as Ellen's dependent.

Under the prior law, Jane would not be entitled to claim Sam as her dependent, since she did not provide more than half of his support. However, under the new law, Sam is Jane's qualifying child, because he is her son, and he lived in her principal place of abode for more than half of the year. Ellen would be otherwise qualified to claim Sam as her dependent, since Sam is also a qualifying child of Ellen; however, under the tie-breaking rules, Jane is entitled to claim the exemption, since Sam is Jane's son.

Notwithstanding the tie-breaking rules, divorced or legally-separated parents can still agree to which parent will claim the dependency exemption. However, the noncustodial parent cannot claim the exemption unless the custodial parent completes a Form 8332, Release of Claim to Exemption for Child of Divorced or Separated Parents, or a similar statement indicating that he or she is not claiming the exemption. The noncustodial parent attaches this form or statement to his or her return.

For further information on this subject, consult any of the following CCH reporter explanations:

- Standard Federal Tax Reporter, 2004FED ¶3340.01, ¶3507.01, ¶8005.01 and ¶8251.01

- Federal Tax Service, FTS § A:3.80

- Federal Tax Guide, 2004FTG ¶6110

★ *Effective date.* The provisions apply to tax years beginning after December 31, 2004 (Act Sec. 208 of the Working Families Tax Relief Act of 2004).

Act Sec. 201 of the Working Families Tax Relief Act of 2004, amending Code Sec. 152; Act Sec. 207(1), amending Code Sec. 2(a)(1)(B)(i); Act Sec. 207(2), amending Code Sec. 21(e)(5); Act Sec. 207(3), amending Code Sec. 21(e)(6)(B); Act Sec. 207(4), amending Code Sec. 25B(c)(2)(B); Act Sec. 207(5), amending Code Sec. 51(i)(1)(A), (B) and (C); Act Sec. 207(6) and (7), amending Code Sec. 72(t)(2)(D)(i)(III) and (7)(A)(iii); Act Sec. 207(8), amending Code Sec. 42(i)(3)(D)(ii)(I); Act Sec. 207(9), amending Code Sec. 105(b) and (c)(1); Act Sec. 207(10), amending Code Sec. 120(d)(4); Act Sec. 207(11), amending Code Sec. 125(e)(1)(D); Act Sec. 207(12), amending Code Sec. 129(c)(2); Act Sec. 207(13), amending Code Sec. 132(h)(2)(B); Act Sec. 207(14), amending Code Sec. 153; Act Sec. 207(15) and (16), amending Code Sec. 170(g)(1) and (3); Act Sec. 207(17) and (18), amending Code Sec. 213(a) and (d)(11); Act Sec. 207(19), amending Code Sec. 220(d)(2)(A); Act Sec. 207(20), amending Code Sec. 221(d)(4); Act Sec. 207(21), amending Code Sec. 529(e)(2)(B); Act Sec. 207(22), amending Code Sec. 2032A(c)(7)(D); Act Sec. 207(23), amending Code Sec. 2057(d)(2)(B); Act Sec. 207(24), amending Code Sec. 7701(a)(17); Act Sec. 207(25), amending Code Sec. 7702B(f)(2)(C)(iii); Act Sec. 207(26), amending Code Sec. 7703(b)(1); Act Sec. 208. Law at ¶ 5010, ¶ 5015, ¶ 5025, ¶ 5055, ¶ 5075, ¶ 5110, ¶ 5115, ¶ 5120, ¶ 5125, ¶ 5140, ¶ 5145, ¶ 5150, ¶ 5165, ¶ 5185, ¶ 5190, ¶ 5195, ¶ 5250, ¶ 5355, ¶ 5360, ¶ 5400, ¶ 5405, ¶ 5410. Committee Report at ¶ 10,100.

¶ 150
Definition of Head of Household

Background

In order to qualify for the favorable income tax rates as a head of household under Code Sec. 1(b), a taxpayer must meet several requirements. The taxpayer must not be married at the close of the tax year, and must not be a surviving spouse within the meaning of Code Sec. 2(a). The taxpayer must also maintain a household for more than one-half of the tax year that is the principal place of abode for at least one qualifying individual (Code Sec. 2(b)(1)).

Qualifying individuals are the taxpayer's unmarried sons, daughters, and their descendants and the taxpayer's unmarried step-sons and step-daughters (Code Sec. 2(b)(1)(A)(i)). A legally adopted child is treated the same as a child by blood (Code Sec. 2(b)(2)(A)). Other persons related to the taxpayer can also be qualifying individuals, but only if the taxpayer is entitled to claim them as dependents (Code Sec. 2(b)(1)(A)(ii) and (b)(3)(B)(i)). Thus, the following persons must meet the five dependency exemption tests (see the Background in ¶ 145) in order to be considered qualifying individuals:

- the taxpayer's married children and their married descendants, and the taxpayer's married step-children (but only if the taxpayer is entitled to claim them as dependents, or would be so entitled but for having released the dependency exemption to the noncustodial parent (Code Sec. 2(b)(1)(A)(i));

- the taxpayer's siblings, including step-siblings and half-siblings;

- the taxpayer's parents and their ancestors, and the taxpayer's step-parents;

- the taxpayer's nephews, nieces, aunts and uncles, related by blood;

- the taxpayer's in-laws (mother-in-law, father-in-law, daughter-in-law, son-in-law, sister-in-law and brother-in-law); and

- the taxpayer's foster children who live with the taxpayer for the entire tax year.

These relatives are not qualifying individuals if the taxpayer is entitled to claim them as dependents under a multiple support agreement (Code Sec. 2(b)(3)(B)(ii)). Persons who are not related to the taxpayer are not qualifying individuals, even if the taxpayer may claim them as dependents.

Additionally, if certain requirements are met, a taxpayer's maintenance of a separate household for a parent will qualify the taxpayer for head-of-household status (Code Sec. 2(b)(1)(B)).

Working Families Tax Act Impact

Head of household redefined.—Consistent with changes intended to provide a uniform definition of a "qualifying child," for purposes of determining a taxpayer's right to claim head-of-household filing status, the Working Families Tax Relief Act of 2004 deletes all references to a "son, stepson, daughter, or stepdaughter of the taxpayer, or descendent of a son or daughter of the taxpayer" (Code Sec. 2(b)(1)(A)(i), as amended by the Working Families Tax Relief Act of 2004). Instead, the taxpayer's head-of-household status will depend on the taxpayer's maintainance of a household for a "qualifying child," as defined by Code Sec. 152(c), but determined without regard to Code Sec. 152(e) (relating to a custodial parent's release of the child's dependency exemption to the noncustodial parent) (see ¶145). Qualifying children include the taxpayer's children, siblings and step-siblings, and their descendants (Code Sec. 152(c)(2), as amended by the 2004 Working Families Tax Act). However, a taxpayer will not be deemed to be a head of household with respect to a qualifying child who is married at the close of the taxpayer's tax year, and who is not the taxpayer's dependent because of the operation of Code Sec. 152(b)(2) (generally applying a more demanding dependency test to married dependents) or Code Sec. 152(b)(3) (generally requiring a dependent to be a citizen or national of the United States, Canada, or Mexico) (see ¶145).

For tax years after 2004, the Act deletes Code Sec. 2(b)(2)(A), which provides that, for purposes of determining head-of-household status, a legally adopted child is considered to be the taxpayer's child by blood. However, Code Sec. 2(b)(1)(A)(i) (as amended by the 2004 Working Families Tax Act) incorporates the definition of a "qualifying child" contained in Code Sec. 152(c), by reference. Accordingly, a qualifying child can be an adopted child, defined as a child legally adopted by the taxpayer or lawfully placed with the taxpayer for legal adoption by the taxpayer. A qualifying child can also be an eligible foster child, defined as a person placed with the taxpayer by an authorized placement agency or by a judgment, decree or other court order (Code Sec. 152(f)(1)(B) and (C), as amended by the 2004 Working Families Tax Act) (see ¶145). The requirement under current law that a foster child live with the taxpayer for the entire tax year is removed.

The other rules governing relatives who can be qualifying individuals are unchanged.

PRACTICAL ANALYSIS. Vincent O'Brien, President of Vincent J. O'Brien, CPA, PC, Lynbrook, New York, observes that under the prior law, an unmarried taxpayer who provided for more than half of the cost of maintaining a principal residence shared with his or her unmarried child could claim head-of-household status, even if the taxpayer could not claim the child as his or her dependent.

Under the new law, a child must be a qualifying child or otherwise qualify as a dependent of the taxpayer in order to entitle the taxpayer to be a head of household.

Example. Mary is unmarried. She provides for more than half of the cost of her principal residence that she shares with her unmarried daughter Cheryl. Cheryl is 25, and her income exceeds the dependent exemption amount; thus, Mary is not entitled to claim Cheryl as her dependent. Under prior law, Mary was still entitled to head-of-household status. Under the new law, she is no longer entitled to that status, since Cheryl is not a qualifying child and is not otherwise qualified to be Mary's dependent.

¶150

For further information on this subject, consult any of the following CCH reporter explanations:

- Standard Federal Tax Reporter, 2004FED ¶3340.01
- Federal Tax Service, FTS § A:2.80
- Federal Tax Guide, 2004FTG ¶6070

★ *Effective date.* The provision applies to tax years beginning after December 31, 2004 (Act Sec. 208 of the Working Families Tax Relief Act of 2004).

Act Sec. 202(a) of the Working Families Tax Relief Act of 2004, amending Code Sec. 2(b)(1)(A)(i); Act Sec. 202(b), amending Code Sec. 2(b)(2), (3)(B)(i), and (3)(B)(ii); Act Sec. 208. Law at ¶5010. Committee Report at ¶10,120.

¶155
Dependent Care Credit

Background

A nonrefundable credit is allowed for a portion of qualifying child or dependent care expenses paid by an individual in order to be gainfully employed. Taxpayers with adjusted gross income of $15,000 or less are allowed a credit equal to 35 percent of employment-related expenses. The credit is reduced by one percentage point for each $2,000 of adjusted gross income, or fraction thereof, above $15,000 through $43,000. Taxpayers with adjusted gross income over $43,000 are allowed a credit equal to 20 percent of employment-related expenses (Code Sec. 21(a)). The maximum amount of employment-related expenses to which the credit may be applied is $3,000 if there is one qualifying individual or $6,000 if two or more qualifying individuals are involved (Code Sec. 21(c)). These amounts are subject to the sunset provision of the Economic Growth and Tax Relief Reconcilation Act of 2001 (Sec. 901 of P.L. 107-16) under which these amounts will return to pre-2001 levels for tax years beginning after December 31, 2010.

To be eligible for the dependent care credit, the taxpayer must maintain a household for one or more of the following qualifying individuals:

- a dependent under the age of 13 for whom a dependency exemption may be claimed,

- a dependent who is physically or mentally incapable of taking care of himself or herself, or

- the taxpayer's spouse, if the spouse is physically or mentally incapable of taking care of himself or herself.

A taxpayer is considered to have maintained a household for any period if he or she furnishes over one-half of the costs incurred in maintaining the household. Such costs include property taxes, mortgage interest, rent, utility charges, repairs, property insurance, and food consumed on the premises. The household must be both the taxpayer's and the qualifying individual's principal place of abode for the tax year (Code Sec. 21(e)(1) and Reg. § 1.44A-1(d)(3)).

Working Families Tax Act Impact

Dependent care credit modified.—The Working Families Tax Relief Act of 2004 makes several changes with respect to the dependent care credit. First, if all other requirements are satisfied, a taxpayer may claim the dependent care credit with respect to a qualifying individual who lives with the taxpayer for more than one-half of the year, even if the taxpayer does not provide more than one-half of the cost of maintaining the household (Code Sec. 21(a)(1), as amended by the 2004 Working Families Tax Act).

To be a qualifying individual for purposes of the dependent care credit, a disabled dependent or spouse of the taxpayer will have to have the same principal place of abode as the taxpayer for more than one-half of the tax year (Code Sec. 21(b)(1), as amended by the 2004 Working Families Tax Act). Morever, an individual will not be treated as having the same principal place of abode as the taxpayer if, at any time during the tax year, the relationship between the individual and the taxpayer is in violation of local law (Code Sec. 21(e)(1), as amended by the 2004 Working Families Tax Act).

> **Compliance Tip:** The dependent care credit is claimed on Form 2441, Dependent Care Expenses, for taxpayers who file Form 1040. Taxpayers who file Form 1040A must claim the credit using Schedule 2, Child and Dependent Care Expenses for Form 1040A Filers.

For further information on this subject, consult any of the following CCH reporter explanations:

- Standard Federal Tax Reporter, 2004FED ¶3507.01
- Federal Tax Service, FTS § A:19.41
- Federal Tax Guide, 2004FTG ¶2181

★ *Effective date.* The provision applies to tax years beginning after December 31, 2004 (Act Sec. 208 of the Working Families Tax Relief Act of 2004).

Act Sec. 203(a) of the Working Families Tax Relief Act of 2004, amending Code Sec. 21(a)(1); Act Sec. 203(b), amending Code Sec. 21(b)(1); Act Sec. 203(c), amending Code Sec. 21(e)(1); Act Sec. 208. Law at ¶5015. Committee Report at ¶10,130.

¶160

Child Tax Credit Requirements Modified

Background ————————————————————————————————

Child-related tax benefits affect millions of individual tax returns. The existence of a qualifying child or children can determine whether a taxpayer is entitled to a dependency exemption; whether the taxpayer qualifies as a head of household; and whether the taxpayer can claim the child tax credit, the earned income credit, and the dependent care credit. Each of these items has its own independent definition of a qualifying child, and these varying definitions add to the complexity of the tax code. Factors relevant to the definitions of a qualifying child include the child's age, the child's relationship to the taxpayer, the child's income, the child's residence and who maintains it, and the level of support provided by the taxpayer. Note that a taxpayer must determine eligibility for each of these benefits separately, and an individual who qualifies the taxpayer for benefits under one provision may not necessarily qualify the taxpayer for benefits under another provision.

Taxpayers with incomes below certain amounts are eligible for a child tax credit for each qualifying child, and a portion of this credit is refundable under certain circumstances. The maximum amount of the child tax credit is $1,000 per child in the case of tax years beginning in 2003 or 2004. The credit is scheduled to revert to $700 for tax years beginning in 2005 through 2008, $800 for tax years beginning in 2009, and back to $1,000 for tax years beginning in 2010. The credit then declines to $500 in tax year 2011 (Code Sec. 24(a)).

Background _____

For purposes of the child credit, a "qualifying child" is an individual: (1) with respect to whom the taxpayer is entitled to a dependency exemption for the year; (2) who satisfies the same relationship test applicable to the earned income credit (see ¶165); and (3) who has not attained age 17 as of the close of the calendar year (Code Sec. 24(c)). In Rev. Rul. 2003-72, the IRS stated that for purposes of the child tax credit, an individual attains a specific age on the anniversary of the date that the child was born.

> **Example:** Amie St. Claire was born on January 1, 1988. She will attain the age of 17 on January 1, 2005.

For purposes of the child tax credit, the relationship test is satisfied by:

- the taxpayer's children and step-children, and their descendants;

- the taxpayer's siblings and step-siblings and their descendants, if they are cared for as the taxpayer's own children;

- a child who was legally adopted by the taxpayer or who was placed with the taxpayer by an authorized placement agency for adoption by the taxpayer; and

- a foster child who was placed with the taxpayer by an authorized placement agency, and is cared for as the taxpayer's own child (Code Sec. 32(c)(3)(B)).

A qualifying child must also be a citizen or resident of the United States (Code Sec. 24(c)(2)). The child tax credit does not apply with respect to a child who is a resident of Canada or Mexico and is not a U.S. citizen, even if a dependency exemption is available with respect to the child.

> **Comment:** The Conference Committee Report states that under current law, the child tax credit is available with respect to a child dependent who is not a resident or citizen of the United States if the child has been legally adopted by the taxpayer, the child's principal place of abode is the taxpayer's home, and the taxpayer is a U.S. citizen or national (Conference Committee Report to the Working Families Tax Relief Act of 2004, H.R. Conf. Rep. No. 108-696). However, this statement appears to conflict with the existing statutory language (Code Secs. 24(c)(2) and 152(b)(3)).

Working Families Tax Act Impact

Child defined for child tax credit.—The child tax credit generally uses the same relationships to define an eligible child as are used in the new uniform definition of a child for purposes of the dependency exemption (see ¶145) (Code Sec. 24(c)(1), as amended by the Working Families Tax Relief Act of 2004). This means that a qualifying child for purposes of the child credit includes the taxpayer's children and their descendants, as well as the taxpayer's siblings (including half-siblings and step-siblings) and their descendants. A qualifying child must share the same principal place of abode as the taxpayer, and must not provide more than one-half of his or her own support for the calendar year in which the taxpayer's tax year begins (Code Sec. 152(c), as amended by the 2004 Working Families Tax Act). A taxpayer's child may also be the taxpayer's stepchild; a child legally adopted by the taxpayer or lawfully placed with the taxpayer for legal adoption by the taxpayer; or a foster child who has been placed with the taxpayer by an authorized placement agency or by a judgment, decree or other order of any court of competent jurisdiction (Code Sec. 152(f), as amended by the 2004 Working Families Tax Act).

The definition of a qualifying child for purposes of the child credit still differs from the uniform definition of a child in one significant respect. The child credit retains the present-law requirement that a qualifying child must be under age 17 (Code Sec. 24(c)(1), as amended by the 2004 Working Families Tax Act). However, for purposes of the dependency exemption, all qualifying children can be as old as 19, a student can be as old as 24, and no age limit applies if the child is permanently and totally disabled at any time during the taxpayer's tax year (Code Sec. 152(c)(3), as amended by the 2004 Working Families Tax Act).

> **PRACTICAL ANALYSIS. Vincent O'Brien, President of Vincent J. O'Brien, CPA, PC, Lynbrook, New York, observes that for the purposes of the child credit, the age of an eligible child does not follow the uniform definition. Thus, a qualifying child must still be under the age of 17 for a taxpayer to claim the child credit. Furthermore, a taxpayer still is required to be entitled to claim a child as his or her dependent in order to claim the child credit.**

> *Comment.* **Thus, divorced or legally-separated parents who agree to which parent will claim the dependent exemption for a child must be aware that the same parent that claims the exemption will also be entitled to claim the child credit.**

For further information on this subject, consult any of the following CCH reporter explanations:

- Standard Federal Tax Reporter, 2004FED ¶3770.01
- Federal Tax Service, FTS § A:19.201
- Federal Tax Guide, 2004FTG ¶2222

★ *Effective date.* The provision is effective for tax years beginning after December 31, 2004 (Act Sec. 208 of the Working Families Tax Relief Act of 2004).

Act Sec. 204(a) of the Working Families Tax Relief Act of 2004, amending Code Sec. 24(c)(1); Act Sec. 204(b), amending Code Sec. 24(c)(2); Act Sec. 208. Law at ¶5020. Committee Report at ¶10,140.

¶165
Earned Income Credit Requirements Modified

Background

Child-related tax benefits affect millions of individual tax returns. The existence of a qualifying child or children can determine whether a taxpayer is entitled to a dependency exemption; whether the taxpayer qualifies as a head of household; and whether the taxpayer can claim the child tax credit, the earned income credit, and the dependent care credit. Each of these items has its own independent definition of a qualifying child, and these varying definitions add to the complexity of the tax code. Factors relevant to the definitions of a qualifying child include the child's age, the child's relationship to the taxpayer, the child's income, the child's residence and who maintains it, and the level of support provided by the taxpayer. A taxpayer is required to determine eligibility for each of these benefits separately, and an individual qualifies the taxpayer for benefits under one provision may not necessarily qualify the taxpayer for benefits under another provision.

Generally, the earned income credit is a refundable credit for low-income workers (Code Sec. 32). The amount of the credit depends on the earned income of the taxpayer and whether the taxpayer has one, more than one, or no "qualifying children" (Code Sec. 32(b)). In order to be a qualifying child, an individual must

Background _____

satisfy three tests: (1) a relationship test, (2) a residency test, and (3) an age test (Code Sec. 32(c)(3)). In addition, the name, age, and taxpayer identification number (TIN) of the qualifying child must be included on the taxpayer's return (Code Sec. 32(c)(1)(F)).

Relationship test. An individual satisfies the earned income credit relationship test if the individual is the taxpayer's: (1) son, daughter, step-son, or step-daughter, or a descendant of any such individual; (2) brother, sister, step-brother, or step-sister, or a descendant of any such individual, who the taxpayer cares for as the taxpayer's own child; or (3) eligible foster child. An "eligible foster child" is an individual (1) who is placed with the taxpayer by an authorized placement agency, and (2) who the taxpayer cares for as her or his own child. A married child of the taxpayer is not treated as meeting the relationship test unless the taxpayer is entitled to a dependency exemption with respect to the married child (e.g., the support test is satisfied) or would be entitled to the exemption if the taxpayer had not waived the exemption to the noncustodial parent. A child who is legally adopted or placed with the taxpayer for adoption by an authorized adoption agency is treated as the taxpayer's own child (Code Sec. 32(c)(3)).

Residency test. The residency test is satisfied if the individual has the same principal place of abode as the taxpayer for more than one-half of the tax year (Code Sec. 32(c)(3)(A)(ii)). The residence must be in the United States (Code Sec. 32(c)(3)(E)). The principal place of abode of a member of the Armed Services is treated as in the United States for any period during which the individual is stationed outside the United States on active duty (Code Sec. 32(c)(4)). As with the dependency exemption (see ¶145) and head-of-household filing status (see ¶150), temporary absences due to special circumstances, including absences due to illness, education, business, vacation, and military service, are not treated as absences for purposes of determining whether the residency test is satisfied (Earned Income Credit, IRS Publication 596). The taxpayer is not required to maintain the household in which the taxpayer and the qualifying individual reside.

Age test. The age test is generally satisfied if the individual has not attained age 19 as of the close of the calendar year. In the case of a full-time student, the age test is satisfied if the individual has not attained age 24 as of the close of the calendar year. In the case of an individual who is permanently and totally disabled, no age limit applies (Code Sec. 32(c)(3)(C)).

Working Families Tax Act Impact

Child defined for earned income credit.—The definition of a qualifying child for purposes of the earned income credit is generally the same as the uniform definition of a child that is contained in the new dependency exemption rules (see ¶145). There are many substantive similarities between the old definition and the new one, but they are not entirely identical. For purposes of the earned income credit, the present-law requirement that a foster child and certain other children be cared for as the taxpayer's own child is eliminated. The residency and age tests are not substantively changed.

Relationship test. The relationship test is now provided by the uniform definition of a child, rather than as a separate requirement of the earned income credit (Code Sec. 32(c)(3)(A), as amended by the Working Families Tax Relief Act of 2004). As under current law, a qualifying child must be the taxpayer's son, daughter, step-son, step-daughter, brother, sister, stepbrother, step-sister, or a descendant of any such individual. An adopted child is treated as a child by blood if the child was legally adopted by the taxpayer, or was lawfully placed with the taxpayer for legal adoption

¶165

by the taxpayer. A foster child is also treated as the taxpayer's child if the child was placed with the taxpayer by an authorized placement agency or by judgment, decree, or other order of any court of competent jurisdiction (Code Sec. 152(c), as amended by the 2004 Working Families Tax Act). These provisions eliminate the present-law rule under which the taxpayer's foster children and the taxpayer's siblings, step-siblings, and their descendants, are not qualifying children unless they are cared for as the taxpayer's own children. As under current law, a child who is married at the end of the taxpayer's tax year must qualify as the taxpayer's dependent in order to be a qualifying child (Code Sec. 32(c)(3)(B), as amended by the 2004 Working Families Tax Act).

The uniform definition of a child for purposes of the earned income credit differs from the definition contained in the dependency exemption for a child in two important respects. First, for purposes of the dependency exemption, a qualifying child must not provide more than one-half of his or her own support, but this restriction does not apply to a qualifying child for purposes of the earned income credit. Also, if a custodial parent would be entitled to a child's dependency exemption but for having released it to the noncustodial parent, the child is still a qualifying child for the custodial parent for purposes of the earned income credit (Code Sec. 32(c)(3)(A), as amended by the 2004 Working Families Tax Act).

> **Comment:** If one child is a qualifying child with respect to more than one tax return, the existing tie-breaker rules for the earned income credit continue to apply. These same rules have also been incorporated into the new dependency exemption rules (see ¶145).

Residency test. Under the residency test for the uniform definition of a child, the child must have the same principal place of abode as the taxpayer for more than one-half of the taxpayer's tax year (Code Sec. 152(c)(1)(B), as amended by the 2004 Working Families Tax Act). As under current law, the abode must be in the United States (Code Sec. 32(c)(3)(C), as amended by the 2004 Working Families Tax Act), and temporary absences due to special circumstances, including absences due to illness, education, business, vacation, or military service, are disregarded.

Age test. The substance of the age test does not change, but it is now provided by reference to the uniform definition of a child, rather than as a separate eligibility requirement for the earned income credit. Thus, a child must be under age 19 (or under age 24 in the case of a full-time student) in order to be a qualifying child. However, no age limit applies with respect to individuals who are totally and permanently disabled within the meaning of Code Sec. 22(e)(3) at any time during the calendar year (Code Sec. 152(c)(3), as amended by the 2004 Working Families Tax Act).

Identification requirements. As under current law, the taxpayer's return must provide the qualifying child's name, age and taxpayer identification number (TIN). However, the IRS is given the express authority to prescribe other methods for providing this information (Code Sec. 32(c)(3)(D), as amended by the 2004 Working Families Tax Act).

For further information on this subject, consult any of the following CCH reporter explanations:

- Standard Federal Tax Reporter, 2004FED ¶4082.01
- Federal Tax Service, FTS § A:19.122
- Federal Tax Guide, 2004FTG ¶2275

★ *Effective date.* The provision is effective for tax years beginning after December 31, 2004 (Act Sec. 208 of the Working Families Tax Relief Act of 2004).

Act Sec. 205(a) of the Working Families Tax Relief Act of 2004, amending Code Sec. 32(c)(3); Act Sec. 205(b), amending Code Sec. 32(c)(1), (c)(4) and (m); Act Sec. 208. Law at ¶ 5040. Committee Report at ¶ 10,150.

¶ 170

Dependency Exemption

Background _____

If all of several requirements are met, a taxpayer may claim an income tax exemption for a dependent. In 2004, the exemption amount is $3,100 (Rev. Proc. 2003-85, IRB 2003-49, 1184). The exemption is phased out for higher-income taxpayers with adjusted gross income above certain thresholds (Code Sec. 151(d)(3)).

In addition to the five tests embodied in Code Sec. 152 (relationship or member-of-household test; support test; gross income test; citizen or resident test; and joint return test) (see Background discussion at ¶ 145), Code Sec. 151(c) imposes several additional rules relating to the exemption.

The dependent either must have gross income for the calendar year in an amount that is less than the exemption amount ($3,100 for 2004), *or*

- the dependent must be the taxpayer's child who has not attained age 19 at the close of the calendar year in which the taxpayer's tax year begins, or

- the dependent must be a student who has not attained age 24 at the close of that calendar year (Code Sec. 151(c)(1)).

The dependency exemption is denied with respect to certain married dependents (Code Sec. 151(c)(2)). For purposes of the dependency exemption, a "child" is defined as a son, step-son, daughter or step-daughter of the taxpayer (Code Sec. 151(c)(3)) and a "student" is an individual who during at least five calendar months during the calendar year is either (1) a full-time student at an educational organization or (2) pursuing a full-time, accredited on-farm training course (Code Sec. 151(c)(4)).

For purposes of determining whether the dependent has earned gross income in excess of the exemption amount for the year, income earned at a "sheltered work-shop" by a permanently and totally disabled dependent is disregarded (Code Sec. 151(c)(5)).

Rules are provided that determine the tax treatment of missing children for the purpose of the dependency exemption, the child care tax credit (Code Sec. 24), and the status of a taxpayer as a surviving spouse or head of household (Code Sec. 2). The missing children rules of Code Sec. 151(c)(6) apply to a taxpayer's child who is presumed kidnapped by someone who is not a member of the family, and who otherwise was a dependent of the taxpayer during the portion of the calendar year prior to the kidnapping.

Working Families Tax Act Impact

Dependency exemption rules amended.—The Working Families Tax Relief Act of 2004 modifies the Code Sec. 151(c) rules with respect to the dependency exemption by providing that the exemption will apply to each individual who, for the tax year, is the taxpayer's dependent (as defined in Code Sec. 152). Under the Act, the definition of a dependent is determined according to whether the dependent is a "qualifying child" or a "qualifying relative." For a qualifying child, the existing gross income test is eliminated and the existing support test is relaxed. With respect to qualifying relatives, most of the existing tests for dependents continue to apply. Thus, the gross income and support test, including the special rules applicable to the income of handicapped dependents and the special rules applicable to students, apply. Individuals who meet the existing dependency tests and who are not qualifying children are deemed to be qualifying relatives. Thus, as under pre-2004 Working Families Tax Act law, a taxpayer may claim a parent as a dependent if the taxpayer furnishes more than one-half of the parent's support and the parent's gross income is less than the exemption amount ($3,100 in 2004). Likewise, a grandparent can claim a dependency exemption for a grandchild who does not reside with the grandparent for over half the year, as long as the grandparent provides more than half the support of the grandchild and the grandchild's gross income is less than the exemption amount ($3,100 in 2004) (Conference Committee Report to the 2004 Working Families Tax Act (H.R. Conf. Rep. No. 108-696)).

See ¶145 for a discussion of Code Sec. 152, as amended by the 2004 Working Families Tax Act.

> **Compliance Tip:** Personal exemptions are claimed on Form 1040 or Form 1040A. The taxpayer, his or her spouse, and dependents are listed in the "Exemptions" section of either form. The total number of exemptions is then multiplied by the applicable exemption amount ($3,100 in 2004, subject to the phase-out for high-income taxpayers) and used to figure taxable income. Taxpayer identification numbers (TINs) for dependents must be provided on tax returns. The dependency exemption will be denied to claimants who fail to provide the dependent's correct TIN on the return on which the exemption is claimed (Code Sec. 151(e)).

For further information on this subject, consult any of the following CCH reporter explanations:

- Standard Federal Tax Reporter, 2004FED ¶8005.01
- Federal Tax Service, FTS § A:3.80
- Federal Tax Guide, 2004FTG ¶6110

★ *Effective date.* The provision applies to tax years beginning after December 31, 2004 (Act Sec. 208 of the Working Families Tax Relief Act of 2004).

Act Sec. 206 of the Working Families Tax Relief Act of 2004, amending Code Sec. 151(c); Act Sec. 208. Law at ¶5140. Committee Report at ¶10,100.

MILITARY

¶180

Earned Income Includes Combat Pay

Background

A refundable earned income credit is available to certain low-income individuals who have earned income, meet adjusted gross income thresholds, and do not have more than a certain amount of disqualified income (Code Sec. 32). The term "earned income" generally includes taxable compensation from employment. Wages, salaries, tips, and other employee compensation are common forms of earned income. Earned income does not include nontaxable income such as military pay for housing, subsistence allowances, or combat pay.

Working Families Tax Act Impact

Combat pay treated as earned income.—In an effort to provide assistance to military families in combat zones, the earned income credit (EIC) and refundable child credit amounts are increased for military families in 2004 and 2005 by giving them the option to include combat pay when calculating the EIC and the child tax credit. Now, any taxpayer may elect to treat combat pay that is otherwise excluded from gross income under Code Sec. 112 as earned income for purposes of the earned income credit (Code Sec. 24(d)(1), as amended by the Working Families Tax Relief Act of 2004). Also, combat pay that is otherwise excluded from gross income under Code Sec. 112 is treated as earned income which is taken into account in computing taxable income for purposes of calculating the refundable portion of the child tax credit (Code Sec. 32(c)(2)(B)(vi), as added by the 2004 Working Families Tax Act).

For further information on this subject, consult any of the following CCH reporter explanations:

- Standard Federal Tax Reporter, 2004FED ¶3770.01 and ¶4082.01
- Federal Tax Service, FTS § A:19.124[3]
- Federal Tax Guide, 2004FTG ¶2275

★ *Effective date.* The election to treat combat pay as earned income for the earned income credit is effective for tax years ending after the date of enactment and before January 1, 2006. The provision relating to the treatment of combat pay as earned income for purposes of the child tax credit is effective for tax years beginning after December 31, 2003. (Act Sec. 104(c) of the Working Families Tax Relief Act of 2004).

EGTRRA sunset provision. The amendments made by Title I of the 2004 Working Families Tax Act are subject to the sunset provision found in Title IX of the Economic Growth and Tax Relief Reconciliation Act of 2001 (P.L. 107-16). These 2004 amendments are subject to the EGTRRA sunset provision to the same extent and in the same manner as the provision of EGTRRA to which the amendment relates. (Act Sec. 105). See ¶29,001 for the CCH Explanation of the sunset provision.

Act Sec. 104(a) of the Working Families Tax Relief Act of 2004, amending Code Sec. 24(d)(1); Act Sec. 104(b), amending Code Sec. 32(c)(2)(B); Act Sec. 104(c); Act Sec. 105. Law at ¶5020 and ¶5040. Committee Report at ¶10,070.

TEACHERS

¶185

Teachers' Expense Deduction

Background _____

Eligible educators are entitled to an above-the-line deduction of up to $250 per year for unreimbursed expenses incurred in connection with books, supplies (other than nonathletic supplies for courses of instruction in health or physical education), computer equipment (including related software and services) and other equipment, and supplementary materials used in the classroom (Code Sec. 62(a)(2)(D)). The $250 maximum deduction amount is permitted only to the extent that it exceeds the amount excludable in relation to:

    (1) interest from U.S. Savings Bonds used to pay higher education expenses (Code Sec. 135);

    (2) distributions and earnings from qualified tuition programs (Code Sec. 529(c)(1)); or

    (3) distributions from Coverdell education savings accounts (Code Sec 530(d)(2)).

Background

An eligible educator is an individual who, for at least 900 hours during the school year, is a kindergarten through grade 12 teacher, instructor, counselor, principal or aide. For purposes of the deduction, a school is any school that provides elementary or secondary education as determined under state law (Code Sec. 62(d)).

The deduction for eligible educator classroom expenses was enacted as part of the Job Creation and Worker Assistance Act of 2002 (P.L. 107-147). It applies for classroom expenses paid in 2002 and 2003 (Code Sec. 62(a)(2)(D)).

Working Families Tax Act Impact

Extension of above-the-line deduction for eligible educator expenses.—The deduction for eligible educator expenses now applies to tax years 2002, 2003, 2004, and 2005. It is set to expire for expenses incurred after December 31, 2005 (Code Sec. 62(a)(2)(D), as amended by the Working Families Tax Relief Act of 2004).

> **Compliance Tip:** The above-the-line deduction for eligible educator expenses is claimed on the educator's Form 1040 or Form 1040A individual income tax return.

For further information on this subject, consult any of the following CCH reporter explanations:

- Standard Federal Tax Reporter, 2004FED ¶5504.01
- Federal Tax Service, FTS § A:11.167
- Federal Tax Guide, 2004FTG ¶6460

★ *Effective date.* The provision applies to expenses paid or incurred in tax years beginning after December 31, 2003 (Act Sec. 307(b) of the Working Families Tax Relief Act of 2004).

Act Sec. 307(a) of the Working Families Tax Relief Act of 2004, amending Code Sec. 62(a)(2)(D); Act Sec. 307(b). Law at ¶5095. Committee Report at ¶10,270.

Chapter 2

Business and Government Extensions

BUSINESS INCENTIVES

¶ 205

Research Credit Extended

Background

The credit for increasing research activities (Code Sec. 41, commonly referred to as the "research credit") was first enacted in 1981 for a period of four and one-half years. The purpose behind the credit was, and still is, to encourage companies to increase their spending on research for new and innovative products. Originally, the credit amount was 25 percent of the qualified research expenses over a base amount. Beginning with 1986 legislation and over the next several years:

  • the credit amount was lowered to 20 percent of the expenses over the base amount,

  • the base amount calculation was adjusted,

  • the deduction for research and development expenses (Code Sec. 174) was reduced by 100 percent of the research credit amount claimed,

Background _____

- an alternative incremental research credit calculation was introduced to allow electing taxpayers to claim the research credit at reduced rates based on the amount of expenditures exceeding a lower base amount, and

  - the definition of qualified research expenses was narrowed.

Despite these changes, the research credit is an integral part of many companies' budgeting process and plays a key role in producing jobs. Surveys have shown that between 75 percent and 90 percent of the expenses qualifying for the credit are attributable to wages. The research credit has been acknowledged as a driving force behind the creation of new products, new services and even new companies.

The research credit's expiration date has been extended several times from as short a period as 11 months to as long as five years. At one point, the research credit was allowed to expire and the extension was not made retroactive to the prior expiration date. The latest extension was in 1999 for a period of five years, including two one-year suspension periods. Despite lobbying by numerous manufacturing associations to make it permanent, the research credit expired again on June 30, 2004.

Working Families Tax Act Impact

Extension of the research credit.—The research credit is extended for 18 months for qualified research expenses paid or incurred on or before December 31, 2005 (Code Sec. 41(h)(1)(B), as amended by the Working Families Tax Relief Act of 2004). Expenses that qualify for the Code Sec. 45C credit, Clinical Testing Expenses for Certain Rare Diseases or Conditions ("orphan drug" credit), are defined in part by reference to "qualified research expenses." Thus, changes were made to Code Sec. 45C to reflect the extension of the research credit (Code Sec. 45C(b)(1)(D), as amended by the 2004 Working Families Tax Act).

Compliance Tip: The research credit is computed on Form 6765, Credit for Increasing Research Activities, and, as a component of the general business credit (Code Sec. 38), is subject to the limitations and the carryforward and carryback rules for business credits.

Comment: Several members of Congress have indicated that they will offer amendments to the Foreign Sales Corporation/Extraterritorial Income (FSC/ETI) repeal legislation to either enhance the research credit or make it permanent.

PRACTICAL ANALYSIS. Mark Luscombe, Principal Analyst, CCH Tax and Accounting, notes that several large corporations have been working with Congress to expand the research credit to make the credit more available for research performed in collaborative research consortia and for research contracted to small businesses, universities and federal laboratories. Under language that passed the Senate in the Jumpstart Our Business Strength (JOBS) bill (S. 1637), 20 percent of a taxpayer's research expenses associated with a collaborative research consortia would qualify for the credit regardless of any reference to the expenses exceeding a base amount. Expenses associated with contracted research to small businesses, universities and federal laboratories still would be subject to a base amount test, but 100 percent of those expenses would enter into the calculation, rather than 65 percent as under current law. These changes to the research credit were not picked up as part of this extension legislation but are likely to be revisited by Congress in the future.

¶205

For further information on this subject, consult any of the following CCH reporter explanations:

- Standard Federal Tax Reporter, 2004FED ¶4362.01 and ¶4475.01

- Federal Tax Service, FTS §G:24.80

- Federal Tax Guide, 2004FTG ¶2450

★ *Effective date.* The provision is effective for amounts paid or incurred after June 30, 2004.

Act Sec. 301(a)(1) of the Working Families Tax Relief Act of 2004, amending Code Sec. 41(h)(1)(B); Act Sec. 301(a)(2), amending Code Sec. 45C(b)(1)(D); Act Sec. 301(b). Law at ¶5050 and ¶5070. Committee Report at ¶10,200.

¶ 207

Deduction for Charitable Contribution of Computers Extended

Background

Corporations are entitled to a charitable contributions deduction limited to 10 percent of the corporation's taxable income, computed without adjustments for: (1) the deduction for charitable contributions, (2) the deductions for certain dividends received and for dividends paid on certain preferred stock of public utilities, (3) any net operating loss carryback, and (4) any capital loss carryback (Code Sec. 170(b)(2)). Generally, for contributions of property, the deduction is limited to the corporation's basis in the property up to 10 percent of the corporation's taxable income (Code Sec. 170(e)).

Certain corporate contributions, however, qualify for preferred treatment. An "augmented charitable deduction" is available to C corporations that contribute computer technology and/or equipment to an eligible donee. The augmented charitable deduction is equal to the corporate donor's basis in the donated property plus one-half of the ordinary income that would have been realized if the property had been sold. However, the deduction cannot exceed twice the corporation's basis in the property (Code Sec. 170(e)(6)).

Qualified gifts of computer technology and equipment include contributions of computer software, computer or peripheral equipment, and fiber optic cable related to computer use that are to be used within the United States for educational purposes (Code Sec. 170(e)(6)(F)).

An eligible donee is defined as:

(1) an educational organization that normally maintains a regular faculty and curriculum and has regularly enrolled students in attendance at the place where its educational activities are regularly conducted;

(2) a tax-exempt entity that is organized primarily for purposes of supporting elementary and secondary education;

(3) a private foundation that, within 30 days after receipt of the contribution, contributes the property to an eligible donee described in (1) and (2) above, and notifies the donor of the contribution (Code Secs. 170(e)(6)(B) and (C)); or

(4) a public library, as defined in the Library Services and Technology Act (20 U.S.C. §9122(2)(A)) (Code Sec. 170(e)(6)(B)(i)(III)).

Background

The augmented charitable deduction for contributions of computer technology and/or equipment to schools or public libraries expired for contributions made during any tax year beginning after December 31, 2003 (Code Sec. 170(e)(6)(G)).

Working Families Tax Act Impact

Enhanced charitable deduction for computer technology and equipment extended.—The augmented charitable deduction for computer technology and/or equipment available to eligible donees is extended retroactively for two years. The deduction is now set to expire for computer contributions made during any tax year beginning after December 31, 2005 (Code Sec. 170(e)(6)(G), as amended by the Working Families Tax Relief Act of 2004).

Compliance Tip: Corporations making noncash charitable contributions should file Form 8283, Noncash Charitable Contributions, to report information about the donated property. C corporations, other than personal service corporations and closely held corporations, file Form 8283 only if the amount claimed as a deduction is over $5,000 (Instructions for Form 8283).

For further information on this subject, consult any of the following CCH reporter explanations:

- Standard Federal Tax Reporter, 2004FED ¶11,620.01
- Federal Tax Service, FTS §I:22.164
- Federal Tax Guide, 2004FTG ¶6587

★ *Effective date.* The provision is effective for contributions made in tax years beginning after December 31, 2003.

Act Sec. 306(a) of the Working Families Tax Relief Act of 2004, amending Code Sec. 170(e)(6)(G); Act Sec. 306(b). Law at ¶5165. Committee Report at ¶10,260.

¶209

Election to Deduct Environmental Remediation Costs Extended

Background

A taxpayer can elect to currently deduct certain environmental cleanup costs. The costs must be incurred in connection with the abatement or control of hazardous substances at a qualified contaminated site. In the case of property to which an environmental remediation expenditure otherwise would have to be capitalized, the deduction allowed under the election is treated as a depreciation deduction and is subject to depreciation recapture rules as Code Sec. 1245 property (Code Sec. 198).

The election was enacted by the Taxpayer Relief Act of 1997 (P.L. 105-34). It was extended by the Tax Relief Extension Act of 1999 (P.L. 106-170), and then again by the Community Renewal Tax Relief Act of 2000 (P.L. 106-554) to apply to expenditures paid or incurred before January 1, 2004.

Working Families Tax Act Impact

Extension of election to deduct environmental remediation costs.—The election to deduct environmental remediation costs is extended retroactively for two years to cover expenditures paid or incurred before January 1, 2006 (Code Sec. 198(h), as amended by the Working Families Tax Relief Act of 2004).

Compliance Tip: In general, the election must be made on or before the due date, including extensions, for filing the income tax return for the tax year in which the expenditures are paid or incurred. Each expense must be separately identified. Individuals must include the total amount of the qualified expenses on the line for "other expenses" on Schedule C, Profit or Loss From Business; Schedule E, Supplemental Income or Loss; or Schedule F, Profit or Loss From Farming, which are filed with Form 1040, U.S. Individual Income Tax Return. Wherever the schedule requires that the taxpayer separately identify each expense, the taxpayer must write "Section 198 Election" on the line on which the qualified expenses separately appear. Taxpayers other than individuals must include the total amount of qualified expenses on the line for other deductions, or the equivalent thereof, on their appropriate federal income tax return. A schedule must be attached that separately identifies each expense included in other deductions, or the equivalent thereof, and the taxpayer must write "Section 198 Election" on the line on which the qualified expense amounts separately appear. See Rev. Proc. 98-47, 1998-2 CB 319, for additional information.

For further information on this subject, consult any of the following CCH reporter explanations:

- Standard Federal Tax Reporter, 2004FED ¶12,465.01
- Federal Tax Service, FTS §G:6.323
- Federal Tax Guide, 2004FTG ¶7402

★ *Effective date.* This provision applies to expenditures paid or incurred in tax years beginning after December 31, 2003 (Act Sec. 308(b), Working Families Tax Relief Act of 2004).

Act Sec. 308(a) of the Working Families Tax Relief Act of 2004, amending Code Sec. 198(h); Act Sec. 308(b). Law at ¶5180. Committee Report at ¶10,280.

¶211

Work Opportunity Credit Extended

Background

The work opportunity tax credit provides employers with an incentive to hire individuals from eight targeted groups that have a particularly high unemployment rate or other special employment needs (Code Sec. 51). The credit was designed to help such employers offset the costs of hiring, training, and supervising workers who have little, if any, work experience and few prospects for employment.

Employers hiring members of the following groups are eligible for the credit:

(1) families eligible to receive benefits under the Temporary Assistance for Needy Families (TANF) program (Code Sec. 51(d)(2));

(2) high-risk youth (Code Sec. 51(d)(5));

(3) qualified ex-felons (Code Sec. 51(d)(4));

(4) vocational rehabilitation referrals (Code Sec. 51(d)(6));

(5) qualified summer youth employees (Code Sec. 51(d)(7));

(6) qualified veterans (Code Sec. 51(d)(3));

(7) families receiving food stamps (Code Sec. 51(d)(8)); and

(8) persons receiving certain Supplemental Security Income benefits (Code Sec. 51(d)(9)).

Background

An employer must obtain certification from a state employment security agency that an individual is a member of a targeted group (Code Sec. 51(d)(12)).

The credit is equal to 40 percent of up to $6,000 of the targeted employee's qualified first-year wages ($3,000 for qualified summer youth employees), provided the employee completes a minimum of 400 hours of service (Code Sec. 51(a), (b) and (c)). Thus, the maximum credit per targeted employee is $2,400 ($1,200 for qualified summer youth employees). The credit is reduced to 25 percent for employees who complete less than 400 hours of service, and no credit is allowed for employees who complete less than 120 hours of service (Code Sec. 51(i)(3)). An employer's business expense deduction for wages is reduced by the amount of the work opportunity tax credit (Code Sec. 280C(a)).

The work opportunity credit was enacted by the Small Business Jobs Protection Act of 1996 (P.L. 104-188), replacing the targeted jobs tax credit. As enacted, it applied to wages paid or incurred to a qualified individual who begins work for the employer after September 30, 1996, and before October 1, 1997. The credit, however, has been extended over the years. Most recently, the Job Creation and Worker Assistance Act of 2002 (P.L. 107-147) extended the credit to wages paid or incurred to a qualified individual who began work for an employer before January 1, 2004.

Working Families Tax Act Impact

Extension of the work opportunity credit.—The work opportunity tax credit is retroactively extended for two years through December 31, 2005 (Code Sec. 51(c)(4), as amended by the Working Families Tax Relief Act of 2004).

Compliance Tip: Employers claiming the credit are to use Form 5884, Work Opportunity Credit. Form 8850, Pre-Screening Notice and Certification Request for the Work Opportunity and Welfare-to-Work Credits, is to be used in the pre-screening and certification process. Form 8850 must be sent, along with the appropriate U.S. Department of Labor form, to the state's designated certification agency no later than 21 days after the individual begins work.

PRACTICAL ANALYSIS. Mark Luscombe, Principal Analyst, CCH Tax and Accounting, points out that the Senate has passed legislation, the Jumpstart Our Business Strength (JOBS) bill (S. 1637) that would have consolidated the welfare-to-work credit and work opportunity credit by repealing Code Sec. 51A, the welfare-to-work credit, and adding a new subparagraph to Code Sec. 51, the work opportunity credit, addressing long-term family assistance recipients as one of the many categories of workers qualifying under the work opportunity credit provisions. This proposal also would have made various changes with respect to other categories of disadvantaged workers: ex-felons, food stamp recipients and designated community residents. This simplification effort was not picked up in this legislation as part of the extension of the welfare-to-work credit and work opportunity credit but is likely to be revisited in future legislation.

For further information on this subject, consult any of the following CCH reporter explanations:

- Standard Federal Tax Reporter, 2004FED ¶4803.01
- Federal Tax Service, FTS § G:24.120
- Federal Tax Guide, 2004FTG ¶2800

¶211

★ *Effective date.* The provision applies to individuals who begin work for an employer after December 31, 2003 (Act Sec. 303(b) of the Working Families Tax Relief Act of 2004).

Act Sec. 303(a)(1) of the Working Families Tax Relief Act of 2004, amending Code Sec. 51(c)(4); Act Sec. 303(b). Law at ¶5075. Committee Report at ¶10,220.

¶213
Welfare-to-Work Credit Extended

Background

A tax credit of up to $8,500 per individual is allowed to employers for qualified first- and second-year wages paid to qualified long-term family assistance recipients (Code Sec. 51A). The purpose of the credit is to provide employers with an incentive to hire long-term welfare recipients, to promote the transition from welfare to work by increasing access to employment, and to encourage employers to provide these individuals with training, health coverage, dependent care and better job attachment.

The credit is generally equal to 35 percent of the first $10,000 of eligible wages paid in the first year of employment, plus 50 percent of the first $10,000 of the eligible wages paid in the second year of employment (Code Sec. 51A(a) and (b)). Special rules apply to agricultural and railroad labor (Code Sec. 51A(b)(5)(C)). If a welfare-to-work tax credit is allowed to an employer for an individual for any tax year, that individual is not deemed to be a member of a targeted group for that tax year for purposes of the Code Sec. 51 work opportunity tax credit (Code Sec. 51A(e)).

Enacted by the Taxpayer Relief Act of 1997 (P.L. 105-34), the credit originally applied to wages paid to employees who started work for the employer after December 31, 1997. The credit was extended several times and was last extended by the Job Creation and Worker Assistance Act of 2002 (P.L. 107-147) to cover wages paid to employees who start work no later than December 31, 2003.

Working Families Tax Act Impact

Extension of welfare-to-work credit.—The welfare-to-work tax credit is extended retroactively through 2005. The credit is now scheduled to expire for individuals who begin work for an employer after December 31, 2005 (Code Sec. 51A(f), as amended by the Working Families Tax Relief Act of 2004).

Compliance Tip: Form 8861, Welfare-to-Work Credit, is used to claim the credit. Form 8850, Pre-Screening Notice and Certification Request for the Work Opportunity and Welfare-to-Work Credits, is to be used in the certification process.

For further information on this subject, consult any of the following CCH reporter explanations:

- Standard Federal Tax Reporter, 2004FED ¶4825.01
- Federal Tax Service, FTS §G:24.260
- Federal Tax Guide, 2004FTG ¶2822

★ *Effective date.* The provision applies to individuals who begin work for the employer after December 31, 2003 (Act Sec. 303(b) of the Working Families Tax Relief Act of 2004).

Act Sec. 303(a)(2) of the Working Families Tax Relief Act of 2004, amending Code Sec. 51A(f); Act Sec. 303(b). Law at ¶5080. Committee Report at ¶10,230.

¶ 215

Indian Employment Tax Credit Extended

Background _____

The Omnibus Budget Reconciliation Act of 1993 (P.L. 103-66) provided tax incentives to stimulate economic development and to encourage investment in Indian reservations. A nonrefundable income tax credit is allowed for the first $20,000 of qualified wages and health insurance costs paid or incurred for qualified employees who work on an Indian reservation.

The credit is equal to 20 percent of the employer's cost for a qualified employee's wages and health insurance that exceeds the amount the employer paid or incurred for such costs during 1993. Employees are qualified employees if they or their spouses are enrolled members of an Indian tribe, who work within an Indian reservation, and whose principal place of abode while employed is on or near the reservation where they are working. Employees whose total wages exceed $30,000 per year (as adjusted for inflation) during the tax year are not qualified employees.

Originally scheduled to expire in 2003, the credit was extended through December 31, 2004 by the Job Creation and Worker Assistance Act of 2002 (P.L. 107-147).

_____

Working Families Tax Act Impact

Extension of Indian employment credit.—The Working Families Tax Act of 2004 extends retroactively the Code Sec. 45A Indian employment tax credit through December 31, 2005.

> **Compliance Tip:** Employers should use Form 8845, Indian Employment Tax Credit, to compute the credit. Form 8845 is to be attached to the employer's tax return.

See also ¶ 343 for additional rules that affect the Indian employment credit.

For further information on this subject, consult any of the following CCH reporter explanations:

- Standard Federal Tax Reporter, 2004FED ¶ 4440.01
- Federal Tax Service, FTS § G:24.300
- Federal Tax Guide, 2004FTG ¶ 2775

★ *Effective date.* No specific effective date is provided by the Act. The provision is, therefore, considered effective on the date of enactment.

Act Sec. 315 of the Working Families Tax Relief Act of 2004, amending Code Sec. 45A(f). Law at ¶ 5065. Committee Report at ¶ 10,350.

¶ 217

MACRS Indian Reservation Property Recovery Periods

Background _____

A business incentive designed to encourage the purchase of depreciable property used on Indian reservations substitutes shortened modified accelerated cost recovery system (MACRS) recovery (depreciation) periods for the recovery periods that normally apply (Code Sec. 168(j)). In addition, the MACRS depreciation deduction allowed for regular tax purposes using these shortened recovery periods also applies for alternative minimum tax (AMT) purposes (Code Sec. 168(j)(3)). Consequently, there is no AMT depreciation adjustment. This incentive was scheduled to expire for property placed in service after December 31, 2004 (Code Sec. 168(j)(8)).

The following chart shows the shortened recovery periods.

Property Class	Recovery Period
3-year property	2 years
5-year property	3 years
7-year property	4 years
10-year property	6 years
15-year property	9 years
20-year property	12 years
39-year nonresidential real property	22 years

Comment: The recovery period for MACRS 27.5-year residential rental property used on an Indian reservation is not shortened.

The incentive applies to "qualified Indian reservation property." Qualified Indian reservation property is MACRS 3-, 5-, 7-, 10-, 15-, 20-year property and 39-year nonresidential real property that meets all of these requirements:

• the property must be used predominantly in the active conduct of a trade or business within an Indian reservation,

• the property may not be used or located outside an Indian reservation on a regular basis,

• the property may not be acquired (directly or indirectly) from a related person (as defined in Code Sec. 465(b)(3)(C)), and

• the property may not be used for certain gaming purposes.

Working Families Tax Act Impact

Expiration date of special MACRS Indian reservation property depreciation periods extended through December 31, 2005.—The December 31, 2004, expiration date for the shortened Modified Accelerated Cost Recovery System (MACRS) recovery periods that apply to qualified Indian reservation property has been extended for one year to December 31, 2005. Thus, the shortened recovery periods will continue to apply to qualified Indian reservation property placed in service before January 1, 2006 (Code Sec. 168(j)(8), as amended by the Working Families Tax Relief Act of 2004).

Compliance Tip: The IRS never issued MACRS depreciation table percentages for computing depreciation on qualified Indian reservation property. However, unofficial tables created by CCH editors can be found in the CCH Standard Federal Tax Reporter at ¶11,279.031, the CCH Federal Tax Service at §G:16.83[11], the CCH Federal Tax Guide at ¶9180, and the CCH U.S. Master Depreciation Tax Guide at ¶180.

Example: A machine, 7-year MACRS property subject to the half-year convention, is placed in service in 2004. The depreciable basis of the machine is $100,000. If the machine is not qualified Indian reservation property, the 2004 deduction is $14,290 ($100,000 × 14.29% first-year table percentage for 7-year property). If the property is qualified Indian reservation property, the recovery period is shortened from 7 years to 4 years. The first-year deduction increases to

$25,000 ($100,000 × 25% first-year table percentage for Indian reservation property using a 4-year recovery period).

For further information on this subject, consult any of the following CCH reporter explanations:

- Standard Federal Tax Reporter, 2004FED ¶11,279.01
- Federal Tax Service, FTS § G:16.83[11]
- Federal Tax Guide, 2004FTG ¶9110

★ *Effective date.* No specific effective date is provided by the Act. The provision, is, therefore, considered effective on the date of enactment.

Act Sec. 316 of the Working Families Tax Relief Act of 2004, amending Code Sec. 168(j)(8). Law at ¶5160. Committee Report at ¶10,360.

ALTERNATIVE FUEL VEHICLES

¶ 223

Credit for Qualified Electric Vehicles

Background ————————————————————————————————

Taxpayers are allowed a nonrefundable credit for 10 percent of the cost of any qualified electric vehicle (QEV) placed in service during the tax year (Code Sec. 30). For this purpose, a QEV is any motor vehicle powered primarily by an electric motor drawing current from rechargeable batteries, fuel cells, or other portable sources of electric current. The credit may only be claimed for a QEV that is acquired for original use by the taxpayer (and not acquired for resale).

> **Comment:** Gasoline/hybrid vehicles are not eligible for the credit because they are not considered a QEV powered primarily by an electric motor. These vehicles include: Toyota Prius (Model Years 2001-2004), Honda Insight (Model Years 2000-2004), and Honda Civic Hybrid (Model Years 2003-2004). However, part of the cost of these vehicles may qualify for the deduction for clean-fuel vehicles under Code Sec. 179A. See ¶225.

Limitations. The maximum amount of credit allowed for any vehicle is limited to $4,000. In addition, the amount of credit that is otherwise allowable is phased out for QEVs placed in service after December 31, 2003. The amount of credit that may be claimed must be reduced by 25 percent for property placed in service in 2004, 50 percent for property placed in service in 2005, and 75 percent for property placed in service in 2006. No credit is available for QEVs placed in service after 2006.

Working Families Tax Act Impact

Elimination of phaseouts for QEVs placed in service in 2004 and 2005.—The phaseout limitation for qualified electric vehicles (QEVs) placed in service in 2004 and 2005 has been eliminated. Because of this change, a taxpayer who purchases a QEV in 2004 and 2005 may claim 100 percent of the otherwise allowable credit. However, for property placed in service in 2006, the amount of credit otherwise allowable must still be reduced by 75 percent (Code Sec. 30(b)(2), as amended by the Working Families Tax Relief Act of 2004).

> **Planning Note:** Even though the phaseouts have been eliminated for 2004 and 2005, it is important to note that the credit is still not available for QEVs placed in service after 2006.

Compliance Tip: The credit is computed on Form 8834, Qualified Electric Vehicle Credit.

For further information on this subject, consult any of the following CCH reporter explanations:

- Standard Federal Tax Reporter, 2004FED ¶4056.01
- Federal Tax Service, FTS § A:19.180
- Federal Tax Guide, 2004FTG ¶2425

★ *Effective date.* The provision applies to property placed in service after December 31, 2003 (Act Sec. 318(b) of the Working Families Tax Relief Act of 2004).

Act Sec. 318(a) of the Working Families Tax Relief Act of 2004, amending Code Sec. 30(b)(2); Act Sec. 318(b). Law at ¶5035. Committee Report at ¶10,380.

¶ 225

Deduction for Clean-Fuel Vehicles

Background

Taxpayers are allowed a deduction for the cost of any qualified clean-fuel vehicle property placed in service during the tax year (Code Sec. 179A). A qualified clean-fuel vehicle is any motor vehicle that may be propelled by a clean-burning fuel, such as natural gas, liquefied natural gas, liquefied petroleum gas, hydrogen, electricity, or any other fuel at least 85 percent of which is methanol, ethanol, or any other alcohol or ether. An electric vehicle that qualifies for the 10-percent credit for qualified electric vehicles under Code Sec. 30, will not be treated as a qualified clean-fuel vehicle for this purpose. The deduction may only be claimed for qualified clean-fuel property that is acquired for original use by the taxpayer (and not acquired for resale).

Comment: Gasoline/hybrid vehicles may qualify for the deduction, even if they are not used for business purposes. These vehicles include: Toyota Prius (Model Years 2001-2004), Honda Insight (Model Years 2000-2004), and Honda Civic Hybrid (Model Years 2003-2004).

The maximum amount of deduction allowed for any vehicle is limited to $50,000 for a truck or van with a gross vehicle weight of more than 26,000 pounds (as well as a bus with a seating capacity of 20 or more adults) (Code Sec. 179A(b)). The deduction is limited to $5,000 for a truck or van with gross vehicle weight of more than 10,000 pounds, but not more than 26,000 pounds. The deduction is limited to $2,000 for all other qualified vehicles.

Deduction phaseout. In addition to the maximum limits, the amount of deduction that is otherwise allowable is being phased out for qualified clean-fuel vehicles placed in service after December 31, 2003. The amount of deduction that may be claimed must be reduced by 25 percent for property placed in service in 2004, 50 percent for property placed in service in 2005, and 75 percent for property placed in service in 2006. No deduction is available for vehicles placed in service after 2006 (Code Sec. 179A(f)).

Working Families Tax Act Impact

Elimination of phaseouts for qualified clean-fuel vehicles placed in service in 2004 and 2005.—The phaseout limitation for qualified clean-fuel vehicles placed in service in 2004 and 2005 has been eliminated. Because of this change, a taxpayer who purchases a qualified vehicle in 2004 and 2005 may claim 100 percent of the otherwise allowable deduction. However, for property placed in service in 2006, the amount of the deduction otherwise allowable must still be reduced by 75 percent (Code Sec. 179(b)(1)(B), as amended by the Working Families Tax Relief Act of 2004).

Planning Note: Even though the phaseouts for the deduction have been eliminated for 2004 and 2005, it is important to note that the deduction is still not available for clean-fuel vehicles placed in service after 2006 (Code Sec. 179A(f)).

Compliance Tip: There is no special form used to claim the deduction. Instead, taxpayers enter the allowable amount directly on their tax return. For individuals claiming a nonbusiness deduction for clean-fuel property or employees who use such property for business purposes, the deduction is entered as an adjustment to gross income on Form 1040. Sole proprietors enter the deduction on Schedule C or Schedule F on the line designated for "Other expenses." Partnerships, S corporations and C corporations claim the deduction directly on the appropriate line of their tax return.

PRACTICAL ANALYSIS. Mark Luscombe, Principal Analyst, CCH Tax and Accounting, points out that the extension of the clean-fuel vehicle deduction should contribute to the growth in popularity of hybrid vehicles. The IRS had certified that the 2004 models of three hybrid vehicles qualified for the full deduction allowed under the law: the Toyota Prius, the Honda Insight, and the Honda Civic Hybrid. The deduction, along with high gasoline prices, should also encourage other manufacturers to bring hybrid vehicles to the market. Taxpayers purchasing hybrid vehicles in 2004 who would otherwise have been limited to a deduction of $1,500 due to the start of the phaseout will now qualify for a deduction of $2,000.

Although past extensions of the phaseout of the clean-fuel vehicle deduction had postponed the start of the phaseout, this extension leaves the original levels of phaseout in place following 2005. Prior to the Job Creation and Worker Assistance Act of 2002 (JCWAA), the clean-fuel vehicle deduction was scheduled to be reduced by 25 percent in 2002, 50 percent in 2003 and 75 percent in 2004, before being eliminated after 2004. JCWAA deferred this phaseout for two years with the 25-percent phaseout in 2004, the 50-percent phaseout in 2005 and the 75-percent phaseout in 2006. This legislation eliminated the phaseouts scheduled for 2004 and 2005 but did not postpone the remaining phaseouts. Therefore, rather than the phaseout starting at 25 percent in 2006, the phaseout percentage for 2006 remains at 75 percent, as under prior law. The clean-fuel vehicle deduction still expires in 2007, as under prior law.

For further information on this subject, consult any of the following CCH reporter explanations:

- Standard Federal Tax Reporter, 2004FED ¶ 12,133.01
- Federal Tax Service, FTS § G:6.300
- Federal Tax Guide, 2004FTG ¶ 9065

★ *Effective date.* The provision applies to property placed in service after December 31, 2003 (Act Sec. 319(b) of the Working Families Tax Relief Act of 2004).

Act Sec. 319(a) of the Working Families Tax Relief Act of 2004, amending Code Sec. 179A(b)(1)(B); Act Sec. 319(b). Law at ¶ 5175. Committee Report at ¶ 10,390.

¶225

ENERGY PRODUCTION

¶ 227

Renewable Electricity Production Credit Extended

Background _____

A nonrefundable tax credit is available for the domestic production of electricity from certain "qualified energy resources" (QERs) (Code Sec. 45(a)). The tax credit is named the renewable electricity production credit. The three types of QERs are: (1) wind, (2) closed-loop biomass, and (3) poultry waste (Code Sec. 45(c)). For purposes of the credit, the Internal Revenue Code defines two of the three QERs:

(1) *Closed-loop biomass.* The term "closed-loop biomass" means any organic material from a plant which is planted exclusively for the purpose of being used at a qualified facility to produce electricity (Code Sec. 45(c)(2)).

(2) *Poultry waste.* The term "poultry waste" means poultry manure and litter, including wood shavings, straw, rice hulls, and other bedding material used for the disposition of manure (Code Sec. 45(c)(4)).

In order to be eligible for the renewable electricity production credit, the electricity must be produced from a QER and it must be produced at a "qualified facility" (QF). The three types of QFs are:

(1) closed-loop biomass facilities placed in service after 1992 and before January 1, 2004,

(2) wind energy facilities placed in service after 1993 and before January 1, 2004, and

(3) poultry waste facilities placed in service after 1999 and before January 1, 2004.

Comment: With regard to *wind energy facilities* and the type of property (e.g., wind turbines) that will qualify for the credit, the IRS has provided the needed information in Rev. Rul. 94-31, 1994-1 CB 16.

The electricity produced at the QF will only be eligible for the tax credit during the 10-year period beginning on the date the facility was originally placed in service (Code Sec. 45(a)(2)(A)(ii)). The QF must be owned by the taxpayer and the electricity must be sold to an unrelated person during the tax year in order to be eligible for the tax credit (Code Sec. 45(a)(2)(B)).

Only sales of electricity that is produced in the United States or in a United States possession are taken into account (Code Sec. 45(d)(1)). When a facility has more than one owner, production must be allocated in proportion to the respective ownership interests in the gross sales from the facility (Code Sec. 45(d)(3)).

_____

Working Families Tax Act Impact

"Placed in service" date extended for qualified facilities.—The placed in service date for qualified facilities (i.e., wind, closed-loop biomass, and poultry waste facilities) is extended to include facilities placed in service by December 31, 2005 (Code Sec. 45(c)(3)(A), (B) and (C), as amended by the Working Families Tax Relief Act of 2004).

Planning Note: This extension of the "placed in service date" allows electricity produced from renewable resources to be eligible for the tax credit, even though the facility producing the electricity was placed in service after December 31, 2003.

> **Comment:** The American Wind Energy Association (AWEA), an industry trade group, announced that the two-year extension will allow some $3 billion in wind energy projects to "get back on track" and permit hundreds of furloughed wind industry employees to return to work. The AWEA continues to support an extension of the credit for an additional year to December 31, 2006.

For 2004, the renewable electricity production credit amount is 1.8 cents multiplied by the kilowatt hours of electricity sold by the taxpayer during the tax year and produced from qualified energy resources at a qualified facility (Notice 2004-29, I.R.B. 2004-17, 828). The amount of the credit is subject to an annual inflation adjustment. The IRS has not yet announced the amount of the credit for 2005.

> **Comment:** According to the House Ways and Means Committee Report to H.R. 4520, American Jobs Creation Bill of 2004 (H. Rept. No. 108-548), that was released earlier this year, the Committee recognized that the tax credit allowed for the production of electricity from wind power has fostered additional production of electricity. It stated that the extension of the credit for two years would encourage more production from this non-polluting source of electricity. According to the American Wind Energy Association (AWEA), at the present time, the United States receives about $3/10$ of 1% of its electricity from wind power. The U.S. Department of Energy states that the long-term goal is to produce 5% of the nation's electricity by 2020 and the ultimate goal is to produce 20%.

> The Committee also commented that the credit for closed-loop biomass production was extended because it believed that this extension would encourage entrepreneurs to explore alternative sources for generating electricity.

> **Compliance Tip:** As a general rule, taxpayers claim their allowable credit on Form 8835, Renewable Electricity Production Credit. However, in some situations (e.g., the credit is from a passive activity), the taxpayer must also file Form 3800, General Business Credit, in order to claim the credit.

For further information on this subject, consult any of the following CCH reporter explanations:

- Standard Federal Tax Reporter, 2004FED ¶4415.01
- Federal Tax Service, FTS § G:24.240
- Federal Tax Guide, 2004FTG ¶2575

★ *Effective date.* The provision applies to qualified wind, closed-loop biomass, and poultry waste facilities placed in service after December 31, 2003 (Act Sec. 313(b) of the Working Families Tax Relief Act of 2004).

Act Sec. 313(a) of the Working Families Tax Relief Act of 2004, amending Code Sec. 45(c)(3)(A), (B), and (C); Act Sec. 313(b). Law at ¶5060. Committee Report at ¶10,330.

¶ 229

Suspension of Percentage Depletion Limitation for Marginal Production

Background _____

Code Sec. 613A imposes substantial limitations on the allowance for percentage depletion of oil and gas wells. Code Sec. 613A(c) allows percentage depletion only

Background ——————————————————————————————

with respect to up to 1,000 barrels of average daily production of domestic crude oil or the equivalent amount of natural gas (6 million cubic feet) to independent producers and royalty owners. For producers of both oil and natural gas, this limitation applies on a combined basis. This exemption is limited to 65 percent of the taxpayer's taxable income for the year (Code Sec. 613A(d)). Amounts disallowed under this provision are treated as a deduction in the succeeding tax year subject, again, to the 65-percent limitation.

The percentage depletion allowance for producers and royalty owners of oil and natural gas produced from marginal wells cannot exceed 100 percent of the taxpayer's net income from the property (computed without allowances for depletion) (Code Sec. 613(a)). This 100-percent net income limitation requires percentage depletion to be calculated on a property-by-property basis. The 100-percent limitation on percentage depletion based on the net income from the property operates independently of the 65-percent taxable income limitation. The 100-percent net income deduction was suspended for tax years after December 31, 1997, and before January 1, 2004.

——

Working Families Tax Act Impact

Extension of suspension of taxable income limit with respect to marginal production.—The temporary suspension of the taxable income limit on the percentage depletion allowance for oil and gas produced from marginal wells has been extended to include tax years 2004 and 2005. Thus, the limitation on the amount of a percentage depletion deduction to 100 percent of the net income from an oil or gas producing property does not apply to domestic oil and gas produced from marginal properties during tax years beginning after December 31, 1997, and before January 1, 2006 (Code Sec. 613A(c)(6)(H), as amended by the Working Families Tax Relief Act of 2004).

> **Comment:** Marginal production means domestic crude oil or natural gas that is produced from a property that is a stripper well property for the calendar year in which the tax year begins or a property in which substantially all of the production during such calendar year is heavy oil (Code Sec. 613A(c)(6)(D)).

> **Comment:** The Interstate Oil and Gas Compact Commission's annual survey on marginal oil and natural gas wells found that some of the smallest producing wells accounted for a major portion of the on-shore natural gas production increase in 2002. Although marginal wells collectively represent 10 percent of the natural gas production on-shore in the lower 48 states, they accounted for 43 percent of the overall rise in natural gas production in 2002. There are nearly 500,000 marginal wells in the United States, and together they produce about the same amount of oil as the United States imports from Saudi Arabia. The United States Department of Energy (DOE) has expressed concern that these wells are at risk of being prematurely abandoned. The DOE estimates that between 1993 and 2000, 150,000 marginal wells were abandoned, costing the United States more than $3.5 billion in lost economic output. Although the number of natural gas stripper wells that have been abandoned is less than marginal oil wells, the DOE has also expressed a growing concern about the premature abandonment of stripper wells.

For further information on this subject, consult any of the following CCH reporter explanations:

- Standard Federal Tax Reporter, 2004FED ¶ 23,988.01

¶229

- Federal Tax Service, FTS § L:4.140
- Federal Tax Guide, 2004FTG ¶ 9645

★ *Effective date.* The provision applies to tax years beginning after December 31, 2003 (Act Sec. 314(b) of the Working Families Tax Relief Act of 2004).

Act Sec. 314(a) of the Working Families Tax Relief Act of 2004, amending Code Sec. 613A(c)(6)(H); Act Sec. 314(b). Law at ¶ 5260. Committee Report at ¶ 10,340.

ECONOMIC DEVELOPMENT

¶ 235

Authority to Issue New York Liberty Zone Bonds Extended

Background

In order to finance the rebuilding of property damaged by the September 11 terrorist attacks, the Job Creation and Worker Assistance Act of 2002 (P.L. 107-147) authorized tax-exempt bond financing for New York City. Code Sec. 1400L(d) allows the State and City of New York to issue an additional $8 billion worth of qualified New York Liberty Bonds to finance the construction and rehabilitation of real estate and infrastructure within the designated "Liberty Zone" (the "Zone") of New York City. A bond is a qualified New York Liberty Zone Bond when: (1) 95 percent or more of the net proceeds of the issue are to be used for qualified project costs; (2) the bond is issued by the State of New York or a political subdivision thereof; (3) the Governor of New York or the Mayor of New York City designates the bond as a New York Liberty Bond; and (4) the bond is issued before January 1, 2005 (Code Sec. 1400L(d)(2)).

The Zone is an area located on or south of Canal Street, East Broadway (east of its intersection with Canal Street), or Grand Street (east of its intersection with East Broadway) in the Borough of Manhattan in New York City (Code Sec. 1400L(h)). Property eligible for financing under these bonds includes buildings and their structural components, including both nonresidential and residential real property, fixed tenant improvements, and public utility property (e.g., gas, water, electric, and telecommunication lines). Projects within and outside of the Liberty Zone are authorized, provided all are within New York City (Code Sec. 1400L(d)(4)).

In addition, certain types of bonds used to fund facilities located in New York City are permitted one additional advanced refunding after March 9, 2002, and before January 1, 2005 (Code Sec. 1400L(e)). Advance funding occurs when the refunded debt is not redeeemed within 90 days after the refunding bonds are issued. Advance refunding is normally prohibited by the Internal Revenue Code except for certain government and Code Sec. 501(c)(3) issues.

Working Families Tax Act Impact

Extension of authority to issue NY Liberty Bonds.—The authority to issue New York Liberty Bonds has been extended through December 31, 2009 (Code Sec. 1400L(d)(2), as amended by the Working Families Tax Relief Act of 2004). Thus, such bonds may be issued before January 1, 2010. Such authority was made in order to facilitate the full designation of New York Liberty Bond Authority. The Conference Committee Report notes that such authority could be further extended if justified.

Advanced refunding. In addition, advanced refunding authority has been extended through December 31, 2005 (Code Sec. 1400L(e)(1), as amended by the 2004

Working Families Tax Act). Bonds of the Municipal Assistance Corporation have been included in the list of bonds eligible for additional advanced refunding after March 9, 2002, and before January 1, 2010 (Code Sec. 1400L(e)(2)(B), as amended by the 2004 Working Families Tax Act).

Comment: New York Liberty Bonds are "private activity bonds." The interest on such bonds is tax exempt if the bonds are issued for an approved purpose. Because these bonds confer a tax benefit, the aggregate volume of bonds that a State may issue generally is restricted. For calendar year 2004, the annual volume limit is the greater of $80 per resident of the state or $234 million. However, New York Liberty Bonds are not subject to the annual volume limit. Further, these bonds may be issued only for projects approved by the Mayor of New York City or the Governor of New York State, each of whom may designate up to $4 billion of the bonds authorized.

Compliance Tip: As issuer of Liberty Bonds must complete Form 8038, Information Return for Tax-Exempt Private Activity Bond Issues. An issuer of Liberty Advance Refunding Bonds must complete the appropriate Form 8038 series (Form 8038, 8038-G, 8038-GC) (Notice 2002-42, 2002-2 CB 36).

For further information on this subject, consult any of the following CCH reporter explanations:

- Standard Federal Tax Reporter, 2004FED ¶ 32,477.01
- Federal Tax Service, FTS § E:17.110
- Federal Tax Guide, 2004FTG ¶ 8610

★ *Effective date.* No specific effective date is provided by the Act with respect to the Liberty Zone Bonds and the general advanced refunding provisions. These provisions are, therefore, considered effective on the date of enactment. The provision relating to the advance refunding of bonds by the Municipal Assistance Corporation is effective March 9, 2002 (Act Sec. 309(d) of the Working Families Tax Relief Act of 2004; Act Sec. 301 of the Job Creation and Worker Assistance Act of 2002 (P.L. 107-147)).

Act Sec. 309(a) of the Working Families Tax Relief Act of 2004, amending Code Sec. 1400L(d)(2)(D); Act Sec. 309(b), amending Code Sec. 1400L(e)(1); Act Sec. 309(c), amending Code Sec. 1400L(e)(2)(B); Act Sec. 309(d). Law at ¶ 5350. Committee Report at ¶ 10,290.

¶ 237

District of Columbia Enterprise Zone and D.C. Homebuyer Credit Provisions Extended

Background

Parts of the District of Columbia are treated as an empowerment zone, called the District of Columbia Enterprise Zone (DC Zone) (Code Sec. 1400). The designation of the area as the DC Zone is scheduled to end on December 31, 2003 (Code Sec. 1400(f)).

As with other empowerment zones, special tax incentives are provided for the DC Zone in order to attract businesses to the area. One tax break for DC Zone businesses is an exclusion from income for qualified capital gain from the sale or exchange of a DC Zone asset held for more than five years (Code Sec. 1400B). The DC Zone assets, including DC Zone business stock, DC Zone partnership interests and DC Zone business property, must be acquired before January 1, 2004, and the gain

Background

cannot be attributable to periods before January 1, 1998, or after December 31, 2008 (Code Sec. 1400(B)(e)(2)).

The DC Zone also receives special tax-exempt financing incentives that apply to bonds issued from January 1, 1998, through December 31, 2003 (Code Sec. 1400A). Generally, the limit on the amount of bonds that can be allocated to a particular DC Zone business in the DC Zone is $15 million. This is higher than the $3 million that can be allocated to a particular enterprise zone business in an empowerment zone or enterprise community (Code Sec. 1400A and Code Sec. 1394(c)).

First-time homebuyers of a principal residence in the District of Columbia are allowed a credit of up to $5,000 of the purchase price of the residence. The maximum amount of the credit is $2,500 for each married taxpayer filing a separate return (Code Sec. 1400C(a) and (e)(1)(A)). The credit phases out for individual taxpayers with adjusted gross income between $70,000 and $90,000 ($110,000 and $130,000 for joint filers) (Code Sec. 1400C(b)). A first-time homebuyer means any individual who did not have a present ownership interest in a principal residence in the District of Columbia in the one-year period ending on the date of the purchase of the residence to which the credit applies (Code Sec. 1400C(c)).

To qualify for the credit, the residence must have been purchased after August 4, 1997, and before January 1, 2004 (Code Sec. 1400C(i)). If the D.C. residence is newly constructed by the taxpayer, the date that the taxpayer first occupies the residence is treated as the purchase date (Code Sec. 1400C(e)(2)(B)).

Working Families Tax Act Impact

Extension of District of Columbia enterprise zone and D.C. homebuyer credit provisions.—The Working Families Tax Relief Act of 2004 extends for two years the designation of the applicable DC area as the DC Enterprise Zone from December 31, 2003, to December 31, 2005 (Code Sec. 1400(f), as amended by the 2004 Working Families Tax Act). With respect to the zero percent capital gain rate provisions of Code Sec. 1400B, (1) it extends the DC Zone business stock acquisition date from January 1, 2004, to January 1, 2006 (Code Sec. 1400B(b), as amended by the 2004 Working Families Tax Act); (2) for the definition of qualified capital gain, the change is from December 31, 2008, to December 31, 2010 (Code Sec. 1400B(e)(2), as amended by the 2004 Working Families Tax Act); and (3) for the qualified capital gain period for sales and exchanges of interests in partnerships and S corporations that are in DC businesses, the change is from December 31, 2008, to December 31, 2010 (Code Sec. 1400B(g)(2), as amended by the 2004 Working Families Tax Act). The first-time homebuyer credit for DC is extended from January 1, 2004, to January 1, 2006 (Code Sec. 1400C(i), as amended by the 2004 Working Families Tax Act). The DC zone tax-exempt bond financing incentives have also been extended to apply to bonds issued from January 1, 1998, through December 31, 2005, for bonds issued after the date of enactment (Code Sec. 1400A(b), as amended by the 2004 Working Families Tax Act; Act Sec. 310(d)).

> **Compliance Tip:** Taxpayers eligible for the District of Columbia first-time homebuyer credit must file Form 8859, District of Columbia First-Time Homebuyer Credit, with their Form 1040 to claim the credit.

For further information on this subject, consult any of the following CCH reporter explanations:

¶237

- Standard Federal Tax Reporter, 2004FED ¶32,423.01, ¶32,425.01, ¶32,427.01 and ¶32,429.01
- Federal Tax Service, FTS § E:5.160
- Federal Tax Guide, 2004FTG ¶2226

★ *Effective date.* The provisions are generally effective on January 1, 2004, except that the tax-exempt bond provision is effective on the date of enactment (Act Sec. 310(d) of the Working Families Tax Relief Act of 2004).

Act Sec. 310(a) of the Working Families Tax Relief Act of 2004, amending Code Sec. 1400(f); Act Sec. 310(b), amending Code Sec. 1400A(b); Act Sec. 310(c)(1), amending Code Sec. 1400B(b); Act Sec. 310(c)(2), amending Code Sec. 1400B(e)(2), Code Sec. 1400B(g)(2) and Code Sec. 1400F(d); Act Sec. 310(d), amending Code Sec. 1400C(i); Act Sec. 310(e). Law at ¶5325, ¶5330, ¶5335, ¶5340 and ¶5345. Committee Report at ¶10,300.

¶ 239

Qualified Zone Academy Bond Program Extended

Background

Traditionally, bonds are issued by states and local school districts to fund school renovation and expansion projects. Under Code Sec. 103(a), the interest earned on these bonds is exempt from federal taxes. The tax-exempt nature of these bonds make them attractive to many investors and, therefore, the issuing authorities can sell them at a lower interest rate than the rate attached to standard corporate bonds. Generally, interest payments can equal up to 50 percent of the economic cost of a bond. The lower rate saves the issuing authorities about 20 percent of the interest costs in the current market.

The Taxpayer Relief Act of 1997 (P.L. 105-34) created a new financial tool known as a qualified zone academy bond that can be used by state education agencies to encourage the formation of partnerships between public schools and local businesses. The federal government provides bond holders with a tax credit in lieu of cash interest payments, and the school district or other issuer is then only responsible for repaying the amount borrowed.

Qualified zone academy bonds are bonds issued by a state or local government where at least 95 percent of the funds raised are used to renovate, provide equipment to, develop course materials for use at, or train teachers and others at certain public schools (qualified zone academies) that provide education or training below the college level. These public schools must be located in empowerment zones or enterprise communities or have a reasonable expectation that at least 35 percent of the students will be eligible for free or reduced-cost lunches under the National School Lunch Act. In addition, private businesses must promise to contribute equipment, technical assistance or training, employee services, or other property or services with a value equal to at least 10 percent of the value of the bond proceeds (Code Sec. 1397E(d)).

Banks, insurance companies, and certain corporate lenders may hold these taxable qualified zone academy bonds and are entitled to the nonrefundable credit (Code Sec. 1397E(a) and (d)(6)). The credit is allowed to eligible taxpayers holding a qualified zone academy bond on the credit allowance date (the anniversary of the issuance of the bond) for each year in which the bond is held (Code Sec. 1397E(f)(1)). The amount of the credit is equal to a credit rate set monthly by the Treasury Department multiplied by the face amount of the bond (Code Sec. 1397E(b); Reg.

Background ——————————————————————————————————————

§ 1.1397E-1(b)). The credit is includible in income as if it were an interest payment on the bond and may be claimed against regular income tax and alternative minimum tax (AMT) liability (Code Sec. 1397E(g); Reg. § 1.1397E-1(a)).

Up to $400 million in qualified zone academy bonds may be issued nationally in each calendar year beginning in 1998 and ending in 2003 (Code Sec. 1397E(e)(1)). The annual $400 million amount is allocated among the states based upon their population below the poverty level (Code Sec. 1397E(e)(2)). Each state's educational agency is responsible for apportionment of the allocation within its boundaries. A state was permitted a three-year carryforward of unused allocations from 1998 and 1999; however, the carryforward is only two years for unused allocations from subsequent years (Code Sec. 1397E(e)(4)).

This provision, originally due to expire in 2001, was extended to calendar years 2002 and 2003 by the Job Creation and Worker Assistance Act of 2002 (P.L. 107-147).

Working Families Tax Act Impact

Extension of qualified zone academy bond program.—The Working Families Tax Relief Act of 2004 extends the existing qualified zone academy bond program by authorizing issuance of up to $400 million of qualified zone academy bonds annually for calendar years 2004 and 2005.

For further information on this subject, consult any of the following CCH reporter explanations:

- Standard Federal Tax Reporter, 2004FED ¶ 32,407.01
- Federal Tax Service, FTS § G:1.80
- Federal Tax Guide, 2004FTG ¶ 8501

★ *Effective date.* The provision applies to obligations issued after December 31, 2003 (Act Sec. 304(b) of the Working Families Tax Relief Act of 2004).

Act Sec. 304(a) of the Working Families Tax Relief Act of 2004, amending Code Sec. 1397E(e)(1); Act Sec. 304(b). Law at ¶ 5320. Committee Report at ¶ 10,240.

HEALTH PLANS

¶ 245

Archer Medical Savings Accounts

Background ——————————————————————————————————————

The Health Insurance Portability and Accountability Act of 1996 (P.L. 104-91) added Code Sec. 220, permitting employees of small employers and self-employed individuals to establish Archer medical savings accounts (MSAs). Archer MSAs are similar in design to individual retirement arrangements in that they are tax-exempt trusts or custodial accounts established to help pay for medical expenses in conjunction with a high deductible health plan purchased by the participant.

A high deductible health plan is a health insurance plan (not merely a reimbursement arrangement) with deductibles and out-of-pocket limitations that are indexed for inflation (Code Sec. 220(c)(2)). For 2004, the annual deductible for individuals must be at least $1,700 and not more than $2,600. For family coverage, the annual deductible must be at least $3,450 and not more than $5,150. The maximum out-of-pocket expenses, including the deductible, must not be more than $3,450 for individuals and not more than $6,300 for family coverage.

> **Comment:** The Medicare Prescription Drug, Improvement, and Modernization Act of 2003 (P.L. 108-173) established health savings accounts (HSAs), which provide tax-favored treatment for amounts that are contributed and used to pay an account beneficiary's medical expenses (Code Sec. 223). HSAs are generally identical to Archer MSAs but with a less restrictive definition of a high-deductible health plan. For HSAs, a high-deductible plan is one in which the deductible for individuals is at least $1,000 and out-of-pocket expenses are limited to no more than $5,000. For family coverage, the deductible must be at least $2,000 and the out-of-pocket expense limit must not be more than $10,000. Like Archer MSAs, these dollar figures are to be indexed annually for inflation. However, unlike an Archer MSA, an HSA has no maximum deductible limit and is not tied to an individual's employment.

Contributions by a participant to an Archer MSA may be deductible in determining gross income. Contributions by an eligible employer on behalf of a participant are excluded from the account holder's gross income (unless made through a cafeteria plan (Code Sec. 125). Although employer contributions must be reported on an employee's Form W-2 for the tax year, they are not subject to income tax withholding or other employment taxes.

Amounts earned in an Archer MSA are not subject to current taxation. However, distributions are included in the account holder's gross income unless they are made for qualified medical expenses incurred for the benefit of the account holder, a spouse, or dependents (Code Sec. 220(f)). No exclusion is available if the medical care is rendered for an individual covered under a high-deductible health plan and such individual is also covered under any other health plan that is not a high-deductible health plan. Distributions may also be excluded from gross income if: (1) they are rolled over to a new Archer MSA or an HSA within 60 days; or (2) they are incident to the participant's divorce. If an Archer MSA distribution is included in gross income, then an additional 15-percent penalty tax will apply unless the distribution is made after age 65 or upon death or disability.

Archer MSAs are a pilot project and may be established for tax years beginning after 1996. However, new Archer MSAs may not be established after December 31, 2003. The pilot project provided that the prohibition against new accounts could be cut off sooner if the number of taxpayers benefitting from an Archer MSA exceeds 750,000 for a particular tax year. To determine if this threshold is met, each person who is a trustee of an Archer MSA must report to the IRS by August 1 of each calendar year the number of accounts established before July 1 of that year (Code Sec. 220(j)). The IRS must announce by October 1 whether the threshold is met. After the cutoff date (i.e., December 31, 2003, or the date announced by the IRS, if earlier), contributions may only be made to existing Archer MSAs. Special rules prevent year-end adoptions of Archer MSAs for purposes of avoiding the cutoff date.

Working Families Tax Act Impact

Availability of medical savings accounts extended.—The Working Families Tax Relief Act of 2004 extends the Archer medical savings account (MSA) program by allowing taxpayers to establish new accounts through December 31, 2005 (Code Sec. 220(i)(2) and (3)(B), as amended by the 2004 Working Families Tax Act).

¶245

Comment: There is little incentive for taxpayers to establish a new Archer MSA in 2004 or 2005 given that they may set up a health savings account (HSA) as of January 1, 2004. However, given the early reluctance of many institutions in offering HSAs, taxpayers may, nonetheless, wish to establish a new MSA to use as a transition vehicle until HSAs are more fully developed. This can be accomplished tax free, because a distribution from an Archer MSA will not be treated as a taxable distribution if it is rolled over into an HSA within 60 days of disbursement.

Trustees of Archer MSAs who were required to report the number of accounts established by August 1, 2004, will be considered to meet this requirement if they file the report within 90 days of the date of enactment of the 2004 Working Families Tax Act (Act Sec. 322(d)(1) of the 2004 Working Families Tax Act).

In addition, the IRS determination and publication of whether the 750,000 threshold level is met for 2004 will be treated as timely made if it is made within the 120-day period beginning on the date of enactment. If the IRS determines that 2004 is a cut-off year, then the cut-off date for establishing a new Archer MSA in 2004 will be the final day of the 120-day period (Act Sec. 322(d)(2) of the 2004 Working Families Tax Act).

There is no numerical limitation for the number of Archer MSAs that may be established in 2003 (Code Sec. 220(j)(2)(C), as amended by the 2004 Working Families Tax Act).

For further information on this subject, consult any of the following CCH reporter explanations:

- Standard Federal Tax Reporter, 2004FED ¶ 12,675.01
- Federal Tax Service, FTS § A:14.200
- Federal Tax Guide, 2004FTG ¶ 4153

★ *Effective date.* The amendment takes effect on January 1, 2004 (Act Sec. 322(c) of the Working Families Tax Relief Act of 2004).

Act Sec. 322(a) of the Working Families Tax Relief Act of 2004, amending Code Sec. 220(i)(2) and (3)(B); Act Sec. 322(b), amending Code Sec. 220(j)(2) and (4)(A); Act Sec. 322(c); Act Sec. 322(d). Law at ¶ 5190 and ¶ 7023. Committee Report at ¶ 10,420.

¶ 247

Parity in the Application of Certain Limits to Mental Health Benefits

Background ―――――――――――――――――――――――――――――――

The Taxpayer Relief Act of 1997 (P.L. 105-34) incorporated provisions of the Mental Health Parity Act of 1996 that had previously amended the Employee Retirement Income Security Act of 1974 (ERISA) and the Public Health Service Act (PHSA) into the Internal Revenue Code. Under Code Sec. 9812, group health plans that provide mental health benefits and have lifetime or annual limits on what the plans will spend for medical or surgical services must either include services for mental illness in their total limit or maintain a separate limit for mental illness that is no more restrictive than the medical/surgical limit. Group health plans are not required to provide any mental health benefits under the plan (Code Sec. 9812(b)(1)). However, in the case of a group health plan that provides both medical and surgical benefits and mental health benefits, plans that do not include a lifetime or annual

Background

limit on medical and surgical benefits may not impose any lifetime or annual limit on mental health benefits.

Employers whose group health plans fail to comply with the mental health parity rules are subject to the excise tax provisions under Code Sec. 4980D, which impose a $100 per day penalty per individual during the period of noncompliance (Code Sec. 4980D(b)(1)). The maximum tax that can be imposed during a tax year cannot exceed the lesser of 10 percent of the employer's group health plan expenses for the prior year or $500,000 (Code Sec. 4980D(c)(3)). No excise tax will be imposed if the IRS determines that the person otherwise liable for the tax did not know and could not have reasonably known that such noncompliance existed within the plan (Code Sec. 4980D(c)(1)).

Small employers, as defined in Code Sec. 4980D(d), are exempt from the mental health benefits parity requirements (Code Sec. 9812(c)(1)). Also, the parity provisions do not apply if the application would result in an increase in the cost under the plan of at least one percent (Code Sec. 9812(c)(2)).

Comment: The term "mental health benefits" does not include benefits with respect to treatment of substance abuse or chemical dependency (Code Sec. 9812(e)(4)).

Comment: The excise provisions of the mental health parity rules were initially effective for plan years beginning on or after January 1, 1998. The excise tax does not apply to benefits for services furnished on or after September 30, 2001, and before January 10, 2002, during which period the parity provisions had expired.

Working Families Tax Act Impact

Parity in the application of certain limits to mental health benefits.—The mental health parity provisions are extended through December 31, 2005 (Code Sec. 9812(f)(2) and (3), as added by the Working Families Tax Relief Act of 2004). This extension also clarifies that no excise penalties under Code Sec. 4980D are applicable for group health benefits in effect beginning on or after January 1, 2004, and the date of enactment of this provision.

This extension also applies to the relevant provisions of the Employee Retirement Income Security Act of 1974 and the Public Health Service Act.

For further information on this subject, consult any of the following CCH reporter explanations:

- Standard Federal Tax Reporter, 2004FED ¶44,088.01
- Federal Tax Service, FTS § B:13.112[3]
- Federal Tax Guide, 2004FTG ¶21,475

★ *Effective date.* The provision is effective on the date of enactment (Act Sec. 302(d) of the Working Families Tax Relief Act of 2004).

Act Sec. 302(a) of the Working Families Tax Relief Act of 2004, amending Code Sec. 9812(f); Act Sec. 302(b), amending Sec. 712(f) of the Employee Retirement Income Security Act of 1974 (ERISA); Act Sec. 302(c), amending Section 2705(f) of the Public Health Service Act; Act Sec. 302(d). Law at ¶5425 and ¶7015. Committee Report at ¶10,210.

DISCLOSURES AND IRS ADMINISTRATION

¶ 253

Combined State-Federal Employment Tax Reporting

Background

Returns and return information concerning income, estate, gift, Social Security, unemployment, withholding and certain excise taxes, including windfall profit, alcohol and tobacco taxes, can be inspected by or disclosed to any state agency, body or commission responsible for administering state tax laws. Disclosure is permitted only for the purpose of, and only to the extent necessary to, administer state tax laws (Code Sec. 6103(d)(1)). However, disclosure to state officials who administer certain non-tax-related laws and programs is also permitted for purposes of administering those laws and programs.

The IRS and the state of Montana jointly entered into a five-year demonstration project to assess the feasibility and desirability of combined federal and state tax reporting on one form. The demonstration project was limited to employment tax reporting. The form contained exclusively federal data, exclusively state data, and data common to both. Disclosure was limited to the taxpayer's name, address, taxpayer identification number, and signature. The demonstration project expired on August 5, 2002 (Code Sec. 6103(d)(5), as amended by the Taxpayer Relief Act of 1997 (P.L. 105-34)).

For purposes of the project, the criminal penalties for unauthorized disclosure (Code Sec. 7213) or inspection (Code Sec. 7213A) of returns or return information, as well as the rules prohibiting disclosure of returns and return information by state or local officials (Code Sec. 6103(a)(2)) and the rules on safeguards for disclosed information (Code Sec. 6103(p)(4)) did not apply.

Working Families Tax Act Impact

Disclosure of tax information for expanded federal/state employment tax programs.—Any state may now participate in a combined federal and state employment tax reporting program through December 31, 2005 (Code Sec. 6103(d)(5), as amended by the Working Families Tax Relief Act of 2004). However, the Secretary must approve the program. The IRS may disclose taxpayer identity information and signatures to any agency, body, or commission of any state for purposes of the combined employment tax reporting program. As under the earlier demonstration project, the criminal penalties for unauthorized disclosure (Code Sec. 7213) or inspection (Code Sec. 7213A) of return or return information will not apply to the program. Likewise, the rules prohibiting disclosure of returns and return information by state or local officials (Code Sec. 6103(a)(2)) and the rules on safeguards for disclosed information (Code Sec. 6103(p)(4)) will not apply.

For further information on this subject, consult any of the following CCH reporter explanations:

- Standard Federal Tax Reporter, 2004FED ¶ 36,894.01
- Federal Tax Service, FTS § P:9.80
- Federal Tax Guide, 2004FTG ¶ 22,221

★ *Effective date.* The provision takes effect on the date of enactment (Act Sec. 311(b) of the Working Families Tax Relief Act of 2004).

Act Sec. 311(a) of the Working Families Tax Relief Act of 2004, amending Code Sec. 6103(d)(5); Act Sec. 311(b). Law at ¶ 5390. Committee Report at ¶ 10,310.

¶ 255
Authority to Disclose Student Loan Information Extended

Background

Tax returns and return information are confidential and not subject to disclosure, except as provided under Code Sec. 6103. Code Sec. 6103(l)(13) authorizes the disclosure of certain information to the Department of Education for purposes of determining an appropriate income-contingent repayment amount for an "applicable student loan." The information that may be disclosed to the Department of Education is limited to the former student's name, mailing address, taxpayer identification number, filing status and adjusted gross income. The term "applicable student loan" means loans made under the direct student loan program (loans under part D of title IV of the Higher Education Act of 1965) and other student loans (under part B or E of title IV of the Higher Education Act of 1965) that are in default and have been referred to the Department of Education for collection.

The disclosure provisions of Code Sec. 6103(l)(13) do not allow for the disclosure of information to contractors of the Department of Education. A taxpayer may, however, consent to the disclosure of information to another person under Code Sec. 6103(c). The Department of Education uses contractors for the income-contingent loan verification program and so must obtain the taxpayer information with Code Sec. 6103(c) consents, rather than under Code Sec. 6103(l)(13) (Department of Treasury, Report to Congress on Scope and Use of Taxpayer Confidentiality and Disclosure Provisions, Volume I: Study of General Provisions, October 2000, p. 91, cited in the House Ways and Means Committee Report for H.R. 4520, American Jobs Creation Bill of 2004 (H. Rept. No. 108-548)).

The authority to disclose tax information to the Department of Education was initially scheduled to expire on September 30, 1998, but was extended to December 31, 2004, by P.L. 108-89.

Working Families Tax Act Impact

One-year extension of disclosure authority related to student loan information.—The authority to disclose information to the Department of Education for purposes of establishing an appropriate income-contingent repayment amount is extended for one year until December 31, 2005 (Code Sec. 6103(l)(13)(D), as amended by the Working Families Tax Relief Act of 2004). Only the taxpayer's identity information, filing status, and adjusted gross income may be disclosed.

> **Comment:** It does not appear that the one-year extension of the disclosure authority will solve the problems that result from the use of Code Sec. 6103(c) consents. Use of the consents places an administrative burden on the IRS because some 100,000 consents are processed per year. Additionally, the consents do not provide use restrictions and are not subject to statutory safeguards (General Explanations of the Administration's Fiscal Year 2004 Revenue Proposals, Department of Treasury, February 2003, p. 133, cited in the House Ways and Means Committee Report for H.R. 4520 (H. Rept. No. 108-548)). Past proposals have gone further by permanently extending the disclosure authority and expanding disclosure to the Department of Education and its contractors (see, for example, General Explanations of the Administration's Fiscal Year 2005 Revenue Proposals, Department of Treasury, February 2004, p. 169).

For further information on this subject, consult any of the following CCH reporter explanations:

- Standard Federal Tax Reporter, 2004FED ¶36,894.01
- Federal Tax Service, FTS § P:9.106
- Federal Tax Guide, 2004FTG ¶22,221

★ *Effective date.* No specific effective date is provided by the Act. The provision is, therefore, considered effective on the date of enactment.

Act Sec. 317 of the Working Families Tax Relief Act of 2004, amending Code Sec. 6103(l)(13)(D). Law at ¶5390. Committee Report at ¶10,370.

¶ 257

Authority to Disclose Terrorist Activity Information Extended

Background

Because the IRS probably has more information about more people than any other agency in the United States, any federal or state agency needing information about U.S. citizens tends to seek it from the IRS. To protect taxpayers, tax returns and return information are confidential and are not subject to disclosure to federal or state agencies or employees except as provided in Code Sec. 6103.

Special disclosure rules apply to disclosures related to terrorist incidents, threats or activities (terrorist activities), for disclosures made on or after January 23, 2002, but before January 1, 2004 (Code Sec. 6103(i)(3)(C) and (7)). Federal law enforcement agencies and federal intelligence agencies may request that return information be disclosed for purposes of responding to and investigating terrorist activities and collecting and analyzing related intelligence and counterintelligence information. Specifically, disclosure is to be made only to those officers and employees of the agencies that are personally and directly involved in these activities (Code Sec. 6103(i)(7)(A) and (B)). If taxpayer return information is requested, disclosure must be made pursuant to the *ex parte* order of a federal district court judge or magistrate (Code Sec. 6103(i)(7)(C)).

The IRS may, on its own initiative, disclose return information (other than taxpayer return information) to the head of the appropriate federal law enforcement agency responsible for responding to or investigating terrorist activities (Code Sec. 6103(i)(3)(C)(i)). If the IRS wants to disclose taxpayer return information, however, it must seek an *ex parte* order from a federal district court judge or magistrate (Code Sec. 6103(i)(7)(D)). For purposes of these disclosure rules, taxpayer return information does not include the taxpayer's identity (Code Sec. 6103(i)(3)(C)(iii) and (7)(B)(iv)). A terrorist incident, threat or activity means an incident, threat or activity involving an act of domestic terrorism as defined by 18 U.S.C. § 2331(5) or international terrorism as defined by 18 U.S.C. § 2331(1) (Code Sec. 6103(b)(11)).

Working Families Tax Act Impact

Disclosure authority related to terrorist activities extended.—The Working Families Tax Relief Act of 2004 extends for two years the disclosure authority relating to terrorist activities. No disclosures can be made after December 31, 2005 (Code Sec. 6103(i)(3)(C)(iv) and (7)(E), as amended by the Working Families Tax Relief Act of 2004). Extension of the authority will provide additional time to evaluate the effectiveness of the provision and whether any modifications need to be made.

In addition, a technical correction clarifies that a taxpayer's *identity* is not treated as taxpayer return information for purposes of disclosures to law enforcement agencies regarding terrorist activities (Code Sec. 6103(i)(7)(A)(v), as added by the 2004 Working Families Tax Act).

Caution Note: The change regarding a taxpayer's identity is retroactive and is effective for disclosures made after January 22, 2002.

For further information on this subject, consult any of the following CCH reporter explanations:

- Standard Federal Tax Reporter, 2004FED ¶ 36,894.01
- Federal Tax Service, FTS § P:9.104[1]
- Federal Tax Guide, 2004FTG ¶ 22,221

★ *Effective date.* The provision extending disclosure authority applies to disclosures on or after the date of enactment. The technical change providing that identity is not treated as taxpayer return information is effective for disclosures made on or after January 23, 2002 (P.L. 107-134) (Act Sec. 320(c) of the Working Families Tax Relief Act of 2004, Sec. 201 of the Victims of Terrorism Tax Relief Act of 2001 (P.L. 107-134)).

Act Sec. 320(a) of the Working Families Tax Relief Act of 2004, amending Code Sec. 6103(i)(3)(C)(iv) and (7)(E); Act. Sec. 320(b), adding Code Sec. 6103(i)(7)(A)(v); Act Sec. 320(c). Law at ¶ 5390. Committee Report at ¶ 10,400.

¶ 259

Annual Joint Congressional Review of IRS Plans and Budget

Background

A joint congressional review of the strategic plans and budget of the IRS was required to be held once a year as part of the effort to coordinate ongoing high-level oversight of the IRS. The joint review was held at the call of the Chair of the Joint Committee on Taxation, before June 1 of each year from 1999 to 2003. Participants in the hearings included three members (two majority and one minority) from each of the committees with shared jurisdiction over the IRS. The participating Senate committees are Finance, Appropriations, and Governmental Affairs. The participating House committees are Ways and Means, Appropriations, and Government Reform and Oversight (Code Sec. 8021(f)(2)).

The topics that were to be covered in an annual report based on the joint review included: (1) the IRS strategic and business plans; (2) IRS progress in meeting its objectives; (3) the IRS budget and whether the budget supported IRS objectives; (4) IRS progress in improving taxpayer service and compliance; (5) IRS progress on technology modernization; and (6) the annual filing season.

The Chief of Staff of the Joint Committee on Taxation, as well as the Joint Committee staff, are directed to provide assistance as needed to facilitate the joint reviews.

Working Families Tax Act Impact

Joint review of strategic plans and budget for the IRS.—The Joint Committee on Taxation is required to complete a joint review of the IRS before June 1, 2004. Without this extension the last review would have been before June 1, 2003 (Code Sec. 8021(f)(2), as amended by the Working Families Tax Relief Act of 2004). The joint review required to be made before June 1, 2004, will be treated as timely if made before June 1, 2005 (Act Sec. 321(c)). The annual report to the committees that are represented on the Joint Committee is also extended to include calendar year 2004 (Code Sec. 8022(3)(C), as amended by the 2004 Working Families Tax Act). In addition, the six listed topics that the Joint Committee was to have addressed in its report have been eliminated. Instead, the Joint Committee's report is to include a review of the IRS's strategic plans and budget, as well as any other matters that the Chair of the Joint Committee deems appropriate (Code Sec. 8022(3)(C), as amended by the 2004 Working Families Tax Act).

For further information on this subject, consult any of the following CCH reporter explanations:

- Standard Federal Tax Reporter, 2004FED ¶44,004.01
- Federal Tax Service, FTS § P:9.101

★ *Effective date.* No specific effective date is provided by the Act. This provision is, therefore, considered effective on the date of enactment.

Act Sec. 321(a) of the Working Families Tax Relief Act of 2004, amending Code Sec. 8021(f)(2); Act Sec. 321(b), amending Code Sec. 8022(3)(C); Act Sec. 321(c). Law at ¶5415, ¶5420 and ¶7022. Committee Report at ¶10,410.

EXCISE TAX

¶ 265

Cover Over of Tax on Distilled Spirits

Background

A $13.50 per proof gallon excise tax is imposed on all distilled spirits produced in, or imported into, the United States (Code Sec. 5001(a)(1)). This excise tax does not apply to distilled spirits that are exported from the United States or to distilled spirits that are consumed in U.S. possessions, such as Puerto Rico and the Virgin Islands.

Puerto Rico and the Virgin Islands receive a payment ("cover over") limited to the amount of $10.50 per proof gallon of the excise tax imposed on rum brought into the United States, regardless of the country of origin (Code Sec. 7652(f)). The cover over payment limit was temporarily set at $13.25 per proof gallon for the period July 1, 1999, through December 31, 2003.

Tax amounts from rum produced in Puerto Rico are covered over to Puerto Rico and tax amounts from rum produced in the Virgin Islands are covered over to the Virgin Islands. Tax amounts from rum produced in neither Puerto Rico nor the Virgin Islands are divided and covered over to the two possessions under a formula. All amounts covered over are subject to the dollar limitation.

Working Families Tax Act Impact

Increased cover over limit extended.—The $13.25 per proof gallon cover over amount for rum brought into the United States is extended for two more years, through December 31, 2005 (Code Sec. 7652(f)(1), as amended by the Working Families Tax Relief Act of 2004). After December 31, 2005, the cover over amount reverts to $10.50 per proof gallon.

For further information on this subject, consult any of the following CCH reporter explanations:

- Standard Federal Tax Reporter, 2004FED ¶42,968F.01
- Federal Tax Guide, 2004FTG ¶21,740

★ *Effective date.* The provision applies to articles brought into the United States after December 31, 2003 (Act Sec. 305(b) of the Working Families Tax Relief Act of 2004).

Act Sec. 305(a) of the Working Families Tax Relief Act of 2004, amending Code Sec. 7652(f)(1); Act Sec. 305(b). Law at ¶ 5395. Committee Report at ¶ 10,250.

Chapter 3

Technical Corrections

DIVIDENDS AND INVESTMENT

¶ 305

Clarification of Holding Periods Applicable to Dividends

Background _____

The top federal tax rate for dividends received by a taxpayer other than a corporation (including individuals, estate and trusts) was reduced to 15 percent by the Jobs and Growth Tax Relief Reconciliation Act of 2003 (P.L. 108-27) (Code Sec.

Background _____

1(h)(11)). The qualified dividend rate is 5 percent for those whose incomes fall in the 10- or 15-percent rate brackets. The reduced tax rate applies to dividends received during the tax year from a domestic corporation or a qualified foreign corporation. Corporate stock dividends passed through to investors by a mutual fund or other regulated investment company, partnership, real estate investment trust, or held by a common trust fund are also eligible for the reduced rate assuming the distribution would otherwise be classified as qualified dividend income.

A holding period applies to stock purchased close to the ex-dividend date (the date following the record date on which the corporation finalizes the list of share-holders who will receive the dividend). The holding period rule prevents the tax-payer from using price drops due to dividends to generate capital loss to offset ordinary income while paying tax on the dividend at a lower rate. As the provision was originally drafted, an investor was required to hold the stock for more than 60 days (i.e., at least 61 days) in the 120-day period beginning 60 days before the ex-dividend date for the reduced rates to apply (Code Sec. 1(h)(11)(B)(iii)). This meant that an investor who purchased stock one day before the ex-dividend date did not qualify for the special rate. In practice, the IRS applied a 61-out-of-121-day holding period for 2003 returns, taking the liberty of adopting changes to the rules before Congress enacted the technical corrections (IRS News Release IR-2004-22, February 19, 2004). The original law did not contain a clear provision for a preferred stock holding period; however, IRS instructions issued subsequent to the 2003 Act indicated that a 90-out-of-181 day holding period should apply to cumulative preferred stock.

A similar holding period applies to the dividend received deduction for corporations, and the qualified dividend holding period is drafted by referring to these rules under Code Sec. 246(c). A corporation is not entitled to a dividends received deduction if the dividend paying stock is held less than 46 days during the 90-day period that begins 45 days before the stock becomes ex-dividend (Code Sec. 246(c)(1)(A)). The holding period for dividends on preferred stock attributable to a period or periods in excess of 366 days (cumulative preferred stock dividends) is increased to 91 days during the 180-day period that begins 90 days before the stock becomes ex-dividend with respect to the dividend (Code Sec. 246(c)(2)).

A holding period requirement is also imposed for purposes of crediting foreign taxes associated with foreign-source dividends. In general, a taxpayer is not entitled to a tax credit for foreign withholding taxes paid with respect to a dividend if a 16-day holding period for the dividend-paying stock (or a 46-day holding period for certain dividends on preferred stock) is not satisfied. The 16-day holding period requirement must be met within the 30-day period beginning 15 days before the ex-dividend date. If the stock is held for 15 days or less during the 30-day period, the foreign tax credit for the withholding tax on the dividend is disallowed (Code Sec. 901(k)).

The dividends received holding period and the foreign tax credit holding period share the common consequence that a taxpayer who acquires stock the day before the ex-dividend date cannot satisfy the holding period requirements with respect to the dividend. This situation has been viewed as unfair since the provision is designed to penalize traders who dodge in and out of a stock position, and should not penalize purchasers who "buy the dividend" but subsequently hold the stock for the duration of the tax year.

¶305

Working Families Tax Act Impact

Clarification of holding periods applicable to dividends.—The holding period requirements for the qualified dividend tax rate, the dividends received deduction, and the holding period for claiming foreign tax credits with respect to dividends have been amended to ensure that taxpayers can satisfy the holding period requirements when they purchase stock one day before the ex-dividend date. The revised holding periods are:

- **qualified dividends**: the stock must be held for 61 days during the 121 day period beginning 60 days before the ex-dividend date (Code Sec. 1(h)(11)(B)(iii), as amended by the Working Families Tax Relief Act of 2004);

- **qualified dividends paid on preferred stock**: the stock must be held for 91 days during the 181-day period beginning 90 days before the ex-dividend date (Code Sec. 1(h)(11)(B)(iii), as amended by the 2004 Working Families Tax Act);

- **dividends received deduction for corporations**: the stock must be held for 46 days during the 91 day period beginning 45 days before the ex-dividend date to qualify for the dividends received deduction under (Code Sec. 246(c)(1)(A), as amended by the 2004 Working Families Tax Act);

- **dividends received deduction for preferred stock**: the stock must be held for 91 days during the 181 day period beginning 90 days before the ex-dividend date (Code Sec. 246(c)(2)(B), as amended by the 2004 Working Families Tax Act);

- **foreign tax credit with respect to dividend income**: the stock must be held for 16 days within the 31-day period beginning 15 days before the ex-dividend date (Code Sec. 901(k)(1)(A)(i), as amended by the 2004 Working Families Tax Act); and

- **foreign tax credit for dividends on cumulative preferred stock**: the stock must be held for 46 days within the 91-day period beginning 45 days before the ex-dividend date (Code Sec. 901(k)(3)(B), as amended by the 2004 Working Families Tax Act).

Holding period for stock to qualify for reduced dividend rate. To qualify for the lower tax rates, the taxpayer must now hold the dividend-paying stock for at least 61 days during the 121-day period (instead of the former 120-day period) beginning 60 days before the ex-dividend date (the first date that the buyer will not be entitled to receive that dividend). Thus, a stock bought on the last day before the ex-dividend date, i.e. the latest purchase date for collecting a dividend, could still meet the holding period test for that dividend, since there would have been 61 days left in the 121-day period. A stock sold on the ex-dividend date (the earliest selling date after entitlement to a dividend) can also meet the test, since that is the 61st day in the period. As long as the taxpayer holds the stock for at least 61 continuous days, the holding period test will be met for any dividend received (unless another restriction applied, such as a diminished risk of loss).

A similar holding period applies for preferred stock dividends attributable to a more-than-366-day period (dividends paid on cumulative preferred stock). This holding period is at least 91 days during a 181-day period beginning 90 days before the ex-dividend date.

Planning Note: The IRS allowed taxpayers to apply the 61-out-of-121 and 91-out-of-181 holding periods for the 2003 tax year even though these technical changes had not yet been made to the tax code. In IRS News Release IR-2004-22, issued February 19, 2004, the IRS announced that mutual fund holders and other investors filing 2003 returns could proceed as if the corrections then contained in

¶305

Act Section 2 of the Tax Technical Corrections Act of 2003 had already been enacted. Their early application of the technical correction probably means that no corrected returns will need to be filed as a result of the revised holding period rules.

Example: The ex-dividend date for General Electric is September 23, 2004. On September 22, 2004, Joe Rowley purchases 10,000 shares of GE for $320,000. Joe will receive a GE dividend because he owned the stock on the day of record. The dividend will qualify for the reduced rate if he holds the stock for at least 61 days in the 121-day period beginning 60 days before the ex-dividend date (September 23), or 61 days in the period beginning July 25, 2004. The earliest date he can sell and still claim the reduced dividend rate is November 22, 2004.

Compliance Tip: For purposes of counting the number of days, the day of disposition, but not the day of acquisition, is included (Code Sec. 246(c)(3)).

Dividend holding periods for mutual fund shareholders and other pass-throughs. Mutual funds, other regulated investment companies, and real estate investment trusts that pass through dividend income to their shareholders must meet the holding period test for the dividend-paying stocks that they hold in order for corresponding amounts that they pay out to be reported as qualified dividends on Form 1099-DIV. Investors must meet the holding period for their shares in a mutual fund or other pass-through entity to be entitled to treat "qualified dividends" passed through to them as qualified dividends on their returns.

Holding period for dividends received deduction. The holding period requirement for the dividends received deduction under Code Sec. 246(c) now requires a corporation to have held a stock for at least 46 days during the 91-day period (instead of the former 90 days) that begins 45 days before the stock becomes ex-dividend in order to claim the dividends received deduction (Code Sec. 246(c)(1)(A), as amended by the 2004 Working Families Tax Act). As with the qualifying dividends holding period, this change allows a purchaser who acquired stock one day before the ex-dividend date to be able to meet the holding period requirement. A similar amendment changes the holding period requirement for preferred stock to 90 days during the 181-day period (instead of the former 180 days) beginning 90 days before the ex-dividend date. This change was enacted as a retroactive amendment to the original holding period rules enacted under the Taxpayer Relief Act of 1997, and accordingly the change is retroactive for dividends paid after September 4, 1997.

Comment: The IRS did not pre-adopt the technical correction to the dividends received holding period, as it did with the qualified dividends holding period. Accordingly, there may be corporate investors that now meet the holding period and did not reflect this on their tax returns for 1997 through 2003.

Holding period for foreign tax credits with respect to dividends. The holding period that applies in order for a taxpayer to be able to claim the foreign tax credit for foreign withholding taxes paid with respect to a dividend is 16 days within the 31-day period (instead of the former 30 days) beginning 15 days before the ex-dividend date (Code Sec. 901(k)(1)(A)(i), as amended by the 2004 Working Families Tax Act). For dividends on preferred stock attributable to a period in excess of 366 days (cumulative), the required holding period is 46 days within the 91-day period (instead of the former 90 days) beginning 45 days before the ex-dividend date (Code Sec. 901(k)(3)(B), as amended by the 2004 Working Families Tax Act).

PRACTICAL ANALYSIS. Arthur Seltzer of Brown Smith Wallace, LLC, St. Louis, Missouri, notes that a technical correction eliminates a mechanical problem that would apply to stock acquired on the day

before an ex-dividend date. For example, to qualify for the lower tax rate, stock must be owned for 60 days during the 120-day period beginning 60 days before the ex-dividend date. The change would permit such a dividend to qualify by adding an extra day to the qualification period.

For further information on this subject, consult any of the following CCH reporter explanations:

- Standard Federal Tax Reporter, 2004FED ¶3285.01, ¶13,057.034 and ¶27,826.026

- Federal Tax Service, FTS § E:5.101[11], § I:2.102 and § M:10.101[8]

- Federal Tax Guide, 2004FTG ¶3205, ¶12,570 and ¶17,240

★ *Effective date.* The qualifying dividends holding period provision applies to tax years beginning after December 31, 2002 (Act Sec. 402(b) of the Working Families Tax Relief Act of 2004; Act Sec. 302(f)(1) of the Jobs and Growth Tax Relief Reconciliation Act of 2003). It is subject to a sunset provision indicating that it will not apply to tax years beginning after December 31, 2008 (Act Sec. 303 of the Jobs and Growth Tax Relief Reconciliation Act of 2003) (see ¶29,001 for a discussion of the sunset provision). The dividends received deduction holding period applies to dividends received or accrued after September 4, 1997 (Act Sec. 406(h) of the 2004 Working Families Tax Act; Act Sec. 1015(c) of the Taxpayer Relief Act of 1997). The foreign tax credit holding period provision applies to dividends paid or accrued after September 4, 1997 (Act Sec. 406(h) of the 2004 Working Families Tax Act and Act Sec. 1053(c) of the Taxpayer Relief Act of 1997).

Act Sec. 402(a)(2) of the Working Families Tax Relief Act of 2004, amending Code Sec. 1(h)(11)(B)(iii)(I); Act Sec. 402(b); Act Sec. 406(f)(1), amending Code Sec. 246(c)(1)(A); Act Sec. 406(f)(2), amending Code Sec. 246(c)(2)(B); Act Sec. 406(g)(1), amending Code Sec. 901(k)(1)(A)(i); Act Sec. 406(g)(2), amending Code Sec. 901(k)(3)(B); Act Sec. 406(h). Law at ¶5005, ¶5200, and ¶5280. Committee Reports at ¶10,510 and ¶10,550.

¶ 307

Qualified Dividends Paid By Mutual Funds, REITs, and Other Pass-Through Entities

Background

The top federal tax rate for dividends received by a taxpayer other than a corporation (including individuals, estate and trusts) was reduced to 15 percent by the Jobs and Growth Tax Relief Reconciliation Act of 2003, P.L. 108-27 (the rate is 5 percent for those whose incomes fall in the 10- or 15-percent rate brackets) (Code Sec. 1(h)(11)). Corporate stock dividends passed through to investors by a mutual fund or other regulated investment company, partnership, real estate investment trust, or held by a common trust fund are also eligible for the reduced rate assuming the distribution would otherwise be classified as qualified dividend income.

Dividends paid by a real estate investment trust (REIT) are not generally eligible for the reduced dividend rate. These sums largely represent rents and other income that are passed through to shareholders as dividends deductible to the REIT, rather than corporate earnings subject to the corporate income tax. However, REIT distributions will qualify for the reduced dividend rate to the extent they represent qualified corporate dividends.

Working Families Tax Act Impact

Clarification of qualified dividends rules for RICs, REITs and other pass-through entities.—The new law adds several specific provisions for applying the qualified dividend rules to mutual funds (regulated investment companies), real estate investment trusts, and other pass-through entities. When the qualified dividend rate was originally enacted, the treatment of shareholders in RICs and REITS was indicated by referring to the rules allowing RICs and REITS to designate certain dividends as eligible for the dividends received deduction. Now, the RIC and REIT rules each contain explicit instructions for passing through qualifying dividends eligible for the reduced tax rate (Code Sec. 854(b)(1)(B) and Code Sec. 857(c)(2), as amended by the 2004 Working Families Tax Act). The new law also expands the specific list of pass-through entities from which distributions of qualifying corporate dividends may be received.

> **Comment:** The qualified dividend rules for the treatment of qualified dividends received from a regulated investment company (RIC) or a real estate investment trust (REIT) are not significantly changed; however, the tax code has been changed to set forth these rules explicitly instead of by reference to rules applicable to dividends received by corporate shareholders.

Qualifying dividends paid by partnerships, S corporations, estates, and trusts. Partnerships, S corporations, estates, revocable trusts treated as part of an estate, or common trust fund can pass through dividends received to their partners, shareholders and beneficiaries as dividends qualifying for the lower tax rates, to the extent that the dividends are otherwise qualified. However, a technical correction clarifies that dividends received by an entity before December 31, 2002 should not be treated as qualified dividend income, regardless of when the dividends are distributed (Act Sec. 402(a)(6) of the 2004 Working Families Tax Act, amending Act. Sec. 302(f) of the Jobs and Growth Tax Relief Reconciliation Act of 2003).

Qualifying dividends paid by mutual funds. A mutual fund (or other regulated investment company) shareholder can include as part of qualifying dividend income any dividends designated by the mutual fund as qualifying dividends (Code Sec. 854(b)(1)(B)(i), as amended by the 2004 Working Families Tax Act). In order for the regulated investment company to designate the amount as qualified dividend income, the entity's qualified dividend income must be less than 95 percent of its gross income. The aggregate amount designated as qualified dividends may not exceed the aggregate dividends received during the year (Code Sec. 854(b)(1)(C), as amended by the 2004 Working Families Tax Act). In addition, the amount designated as qualifying dividend income may not exceed the sum of:

(1) the qualified dividend income of the RIC for the tax year; and

(2) the amount of any earnings and profits distributed for the tax year accumulated in a tax year in which the RIC rules did not apply (Code Sec. 854(b)(1)(C)(ii), as amended by the 2004 Working Families Tax Act).

> **Comment:** Under the formula for calculating the maximum amount that can be designated as qualifying dividends, note that all distributions by a mutual fund of the earnings and profits from C corporation years (before the entity became a regulated investment company) can be treated as qualifying dividends eligible for the reduced rate (see Code Sec. 854(b)(1)(C)(ii)(II), as amended by the 2004 Working Families Tax Act).

Qualifying dividends paid by REITs. A portion of a REIT's distribution may be classified as "qualified dividend income" if it was either attributable to income that was subject to corporate tax at the REIT level or if it was a corporate dividend received as investment income by the REIT (it was qualified dividend income when it was received by the REIT). The amount of dividends paid by a REIT that will qualify for the reduced rate may not exceed the amount of aggregate qualifying dividends received by the REIT, and the aggregate amount of qualifying dividends received by the REIT must be less than 95 percent of its gross income (Code Sec. 857(c)(2)(B), as amended by the 2004 Working Families Tax Act). The most that can be designated as qualified dividend income is the sum of:

(1) the qualified dividend income of the REIT for the tax year;

(2) the excess of (a) the REIT taxable income under Code Secs. 857(b)(2) and 337(d) for the preceding tax year over (b) the taxes payable by the REIT under Code Sec. 857(b)(1) for that preceding tax year; and

(3) the amount of earnings and profits distributed by the REIT during the preceding tax year that were accumulated in a tax year to which the REIT rules did not apply (Code Sec. 857(c)(2)(B), as amended by the 2004 Working Families Tax Act).

Comment: The revised formula allows "flush out" dividends that a C Corp pays when electing REIT status to be taxed as qualifying dividends even if paid after the REIT election.

Notification date for mutual funds and REITs. A regulated investment company or REIT is required to provide notice to shareholders of the amount to be treated as qualified dividend income within 60 days after the close of its tax year (Code Sec. 854(b)(2); Code Sec. 857(c)(2)(C), as amended by the 2004 Working Families Tax Act). A retroactive technical amendment adds that the notification date for tax years ending on or before November 30, 2003, was extended until the due date for the 2003 1099-DIV forms (Act Sec. 402(a)(5)(F) of the 2004 Working Families Tax Act).

PRACTICAL ANALYSIS. Arthur Seltzer of Brown Smith Wallace, LLC, St. Louis, Missouri, observes that this is a significant change affecting dividends from pass-through entities for fiscal years ending in 2003. A specific provision of the Jobs and Growth Tax Relief Reconciliation Act of 2003 (JGTRRA) treated dividends earned after December 31, 2002, and passed through by RICs and REITs as eligible for the lower rate. In the absence of a specific provision or a disclosure on the K-1, there was a question as to whether this treatment was available for dividends earned by partnerships, S corporations and other pass-through entities.

Comment. **This provision will be particularly helpful to estates, and trusts covered by elections under Code Sec. 645, that have elected a fiscal tax year.**

For further information on this subject, consult any of the following CCH reporter explanations:

- Standard Federal Tax Reporter, 2004FED ¶26,433.01, ¶26,465.01 and ¶26,533.025

- Federal Tax Service, FTS §E:5.101[11], §F:9.80 and §I:21.180

- Federal Tax Guide, 2004FTG ¶16,610, ¶16,650 and ¶16,670

★ *Effective date.* The provisions apply to tax years ending after December 31, 2002 (Act Sec. 402(b) of the Working Families Tax Relief Act of 2004 and Act Sec. 302(f) of the Jobs and Growth Tax Relief Reconciliation Act of 2003). The amendments are subject to a sunset provision indicating that they will not apply to tax years beginning after December 31, 2008 (Act Sec. 303 of the Jobs and Growth Tax Relief Reconciliation Act of 2003) (see ¶29,001 for a discussion of the sunset provision).

Act Sec. 402(a)(5)(A)-(E) of the Working Families Tax Relief Act of 2004, amending Code Sec. 854(b)(1)(B), Code Sec. 854(b)(1)(C), Code Sec. 854(b)(2), Code Sec. 854(b)(5) and Code Sec. 857(c)(2); Act Sec. 402(a)(5)(F); Act Sec. 402(a)(6), amending Act Sec. 302(f)(2) of the Jobs and Growth Tax Relief Reconciliation Act of 2003; Act Sec. 402(b). Law at ¶5270, ¶5275 and ¶7025. Committee Report at ¶10,510.

¶ 309

Clarification of Qualified Dividend Calculations and Reporting

Background

The top federal tax rate for dividends received by a taxpayer other than a corporation (including individuals, estate and trusts) was reduced to 15 percent by the Jobs and Growth Tax Relief Reconciliation Act of 2003, P.L. 108-27 (the rate is 5 percent for those whose incomes fall in the 10- or 15-percent rate brackets) (Code Sec. 1(h)(11)). The new dividend rate is the same as the reduced rate for capital gains, and qualified dividends and net capital gain are generally combined for reporting purposes. When the dividend rate was passed, several provisions in the tax law that incorporate references to amounts taxed at the reduced capital gains rate were not updated to explicitly include or exclude qualified dividends.

Working Families Tax Act Impact

Qualified dividend rules coordinated with estate tax deduction, extraordinary dividend rules for noncorporate taxpayers, and calculation of tax on unrecaptured section 1250 gain.—Several outstanding details about the application of the qualified dividend rules have been clarified by technical corrections. The formula for computing the amount of gain subject to the 25-percent rate of tax (unrecaptured section 1250 gain) has been revised to exclude qualified dividends (Code Sec. 1(h)(1)(D)(i), as amended by the Working Families Tax Relief Act of 2004). The formula for calculating the estate tax deduction for estate taxes attributable to amounts taxed at favorable capital gain rates has been amended to specifically include qualified dividends (Code Sec. 691(c)(4), as amended by the 2004 Working Families Tax Act). The treatment of extraordinary dividends has also been clarified so that the long term capital loss treatment applies not just to individuals, but to any noncorporate taxpayer eligible for the reduced dividend tax rate, including trusts and estates (Code Sec. 1(h)(11)(D), as amended by the 2004 Working Families Tax Act).

Decedent's deduction for estate taxes reduces amount eligible for reduced dividend rate. A person reporting dividend as income in respect of a decedent on a decedent's final return can claim a deduction for estate taxes paid to the extent that the dividend was included in the decedent's gross estate (Code Sec. 691(c); Reg. §1.691(c)-1). The recipient of the dividend must also reduce the amount reported as eligible for the reduced dividend rate by the amount claimed as a deduction for estate taxes (Code Sec. 691(c)(4), as amended by the 2004 Working Families Tax Act). This has the effect of reducing the amount decedent's income eligible for the reduced dividend tax rate by the deduction attributable to estate taxes. Prior to the amendment, the provision coordinating the estate tax deduction with the capital gains tax rate indicated that the amount of "gain" that was included as income in respect of a decedent and taxed at the net capital gain rate should be reduced by the amount of any applicable deduction for estate taxes attributable (Code Sec. 691(c)(4)). The use of the word "gain" instead of simply referring to the amounts eligible for the net capital gain tax rate caused some confusion over whether qualifying dividends were also included in the rule.

Comment: The deduction for estate taxes may be claimed only as an itemized deduction and may not be claimed as a deduction from gross income in arriving at adjusted gross income. The amendment thus does not affect non-itemizers. Also, with the steady rise in the amount of an estate that is exempt from estate tax (to $1,500,000 in 2004), it is likely that many individuals will not pay estate tax and thus will not claim a deduction attributable to estate taxes paid.

Long-term capital loss treatment for extraordinary dividends. A technical correction clarifies that the long-term capital loss treatment of qualified extraordinary dividends applies to any taxpayer to whom the provision may apply, including trusts and estates, and not just to individuals (Code Sec. 1(h)(11)(D)(ii), as amended by the 2004 Working Families Tax Act). The rule for extraordinary dividends states that if a taxpayer receives a dividend qualifying for the reduced rate, and the dividend exceeds 10 percent of the shareholder's basis in the stock, then any loss on the sale of the stock to the extent of the dividends will be treated as long-term capital loss (Code Sec. 1(h)(11)(D)(ii) and Code Sec. 1059(c)). The holding period of the stock on which the extraordinary dividend is paid is not taken into account in determining whether an individual is subject to the extraordinary dividend rule or whether the loss on the stock (to the extent of the extraordinary dividends) is long-term capital loss.

Compliance Tip: This rule was incorporated into IRS income tax return instructions for 2003. Amended returns should not be needed.

Comment: The long-term capital loss characterization rule affects taxpayers with both short-term capital gain and long-term capital gain from other transactions in excess of the loss generated by the extraordinary dividend transaction. The characterization makes no difference to a taxpayer having no capital gains, capital gain not in excess of the dividend transaction loss, or only capital losses.

Dividends excluded from 25-percent rate calculations on depreciated realty recapture. Qualified dividends are excluded from calculations of the net capital gain limit on the amount of gain taxed at the 25-percent rate (Code Sec. 1(h)(1)(D), as amended by the 2004 Working Families Tax Act). Gain attributable to prior depreciation claimed on real property is taxed at a 25-percent rate, and is referred to as "unrecaptured section 1250 gain." Recapture occurs to prevent a taxpayer from obtaining favorable capital gain treatment on gain attributable to depreciation deductions that were used to offset ordinary income taxed at a higher rate.

In general, unrecaptured section 1250 gain is the amount of depreciation claimed on section 1250 property which is not recaptured as ordinary income. Since MACRS real property is not subject to ordinary income recapture, all depreciation on such property, to the extent of gain, is potentially characterized as unrecaptured section 1250 gain taxed at the 25 percent rate. The maximum amount subject to the 25-percent rate is the taxpayer's net capital gain.

Compliance Tip: Section 1250 recapture, if any, is computed in Part III of Form 4797, Sales of Business Property.

The revised technical formula for computing the tax on unrecaptured section 1250 gain imposes a tax rate of 25 percent on the excess of:

(1) the unrecaptured section 1250 gain (or, if less, net capital gain determined without regard to qualified dividends), over

(2) the sum of the amount subject to tax at ordinary income rates, plus the net capital gain determined without regard to qualified dividends; over taxable income (Code Sec. 1(h)(1)(D), as amended by the 2004 Working Families Tax Act).

¶309

Comment: Section 1250 net capital gain is the excess of net long-term capital gain over net short-term capital loss, increased by qualified dividend income.

PRACTICAL ANALYSIS. Arthur Seltzer of Brown Smith Wallace, LLC, St. Louis, Missouri, observes that under Code Sec. 691(a)(4), the amount of capital gain taxed at the lower rate is reduced by the amount of the Code Sec. 691(c) deduction attributable to capital gain IRD items reported for the tax year. A technical correction extends this treatment to qualifying dividend IRD items.

For further information on this subject, consult any of the following CCH reporter explanations:

- Standard Federal Tax Reporter, 2004FED ¶3285.01 and ¶24,911.01
- Federal Tax Service, FTS §E:5.100 and §E:5.140
- Federal Tax Guide, 2004FTG ¶1010, ¶5581, ¶16,665, ¶19,500 and ¶19,525

★ *Effective date.* The provisions are effective for tax years beginning after December 31, 2002 (Act Sec. 402(b) of the Working Families Tax Relief Act of 2004 and Act Sec. 302(f) of the Jobs and Growth Tax Relief Reconciliation Act of 2004). The amendments are subject to a sunset provision indicating that they will not apply to tax years beginning after December 31, 2008 (Act Sec. 303 of the Jobs and Growth Tax Relief Reconciliation Act of 2003) (see ¶29,001 for a discussion of the sunset provision).

Act Sec. 402(a)(1) of the Working Families Tax Relief Act of 2004, amending Code Sec. 1(h)(1)(D)(i); Act Sec. 402(a)(3), amending Code Sec. 1(h)(11)(D)(ii); Act Sec. 402(a)(4), amending Code Sec. 691(c)(4); Act Sec. 402(b). Law at ¶5005 and ¶5265. Committee Report at ¶10,510.

¶ 311

Tax Treatment of Options and Securities Futures Contracts

Background ───

Under the end-of-year mark-to-market rules, gain or loss on a section 1256 contract is treated as 60 percent long-term and 40 percent short-term (Code Sec. 1256(a)(3)). A section 1256 contract is defined to include dealer equity options, (Code Sec. 1256(b)(4), (g)(4), and (g)(6)). Only options dealers are eligible for section 1256 treatment with respect to equity options.

The Community Renewal Tax Relief Act of 2000 (P.L. 106-554) amended the mark-to-market provisions of Code Sec. 1256 to change the definition of an equity option (Code Sec. 1256(g)(6), as amended by P.L. 106-554). As amended, equity options are defined to include (in addition to options to buy or sell stock) any option the value of which is determined by reference to any narrow-based security index as defined under section 3(a)(55) of the Securities and Exchange Act. The term "equity option" includes an option on a group of stocks only if the group meets the requirements for a narrow-based security index (Code Sec. 1256(g)(6), as amended by P.L. 106-554). Prior to amendment, the definition of an equity option was more broadly defined to include (in addition to options to buy or sell stock) any option the value of which is determined directly or indirectly by reference to any stock (or group of stock) or stock index. An exception was provided which excluded certain options regulated by the Commodities Futures Trading Commission from the definition of an equity option (Code Sec. 1256(g)(6), prior to amendment by P.L. 106-554).

Both prior to and after amendment by the Community Renewal Tax Relief Act, listed options that are not "equity options" are considered nonequity options to

Background _____

which Code Sec. 1256 applies for all taxpayers (Code Sec. 1256(b)(3) and Code Sec. 1256(g)(3)). Options relating to broad-based groups of stocks and broad-based stock indexes continue to be treated as nonequity options under Code Sec. 1256, according to the Conference Committee Report to P.L. 106-554.

The amendments by the Community Renewal Tax Relief Act did not specifically address the treatment of an option whose value is determined by reference to an index which changes its status to or from a narrow-based securities index after the option was purchased. Thus, it was unclear whether a dealer equity option lost its status and became a nonequity option if its value was tied to a narrow-based security index which later failed to meet the requirements for a narrow-based security index. Conversely, the treatment of an option whose value is tied to a non-narrow based index which later satisfies the narrow-based index requirements was also uncertain.

P.L. 106-554 also added a new provision, Code Sec. 1234B, which deals with a new type of financial instrument, a "securities futures contract," which was created by the Commodities Futures Modernization Act of 2000 (P.L. 103-556). "Dealer securities futures contracts" are treated as section 1256 contracts and marked-to-market (Code Sec. 1256(b)(5)). Thus, gains and losses are treated as 60-percent long-term and 40-percent short-term. Investors in a "securities futures contract" generally recognize short term gain or loss upon disposition of the contract (Code Sec. 1234B(b)).

A securities futures contract is defined by reference to section 3(a)(55)(A) of the Securities Exchange Act of 1934, which was added by P.L. 106-554. In general, that section defines a securities futures contract as "a contract of sale for future delivery of a single security or a narrow-based securities index, including any interest therein or based on the value therefor".

As in the case of an option whose value is determined by reference to an index which changes status, Code Sec. 1234B is silent with regard to the treatment of a contract whose value is determined with respect to an index that changes status to or from a narrow-based securities index.

_____

Working Families Tax Act Impact

Regulatory authority over options and contracts clarified.—The technical correction gives the Secretary of the Treasury authority to prescribe regulations regarding the status of an option or a contract, the value of which is determined directly or indirectly by reference to an index which becomes (or ceases to be) a narrow-based security index (as defined in Code Sec. 1256(g)(6)). This authority includes, but is not limited to, regulations that provide for preserving the status of such an option or contract as appropriate (Code Secs. 1234B(c) and 1256(g)(6), as amended by the Working Families Tax Relief Act of 2004).

For further information on this subject, consult any of the following CCH reporter explanations:

- Standard Federal Tax Reporter, 2004FED ¶30,643.01 and ¶31,107.021
- Federal Tax Service, FTS § E:15.240 and § E:16.63
- Federal Tax Guide, 2004FTG ¶5840 and ¶5864

★ *Effective date.* The provision is effective on December 21, 2000 (Act Sec. 405(b) of the Working Families Tax Relief Act of 2004; Act Sec. 401(j) of the Community Renewal Tax Relief Act of 2000 (P.L. 107-16)).

Act Sec. 405(a)(1) of the Working Families Tax Relief Act of 2004, amending Code Sec. 1234B(c); Act Sec. 405(a)(2), amending Code Sec. 1256(g)(6); Act Sec. 405(b). Law at ¶5295 and ¶5300. Committee Report at ¶10,540.

¶313

Constructive Sales of Appreciated Financial Positions

Background _____

Under Code Sec. 1259, which was enacted by the Taxpayer Relief Act of 1997 (P.L. 105-34), certain hedging transactions that involve appreciated financial positions, generally result in constructive sales. As a result of these constructive sale rules, taxpayers are required to recognize gain even though the transaction has not really been closed. In essence, the taxpayers are taxed on their paper profits. However, some limited exceptions are made from these constructive sales rules.

Appreciated financial position. The term "appreciated financial position" is generally defined to mean any interest in stock, partnership, or debt, if disposing of the interest would result in gain (Code Sec. 1259(b)(1)). The term "position" includes futures or forward contracts, short sales, or options (Code Sec. 1259(b)(3)).

Constructive sales. Taxpayers will be treated as having made a constructive sale of an appreciated financial positions when they engage in a number of transactions. These transactions include (Code Sec. 1259(c)(1)):

(1) entering into a short sale of the same or substantially identical property,

(2) entering into an offsetting notional principal contract relating to the same or substantially identical property, or

(3) acquiring the same or substantially identical property when the appreciated financial position is a short sale, an offsetting notional principal contract, or a futures or forward contract.

Exceptions. There are three main exceptions to the constructive sales rules:

(1) *Nonmarketable securities.* A contract for the sale of a nonmarketable security is not a constructive sale if the contract settles within one year of the date the taxpayer entered into the contract (Code Sec. 1259(c)(2)).

(2) *Certain closed transactions.* A transaction will not be treated as a constructive sale when it meets the requirements of a closed transactions (e.g., certain time limits are met) (Code Sec. 1259(c)(3)).

(3) *Reestablished closed positions.* A reestablished position after a position has been closed will not be treated as a constructive sale if certain time limits are met (Code Sec. 1259(c)(3)).

Planning Note: With regard to "closed transaction," the IRS has issued information that will help taxpayers determine if they qualify for this exception to the constructive sale rules (Rev. Rul. 2003-1).

Working Families Tax Act Impact

Clarification of exceptions to closed transaction rule.—The Working Families Tax Relief Act of 2004 has made several technical corrections to the exceptions to the constructive sales rules for appreciated financial positions (AFPs). The technical corrections pertain to: (1) nonpublicly traded property, (2) closed transactions, in general, and (3) certain closed transactions where risk of loss is diminished. The technical changes are:

(1) *Nonpublicly traded property.* A technical correction modifies the rule covering the exception for nonpublicly traded property. Under this modification, a taxpayer will not be treated as having made a constructive sale of an AFP solely because the taxpayer entered into a contract to sell certain nonmarketable property as defined by Code Sec. 453(f), provided the contract settles within one year (Code Sec. 1259(c)(2), as amended by the 2004 Working Families Tax Act).

Comment: This modification has narrowed the exception allowed for nonpublicly traded property. Under the original wording of Code Sec. 1259(c)(2), *any* contract to sell nonpublicly traded property qualified for the exception to the constructive sale rules. Under the change in wording made to Code Sec. 1259(c)(2) by the 2004 Working Families Tax Act, a contract to sell nonpublicly traded property may not always be sufficient to qualify the transaction for the exception. As a result, other factors may have to be taken into account when making the determination if a sale of nonpublicly traded property qualifies for the exception.

(2) *Closed transactions, in general.* The amendment clarifies that certain closed transactions will not cause the constructive sale of the original AFP (Code Sec. 1259(c)(3)(A), as amended by the 2004 Working Families Tax Act). Before this amendment, it appeared that the closed transaction itself had to be treated as a constructive sale. The amendment also clarifies that the transaction must be closed *on or before* the end of the 30th day after the close of the tax year (Code Sec. 1259(c)(3)(A)(i), as amended by the 2004 Working Families Tax Act). Prior wording stated that the transaction had to be closed *before* the 30th day.

(3) *Closed transactions where risk of loss diminished.* An amendment clarifies that the exception that existed for "reestablished positions," applies to all closed transactions, including reestablished positions, provided the required time limits are followed (Code Sec. 1259(c)(3)(B), as amended by the 2004 Working Families Tax Act).

Comment: The exception for closed transactions has been greatly expanded by eliminating the terms "reestablished position" and "substantially identical." The exception now applies to transactions that diminish the risk of loss in the original AFP. Thus, taxpayers have been given a great deal of latitude when constructing transactions that will reduce the possibility of loss in their AFPs.

Planning Note: In Rev. Rul. 2003-1, the IRS illustrates, through the use of several examples, when a taxpayer's short sales of stock will not cause the constructive sale of an AFP. In addition, the ruling anticipated the technical corrections made by the 2004 Working Families Tax Act by using some of the same terms that have now been incorporated into the Tax Code.

PRACTICAL ANALYSIS. Arthur Seltzer of Brown Smith Wallace, LLC, St. Louis, Missouri, notes that prior legislation restricted the viability of the "short sale against the box" and similar techniques designated as constructive sales. Unfavorable recognition treatment is avoided if the taxpayer remains at risk for the re-established position for 60 days after closing the original transaction. The 2004 Working Families Act clarifies that where the re-established position is closed and replaced within the 60-day period, the same rule applies to the liquidation of the replacement position.

For further information on this subject, consult any of the following CCH reporter explanations:

- Standard Federal Tax Reporter, 2004FED ¶31,130G.01
- Federal Tax Service, FTS § E:15.203
- Federal Tax Guide, 2004FTG ¶5731

★ *Effective date.* The provisions are generally effective for constructive sales entered into after June 8, 1997 (Act Sec. 406(h) of the Working Families Tax Relief Act of 2004; Act Sec. 1001(d)(1) of the Taxpayer Relief Act of 1997 (P.L. 105-34)). Special transition rules apply for sales of positions held before June 9, 1997, and decedents dying after June 8, 1997 (Act Sec. 1001(d)(2) and (3) of the Taxpayer Relief Act of 1997 (P.L. 105-34).

Act Sec. 406(e)(1) of the Working Families Tax Relief Act of 2004, amending Code Sec. 1259(c)(2); Act Sec. 406(e)(2), amending Code Sec. 1259(c)(3)(A) and (B)(i); Act Sec. 406(e)(3), amending Code Sec. 1259(c)(3)(A)(i); Act Sec. 406(e)(4), amending Code Sec. 1259(c)(3)(B)(ii); Act Sec. 406(e)(5), amending Code Sec. 1259(c)(3)(B)(ii)(I); Act Sec. 406(e)(6), amending Code Sec. 1259(c)(3)(B)(ii)(II); Act Sec. 406(e)(7), amending Code Sec. 1259(c)(3)(B); Act Sec. 406(h). Law at ¶5305. Committee Report at ¶10,550.

ALTERNATIVE MINIMUM TAX

¶315

Capital Gain

Background ——————————————————————————

For noncorporate taxpayers, the maximum rate of the alternative minimum tax (AMT) on net capital gain is limited (Code Sec. 55(b)(3)), as it is limited for regular income tax purposes (Code Sec. 1(h)). Starting after May 5, 2003, the maximum capital gains rate is generally either 5 percent or 15 percent, depending on the taxpayer's highest marginal tax bracket (Code Sec. 1(h)(1)). Higher capital gains tax rates may apply to certain types of gains. For example, long-term capital gains from collectibles may be subject to a capitals gains tax rate as high as 28 percent.

When computing a noncorporate taxpayer's AMT, part of the process requires that a determination be made as to what portion of the adjusted net capital gain is eligible to be taxed at 5 percent for AMT purposes (Code Sec. 55(b)(3)).

Example 1: Nick and Nora file a join tax return for 2004 and they have no dependents. For 2004, their income and deductions consisted of: (1) $32,100 in salary, (2) $82,000 in long-term capital gains from the sale of shares in Afta, Inc., (3) $73,000 in itemized deductions, from state and local taxes and allowable miscellaneous itemized deductions, and (4) $6,200 in personal exemptions. As a result, their taxable income for 2004 is $34,900. For AMT purposes, their taxable excess is $56,100 ($32,100 wages + $82,000 in long-term capital gain − $58,000 AMT exemption amount).

In computing their regular income tax for 2004, the amount of their income taxed at the 5-percent long-term rate would be the *lesser* of: (1) taxable income ($34,900), (2) adjusted net capital gain ($82,000), or (3) the excess of the maximum amount of long-term capital gains taxed at the 15-percent rate ($58,100 for 2004), over the ordinary taxable income ($0). As a result, the regular income tax imposed on their long-term capital gain is $1,745 ($34,900 × 5%).

Before the changes enacted by the Working Families Tax Relief Act of 2004, Nick and Nora determining their potential AMT would have used the following computations: (1) the amount taxed at 5 percent would have been the $34,900 (i.e., the *lesser* of (a) $34,900, the amount of adjusted net capital gain taxed at the

Background _____

5% regular income tax rate, or (b) $56,100, the taxable excess) and (2) the remaining $21,200 of taxable excess ($56,100 – $34,900) would have been taxed at 15%. As a result of these computations, Nick and Nora's tentative minimum tax for AMT purposes would have been $4,925 (($34,900 × 5% = $1,745) + ($21,200 × 15% = $3,180)).

Working Families Tax Act Impact

Change in required computations.—The provision changes the required AMT computation (Code Sec. 55(b)(3)(B), as amended by the Working Families Tax Relief Act of 2004). Under this change, the maximum amount of adjusted net capital gain eligible for the 5-percent rate is the *excess* of the maximum taxable income that may be taxed at a rate of less than 25 percent under the regular tax (i.e., $58,100 on a 2004 joint tax return), over taxable income reduced by the adjusted net capital gain.

Example 2: Assume the same facts as in Example 1, above, except that Nick and Nora are computing their AMT under the new provision. The amount taxed at 5% is the *lesser* of: (1) $56,100, taxable excess, (2) $82,000, adjusted net capital gain, or (3) the excess of the amount taxed at the 15% rate under the regular income tax ($58,100), over the ordinary taxable income ($0). Under this computation, Nick and Nora's tentative minimum tax is $2,805 ($56,100 × 5%).

For further information on this subject, consult any of the following CCH reporter explanations:

- Standard Federal Tax Reporter, 2004FED ¶5101.01
- Federal Tax Service, FTS § E:5.100
- Federal Tax Guide, 2004FTG ¶1320

★ *Effective date.* The amendment applies to tax years ending after May 6, 1997 (Act Sec. 406(h) of the Working Families Tax Relief Act of 2004; Act Sec. 311(d) of the Taxpayer Relief Act of 1997 (P.L. 105-34)).

Act Sec. 406(d) of the Working Families Tax Relief Act of 2004, amending Code Sec. 55(b)(3)(B); Act Sec. 406(h). Law at ¶5085. Committee Report at ¶10,550.

NET OPERATING LOSSES

¶ 321

Five-Year 2001 and 2002 NOL Carryback Clarified

Background _____

The net operating loss (NOL) carryback period was extended from two years (or three years in certain cases) to five years for "a taxpayer which has" an NOL for any tax year ending in 2001 and 2002 (Code Sec. 172(b)(1)(H), as amended by the Job Creation and Worker Assistance Act of 2002 (P.L. 107-147). This language caused some concern about whether the five-year carryback might not apply to any NOL that "a taxpayer which has" a 2001 or 2002 NOL might have.

A more pressing concern was the transition with respect to the selection of the five-year period, the two-year period, or a carryfoward for NOLs from tax years ending in 2001 or 2002, and the resulting adjustment to tentative carrybacks that would result from this choice. Independent of the 2002 amendments, taxpayers could (and still can) waive a carryback in favor of a carryforward (Code Sec. 172(b)(3)) if done by the due date of the return for the tax year of the NOL. The P.L. 107-147

Background

amendments provide a similar waiver provision to enable a taxpayer to waive the automatic five-year carryback in favor of the two-year (or three-year) carryback to which they would otherwise be entitled (Code Sec. 172(j)), as added by the Job Creation and Worker Assistance Act of 2002 (P.L. 107-147). Adjustments to tentative carrybacks required by Code Sec. 6411(a) are of course affected by the manner in which an NOL is carried over. Because P.L. 107-147 was enacted on March 9, 2002, some taxpayers had already filed their 2001 tax returns thinking their choice was either a two- (or three-) year carryback or no carryback. Furthermore, their adjustments to tentative carrybacks were made based on whatever they selected or thought they were selecting. In response to these concerns, the IRS issued Rev. Proc. 2002-40, 2002-1 CB 1096, which gave taxpayers until October 31, 2002, to decide whether to waive the five-year period or waive a carryback altogether. These taxpayers also had until October 31, 2002, to make resulting carryback adjustments.

P.L. 107-147 amended Code Sec. 56(d) to provide favorable alternative minimum tax treatment for 2001 and 2002 NOLs and NOL carryovers taken in those years. The amendments provided that 100 percent rather than the usual 90 percent of NOLs can be deducted from alternative tax income for 2001 and 2002 NOLs.

Working Families Tax Act Impact

Transition rules written into law.—The Working Families Tax Relief Act of 2004 adopts the transition deadlines found in Rev. Proc. 2002-40. The 2004 Working Families Tax Act (Act Sec. 403(b)(2)) provides that taxpayers with NOLs from 2001 or 2002 have until October 31, 2002, to make carryback adjustments under Code Sec. 6411(a), elect to waive the five-year carryback under Code Sec. 172(j), or elect to wave carrybacks altogether under Code Sec. 172(b)(3).

> **Comment:** The 2004 Working Families Tax Act transition corrections leave the Code itself unchanged.

> **Comment:** One reason that Congress might have felt a need to reinforce the deadlines that the IRS already adjusted in Rev. Proc. 2002-40 is that the IRS might have stretched its authority when it relaxed three deadlines contained in the Code.

Ambiguities removed. The 2004 Working Family Tax Act clarifies that only NOLs from 2001 and 2002 can qualify for the five-year carryback. Act Sec. 403(b)(1) strikes the confusing "a taxpayer which has" language from the phrase "in the case of a taxpayer which has a net operating loss for any taxable year ending in 2001 or 2002" so that it reads "in the case of a net operating loss for any taxable year ending in 2001 or 2002."

> **Compliance Tip:** The application for a tentative carryback adjustment must be filed on Form 1139, Corporation Application for Tentative Refund, by a corporation, or on Form 1045, Application for Tentative Refund, by all other taxpayers. See Reg. § 1.6411-1 for further discussion.

Alternative minimum tax benefits clarified. Act Sec. 403(b)(4) of the 2004 Working Families Tax Act clarifies that favorable alternative minimum tax treatment applies to NOLs generated in 2001 and 2002, and to NOLs carried over to 2001 and 2002. Also, Act Sec. 403(b)(3) changes the effective date of the 2002 alternative minimum tax amendment from tax years ending before January 1, 2003, to tax years ending after December 31, 1990.

¶321

For further information on this subject, consult any of the following CCH reporter explanations:

- Standard Federal Tax Reporter, 2004FED ¶5210.03 and ¶12,014.023
- Federal Tax Service, FTS § A:22.83[2], § G:14.82 and § I:24.126[2]
- Federal Tax Guide, 2004FTG ¶1350 and ¶10,875

★ *Effective date.* The corrections apply to net operating losses for tax years beginning after December 31, 2000, except the alternative minimum tax corrections which are effective for tax years ending after December 31, 1990 (Act. Sec. 403(f) of the Working Families Tax Relief Act of 2004; Act Sec. 102(d) of the Job Creation and Worker Assistance Act of 2002 (P.L. 107-147)).

Act Sec. 403(b)(1) of the 2004 Working Families Tax Relief Act of 2004, amending Code Sec. 172(b)(1)(H); Act Sec. 403(b)(2); Act Sec. 403(b)(3), amending Act Sec. 102(c)(2) of the Job Creation and Worker Assistance Act of 2002; Act Sec. 403(b)(4), amending Code Sec. 56(d)(1)(A); Act Sec. 403(f). Law at ¶5090, ¶5170 and ¶7030. Committee Report at ¶10,520.

BONUS DEPRECIATION

¶327

Syndicated Leasing Transactions

Background _____

In order to qualify for the additional bonus depreciation allowance (Code Sec. 168(k)), the original use of the property must commence with the taxpayer claiming the bonus depreciation deduction after September 10, 2001 (Code Sec. 168(k)(2)(A)(ii)). This rule is intended to prevent used property from qualifying for bonus depreciation. In addition, the taxpayer must place the property in service before January 1, 2005 (Code Sec. 168(k)(2)(A)(iv)).

A limited exception to the original use requirement applies to certain sale-leaseback transactions.

The exception applies if a person originally places property in service after September 10, 2001, and within three months both sells the property and reacquires it in a leaseback transaction. In this situation the lessor is treated as having originally placed the property in service no sooner than the date on which the property is used under the leaseback (Code Sec. 168(k)(2)(D)(ii), prior to amendment by the Working Families Tax Act of 2004). Consequently, the lessor is entitled to claim the bonus depreciation deduction.

Example: ABC Corporation purchases a new airplane from the manufacturer on October 1, 2003. If ABC sells the airplane to DEF Corporation and leases it back from DEF before January 1, 2004, DEF is treated as originally placing the airplane in service on the date that the airplane is used under the leaseback. DEF may claim bonus depreciation on the airplane.

Comment: After enactment of the bonus depreciation provision, it appeared that the ultimate purchaser of leased property in a syndicated leasing transaction would not be able to qualify for bonus depreciation. For example, if DEF in the example above syndicated the transaction by selling the airplane to a partnership, it appeared that the partnership could not qualify for bonus depreciation and could not pass the deduction through to its partners. Furthermore, it appeared that if DEF purchased the airplane directly from the manufacturer, leased it to ABC, and then syndicated the transaction, the investors would not qualify for bonus depreciation. Moreover, it appeared that if the syndicator purchased and sold the leased property to investors in the same tax year, the syndicator would not qualify for bonus depreciation and the benefit of the deduction would be entirely lost. (Property acquired and disposed of in the same tax year by a taxpayer may not be depreciated.) The inability of syndicators and their investors to claim bonus depreciation was understandably of major concern to the equipment leasing industry and it immediately called for a technical correction and the issuance of regulations to clarify the issue. The Equipment Leasing Association (ELA) estimates that between 20 and 25 billion dollars is invested annually in syndicated leasing transactions.

The IRS responded favorably and, without prior passage of a technical correction, issued regulations that allow investors who acquire their interests in syndicated leasing transactions to claim the bonus depreciation deduction if certain requirements are satisfied (Temporary Reg. §1.168(k)-1T(b)(3)(iii)(B) and Temporary Reg. §1.168(k)-1T(b)(5)(ii)(B), adopted by T.D. 9091, filed with the Federal Register on September 5, 2003). The regulations were made retroactive to apply to property acquired after September 10, 2001 (Temporary Reg. §1.168(k)-1T(g)(1)).

Under temporary regulations, if qualified property is originally placed in service by a lessor after September 10, 2001 (after May 5, 2003, for the 50-percent bonus depreciation rate to apply), and is sold by the lessor or any later purchaser within three months after the date the property was originally placed in service by the lessor, and the user of the property does not change during this three-month period, then the purchaser of the property in the last sale is considered to be the original user of the property (Temporary Reg. §1.168(k)-1T(b)(3)(iii)(B)) and the property is treated as originally placed in service not earlier than the date of the last sale by the purchaser of the property in the last sale (Temporary Reg. §1.168(k)-1T(b)(5)(ii)(B)).

The regulations further provide that if a sale-leaseback transaction in which a lessor is treated as the original user under Code Sec. 168(k)(2)(D)(ii) is followed by a syndication transaction, then the original user and placed-in-service date is determined in accordance with the rule for syndication transactions (Temporary Reg. §1.168(k)-1T(b)(3)(iii)(C) and Temporary Reg. §1.168(k)-1T(b)(5)(ii)(C)). Thus, the rule for syndicated leasing transactions preempts the rule for sale-leasebacks and the investor in the syndicated leasing transaction may claim the bonus allowance.

Working Families Tax Act Impact

Bonus depreciation allowed in syndicated leasing transactions.—The new law contains a retroactive technical correction that allows investors in a syndicated leasing transaction to claim the bonus depreciation deduction (Code Sec. 168(k)(2)(D)(iii), as added by the Working Families Tax Relief Act of 2004).

The technical correction provides that if:

(1) a lessor of property originally places the property in service after September 10, 2001 (or is considered to have originally placed it in service after September 10, 2001 by operation of the sale-leaseback rule (Code Sec. 168(k)(2)(D)(ii), as described in the Background section, above);

(2) the property is sold by the lessor (or any subsequent purchaser) within three months after the lessor places the property in service; and

(3) the user of the property after the last sale during the three-month period remains the same as when the property was originally placed in service;

then the property is treated as originally placed in service not earlier than the date of the last sale within the three-month period.

Example 1: ABC Manufacturing Corporation purchases a new cargo container on January 1, 2004. It sells the cargo container to SYND corporation and leases it back from SYND on March 1, 2004. Both before and after issuance of the temporary regulations and passage of the technical correction, if there are no further transactions, SYND is considered to have originally placed the container in service on March 1, 2004, and may claim bonus depreciation. However, by reason of the temporary regulations and the technical correction, if SYND resells the container to an investor within three months after March 1, 2004, and ABC continues to use the container, the investor is considered to have originally placed the container in service on the date of purchase from SYND and may claim the bonus depreciation deduction.

Comment: The last purchaser within the three-month period is entitled to the bonus depreciation deduction as long as the original user (i.e., the lessee) remains the same. However, if the syndicator retains an interest in the leased equipment, it may also claim bonus depreciation with respect to that retained interest.

Example 2: Assume the same facts as in Example 1, above, except that the first investor sells the container to a second investor within three months after March 1, 2004. Assuming that ABC continues to use the container, the second investor is entitled to claim the bonus depreciation deduction.

The technical correction and temporary regulations also cover situations in which a syndicator is the original purchaser of the equipment, leases the equipment, and then sells the equipment subject to the lease to investors.

Example 3: SYND corporation purchases a new cargo vessel on January 1, 2004, from a ship manufacturer and leases it on the same date to GHI corporation. If SYND sells the vessel to one or more investors before April 1, 2004, and GHI is still the lessee, the investors may claim the bonus depreciation deduction. However, if any investor resells its interest in the vessel before April 1, 2004, and GHI continues to lease the vessel, then the subsequent purchaser is entitled to the bonus depreciation deduction.

Comment: The syndication rules have no impact on the calculation of regular MACRS depreciation deductions. Depreciation deductions continue to be claimed by any taxpayer who owns the property while it is placed in service provided that the asset is not placed in service and disposed of by the taxpayer in the same tax year.

Comment: An identical version of the technical correction was included in the Tax Technical Corrections Bill of 2002 prior to promulgation of the regulations discussed in the Background section above (H.R. 5713, Act Sec. 2(a)(3)). A similar version also appeared in the Jumpstart Our Business Strength (JOBS) Bill, as passed by the Senate on May 12, 2004 (S. 1637, Act Sec. 621). The JOBS version, however, provided that if multiple properties subject to the same lease are placed in service within a 12-month period, property sold by the lessor within three months after the date the final unit is placed in service may be treated as originally placed in service on the date of the last sale.

New York Liberty Zone. Property placed in service in the New York Liberty Zone may qualify for the bonus depreciation allowance under Code Sec. 1400L(b) if the property does not qualify for bonus depreciation under the more general provision of Code Sec. 168(k). Code Sec. 1400L(b)(2)(D) provides that rules similar to those contained in Code Sec. 168(k)(2)(D) apply to Liberty Zone property. By virtue of this cross reference, the technical correction also applies to leased Liberty Zone property. Regulations under Code Sec. 1400L also incorporate the Code Sec. 168(k) syndication regulations by cross reference (Temporary Reg. § 1.1400L(b)-1T(c)(4) and Temporary Reg. § 1.1400L(b)-1T(c)(6)).

> **Comment:** The Equipment Leasing Association had proposed that syndicators be given up to six months after their acquisition of property in which to resell to investors. The technical correction and temporary regulations, however, limit the resell period to three months.

> **Compliance Tip:** Since the temporary regulations and related technical correction are retroactively effective, taxpayers previously involved in syndicated leasing transactions may need to file amended returns to claim the bonus deduction.

For further information on this subject, consult any of the following CCH reporter explanations:

- Standard Federal Tax Reporter, 2004FED ¶ 11,279.0513 and ¶ 11,279.058
- Federal Tax Service, FTS § G:16.260
- Federal Tax Guide, 2004FTG ¶ 9131

★ *Effective date.* The provision applies to property placed in service after September 10, 2001, in tax years ending after that date (Act Sec. 403(f) of the Working Families Tax Relief Act of 2004; Act Sec. 101(b) of the Job Creation and Worker Assistance Act of 2002 (P.L. 107-147)).

Act Sec. 403(a)(2)(A) of the Working Families Tax Relief Act of 2004, adding Code Sec. 168(k)(2)(D)(iii); Act Sec. 403(a)(2)(B), amending Code Sec. 168(k)(2)(D)(ii); Act Sec. 403(f). Law at ¶ 5160. Committee Report at ¶ 10,520.

¶ 329

Property With Longer Production Periods

Background ————————————————————————————

In order to qualify for the bonus depreciation deduction (Code Sec. 168(k)), qualifying property must be placed into service prior to January 1, 2005 (Code Sec. 168(k)(2)(A)(iv)). The January 1, 2005, placed-in-service date, however, is extended to January 1, 2006, if:

- the property's original use commences with the taxpayer after September 10, 2001;

- the property (1) is acquired by the taxpayer after September 10, 2001, and before January 1, 2005, and no binding written contract for the acquisition was in effect before September 11, 2001, or (2) is acquired pursuant to a written binding contract entered into after September 10, 2001, and before January 1, 2005;

- the property has a recovery period of at least 10 years or is transportation property; and

- the property is subject to the uniform capitalization (UNICAP) rules of Code Sec. 263A by reason of Code Sec. 263A(f)(1)(B)(ii) or (iii).

Code Sec. 263A(f)(1)(B)(ii) applies the UNICAP interest capitalization rules to property produced by a taxpayer and having a production period that exceeds two years. Code Sec. 263A(f)(1)(B)(iii) applies the UNICAP interest capitalization rules to property produced by a taxpayer and having an estimated production period exceeding 1 year and a cost in excess of $1 million.

Background _____

It is possible to interpret the preceding rule to mean that if a property is subject to the UNICAP interest capitalization rules by reason of Code Sec. 263A(f)(1)(B)(i) because it has a long useful life, it is not eligible for the extended placed-in-service date even though the property has a production period that exceeds two years or has an estimated production period exceeding 1 year and a cost in excess of $1 million. Property with a long useful life is defined as real property or property with an MACRS class life of 20 years or more (Code Sec. 263A(f)(4)(A)).

> **Comment:** MACRS class lives for most assets are provided in Rev. Proc. 87-56. The class life of an asset is not necessary (and usually is not) the same as its MACRS recovery period. For example, an asset used in mining has a 7-year recovery period and a 10-year class life (see Asset Class 10.0 in Rev. Proc. 87-56).

Working Families Tax Act Impact

Extended January 1, 2006 bonus depreciation placed-in-service date clarified for property with longer production periods.—A technical correction clarifies that property subject to the UNICAP rules may qualify for the extended January 1, 2006, placed-in-service date under the bonus depreciation rules (Code Sec. 168(k)(2)(B)) so long as the property also meets the requirements of either Code Sec. 263A(f)(1)(B)(ii) (i.e., has an estimated production period exceeding 2 years) or Code Sec. 263A(f)(1)(B)(iii) (i.e., has an estimated production period exceeding 1 year and a cost exceeding $1 million) (Code Sec. 168(k)(2)(B), as amended by the Working Families Tax Relief Act of 2004).

> **Comment:** Temporary Reg. § 1.168(k)-1T(b)(5) deals with the placed-in-service date requirements for the bonus depreciation deduction. However, it provides no guidance regarding the rules that apply for qualification for the extended January 1, 2006, placed-in-service date.

As amended, Code Sec. 168(k)(2)(B) provides that the extended January 1, 2006 placed-in-service date applies if:

- the property's original use commences with the taxpayer after September 10, 2001;

- the property is either (1) acquired by the taxpayer after September 10, 2001, and before January 1, 2005, and no binding written contract for the acquisition was in effect before September 11, 2001, or (2) acquired pursuant to a written binding contract entered into after September 10, 2001, and before January 1, 2005;

- the property has a recovery period of at least 10 years or is transportation property;

- the property is subject to Code Sec. 263A; and

- the property meets the requirements of Code Sec. 263A(f)(1)(B)(ii) or Code Sec. 263A(f)(1)(B)(iii) (determined as if such clauses also apply to property which has a long useful life).

PRACTICAL ANALYSIS. Michael Schlesinger of Schlesinger & Sussman of New York, New York, observes that in the Working Families Tax Relief Act of 2004, Congress has let Code Sec. 168(k)'s bonus depreciation expire. Fortuitously, the bonus depreciation rules do not expire on passage of the bill; rather, taxpayers have until January 1, 2005, to place property in service with an exception made for property placed in

service in the New York Liberty Zone, providing it is placed in service after December 31, 2005, and before December 31, 2006.

Notwithstanding Congress's desire to allow Code Sec. 168(k)'s bonus depreciation provisions to expire, Congress did make some technical corrections to the provision. One major provision was to amend Code Sec. 168(k)(2)(B) to prescribe that bonus depreciation property includes certain property subject to Code Sec. 263A's capitalization rules. Congress realized that an unintended interpretation of Code Sec. 263A could preclude property from qualifying for bonus depreciation. Accordingly, Congress amended Code Sec. 168(k) to detail that bonus depreciation will apply to Code Sec. 263A property, providing it has an estimated production period exceeding two years, or an estimated production period exceeding one year and a cost exceeding $1 million.

To cover lease situations where there was some confusion (see ¶327), Congress amended Code Sec. 168(k)(2)(D) to prescribe that if property is originally placed in service by a lessor (including by operation of Code Sec. 168(k)(2)(D)(i)), such property is sold within three months after the date that the property was placed in service, and the user of such property does not change, then the property is treated as originally placed in service by the taxpayer not earlier than the date of such sale.

Code Sec. 168(k)'s bonus depreciation provisions are a gift from Uncle Sam and should not be wasted. It is doubtful that Code Sec. 168(k) will be extended by the Republicans and the Bush Administration, because the Bush administration believes that this provision has done its job to stimulate the economy. If Mr. Kerry is elected President, and there is a democratic shift in Congress, it is doubtful that, after election, Congress would extend Code Sec. 168(k)'s bonus depreciation rules, mainly because, judging by the recent reports of Citizens for Tax Justice, and the Institute on Taxation and Economic Policy, major corporations have reduced their taxes tremendously because of this gift from Uncle Sam. Given this tremendous reduction in tax liability for certain major corporations, it is doubtful that the Democrats will want to extend Code Sec. 168(k) to stimulate the economy, since this would be viewed as pandering to rich corporate America.

States will not be pushing Congress to extend the law, either, since only 12 states allowed Code Sec. 168(k) to apply for purposes of their corporate income tax. Twenty-three states decoupled on the passage of Code Sec. 168(k)'s bonus depreciation provisions, and the rest of the states developed special rules for the application of Code Sec. 168(k), such as Nebraska, which required 85 percent of the bonus depreciation taken to be added back, with the amount deducted over five years, beginning with the tax year 2005.

There is an unintended outcome from the expiration of Code Sec. 168(k)'s bonus depreciation provisions—it is likely that the stock market prices for financial institutions and automobile manufacturers will go up. The reason why the stock of automobile manufacturers will rise is because next year, taxpayers will not be able to use the bonus depreciation for the purpose of acquiring a car. As to financial institutions, taxpayers will borrow funds to finance the purchases underCode Sec. 168(k).

¶329

For further information on this subject, consult any of the following CCH reporter explanations:

- Standard Federal Tax Reporter, 2004FED ¶11,279.0513
- Federal Tax Service, FTS §G:16.261
- Federal Tax Guide, 2004FTG ¶9131

★ *Effective date.* The provision applies to property placed in service after September 10, 2001, in tax years ending after that date (Act Sec. 403(f) of the Working Families Tax Relief Act of 2004; Act Sec. 101(b) of the Job Creation and Worker Assistance Act of 2002 (P.L. 107-147)).

Act Sec. 403(a)(1) of the Working Families Tax Relief Act of 2004, amending Code Sec. 168(k)(2)(B)(i); Act Sec. 403(f). Law at ¶5160. Committee Report at ¶10,520.

¶ 331

Bonus Depreciation Limitations Related to Disqualified Users and Related Parties

Background ————————————————————————————————————

The additional first-year bonus depreciation allowance (Code Sec. 168(k)) may be claimed on qualifying property placed in service before January 1, 2005 (January 1, 2006, for certain property with a long production period) if the original use of the property commences with the taxpayer after September 10, 2001. In addition, the property must be acquired by the taxpayer either:

(1) after September 10, 2001, and before January 1, 2005, but only if no written binding contract for the acquisition was in effect before September 11, 2001, or

(2) pursuant to a written binding contract entered into after September 10, 2001, and before January 1, 2005.

Code Sec. 168(k)(2)(D)(i) provides a special rule for self-constructed property. Specifically, in the case of a taxpayer that manufactures, constructs, or produces property for the taxpayer's own use, the acquisition date/binding contract requirements are considered satisfied, and the self-constructed property will qualify for bonus depreciation, if the taxpayer begins manufacturing, constructing, or producing the property after September 10, 2001, and before January 1, 2005.

The IRS issued temporary bonus depreciation regulations (Temporary Reg. §1.168(k)-1T) in September 2003 (T.D. 9091, filed with the Federal Register on September 5, 2003). The regulations were made retroactive to apply to property acquired after September 10, 2001 (Temporary Reg. §1.168(k)-1T(g)(1)). These regulations disqualify property that was acquired pursuant to a pre-September 11, 2001 binding contract by users of the property and persons related to the user. Property for which manufacture, construction, or production began before September 11, 2001 for a related party is also disqualified (Temporary Reg. §1.168(k)-1T(b)(4)(iv)(A)).

Specifically, Temporary Reg. §1.168(k)-1T(b)(4)(iv)(A) (the "disqualified transaction" rule) provides that property does not qualify for bonus depreciation if the user of the property as of the date on which the property was originally placed in service, or a related party to the user, acquired, or had a written binding contract in effect for the acquisition of the property at any time before September 11, 2001. In addition, property manufactured, constructed, or produced for the taxpayer or a related party does not qualify for bonus depreciation if the manufacture, construction, or production of the property for the taxpayer or a related party began at any time before September 11, 2001. If such a binding contract is first effective after May 5, 2003, the

Background ——————————————————————————————

50-percent bonus depreciation rate for property acquired after May 5, 2003, does not apply. For purposes of these rules, persons are related if they have a relationship specified in Code Sec. 267(b) or Code Sec. 707(b) (Temporary Reg. §1.168(k)-1T(b)(4)(iv)(A)).

> **Comment:** Temporary Reg. §1.168(k)-1T(b)(4)(v) contains a number of examples illustrating the application of the disqualified transaction rule.

> Code Sec. 168(k)(2) contains no related party rules similar to those found in Temporary Reg. §1.168(k)-1T(b)(4)(iv)(A).

——————————————————————————————

Working Families Tax Act Impact

Bonus depreciation precluded for pre-September 11, 2001, related party use and related party binding contracts.—The new law includes a technical correction similar to the disqualified transaction rule of Temporary Reg. §1.168(k)-1T(b)(4)(iv) (Code Sec. 168(k)(2)(D)(iv), as added by the Working Families Tax Relief Act of 2004). The technical correction provides that property will not qualify for the bonus depreciation deduction if any of the following persons had a written binding contract in effect for the acquisition of the property at any time on or before September 10, 2001:

(1) the user of the property on the date that the property was originally placed in service;

(2) a person related to a user of the property on the date that the property was originally placed in service; or

(3) a person related to the taxpayer (Code Sec. 168(k)(2)(D)(iv)(I), as added by the 2004 Act).

Likewise, property will not qualify for the bonus depreciation deduction if its manufacture, construction, or production began at any time on or before September 10, 2001, and the property was manufactured, constructed, or produced for:

(1) the user;

(2) a person related to a user of the property on the date that the property was originally placed in service; or

(3) a person related to the taxpayer (Code Sec. 168(k)(2)(D)(iv)(II), as added by the 2004 Act).

As in the case of the regulations, the related party rules of Code Sec. 267(b) and Code Sec. 707(b) are used to determine if two persons are related (Code Sec. 168(k)(2)(D)(iv)(I), as added by the 2004 Act).

> **Example 1:** T.J. Johnson and Partnership ABC are related parties. Johnson enters into a pre-September 11, 2001, contract to purchase production machinery. Prior to placing the property in service, Johnson sells its rights to the machine to ABC. ABC may not claim the bonus depreciation deduction because Johnson had a binding contract for the purchase of the machine in effect before September 11, 2001, and Johnson is related to DEF.

> **Example 2:** Assume that Corp. ABC and Corp DEF are related parties. Corp. ABC began construction on production machinery on January 1, 2001. If Corp. ABC sells rights to the property to DEF prior to using the property and placing it in service, DEF may not claim the bonus depreciation deduction because construction began before September 11, and ABC and DEF are related parties.

> **Example 3:** ABC Corp. has a binding contract to purchase production equipment that is in effect before September 11, 2001. ABC sells the property to

DEF and leases the property back within 3 months of placing the property in service. DEF may not claim the bonus depreciation deduction pursuant to the sale-leaseback rule (Code Sec. 168(k)(2)(D)(ii)) because ABC, the user of the property, had a binding contract for its acquisition in effect prior to September 11, 2001.

New York Liberty Zone. Property placed in service in the New York Liberty Zone may qualify for the bonus depreciation allowance under Code Sec. 1400L(b) if the property does not qualify for bonus depreciation under the more general provision of Code Sec. 168(k). Code Sec. 1400L(b)(2)(D) provides that rules similar to those contained in Code Sec. 168(k)(2)(D) apply to Liberty Zone property. By virtue of this cross reference, this technical correction also applies to Liberty Zone property. Regulations under Code Sec. 1400L also incorporate the Code Sec. 168(k) disqualified transaction regulations by cross reference (Temporary Reg. § 1.1400L(b)-1T(c)(5)).

For further information on this subject, consult any of the following CCH reporter explanations:

- Standard Federal Tax Reporter, 2004FED ¶ 11,279.0513
- Federal Tax Service, FTS § G:16.261
- Federal Tax Guide, 2004FTG ¶ 9131

★ *Effective date.* The provision applies to property placed in service after September 10, 2001, in tax years ending after that date (Act Sec. 403(f) of the Working Families Tax Relief Act of 2004; Act Sec. 101(b) of the Job Creation and Worker Assistance Act of 2002 (P.L. 107-147)).

Act Sec. 403(a)(2)(A) of the Working Families Tax Relief Act of 2004, adding Code Sec. 168(k)(2)(D)(iv); Act Sec. 403(c)(2), amending Code Sec. 1400L(b)(2)(D); Act Sec. 403(f). Law at ¶ 5160 and ¶ 5350. Committee Report at ¶ 10,520.

NEW YORK LIBERTY ZONE

¶ 333

Code Sec. 179 Expense Allowance for New York Liberty Zone Property

Background _____

The Job Creation and Worker Assistance Act of 2002 (P.L. 107-147) created additional Code Sec. 179 expensing allowance incentives for qualified New York Liberty Zone property (Code Sec. 1400L(f), as added by P.L. 107-147).

Specifically, the dollar limitation (Code Sec. 179(b)(1)) is increased by the lesser of:

(1) $35,000, or

(2) the cost of the qualifying New York Liberty Zone property placed in service during the tax year.

Also, the investment limitation (Code Sec. 179(b)(2)) is applied by taking into account only 50 percent of the cost of qualified New York Liberty Zone property placed in service during the tax year.

For tax years beginning in 2001 and 2002, the maximum dollar limit under Code Sec. 179 was $24,000. This amount increases to $100,000 in 2003, 2004, and 2005 and is reduced to $25,000 in 2006. Thus, these dollar amounts may each be increased by up to $35,000 in the case of qualifying New York Liberty Zone property.

The investment limitation requires a taxpayer to reduce the maximum dollar limitation by the cost of qualified section 179 property placed in service during the

Background ―――――――――――――――――――――――――――――

tax year that exceeds $200,000 for a tax year beginning in 2001 and 2002, $400,000 in 2003, 2004, and 2005, and $100,000 in 2006 and later.

> **Comment:** The $100,000 dollar limitation and $400,000 investment limitation are adjusted for inflation in 2004 and 2005. The inflation-adjusted amounts are $102,000 and $410,000, respectively, for 2004 (Rev. Proc. 2003-85, I.R.B. 2003-49, December 8, 2003). The $35,000 bump-up for New York Liberty Zone property is not adjusted for inflation.

> **Comment:** For a tax year that begins in 2004, the maximum amount that may be expensed under Code Sec. 179 in the case of qualifying New York Liberty Zone property is $137,000 ($102,000 + $35,000). Assuming that a taxpayer only places qualified New York Liberty Zone property in service in 2004, the taxpayer may place up to $820,000 of property in service before the dollar limitation is subject to reduction by the investment limitation ($820,000 × 50% = $410,000). For example, if the taxpayer places $1 million of New York Liberty Zone property into service, the $137,000 dollar limitation is reduced by $90,000 (($1,000,000 × 50%) − $410,000).

Only "qualified New York Liberty Zone property" qualifies for the $35,000 additional expensing allowance and the rule allowing only 50 percent of the cost of qualified New York Liberty Zone property to be taken into account in applying the investment limitation.

In general, qualified New York Liberty Zone property is section 179 property that:

- is purchased and placed in service after September 10, 2001, and before January 1, 2007;
- the original use of which in the New York Liberty Zone commences with the taxpayer after September 10, 2001; and
- substantially all the use of which is in the active conduct of a business in the area defined as the New York Liberty Zone (Code Sec. 1400L(b)(2)).

However, qualified New York Liberty Zone property does not include property placed in service in the New York Liberty zone for which bonus depreciation is claimed under Code Sec. 168(k) (Code Sec. 1400L(b)(2)(C)(i)).

> **Comment:** The Job Creation and Worker Assistance Act created two separate bonus depreciation provisions. The generally applicable provision is contained in Code Sec. 168(k). A separate but very similar provision is provided in Code Sec. 1400L(b) for property which is "qualified New York Liberty Zone property." The definition of qualified New York Liberty Zone property excludes property that qualifies for the additional depreciation allowance under Code Sec. 168(k) (Code Sec. 1400L(b)(2)(C)(i)). Thus, property that is placed in service in the New York Liberty Zone is not qualified New York Liberty Zone property if it qualifies for bonus depreciation under the more general bonus depreciation provision of Code Sec. 168(k). Such a property, therefore, cannot qualify for the additional $35,000 section 179 expensing allowance or relaxed investment limitation rule. Congress clearly did not intend this result.

> **Comment:** Most property placed in service in the New York Liberty Zone after September 10, 2001 will qualify for bonus depreciation under the general provision of Code Sec. 168(k). However, there are some exceptions. The most important is that used property cannot qualify for bonus depreciation under Code Sec. 168(k). Used property, however, can qualify for bonus depreciation under Code Sec. 1400L(b) provided that the original use of the property begins

with the taxpayer in the New York Liberty Zone. For example, a second-hand machine that was used in Illinois and then purchased for use in the Liberty Zone will qualify for bonus depreciation under Code Sec. 1400L(b) but not under Code Sec. 168(k). However, if the machine had been purchased from someone currently using it in the Liberty Zone it will not qualify for bonus depreciation under either Code Sec. 1400L(b) or Code Sec. 168(k). If the machine was new when it was purchased by the taxpayer for use in the New York Liberty Zone it qualifies for bonus depreciation under Code Sec. 168(k) and, therefore, is excluded from the definition of New York Liberty Zone property. Since the new machine is excluded from the definition of New York Liberty Zone property it cannot qualify for the additional $35,000 section 179 expense allowance even though it is first placed in service in the New York Liberty Zone.

Comment: The bonus depreciation rate for property acquired after May 5, 2003, and before January 1, 2005, is increased from 30 percent to 50 percent if bonus depreciation is claimed under the general provision of Code Sec. 168(k) (Code Sec. 168(k)(4)). The bonus depreciation rate under Code Sec. 1400L(b) for qualified New York Liberty Zone property was not increased from 30 percent to 50 percent to reflect this change (Code Sec. 1400L(b)(1)(A)).

Working Families Tax Act Impact

Definition of New York Liberty Zone property for purposes of additional section 179 allowances includes property qualifying for bonus depreciation under Code Sec. 168(k).—A technical correction clarifies that the increased section 179 allowance for New York Liberty Zone property also applies to property which would be considered New York Liberty Zone property but for the fact that it also qualifies for the 30-percent or 50-percent additional depreciation allowance under Code Sec. 168(k) (Code Sec. 1400L(f)(2), as amended by the Working Families Tax Relief Act of 2004).

Planning Note: Taxpayers who did not claim the additional section 179 allowance for property placed in service in the New York Liberty Zone (because they qualified for the additional bonus depreciation allowance under the general rule of Code Sec. 168(k)) should file amended returns. The IRS has apparently not corrected this situation administratively. The instructions for Form 4562 (Depreciation and Amortization) allow the $35,000 bump-up only for "qualified New York Liberty Zone property" and regulations issued under Code Sec. 1400L and Code Sec. 179 do not address any aspect of the increased section 179 allowance.

For further information on this subject, consult any of the following CCH reporter explanations:

- Standard Federal Tax Reporter, 2004FED ¶ 32,477.01
- Federal Tax Service, FTS § G:1.121[3]
- Federal Tax Guide, 2004FTG ¶ 9130

★ *Effective date.* The provision is retroactively effective to March 9, 2002, the effective date of Act Sec. 301 of the Job Creation and Worker Assistance Act of 2002 (P.L. 107-147) (Act Sec. 403(f) of the Working Families Tax Relief Act of 2004).

Act Sec. 403(c)(4) of the Working Families Tax Relief Act of 2004, amending Code Sec. 1400L(f)(2); Act Sec. 403(f). Law at ¶ 5350. Committee Report at ¶ 10,520.

¶ 335

Qualified New York Liberty Zone Leasehold Improvement Property

Background

Qualified New York Liberty Zone leasehold improvements to nonresidential real property that are placed in service after September 10, 2001, and before January 1, 2007, are classified as five-year MACRS property. The straight-line method must be used to depreciate this property. A nine-year MACRS alternative depreciation system (ADS) period applies (Code Sec. 1400L(c), as added by the Job Creation and Worker Assistance Act of 2002 (P.L. 107-147)).

Liberty Zone leasehold improvements that are eligible for a five-year recovery period are not also eligible for the 30-percent or 50-percent first-year bonus depreciation allowance under Code Sec. 168(k) or the 30-percent allowance under Code Sec. 1400L(b) (Code Sec. 168(k)(2)(C)(ii) and Code Sec. 1400L(b)(2)(C)(iii)).

In general, qualified leasehold improvement property must satisfy the following requirements (Code Secs. 168(k)(3) and 1400L(c)(2); Temporary Reg. § 1.168(k)-1T(c)):

(1) the improvement must be to the interior portion of a building that is nonresidential real property;

(2) the improvement must be made under or pursuant to a lease by a lessee, sublessee, or lessor, or pursuant to a commitment to enter into a lease;

(3) the lessor and lessee may not be related persons;

(4) the portion of the building that is improved must be exclusively tenant-occupied (by a lessee or sublessee); and

(5) the improvement must be placed in service more than three years after the date that the building was first placed in service.

Although a taxpayer may elect out of the generally applicable Code Sec. 168(k) bonus depreciation provision (Code Sec. 168(k)(2)(C)(iii)) and the Liberty Zone bonus depreciation provision (Code Sec. 1400L(b)(2)(C)(iv)) no similar election out is provided for the five-year qualified New York Liberty Zone leasehold improvement depreciation provision.

Working Families Tax Act Impact

Taxpayer may elect out of 5-year depreciation period for New York Liberty Zone qualified leasehold improvement property.—The new law includes a technical correction that allows a taxpayer to elect out of the five-year recovery period for depreciation of qualified New York Liberty Zone leasehold improvement property (Code Sec. 1400L(c)(5), as added by the Working Families Tax Relief Act of 2004). The new provision does not provide any specific details regarding the election. It simply states that rules similar to those for electing out of bonus depreciation under Code Sec. 168(k)(2)(C)(iii) shall apply.

Comment: The election out of bonus depreciation is made on a property class-by-property class basis. Once made it is revocable only with IRS consent. The election is made by attaching a statement to a timely filed return (including extensions) containing the information described in the instructions to Form 4562 (Depreciation and Amortization). See Temporary Reg. § 1.168(k)-1T(e)(5) for additional details concerning the election out of bonus depreciation.

Since this provision applies retroactively, it seems likely that the IRS will issue administrative guidance detailing how the election out of the 5-year recovery period for qualified leasehold improvement property can be made on an amended return.

Planning Note: If an election out is made, the leasehold improvement property would typically be depreciated as a structural component over a 39-year period. Presumably Congress intended that bonus depreciation could be claimed if the election out is made. Arguably, however, the election does not change the status of the leasehold improvements as "qualified New York Liberty Zone leasehold improvement property," which is made ineligible for bonus depreciation by Code Secs. 168(k)(2)(C)(ii) and 1400L(b)(2)(C)(ii).

Comment: Qualified leasehold improvement property status can only apply to section 1250 property (Temporary Reg. § 1.168(k)-1T(c)(1)). Thus, elements of a building that are personal property (section 1245 property), as opposed to structural components (section 1250 property) may be depreciated under cost segregation principles over shortened recovery periods without regard to the New York Liberty Zone leasehold improvement provision and may qualify for bonus depreciation.

For further information on this subject, consult any of the following CCH reporter explanations:

- Standard Federal Tax Reporter, 2004FED ¶ 32,477.01
- Federal Tax Service, FTS § G:1.121[4]
- Federal Tax Guide, 2004FTG ¶ 9110

★ *Effective date.* The provision is retroactively effective to March 9, 2002, the effective date of Act Sec. 301 of the Job Creation and Worker Assistance Act of 2002 (P.L. 107-147) (Act Sec. 403(f) of the Working Families Tax Relief Act of 2004).

Act Sec. 403(c)(3) of the Working Families Tax Relief Act of 2004, adding Code Sec. 1400L(c)(5); Act Sec. 403(f). Law at ¶ 5350. Committee Report at ¶ 10,520.

¶ 337
Work Opportunity Tax Credit for New York Liberty Zone Businesses

Background

The work opportunity tax credit may be claimed by a "New York Liberty Zone business" with respect to its "New York Liberty Zone business employees." Such employees are treated as members of a targeted group for purposes of the credit (Code Sec. 1400L(a), as added by the Job Creation and Worker Assistance Act of 2002 (P.L. 107-147)).

A New York Liberty Zone business is any trade or business located in:

(1) the New York Liberty Zone, or

(2) the City of New York, but only if it is not within the New York Liberty Zone because its place of business within the New York Liberty Zone was destroyed or damaged as a result of the September 11, 2001 terrorist attack.

The number of employees of a business located in the City of New York (but outside of the New York Liberty Zone) (item (2), above) includes any employee who performs substantially all of his or her services for the business in the City of New York (Code Sec. 1400L(a)(2)(B)(i)). However, only the number of such employees in excess of the number of employees who worked in the Liberty Zone on September 11, 2001, may be taken into account for purposes of the credit (Code Sec. 1400L(a)(2)(B)(ii)). In addition, for purposes of determining the number of employ-

Background

ees, the rules contained in Code Sec. 52 apply (Code Sec. 1400L(a)(2)(D), prior to amendment by the Working Families Tax Relief Act of 2004).

> **Comment:** Code Sec. 52 provides that employees of all corporations that are members of the same controlled group of corporations are treated as employed by a single employer. A controlled group of corporations is determined by reference to Code Sec. 1563(a) but by substituting "more than 50 percent" for "at least 80 percent" each place it appears. Similarly, employees of partnerships, proprietorships, and other businesses (whether or not incorporated) that are under common control are treated as employed by a single employer.

Code Sec. 1400L contains two other rules relating to the determination of the number of employees but, apparently due to a drafting error, the rules of Code Sec. 52 were not made applicable in these instances.

First, large businesses cannot qualify as a New York Liberty Zone business. A large business is any trade or business for any tax year if it employed an average of more than 200 employees on business days during the tax year (Code Sec. 1400L(a)(2)(C)(ii)).

The second rule provides that a New York Liberty Zone business employee includes any employee of a New York Liberty Zone business if substantially all of his or her services are performed in the New York Liberty Zone (Code Sec. 1400L(a)(2)(A)).

Working Families Tax Act Impact

Employee aggregation rules apply when determining the number of employees for purposes of the NY Liberty Zone work opportunity tax credit.—A technical correction clarifies that the Code Sec. 52 employee aggregation rules for controlled groups of corporations and trades or businesses under common control apply in all situations in which a taxpayer must determine the number of employees for purposes of the Code Sec. 1400L(a) work opportunity credit allowed with respect to New York Liberty Zone business employees (Code Sec. 1400L(a)(2)(D)(ii), as amended by the Working Families Tax Relief Act of 2004).

> **Comment:** As a result of this change, a member of a controlled group of corporations will not be entitled to claim the credit if the total number of employees of the controlled group exceeds 200.

The new law also includes a clerical amendment that corrects the text of Code Sec. 1400L(a)(2)(D) by replacing a reference to "subchapter B" with a reference to "subchapter A".

For further information on this subject, consult any of the following CCH reporter explanations:

- Standard Federal Tax Reporter, 2004FED ¶ 32,477.01
- Federal Tax Service, FTS § G:1.121[1]
- Federal Tax Guide, 2004FTG ¶ 8610

★ *Effective date.* The provision is retroactively effective to March 9, 2002, the effective date of Act Sec. 301 of the Job Creation and Worker Assistance Act of 2002 (P.L. 107-147) (Act Sec. 403(f) of the Working Families Tax Relief Act of 2004).

Act Sec. 403(c)(1) of the Working Families Tax Relief Act of 2004, amending Code Sec. 1400L(a)(2)(D) and (D)(ii); Act Sec. 403(f). Law at ¶ 5350. Committee Report at ¶ 10,520.

¶337

EMPLOYER PLANS

¶ 339

Interest Rate for Notices and Reporting for Underfunded Plans

Background

Benefits under a defined benefit pension plan may be funded over a period of years. As a result, plan assets may not be sufficient to provide the benefits owed under the plan to employees and their beneficiaries if the plan terminates before all benefits are paid. In order to protect employees and their beneficiaries, the Pension Benefit Guaranty Corporation (PBGC) insures the benefits owed under defined benefit pension plans. Employers pay premiums to the PBGC for this coverage.

For underfunded plans, additional PBGC premiums must be paid. The amount is based on the amount of unfunded vested benefits. These premiums are referred to as variable rate premiums. Prior to passage of the Job Creation and Worker Assistance Act of 2002 (P.L. 107-147), the interest rate used to determine the amount of unfunded vested benefits was 85 percent of the 30-year Treasury rate for the month preceding the month in which the plan year begins.

Act Sec. 405(c) of the Job Creation Act of 2002 temporarily increased the interest rate used in determining the amount of unfunded vested benefits for variable rate premium purposes, effective for plan years beginning after December 31, 2001, and before January 1, 2004, to 100 percent of the interest rate on 30-year Treasury securities for the month preceding the month in which the plan year begins (Employee Retirement Income Security Act of 1974 (ERISA § 4006(a)(3)(E)). However, the change in the variable premium interest rate did not apply for purposes of determining whether certain notices to plan participants were required. Accordingly, plan administrators may have been required to provide a notice to participants for the 2002 and 2003 plan years even if a variable rate premium was not payable for that plan year.

Working Families Tax Act Impact

Interest rate increases.—The Working Families Tax Relief Act of 2004 amends the rules applicable to notices and reporting required under Title IV of ERISA with respect to underfunded plans to reflect the temporary increase in the interest rate used in determining the amount of unfunded vested benefits for PBGC variable rate premium purposes. That rate was increased for plan years beginning in 2002 and 2003 from 85 percent to 100 percent of the interest rate on 30-year Treasury securities (ERISA § 4006(a)(3)(E)). This change means that a participant notice is required for 2002 and 2003 plan years *only* if a variable rate premium is payable for that plan year.

Comment: Prior to passage of the 2004 Working Families Tax Act, the PBGC had instituted a Participant Notice Voluntary Correction Program (VCP) allowing plan administrators to avoid penalties for failure to provide required notices for the 2002 and 2003 plan years by filing a corrective notice. The Pension Funding Equity Act of 2004 (P.L. 108-218) modified the rules for determining the required interest rate for premium payments in plan years beginning in 2004 and 2005. For those years, plan administrators are authorized to use the revised premium interest rate in determining whether a participant notice is required. Accordingly, a participant notice is required for 2004 and 2005 plan years *only* if a variable rate premium is payable for that plan year (PBGC Notice, 5-7-04, (60 FR 25791)).

For further information on this subject, consult any of the following CCH reporter explanations:

- Standard Federal Tax Reporter, 2004FED ¶19,125.03
- Federal Tax Service, FTS §C:11.81
- Federal Tax Guide, 2004FTG ¶11,040

★ *Effective date.* The amendment is retroactively effective to March 9, 2002 (Act Sec. 403(f) of the Working Families Tax Relief Act of 2004; Act Sec. 405 of the Job Creation and Worker Assistance Act of 2002 (P.L. 107-147)).

Act Sec. 403(d) of the Working Families Tax Relief Act of 2004, amending ERISA Sec. 4006(a)(3)(E)(iii)(IV); Act Sec. 403(f). Law at ¶7030. Committee Report at ¶10,520.

¶ 341

Employer Adoption Assistance Programs

Background _____

For employer-paid or employer-reimbursed adoption expenses paid pursuant to an adoption assistance plan, there is an exclusion from the employee's income of up to $10,000 in tax years 2002 through 2010 (Code Secs. 137(a) and (b)(1)). In the case of a child with special needs, the $10,000 income exclusion is allowed regardless of the actual expenses incurred. The income exclusion for a special needs adoption is increased by the excess, if any, of $10,000 over the aggregate adoption expenses for the tax year the adoption becomes final and all prior tax years (Code Sec. 137(a)(2)). This special needs adoption provision is applicable for tax years beginning in 2003 through 2010.

The provision allowing an income exclusion of $10,000 for a special needs adoption, regardless of the actual total of the expenses incurred, does not *specifically state* that the *maximum* allowable expenses for a special needs adoption is $10,000 (Code Sec. 137(a)(2)). Furthermore, the dollar limitation provision of Code Sec. 137(b)(1) currently only applies to non-special needs adoptions.

The $10,000 income exclusion for qualified adoption expenses in the case of a non-special needs adoption and for a special needs adoption is subject to cost-of-living adjustments in tax years 2003 through 2010 (Code Sec. 137(f)). For tax years beginning in 2004, the amount of qualified adoption expenses and special needs adoption expenses that can be excluded from an employee's gross income is $10,390 (Rev. Proc. 2003-85). In 2005, the **CCH** INCORPORATED projected income exclusion amount is $10,630.

The provisions applicable to the adoption of a child with special needs, the inflation adjustment, and the $10,000 maximum expense limitation are subject to a sunset provision for tax years beginning after December 31, 2010 (Act Sec. 901 of the Economic Growth and Tax Relief Reconciliation Act of 2001 (P.L. 107-16)).

Working Families Tax Act Impact

Aggregate amount of exclusion for special needs adoptions is $10,000.—A technical correction clarifies that the maximum amount of aggregate special needs adoption expenses (actually incurred, or not) that may be excluded from an employee's income as part of an employer adoption assistance program is $10,000 per child, adjusted for inflation (Code Sec. 137(b)(1), as amended by the Working Families Tax Relief Act of 2004). This amendment to the *dollar limitation* provision specifically applies the $10,000 maximum limitation to:

(1) qualified adoption expenses in the case of a non-special needs adoption (Code Sec. 137(a)(1)), and

(2) special needs adoption expenses, regardless of the actual total of the expenses incurred, in the case of a special needs adoption (Code Sec. 137(a)(2)).

Comment: The amendment to the dollar limitation provision to clarify its application in the case of a special needs adoption may initially appear redundant. However, a closer analysis of the special needs adoption provision (Code Sec. 137(a)(2)) indicates that its purpose is to make clear that $10,000 may be excluded from the employee's income, whether incurred or not, and it is only by implication that the reader could infer a $10,000 maximum limit. The amendment leaves no doubt that the $10,000 per child maximum, as adjusted for inflation, applies to all adoptions, including those of a child with special needs.

Planning Note: For tax years beginning in 2004, the maximum amount of qualified adoption expenses and special needs adoption expenses that can be excluded from an employee's gross income is $10,390. In 2005, the **CCH** INCORPORATED projected maximum income exclusion is $10,630. For purposes of the income exclusion, amounts are generally excludable from the employee's gross income for the year in which the employer pays the qualified adoption or special needs adoption expense (Notice 97-9, 1997-1 CB 365, as modified by Notice 97-70, 1997-2 CB 332). In the case of a foreign adoption, the general rule is modified since adoption expenses incurred for a child who is not a citizen or resident of the U.S. are not excludable until the year the adoption is finalized. See Part II, Section H. 2 of Notice 97-9.

For further information on this subject, consult any of the following CCH reporter explanations:

- Standard Federal Tax Reporter, 2004FED ¶ 7625.01

- Federal Tax Service, FTS § B:10.282

- Federal Tax Guide, 2004FTG ¶ 4760

★ *Effective date.* This provision applies to tax years beginning after December 31, 2001 (Act Sec. 403(f) of the Working Families Tax Relief Act of 2004; Act Sec. 411(c)(3) of the Job Creation and Worker Assistance Act of 2002 (P.L. 107-147)). See ¶ 29,001 for a discussion of the impact of the sunset rule on this technical correction.

Act Sec. 403(e) of the Working Families Tax Relief Act of 2004, amending Act Sec. 411(c)(2)(B) of the Job Creation and Worker Assistance Act of 2002; Act Sec. 403(f). Law at ¶ 7030. Committee Report at ¶ 10,520.

¶ 343

Rounding Rule Clarified

Background _____

The Economic Growth and Tax Relief Reconciliation Act of 2001 (P.L. 107-16) increased the dollar limits on qualified retirement plan benefits and contributions under Code Sec. 415. P.L. 107-16 also added a new rounding rule for cost-of-living adjustments to the dollar limit on annual additions to defined contribution plans. This new rounding rule is in addition to a pre-existing rounding rule that applies to benefits payable under defined benefit plans.

Background _____

Other provisions in the Internal Revenue Code refer to the cost-of-living rules of Code Sec. 415.

The Indian employment tax credit is not available with respect to an employee whose wages exceed $30,000 (Code Sec. 45A). For years after 1994, this $30,000 amount is adjusted for cost-of-living increases at the same time, and in the same manner, as cost-of-living adjustments to the dollar limits on qualified retirement plan benefits and contributions under Code Sec. 415. As noted above, P.L. 107-16 increased the dollar limits under Code Sec. 415 and added a new base period for making cost-of-living adjustments.

Working Families Tax Act Impact

Pre-existing rounding rule applies.—A technical correction clarifies that the pre-existing rounding rule applies for purposes of other Code provisions that refer to Code Sec. 415 and do not contain a specific rounding rule (Code Sec. 415(d)(4)(A), as added by the Working Families Tax Relief Act of 2004).

The provision specifically clarifies that the pre-existing base period continues to apply for purposes of calculating the cost-of-living increases for the Indian employment credit (Code Sec. 45A(c)(3), as added by the 2004 Working Families Tax Act). Another provision of the 2004 Working Families Tax Act extends the Indian employment credit incentive for one year, to tax years beginning before January 1, 2006 (see ¶215).

For further information on this subject, consult any of the following CCH reporter explanations:

- Standard Federal Tax Reporter, 2004FED ¶4440.01
- Federal Tax Service, FTS §C:13.102
- Federal Tax Guide, 2004FTG ¶2775 and ¶11,035

★ *Effective date.* The provision is generally effective for years beginning after December 31, 2001 (Act Sec. 404(f) of the Working Families Tax Relief Act of 2004; Act Sec. 611(h) of the Economic Growth and Tax Relief Reconciliation Act of 2001 (EGTRRA) (P.L. 107-16)).

Act Sec. 404(b)(1) of the Working Families Tax Relief Act of 2004, amending Code Sec. 45A(c)(3); Act Sec. 404(b)(2), amending Code Sec. 415(d)(4)(A); Act Sec. 404(f). Law at ¶5065 and ¶5240. Committee Report at ¶10,530.

¶345

Excise Tax on Employer's Nondeductible Contributions to Qualified Plans Conformed

Background _____

Before the Economic Growth and Tax Relief Reconciliation Act of 2001 (EGTRRA) (P.L. 107-16), the limits on deductions for employer contributions to qualified retirement plans applied to elective deferrals, and elective deferrals were taken into account in applying the deduction limits to other contributions. Under Code Sec. 404(n), which was added by EGTRRA, the limits on deductions for employer contributions to qualified plans no longer apply to elective deferrals, and elective deferrals are no longer taken into account in applying the deduction limits to other contributions. A 10-percent excise tax is imposed under Code Sec. 4972 on nondeductible employer contributions, though an exception is made for elective deferrals (Code Sec. 4972(c)(6)(A)(ii)).

Working Families Tax Act Impact

Excise tax provision on nondeductible contributions conformed.—Code Sec. 4972, which imposes an excise tax on nondeductible contributions, provided an exception for elective deferrals for purposes of determining the amount of nondeductible contributions. Because elective deferrals are no longer taken into account when determining the limits on employer deductions, Act Sec. 404(c) of the Working Families Tax Act amends Code Sec. 4972(c)(6)(A)(ii) by removing reference to elective deferrals.

For further information on this subject, consult any of the following CCH reporter explanations:

- Standard Federal Tax Reporter, 2004FED ¶34,342.01
- Federal Tax Service, FTS § C:12.241
- Federal Tax Guide, 2004FTG ¶21,410

★ *Effective date.* This correction is effective for tax years beginning after December 31, 2001 (Act Sec. 404(f) of the Working Families Tax Relief Act of 2004; Act Sec. 614(b) of the Economic Growth and Tax Relief Reconciliation Act of 2001 (P.L. 107-16).

Act Sec. 404(c) of the Working Families Tax Relief Act of 2004, amending Code Sec. 4972(c)(6)(A)(ii); Act Sec. 404(f). Law at ¶5365. Committee Report at ¶10,530.

¶ 347

Contributions to SIMPLE Plans for Household Workers

Background —————————————————————————

Prior to enactment of the Economic Growth and Tax Relief Reconciliation Act of 2001 (EGTRRA) (P.L. 107-16), contributions by employers to retirement plans for domestic or household workers were subject to a 10-percent excise tax because the employers were not engaged in a trade or business. To encourage retirement plans for household workers, Act Sec. 637 of EGTRRA amended Code Sec. 4972(c)(6)(B) to except from the excise tax nondeductible retirement plan contributions when the sole reason that a contribution is considered nondeductible is that it was not made in connection with the employer's trade or business.

One of the requirements for making qualified contributions to a savings incentive match plan for employees (SIMPLE) plan is that contributions must be made from compensation (including deferral income) subject to withholding for income and employment taxes and reported on a W-2 form (Code Sec. 408(p)(6)(A)(i)). However, under Code Sec. 3401(a)(3), wages paid to domestic workers are not subject to income tax withholding. Accordingly, unless the household worker and the worker's employer elect to subject the worker's wages to income tax withholding, SIMPLE contributions do not qualify as an excludable retirement plan contribution for employees, nor do they qualify for any matching employer contributions. Since the wages are not subject to withholding, the employer cannot take advantage of the exception to the excise tax on nondeductible contributions.

Working Families Tax Act Impact

Clarification of household worker's qualifying compensation for SIMPLE plan contributions.—The definition of compensation found in Code Sec. 408(p)(6)(A) for purposes of determining contributions to a SIMPLE plan is revised to include wages paid to domestic workers, even though such amounts are not subject to income tax withholding. This correction clarifies that, for purposes of contributions to SIMPLE plans, wages of household workers need not be subject to withholding to qualify for excludible retirement plans.

> **Caution:** Tax practitioners need to be aware that the law concerning the nondeductibility of contributions to a pension plan for a domestic or household worker did not change. These contributions remain nondeductible, and the contribution limits and nondiscrimination rules continue to apply. The clarification affects only the 10-percent excise tax.

For further information on this subject, consult any of the following CCH reporter explanations:

- Standard Federal Tax Reporter, 2004FED ¶ 18,922.01
- Federal Tax Service, FTS § C:21.281
- Federal Tax Guide, 2004FTG ¶ 11,475 and ¶ 21,410

★ *Effective date.* The amendment is effective for tax years beginning after December 31, 2001 (Act Sec. 404(f) of the Working Families Tax Relief Act of 2004; Act Sec. 637(d) of the Economic Growth and Tax Relief Reconciliation Act of 2001 (P.L. 107-16)).

Act Sec. 404(d) of the Working Families Tax Relief Act of 2004, amending Code Sec. 408(p)(6)(A)(i); Act Sec. 404(f). Law at ¶ 5225. Committee Report at ¶ 10,530.

¶ 349

Rollover Distributions from Qualified Annuity Plans

Background ──

Distributions of retirement savings can be excluded from the distributee's income if they are rolled over into another retirement plan, subject to certain limitations. Code Sec. 402, which applies by its terms to distributions from exempt trusts holding assets of qualified retirement plans, contains many of these limitations. For example, the rollover into the new plan must be made within 60 days of the receipt of the distribution (Code Sec. 402(c)(3)) and, when a distribution is made to a deceased employee's surviving spouse, the rollover rules must be applied as though the surviving spouse were the employee (Code Sec. 402(c)(9)). This allows the surviving spouse to combine the inherited account with his or her own retirement accounts. In addition, plan administrators must provide certain information regarding rollovers to participants receiving distributions that are eligible to be rolled over (Code Sec. 402(f)).

Many of the rollover rules in Code Sec. 402 governing exempt trusts are explicitly adopted by reference for purposes of distributions from qualified annuity plans (Code Sec. 403(a)(4)(B)). However, the rule regarding distributions to a deceased employee's surviving spouse and the rule regarding rollover information that must be sent to participants have not been explicitly adopted for purposes of qualified annuity plans.

Working Families Tax Act Impact

Additional rollover rules apply to qualified annuity plan distributions.—The Working Families Tax Relief Act of 2004 amends Code Sec. 403(a)(4)(B) to expand the list of rollover provisions from Code Sec. 402 that apply to distributions from qualified annuity plans. For distributions from a qualified annuity plan after December 31, 2001, a distribution to the employee's surviving spouse must be treated as though the spouse were the employee, and the plan administrator must provide the rollover notice to the distributee.

> **Compliance Tip:** The IRS has already provided a safe harbor notice form appropriate for dissemination by administrators of qualified annuity plans, even though the enactment of this change suggests that dissemination of a notice was not previously required (see Notice 2002-3, 2002-1 CB 289, for the safe harbor notice form).

For further information on this subject, consult any of the following CCH reporter explanations:

- Standard Federal Tax Reporter, 2004FED ¶18,282.0435
- Federal Tax Service, FTS § C:14.200
- Federal Tax Guide, 2004FTG ¶11,435

★ *Effective date.* The provision is effective for distributions after December 31, 2001 (Act Sec. 404(f) of the Working Families Tax Relief Act of 2004; Act Sec. 641(f)(1) of the Economic Growth and Tax Relief Reconciliation Act of 2001 (P.L. 107-16)).

Act Sec. 404(e) of the Working Families Tax Relief Act of 2004, amending Code Sec. 403(a)(4)(B); Act Sec. 404(f). Law at ¶5220. Committee Report at ¶10,530.

¶ 351

Former Participation Requirement for Defined Contribution Plans

Background

A minimum participation requirement provided that a retirement plan could not be a qualified plan unless it benefited no fewer than the lesser of: (1) 50 employees of the employer or (2) 40 percent of all employees of the employer. In the case of a defined contribution plan, employees who were eligible to make salary reduction contributions or receive matching contributions were treated as benefiting under the plan (Code Sec. 401(a)(26)(C)). In 1996, the minimum participation rule was amended so that it no longer applied to defined contribution plans, but the provision regarding employees who benefited under such a plan was not repealed.

Working Families Tax Act Impact

Obsolete provision regarding repealed participation requirement removed.—The obsolete provision stating that employees who were eligible to make salary reduction contributions or receive matching contributions to a defined contribution plan were treated as benefiting under the plan is repealed.

For further information on this subject, consult any of the following CCH reporter explanations:

- Standard Federal Tax Reporter, 2004FED ¶17,921.01
- Federal Tax Service, FTS § C:2.20
- Federal Tax Guide, 2004FTG ¶11,020

★ *Effective date.* This provision is effective for years beginning after December 31, 1996 (Act Sec. 407(c) of the Working Families Tax Relief Act of 2004; Act Sec. 1432(c) of the Small Business Job Protection Act of 1996 (P.L. 104-188)).

Act Sec. 407(b) of the Working Families Tax Relief Act of 2004, amending Code Sec. 401(a)(26); Act Sec. 407(c). Law at ¶ 5215. Committee Report at ¶ 10,560.

HSAs AND MSAs

¶ 357

Distributions from Health Savings Accounts (HSAs)

Background ⎯⎯⎯⎯⎯⎯⎯⎯⎯⎯⎯⎯⎯⎯⎯⎯⎯⎯⎯⎯⎯⎯⎯⎯⎯⎯⎯⎯⎯⎯⎯

The alternative minimum tax (AMT) is a parallel, alternative system of income taxation intended to make sure higher-income individuals pay some income tax, regardless of their deductions and credits. The AMT applies only if AMT liability exceeds a taxpayer's "regular tax liability" (Code Sec. 55). The term "regular tax liability" generally means the tax imposed by Chapter 1 of the Internal Revenue Code for the tax year, but a number of taxes are not taken into account in computing regular tax liability (Code Sec. 26).

Qualified individuals who are eligible for a Trade Readjustment Allowance (TRA) or who are receiving benefits from the Pension Benefit Guarantee Corporation (PBGC) may claim a credit against their regular tax liability for a portion of their health insurance costs. The amount of the credit is equal to 65 percent of the amount paid by the taxpayer for coverage of the taxpayer and qualifying family members for qualified health insurance (Code Sec. 35(a)). However, amounts distributed from an Archer medical savings account (MSA) cannot be taken into account in computing the amount of the credit. An MSA is a tax-advantaged savings account, similar to an individual retirement account (IRA), that is available to taxpayers who are self-employed or who work for small employers (Code Sec. 220). Account distributions used to pay medical costs are generally excluded from gross income. Distributions that are not used for medical expenses are generally included in the account holder's gross income and are subject to an additional tax equal to 15 percent of the includible amount (Code Sec. 220(f)(4)). For purposes of determining whether a taxpayer is liable for the AMT, this additional tax is not included in the taxpayer's regular tax liability.

Health savings accounts (HSAs) are similar to MSAs, but they are available to any taxpayer whose health insurance coverage is provided by a high deductible health plan (Code Sec. 223). Contributions up to the annual limit, and distributions used to pay medical costs, are excludable from the account holder's gross income. Distributions that are not used for medical expenses are generally included in the account holder's income, and are also subject to an additional tax equal to 10 percent of the includible amount (Code Sec. 223(f)(4)).

Working Families Tax Act Impact

Tax treatment of HSA distributions conformed to MSA distributions.—Health savings account (HSA) distributions will be treated like Archer medical savings account (MSA) distributions for purposes of: (1) the additional tax on distributions that are not used for medical expenses, and (2) the restriction on distributions used to pay health insurance premiums that would otherwise qualify for the health insurance credit (Code Secs. 26(b) and 35(g)(3), as amended by the Working Families Tax Relief Act of 2004).

¶357

The term "regular tax liability" means the tax imposed by Chapter 1 of the Internal Revenue Code for the tax year. However, the additional tax on HSA distributions that are not used for qualified medical expenses (Code Sec. 223(f)(4)) is added to the list of taxes that are excluded from the definition of "regular tax liability" because they are not treated as a tax imposed by Chapter 1 of the Code (Code Sec. 26(b)(2)(S), as added by the 2004 Working Families Tax Act).

> **Comment:** Although the additional tax on HSA distributions that are not used for medical expenses is payable by the taxpayer to the same extent as any other additional tax "penalty," it cannot be used to reduce any alternative minimum tax (AMT) liability of the taxpayer. Generally, AMT is payable to the extent that it exceeds the taxpayer's regular tax liability (Code Sec. 55). Since this HSA penalty is not included in the regular tax liability, it cannot be used to offset the AMT, even though the taxpayer is still liable for payment of this HSA tax.

HSA distributions also cannot be used to generate a medical insurance credit (Code Sec. 35(g)(3) as amended by the 2004 Working Families Tax Act). Although a qualified individual may claim a credit for a portion of his or her health insurance costs, amounts distributed from either an HSA (Code Sec. 223(d)) or from an Archer MSA (Code Sec. 220(d)) cannot be used to compute the credit.

For further information on this subject, consult any of the following CCH reporter explanations:

- Standard Federal Tax Reporter, 2004FED ¶3851.03
- Federal Tax Service, FTS § B:13.45[6] and § B:13.47[5]
- Federal Tax Guide, 2004FTG ¶4152

★ *Effective date.* These amendments are effective for tax years beginning after December 31, 2003 (Act Sec. 401(b) of the Working Families Tax Relief Act of 2004; Act Sec. 1201(k) of the Medicare Prescription Drug, Improvement, and Modernization Act of 2003 (P.L. 108-173)).

Act Sec. 401(a)(1) of the Working Families Tax Relief Act of 2004, adding Code Sec. 26(b)(2)(S); Act Sec. 401(a)(2), amending Code Sec. 35(g)(3); Act Sec. 401(b). Law at ¶5030 and ¶5045. Committee Report at ¶10,500.

¶ 359

Medicare+Choice MSA Renamed as Medicare Advantage MSA

Background

The Medicare Prescription Drug, Improvement and Modernization Act (P.L. 108-173) established a new Medicare managed care program called Medicare Advantage. The Medicare Advantage program is replacing the former Medicare+Choice program beginning in 2004.

Medical savings accounts (MSAs) are tax-favored savings plans that allow eligible individuals to save money for paying their medical expenses (Code Sec. 220). Contributions by the Secretary of Health and Human Services directly into a Medicare+Choice MSA are excluded from the account holder's gross income (Code Sec. 138(a)). Distributions from a Medicare+Choice MSA are also excluded from income if the amounts are used to pay qualified medical expenses (Code Sec. 138(c)).

Working Families Tax Act Impact

Medicare Advantage MSA.—References in the Internal Revenue Code to the Medicare+Choice MSA have now been changed to the Medicare Advantage MSA

(Code Secs. 26(b)(2) and 138, as amended by the Working Families Tax Relief Act of 2004). This renaming of Medicare-related MSAs reflects the replacement of the Medicare+Choice program with the Medicare Advantage program by the Medicare Prescription Drug, Improvement and Modernization Act (P.L. 108-173). The tax rules, however, did not change. Thus, the tax advantages for MSAs under the former Medicare+Choice program still apply to MSAs established under the new Medicare Advantage program.

For further information on this subject, consult any of the following CCH reporter explanations:

- Standard Federal Tax Reporter, 2004FED ¶3851.03
- Federal Tax Service, FTS § A:14.208
- Federal Tax Guide, 2004FTG ¶4155

★ *Effective date.* No specific effective date is provided by the Act. The provision is, therefore, considered effective on the date of enactment.

Act Sec. 408(a)(5) of the Working Families Tax Relief Act of 2004, amending Code Secs. 26(b)(2) and 138. Law at ¶5030 and ¶5135. Committee Report at ¶10,570.

EDUCATION

¶ 365

Coverdell Education Savings Accounts

Background ───

Among the many education incentives enacted by the Taxpayer Relief Act of 1997 (P.L. 105-34) was a provision that allowed taxpayers to establish education individual retirement accounts or "education IRAs." Despite its name, the education IRA is not a retirement savings vehicle. Rather, it is a trust or custodial account created exclusively to pay the qualified higher education expenses of a single named beneficiary (Code Sec. 530(b)). To reflect this, the name was changed to Coverdell education savings accounts in 2001 (P.L. 107-22).

Contributions to Coverdell education savings accounts are limited to $2,000 annually in tax years beginning after December 31, 2001 (Code Sec. 530(b)(1)(A)).

The Economic Growth and Tax Relief Reconciliation Act of 2001 (EGTRRA) (P.L. 107-16) provided coordination rules that allow a student to take advantage of the Coverdell education savings account provisions, as well as the Hope and lifetime learning credits (Code Sec. 25A) and the qualified tuition program (Code Sec. 529) in the same tax year.

In order to avoid application of the Hope and lifetime learning credits, the taxpayer must elect not to claim the Hope and lifetime learning credits for qualified tuition and related expenses paid during the tax year (Code Sec. 25A; Code Sec. 530(d)(2)(C)).

───

Working Families Tax Act Impact

Coverdell education savings account conforming amendments.—The provision corrects the application of a conforming change to the rule coordinating Coverdell education savings accounts with Hope and lifetime learning credits and qualified tuition programs. The conforming change was made in connection with the expansion of Coverdell education savings accounts to elementary and secondary education expenses by the Economic Growth and Tax Relief Reconciliation Act of 2001 (EGT-RRA) (P.L. 107-16).

For further information on this subject, consult any of the following CCH reporter explanations:

- Standard Federal Tax Reporter, 2004FED ¶22,955.01
- Federal Tax Service, FTS § A:20.101
- Federal Tax Guide, 2004FTG ¶2223, ¶6432 and ¶16,235

★ *Effective date.* The amendment applies to tax years beginning after December 31, 2001 (Act Sec. 404(f) of the Working Families Tax Relief Act of 2004); Act Sec. 401 of the Economic Growth and Tax Relief Reconciliation Act of 2001 (EGTRRA) (P.L. 107-16).

Act Sec. 404(a) of the Working Families Tax Relief Act of 2004, amending Code Sec. 530(d)(2)(C)(i); Act Sec. 404(f). Law at ¶5255. Committee Report at ¶10,530.

¶ 367
Exception to Imposition of Additional Tax on Certain Distributions from an ESA

Background

Education IRAs, which were renamed Coverdell education savings accounts (Coverdell ESAs) by P.L. 107-22, are tax-favored vehicles that help low- and middle-income taxpayers save for education expenses (Code Sec. 530). Distributions receive tax-free treatment provided that they are used to pay the beneficiary's postsecondary education expenses or elementary and secondary education expenses. Distributions from a Coverdell education savings account are taxed under the Code Sec. 72 annuity rules (Code Sec. 530(d)(1)). Those rules treat distributions as consisting of part principal or contributions, which are generally not taxed, and earnings, which may be subject to tax depending on the amount of qualified education expenses (Code Secs. 72(e)(2)(B) and 72(e)(9)).

Example: Tony Tigre receives a $1,000 distribution from his Coverdell education savings account. On the date the distribution is made, the account balance is $10,000, and contributions made to the account total $6,000. The amount of the distribution considered to come from contributions is $600 ($1,000 × ($6,000/$10,000 or .6)). The balance of $400 is considered to come from earnings. Assuming Tigre incurs $750 in qualified education expenses for the year, the amount of earnings excludable from Tigre's income is $300 ($400 × ($750/$1,000 or .75)). The remaining $100 is included in Tigre's income.

There is also an additional 10-percent tax imposed on distributions from a Coverdell ESA that are not used for educational purposes (Code Sec. 530(d)(4)). However, the additional 10-percent tax does not apply to distributions:

(1) made to a beneficiary or the estate of a designated beneficiary after the beneficiary's death;

(2) attributable to the designated beneficiary being disabled (as defined under Code Sec. 72(m)(7));

(3) made on account of a scholarship, allowance, or payment (as defined under Code Sec. 25A(g)(2)) received by the account holder to the extent the amount of the distribution does not exceed the amount of the scholarship allowance, or payment; or

(4) that constitute the return of excess contributions and earnings thereon (although earnings are includible in income) (Code Sec. 530(d)(4)(B)).

Background —————————————————————————————————

Under present law, the first two exceptions to the imposition of the 10-percent additional tax noted above refer to the "designated beneficiary," a term that is used consistently throughout Code Sec. 530 and which is defined elsewhere in the Code. However, the third exception refers instead to the "account holder." The latter term is not used anywhere else in Code Sec. 530.

Working Families Tax Act Impact

Distribution must be received by designated beneficiary.—The Working Families Tax Relief Act of 2004 clarifies that distributions from a Coverdell ESA made on account of a scholarship, allowance, or payment that do not exceed the amount of the scholarship, allowance, or payment will avoid imposition of the 10-percent additional tax on distributions not used for educational purposes, if they are received by the "designated beneficiary" of the ESA (Code Sec. 530(d)(4)(B)(iii), as amended by the Working Families Tax Relief Act of 2004).

> **Comment:** In defining the term "designated beneficiary," Code Sec. 530(b)(2)(B) actually refers to another section of the Code dealing with qualified tuition programs. Specifically, as per Code Sec. 529(e)(1), a designated beneficiary is (1) the individual designated at the commencement of participation in the QTP as the beneficiary of amounts paid, or to be paid, to the program; (2) the new beneficiary (in the case of a change of beneficiaries); or (3) the recipient of a scholarship (in the case of QTP purchased by a state or local government or a qualified charitable organization).

For further information on this subject, consult any of the following CCH reporter explanations:

- Standard Federal Tax Reporter, 2004FED ¶22,955.01
- Federal Tax Service, FTS § A:20.101[3]
- Federal Tax Guide, 2004FTG ¶11,465

★ *Effective date.* The provision is effective for tax years beginning after December 31, 1997 (Act Sec. 406(h) of the Working Families Tax Relief Act of 2004; Act Sec. 213 of the Taxpayer Relief Act of 1997 (P.L. 105-34)).

Act Sec. 406(b) of the Working Families Tax Relief Act of 2004, amending Code Sec. 530(d)(4)(B)(iii); Act Sec. 406(h). Law at ¶5255. Committee Report at ¶10,550.

¶ 369

Permitted Change of Beneficiary in a Qualified Tuition Program

Background —————————————————————————————————

Code Sec. 529 allows the establishment of qualified tuition programs (QTPs) to cover certain costs associated with higher education. Under these plans, after-tax dollars are contributed to a qualified fund on behalf of a beneficiary, and earnings are allowed to grow tax free while invested in the plan. When Code Sec. 529 was first added to the Code by the Small Business Job Protection Act of 1996 (P.L. 104-188), contributions to a QTP were considered incomplete gifts. Therefore, gift tax treatment was determined when a distribution was made from a qualified account.

Pursuant to changes made by the Taxpayer Relief Act of 1997 (P.L. 105-34), effective after August 5, 1997, a contribution to a QTP is treated as a completed gift of a present interest from the contributor to the beneficiary at the time of the contribution. Accordingly, annual contributions are eligible for the gift tax exclusion under

Background

Code Sec. 2503(b) and are excludable for purposes of the generation-skipping transfer (GST) tax, provided that the annual gift tax exclusion limit (currently $11,000 for a single individual, $22,000 for a married couple electing gift splitting) is not exceeded. However, an election is available to treat contributions in excess of the annual gift tax exclusion limit as if they were made ratably over five years, effectively allowing an individual to make a one-time contribution of as much as $55,000 ($110,000 for a married couple electing gift splitting) (Code Sec. 529(c)(2)).

Another change made by P.L. 105-34 allows that, if a beneficiary's interest is rolled over to another beneficiary or there is a change in beneficiary, no gift or GST tax consequences result, provided that the two beneficiaries are of the same generation (Code Sec. 529(c)(5)(B), prior to amendment by the Working Families Tax Relief Act of 2004). Although the legislative history concerning special treatment of a QTP rollover or change in beneficiary (House Committee Report to the Taxpayer Relief Act of 1997 (P.L. 105-34); H.R. Rep. No. 105-148 (Budget), 6/24/97, 1997-4 (Vol. 1) CB 319, 649) indicates that this treatment would apply only if both beneficiaries were also members of the same family, the statutory language adopted did not reflect the family relationship requirement.

Working Families Tax Act Impact

Old and new beneficiaries must be members of the same family.—The Working Families Tax Relief Act of 2004 clarifies that in order for a rollover or change in beneficiary of a QTP to escape gift and GST taxes, the new beneficiary must be (1) of the same (or higher) generation as the old beneficiary and (2) a member of the same family (Code Sec. 529(c)(5)(B)), as amended by the Working Families Tax Relief Act of 2004).

Comment: For purposes of account rollovers and beneficiary changes, the definition of a member of the beneficiary's family includes the beneficiary's spouse, anyone qualifying as a dependent under Code Sec. 152(a), or the spouse of anyone qualifying as a dependent. In addition to spouses, family members include children, siblings, nephews and nieces, certain in-laws, first cousins, and the spouses of those relations (Code Sec. 529(e)(2)).

Example: Alan Able is the designated beneficiary of a QTP. Alan has decided to pursue a career as a professional tennis player rather than attend college. Alan's first cousin, Ben, is designated as the new beneficiary of the QTP. Because Ben is of the same generation as Alan and a member of Alan's family, the designation of Ben as the new beneficiary will not have adverse gift or GST tax consequences.

PRACTICAL ANALYSIS. Arthur Seltzer of Brown Smith Wallace, LLC, St. Louis, Missouri, notes that one of the attractive aspects of the Code Sec. 529 qualified tuition plan technique is the attractive gift tax treatment when there are funds remaining after the beneficiary has completed the college education. Any transfer to a new beneficiary, to the extent reportable, is treated as a gift by the beneficiary rather than the initial donor, and also is eligible for a new five-year election period.

The technical correction clarifies that the transfer to a new beneficiary is not subject to gift tax at all, as long as the new beneficiary is not of a younger generation than the original beneficiary, and also is a member of the beneficiary's family as generously defined.

For further information on this subject, consult any of the following CCH reporter explanations:

- Standard Federal Tax Reporter, 2004FED ¶ 22,945.01
- Federal Tax Service, FTS § A:20.104[3]
- Federal Tax Guide, 2004FTG ¶ 16,230

★ *Effective date.* Clarification of the family relationship requirement among beneficiaries for purposes of the rules governing QTP rollovers is effective for transfers after August 5, 1997 (Act Sec. 406(h) of the Working Families Tax Relief Act of 2004; Act Sec. 211 of the Taxpayer Relief Act of 1997 (P.L. 105-34)).

Act Sec. 406(a) of the Working Families Tax Relief Act of 2004, amending Code Sec. 529(c)(5)(B); Act Sec. 406(h). Law at ¶ 5250. Committee Report at ¶ 10,550.

S CORPORATIONS

¶ 375

Basis Adjustments for QZAB Held by S Corporation

Background

A bank, an insurance company or a corporation actively engaged in the business of lending money may claim a tax credit for each tax year that such an eligible financial institution holds a qualified zone academy bond (QZAB) issued after 1997 (Code Sec. 1397E). Furthermore, a shareholder of an S corporation that is an eligible financial institution may claim a proportional share of the credit with respect to a QZAB held by the S corporation financial institution (Code Sec. 1366(a)(1)(A)). In such a case, the amount of the credit is also included in the gross income of the S corporation shareholder (Code Sec. 1397(g); Code Sec. 1366(a)(1)(A)).

Normally, an S corporation shareholder's stock basis is increased by separately computed items of income (Code Sec. 1367(a)(1)(A)).

Working Families Tax Act Impact

No basis adjustment for QZAB credit by S corporation shareholder.—The basis of stock held by a shareholder in an S corporation that is an eligible financial corporation is not adjusted (under Code Sec. 1367) by the amount of the S corporation's qualified zone academy bond (QZAB) credit that is passed through to the shareholder (Code Sec. 1397E(i), as added by the Working Families Tax Relief Act of 2004). The shareholder continues to take into account its *pro rata* share of the credit. Thus, the S corporation shareholder will continue to claim its share of the credit and include an amount equal to its share of the credit in income, even though the shareholder will not increase its basis in the S corporation's stock by the amount of that income inclusion.

> **PRACTICAL ANALYSIS.** Michael Schlesinger of Schlesinger & Sussman of New York, New York, notes that presently, Code Sec. 1397E prescribes that a shareholder of an S corporation that is an eligible financial institution may claim a credit with respect to a qualified zone academy bond (QZAB) held by the S corporation. The amount of the credit is included in gross income of the shareholder.
>
> Congress realized that Code Sec. 1397E could be interpreted so that the shareholder's basis in the stock of the S corporation could be increased by the amount of the income inclusion, notwithstanding that the bene-

fit of the credit flows directly to the shareholder rather than to the corporation, and the corporation has no additional assets to support the basis increase.

So, to remedy this problem, Congress amended Code Sec. 1397E by adding a new subsection to prescribe that the basis of stock in an S corporation is not affected by this QZAB credit.

For further information on this subject, consult any of the following CCH reporter explanations:

- Standard Federal Tax Reporter, 2004FED ¶970.31 and ¶32,407.01
- Federal Tax Service, FTS §G:1.81
- Federal Tax Guide, 2004FTG ¶13,210

★ *Effective date.* This provision applies to obligations issued after December 31, 1997 (Act Sec. 406(h) of the Working Families Tax Relief Act of 2004; Act Sec. 226(c) of the Taxpayer Relief Act of 1997 (P.L. 105-34)).

Act Sec. 406(c) of the Working Families Tax Relief Act of 2004, adding Code Sec. 1397E(i); Act Sec. 406(h). Law at ¶5320. Committee Report at ¶10,550.

¶ 377

S Corporation Post-Termination Transition Period

Background

Shareholders of an S corporation whose status as an S corporation terminates are allowed a period of time after the termination (the post-termination transition period (PTTP)) to utilize some of the benefits of S corporation status. The shareholders may claim losses and deductions previously suspended due to lack of stock or debt basis up to the amount of the stock basis as of the last day of the PTTP (Code Sec. 1366(d)). Also, shareholders may receive cash distributions from the corporation during the PTTP that are treated as returns of capital to the extent of any balance in the S corporation's accumulated adjustments account (Code Sec. 1371(e)).

The PTTP generally begins on the day after the last day of the corporation's last tax year as an S corporation and ends on the later of the day which is one year after such last day or the due date for filing the return for such last year as an S corporation (including extensions). A provision in the Small Business Job Protection Act of 1996 (P.L. 104-188) added a new 120-day PTTP beginning on the date of any post-termination audit determination that adjusts an S corporation item of income, loss, or deduction arising during the most recent period while the corporation was an S corporation.

Comment: This provision was enacted to allow the tax-free distribution of any additional income determined in the audit.

The definition of "determination" includes a final disposition of a claim for refund by the Secretary of the Treasury and certain other agreements between the Secretary and any person relating to tax liability (Code Sec. 1377(b)(2)).

Comment: This change is significant because distributions made by a former S corporation during its post-termination period are treated as if the distributions were made by an S corporation, whereas distributions made after the post-termination period are generally treated as made by a C corporation.

Working Families Tax Act Impact

S corporation's 120-day PTTP not applicable in allowing suspended losses.— The 120-day post-termination transition period (PTTP) following a post-termination audit determination, does not apply for purposes of allowing suspended losses to be deducted (Code Sec. 1377(b)(3)(A), as added by the Working Families Tax Relief Act of 2004).

Example: At the end of the one-year PTTP following the termination of a corporation's S corporation status, a shareholder has $1 million of suspended losses in the corporation. Later, the shareholder purchases additional stock in the corporation for $1 million. The corporation's audit determines a $25,000 increase in the S corporation's income. Although the $25,000 increase in income would allow $25,000 of suspended losses to be allowed, the shareholder might take the position that the entire $1 million of suspended losses could be utilized during the 120-day PTTP following the end of the audit. The new provision makes it clear that the 120-day PTTP does not apply for purposes of allowing suspended losses to be deducted.

Planning Note: Any amounts of increased income determined in the audit can be offset with the suspended losses.

Also, tax-free distributions of money by the corporation during the 120-day period are allowed only to the extent of any increase in the accumulated adjustments account by reason of adjustments from the audit (Code Sec. 1377(b)(3)(B), as added by the 2004 Working Families Tax Act). Thus, an S corporation that had failed to distribute the entire amount in its accumulated adjustments account during the one-year PTTP following the loss of S corporation status can no longer argue that it could distribute that amount, in addition to the amount determined in the audit, during the 120-day period following the audit.

PRACTICAL ANALYSIS. Michael Schlesinger of Schlesinger & Sussman of New York, New York, observes that, per Code Sec. 1377(b), shareholders of an S corporation whose status as an S corporation terminates are allowed a period of time after the termination (the post-termination transition period [PTTP]) to use certain of the benefits of S corporation status. The shareholders may claim losses and deductions previously suspended due to lack of stock or debt basis up to the amount of the stock basis as of the last day of the PTTP. Also, Code Sec. 1377(b) provides that shareholders may receive cash distributions from the corporation during the PTTP that are treated as returns of capital to the extent of any balance in the S corporation's accumulated adjustments account (AAA).

Code Sec. 1377(b)(1) prescribes three time periods for the computation of PTTP:

(A) The period beginning on the day after the last day of the corporation's last tax year as an S corporation and ending on the later of:

(i) the day which is one year after such last day, or

(ii) the due date for filing the return for such last year as an S corporation (including extensions).

(B) The 120-day period beginning on the date of any determination pursuant to an audit of the taxpayer which follows the termination of the corporation's election and which adjusts a subchapter S item of income, loss or deduction of the corporation arising during the S period (as defined in Code Sec. 1368(e)(2)).

(C) The 120-day period beginning on the date of a determination that the corporation's election under Code Sec. 1362(a) had terminated for a previous tax year.

However, Congress felt that an S corporation shareholder might take the position that an audit adjustment under Code Sec. 1377(b)(1)(B) allows the shareholder to use suspended losses and deductions in excess of the amount of the audit deficiency. For example, assume that, at the end of Code Sec. 1377(b)(1)(A)'s one-year PTTP following the termination of a corporation's S corporation status, a shareholder has $1 million of suspended losses in the corporation. Later the shareholder purchases additional stock in the corporation for $1 million. The corporation's audit determines a $25,000 increase in the S corporation's income. Although the $25,000 increase in income would allow $25,000 of suspended losses to be allowed, the shareholder might take the position that the entire $1 million of suspended losses could be used during the 120-day PTTP following the end of the audit. Similarly, an S corporation that had failed to distribute the entire amount in its AAA during the one-year PTTP following the loss of S corporation status might argue that it could distribute that amount, in addition to the amount determined in the audit, during the 120-day period following the audit.

To clear up any confusion, Congress amended Code Sec. 1377(b) by adding a new section at the end of Code Sec. 1377 to prescribe that Code Sec. 1377(b)(1)(B)'s 120-day PTTP does not apply for purposes of allowing suspended losses to be deducted (since the increased income determined in the audit can be offset with the losses), and tax-free distributions of money by the corporation during the 120-day period will be allowed only to the extent of any increase in the AAA by reason of adjustments from the audit.

For further information on this subject, consult any of the following CCH reporter explanations:

- Standard Federal Tax Reporter, 2004FED ¶ 32,121.03
- Federal Tax Service, FTS § I:18.141[3]
- Federal Tax Guide, 2004FTG ¶ 13,425

★ *Effective date.* This provision applies to determinations made after December 31, 1996 (Act Sec. 407(c) of the Working Families Tax Relief Act of 2004; Act Sec. 1317 of the Small Business Job Protection Act of 1996 (P.L. 104-188); Act Sec. 1601(c)(2) of the Taxpayer Relief Act of 1997 (P.L. 105-34)).

Act Sec. 407(a) of the Working Families Tax Relief Act of 2004, adding Code Sec. 1377(b)(3); Act Sec. 407(c). Law at ¶ 5315. Committee Report at ¶ 10,560.

CODE SECTIONS ADDED, AMENDED OR REPEALED

INTRODUCTION

The Internal Revenue Code provisions amended by the Working Families Tax Relief Act of 2004 (H.R. 1308) are shown in the following paragraphs. Deleted Code material or the text of the Code Section prior to amendment appears in the amendment notes following each amended Code provision. *Any changed or added material is set out in italics.*

[¶ 5005] CODE SEC. 1. TAX IMPOSED.

* * *

(f) PHASEOUT OF MARRIAGE PENALTY IN 15-PERCENT BRACKET; ADJUSTMENTS IN TAX TABLES SO THAT INFLATION WILL NOT RESULT IN TAX INCREASES.—

* * *

⨠➔ *Caution: Code Sec. 1(f)(8), below, was amended by §101(c). For sunset provision, see H.R. 1308, §105, in the amendment notes.*

(8) ELIMINATION OF MARRIAGE PENALTY IN 15-PERCENT BRACKET.—With respect to taxable years beginning after December 31, 2003, in prescribing the tables under paragraph (1)—

(A) the maximum taxable income in the 15-percent rate bracket in the table contained in subsection (a) (and the minimum taxable income in the next higher taxable income bracket in such table) shall be 200 percent of the maximum taxable income in the 15-percent rate bracket in the table contained in subsection (c) (after any other adjustment under this subsection), and

(B) the comparable taxable income amounts in the table contained in subsection (d) shall be ½ of the amounts determined under subparagraph (A).

[CCH Explanation at ¶ 115. Committee Reports at ¶ 10,030.]

Amendments

• **2004, Working Families Tax Relief Act of 2004 (H.R. 1308)**

H.R. 1308, §101(c):

Amended Code Sec. 1(f)(8). **Effective** for tax years beginning after 12-31-2003. Prior to amendment, Code Sec. 1(f)(8) read as follows:

(8) PHASEOUT OF MARRIAGE PENALTY IN 15-PERCENT BRACKET.—

(A) IN GENERAL.—With respect to taxable years beginning after December 31, 2002, in prescribing the tables under paragraph (1)—

(i) the maximum taxable income in the 15-percent rate bracket in the table contained in subsection (a) (and the minimum taxable income in the next higher taxable income bracket in such table) shall be the applicable percentage of the maximum taxable income in the 15-percent rate bracket in the table contained in subsection (c) (after any other adjustment under this subsection), and

(ii) the comparable taxable income amounts in the table contained in subsection (d) shall be ½ of the amounts determined under clause (i).

(B) APPLICABLE PERCENTAGE.—For purposes of subparagraph (A), the applicable percentage shall be determined in accordance with the following table:

For taxable years beginning in calendar year—	The applicable percentage is—
2003 and 2004	200
2005	180
2006	187
2007	193
2008 and thereafter	200.

(C) ROUNDING.—If any amount determined under subparagraph (A)(i) is not a multiple of $50, such amount shall be rounded to the next lowest multiple of $50.

H.R. 1308, §105, provides:

SEC. 105. APPLICATION OF EGTRRA SUNSET TO THIS TITLE.

Each amendment made by this title shall be subject to title IX of the Economic Growth and Tax Relief Reconciliation Act of 2001 to the same extent and in the same manner as the provision of such Act to which such amendment relates.

(g) CERTAIN UNEARNED INCOME OF MINOR CHILDREN TAXED AS IF PARENT'S INCOME.—

* * *

(7) ELECTION TO CLAIM CERTAIN UNEARNED INCOME OF CHILD ON PARENT'S RETURN.—

* * *

(B) INCOME INCLUDED ON PARENT'S RETURN.—In the case of a parent making the election under this paragraph—

* * *

(ii) the tax imposed by this section for such year with respect to such parent shall be the amount equal to the sum of—

* * *

(II) for each such child, *10 percent* of the lesser of the amount described in paragraph (4)(A)(ii)(I) or the excess of the gross income of such child over the amount so described, and

* * *

[CCH Explanation at ¶ 30,050. Committee Reports at ¶ 10,570.]

Amendments

• 2004, Working Families Tax Relief Act of 2004 (H.R. 1308)

H.R. 1308, § 408(a)(1):

Amended Code Sec. 1(g)(7)(B)(ii)(II) by striking "10 percent." and inserting "10 percent". **Effective** on the date of the enactment of this Act.

(h) MAXIMUM CAPITAL GAINS RATE.—

(1) IN GENERAL.—If a taxpayer has a net capital gain for any taxable year, the tax imposed by this section for such taxable year shall not exceed the sum of—

* * *

(D) 25 percent of the excess (if any) of—

(i) the unrecaptured section 1250 gain (or, if less, the net capital gain *(determined without regard to paragraph (11))*), over

(ii) the excess (if any) of—

(I) the sum of the amount on which tax is determined under subparagraph (A) plus the net capital gain, over

(II) taxable income; and

* * *

(6) UNRECAPTURED SECTION 1250 GAIN.—For purposes of this subsection—

(A) IN GENERAL.—The term "unrecaptured section 1250 gain" means the excess (if any) of—

* * *

(ii) the excess (if any) of—

(I) the amount described in paragraph *(4)(B)*; over

(II) the amount described in paragraph *(4)(A)*.

* * *

(11) DIVIDENDS TAXED AS NET CAPITAL GAIN.—

* * *

(B) QUALIFIED DIVIDEND INCOME.—For purposes of this paragraph—

* * *

(iii) COORDINATION WITH SECTION 246(c).—Such term shall not include any dividend on any share of stock—

(I) with respect to which the holding period requirements of section 246(c) are not met (determined by substituting in *section 246(c)* "60 days" for "45 days" each place it appears and by substituting *"121-day period"* for *"91-day period"*), or

(II) to the extent that the taxpayer is under an obligation (whether pursuant to a short sale or otherwise) to make related payments with respect to positions in substantially similar or related property.

* * *

(D) SPECIAL RULES.—

* * *

¶ 5005   Code Sec. 1(g)(7)(B)(ii)(II)

(ii) EXTRAORDINARY DIVIDENDS.—*If a taxpayer to whom this section applies* receives, with respect to any share of stock, qualified dividend income from 1 or more dividends which are extraordinary dividends (within the meaning of section 1059(c)), any loss on the sale or exchange of such share shall, to the extent of such dividends, be treated as long-term capital loss.

* * *

[CCH Explanation at ¶305 and ¶30,050. Committee Reports at ¶10,510 and ¶10,570.]

Amendments

• **2004, Working Families Tax Relief Act of 2004 (H.R. 1308)**

H.R. 1308, §402(a)(1):

Amended Code Sec. 1(h)(1)(D)(i) by inserting "(determined without regard to paragraph (11))" after "net capital gain". **Effective** as if included in section 302 of the Jobs and Growth Tax Relief Reconciliation Act of 2003 (P.L. 108-27) [**effective** generally after 12-31-2002.—CCH].

H.R. 1308, §402(a)(2)(A)-(C):

Amended Code Sec. 1(h)(11)(B)(iii)(I) by striking "section 246(c)(1)" and inserting "section 246(c)", by striking "120-day period" and inserting "121-day period", and by striking "90-day period" and inserting "91-day period". Ef-

fective as if included in section 302 of the Jobs and Growth Tax Relief Reconciliation Act of 2003 (P.L. 108-27) [**effective** generally after 12-31-2002.—CCH].

H.R. 1308, §402(a)(3):

Amended Code Sec. 1(h)(11)(D)(ii) by striking "an individual" and inserting "a taxpayer to whom this section applies". **Effective** as if included in section 302 of the Jobs and Growth Tax Relief Reconciliation Act of 2003 (P.L. 108-27) [**effective** generally after 12-31-2002.—CCH].

H.R. 1308, §408(a)(2)(A)-(B):

Amended Code Sec. 1(h)(6)(A)(ii) by striking "(5)(B)" in subclause (I) and inserting "(4)(B)", and by striking "(5)(A)" in subclause (II) and inserting "(4)(A)". **Effective** on the date of the enactment of this Act.

(i) RATE REDUCTIONS AFTER 2000.—

⫸→ *Caution: Code Sec. 1(i)(1), below, was amended by §101(d)(1)-(2). For sunset provision, see H.R. 1308, §105, in the amendment notes.*

(1) 10-PERCENT RATE BRACKET.—

* * *

(B) INITIAL BRACKET AMOUNT.—For purposes of this paragraph, the initial bracket amount is—

(i) $14,000 in the case of subsection (a),

(ii) $10,000 in the case of subsection (b), and

(iii) ½ the amount applicable under clause (i) (after adjustment, if any, under subparagraph (C)) in the case of subsections (c) and (d).

(C) INFLATION ADJUSTMENT.—*In prescribing the tables under subsection (f) which apply with respect to taxable years beginning in calendar years after 2003—*

(i) the cost-of-living adjustment shall be determined under subsection (f)(3) by substituting "2002" for "1992" in subparagraph (B) thereof, and

(ii) the adjustments under clause (i) shall not apply to the amount referred to in subparagraph (B)(iii).

If any amount after adjustment under the preceding sentence is not a multiple of $50, such amount shall be rounded to the next lowest multiple of $50.

* * *

[CCH Explanation at ¶120. Committee Reports at ¶10,040.]

Amendments

• **2004, Working Families Tax Relief Act of 2004 (H.R. 1308)**

H.R. 1308, §101(d)(1):

Amended Code Sec. 1(i)(1)(B)(i) by striking "($12,000 in the case of taxable years beginning after December 31, 2004, and before January 1, 2008)" following "$14,000". **Effective** for tax years beginning after 12-31-2003.

H.R. 1308, §101(d)(2):

Amended Code Sec. 1(i)(1)(C). **Effective** for tax years beginning after 12-31-2003. Prior to amendment, Code Sec. 1(i)(1)(C) read as follows:

(C) INFLATION ADJUSTMENT.—In prescribing the tables under subsection (f) which apply with respect to taxable years beginning in calendar years after 2000—

(i) except as provided in clause (ii), the Secretary shall make no adjustment to the initial bracket amounts for any taxable year beginning before January 1, 2009,

(ii) there shall be an adjustment under subsection (f) of such amounts which shall apply only to taxable years beginning in 2004, and such adjustment shall be determined under subsection (f)(3) by substituting "2002" for "1992" in subparagraph (B) thereof,

(iii) the cost-of-living adjustment used in making adjustments to the initial bracket amounts for any taxable year beginning after December 31, 2008, shall be determined under subsection (f)(3) by substituting "2007" for "1992" in subparagraph (B) thereof, and

(iv) the adjustments under clauses (ii) and (iii) shall not apply to the amount referred to in subparagraph (B)(iii).

If any amount after adjustment under the preceding sentence is not a multiple of $50, such amount shall be rounded to the next lowest multiple of $50.

H.R. 1308, §105, provides:

SEC. 105. APPLICATION OF EGTRRA SUNSET TO THIS TITLE.

Each amendment made by this title shall be subject to title IX of the Economic Growth and Tax Relief Reconciliation Act of 2001 to the same extent and in the same manner as the provision of such Act to which such amendment relates.

[¶ 5010] CODE SEC. 2. DEFINITIONS AND SPECIAL RULES.

(a) DEFINITION OF SURVIVING SPOUSE.—

(1) IN GENERAL.—For purposes of section 1, the term "surviving spouse" means a taxpayer—

* * *

(B) who maintains as his home a household which constitutes for the taxable year the principal place of abode (as a member of such household) of a dependent (i) who (within the meaning of section 152, *determined without regard to subsections (b)(1), (b)(2), and (d)(1)(B) thereof*) is a son, stepson, daughter, or stepdaughter of the taxpayer, and (ii) with respect to whom the taxpayer is entitled to a deduction for the taxable year under section 151.

* * *

[CCH Explanation at ¶ 145.]

Amendments

• 2004, Working Families Tax Relief Act of 2004 (H.R. 1308)

H.R. 1308, § 207(1):

Amended Code Sec. 2(a)(1)(B)(i) by inserting ", determined without regard to subsections (b)(1), (b)(2), and

(d)(1)(B) thereof" after "section 152". **Effective** for tax years beginning after 12-31-2004.

(b) DEFINITION OF HEAD OF HOUSEHOLD.—

(1) IN GENERAL.—For purposes of this subtitle, an individual shall be considered a head of a household if, and only if, such individual is not married at the close of his taxable year, is not a surviving spouse (as defined in subsection (a)), and either—

(A) maintains as his home a household which constitutes for more than one-half of such taxable year the principal place of abode, as a member of such household, of—

(i) *a qualifying child of the individual (as defined in section 152(c), determined without regard to section 152(e)), but not if such child—*

(I) *is married at the close of the taxpayer's taxable year, and*

(II) *is not a dependent of such individual by reason of section 152(b)(2) or 152(b)(3), or both, or*

(ii) any other person who is a dependent of the taxpayer, if the taxpayer is entitled to a deduction for the taxable year for such person under section 151, or

(B) maintains a household which constitutes for such taxable year the principal place of abode of the father or mother of the taxpayer, if the taxpayer is entitled to a deduction for the taxable year for such father or mother under section 151.

For purposes of this paragraph, an individual shall be considered as maintaining a household only if over half of the cost of maintaining the household during the taxable year is furnished by such individual.

(2) DETERMINATION OF STATUS.—For purposes of this subsection—

(A) an individual who is legally separated from his spouse under a decree of divorce or of separate maintenance shall not be considered as married;

(B) a taxpayer shall be considered as not married at the close of his taxable year if at any time during the taxable year his spouse is a nonresident alien; and

(C) a taxpayer shall be considered as married at the close of his taxable year if his spouse (other than a spouse described in subparagraph (C)) died during the taxable year.

(3) LIMITATIONS.—Notwithstanding paragraph (1), for purposes of this subtitle a taxpayer shall not be considered to be a head of a household—

(A) if at any time during the taxable year he is a nonresident alien; or

(B) by reason of an individual who would not be a dependent for the taxable year but for—

     (i) subparagraph (H) of section 152(d)(2), or

     (ii) paragraph (3) of section 152(d).

[CCH Explanation at ¶ 150. Committee Reports at ¶ 10,120.]

Amendments

● **2004, Working Families Tax Relief Act of 2004 (H.R. 1308)**

H.R. 1308, § 202(a):

Amended Code Sec. 2(b)(1)(A)(i). **Effective** for tax years beginning after 12-31-2004. Prior to amendment, Code Sec. 2(b)(1)(A)(i) read as follows:

(i) a son, stepson, daughter, or stepdaughter of the taxpayer, or a descendant of a son or daughter of the taxpayer, but if such son, stepson, daughter, stepdaughter, or descendant is married at the close of the taxpayer's taxable year, only if the taxpayer is entitled to a deduction for the taxable year for such person under section 151 (or would be so entitled but for paragraph (2) or (4) of section 152(e)), or

H.R. 1308, § 202(b)(1):

Amended Code Sec. 2(b)(2) by striking subparagraph (A) and by redesignating subparagraphs (B), (C), and (D) as subparagraphs (A), (B), and (C), respectively. **Effective** for tax years beginning after 12-31-2004. Prior to being stricken, Code Sec. 2(b)(2)(A) read as follows:

(A) a legally adopted child of a person shall be considered a child of such person by blood;

H.R. 1308, § 202(b)(2):

Amended Code Sec. 2(b)(3)(B)(i)-(ii). **Effective** for tax years beginning after 12-31-2004. Prior to amendment, Code Sec. 2(b)(3)(B)(i)-(ii) read as follows:

(i) paragraph (9) of section 152(a), or

(ii) subsection (c) of section 152.

[¶ 5015] CODE SEC. 21. EXPENSES FOR HOUSEHOLD AND DEPENDENT CARE SERVICES NECESSARY FOR GAINFUL EMPLOYMENT.

(a) Allowance of Credit.—

(1) In General.—*In the case of an individual for which there are 1 or more qualifying individuals (as defined in subsection (b)(1)) with respect to such individual,* there shall be allowed as a credit against the tax imposed by this chapter for the taxable year an amount equal to the applicable percentage of the employment-related expenses (as defined in subsection (b)(2)) paid by such individual during the taxable year.

* * *

[CCH Explanation at ¶ 155. Committee Reports at ¶ 10,130.]

Amendments

● **2004, Working Families Tax Relief Act of 2004 (H.R. 1308)**

H.R. 1308, § 203(a):

Amended Code Sec. 21(a)(1) by striking "In the case of an individual who maintains a household which includes as a member one or more qualifying individuals (as defined in subsection (b)(1))" and inserting "In the case of an individual for which there are 1 or more qualifying individuals (as defined in subsection (b)(1)) with respect to such individual". **Effective** for tax years beginning after 12-31-2004.

(b) Definitions of Qualifying Individual and Employment-Related Expenses.—For purposes of this section—

     (1) Qualifying Individual.—The term "qualifying individual" means—

         (A) a dependent of the taxpayer (as defined in section 152(a)(1)) who has not attained age 13,

         (B) a dependent of the taxpayer who is physically or mentally incapable of caring for himself or herself and who has the same principal place of abode as the taxpayer for more than one-half of such taxable year, or

         (C) the spouse of the taxpayer, if the spouse is physically or mentally incapable of caring for himself or herself and who has the same principal place of abode as the taxpayer for more than one-half of such taxable year.

* * *

[CCH Explanation at ¶ 155. Committee Reports at ¶ 10,130.]

Amendments

• 2004, Working Families Tax Relief Act of 2004 (H.R. 1308)

H.R. 1308, § 203(b):

Amended Code Sec. 21(b)(1). **Effective** for tax years beginning after 12-31-2004. Prior to amendment, Code Sec. 21(b)(1) read as follows:

(1) QUALIFYING INDIVIDUAL.—The term "qualifying individual" means—

(A) a dependent of the taxpayer who is under the age of 13 and with respect to whom the taxpayer is entitled to a deduction under section 151(c),

(B) a dependent of the taxpayer who is physically or mentally incapable of caring for himself, or

(C) the spouse of the taxpayer, if he is physically or mentally incapable of caring for himself.

(e) SPECIAL RULES.—For purposes of this section—

(1) PLACE OF ABODE.—An individual shall not be treated as having the same principal place of abode of the taxpayer if at any time during the taxable year of the taxpayer the relationship between the individual and the taxpayer is in violation of local law.

* * *

(5) SPECIAL DEPENDENCY TEST IN CASE OF DIVORCED PARENTS, ETC.—If—

(A) section 152(e) applies to any child with respect to any calendar year, and

(B) such child is under the age of 13 or is physically or mentally incapable of caring for himself,

in the case of any taxable year beginning in such calendar year, such child shall be treated as a qualifying individual described in subparagraph (A) or (B) of subsection (b)(1) (whichever is appropriate) with respect to the custodial parent (*as defined in section 152(e)(3)(A)*), and shall not be treated as a qualifying individual with respect to the noncustodial parent.

(6) PAYMENTS TO RELATED INDIVIDUALS.—No credit shall be allowed under subsection (a) for any amount paid by the taxpayer to an individual—

(A) with respect to whom, for the taxable year, a deduction under section 151(c) (relating to deduction for personal exemptions for dependents) is allowable either to the taxpayer or his spouse, or

(B) who is a child of the taxpayer (within the meaning of *section 152(f)(1)*) who has not attained the age of 19 at the close of the taxable year.

For purposes of this paragraph, the term "taxable year" means the taxable year of the taxpayer in which the service is performed.

* * *

[CCH Explanation at ¶ 145 and ¶ 155. Committee Reports at ¶ 10,130.]

Amendments

• 2004, Working Families Tax Relief Act of 2004 (H.R. 1308)

H.R. 1308, § 203(c):

Amended Code Sec. 21(e)(1). **Effective** for tax years beginning after 12-31-2004. Prior to amendment, Code Sec. 21(e)(1) read as follows:

(1) MAINTAINING HOUSEHOLD.—An individual shall be treated as maintaining a household for any period only if over half the cost of maintaining the household for such period is furnished by such individual (or, if such individual is married during such period, is furnished by such individual and his spouse).

H.R. 1308, § 207(2)(A)-(B):

Amended Code Sec. 21(e)(5) by striking "paragraph (2) or (4) of" immediately preceding "section 152(e)" in subparagraph (A), and by striking "within the meaning of section 152(e)(1)" and inserting "as defined in section 152(e)(3)(A)". **Effective** for tax years beginning after 12-31-2004.

H.R. 1308, § 207(3):

Amended Code Sec. 21(e)(6)(B) by striking "section 151(c)(3)" and inserting "section 152(f)(1)". **Effective** for tax years beginning after 12-31-2004.

[¶ 5020] CODE SEC. 24. CHILD TAX CREDIT.

>»→ *Caution: Code Sec. 24(a), below, was amended by § 101(a). For sunset provision, see H.R. 1308, § 105, in the amendment notes.*

(a) ALLOWANCE OF CREDIT.—*There shall be allowed as a credit against the tax imposed by this chapter for the taxable year with respect to each qualifying child of the taxpayer an amount equal to $1,000.*

* * *

[CCH Explanation at ¶105. Committee Reports at ¶10,010.]

Amendments

- **2004, Working Families Tax Relief Act of 2004 (H.R. 1308)**

H.R. 1308, §101(a):

Amended Code Sec. 24(a). **Effective** for tax years beginning after 12-31-2003. Prior to amendment, Code Sec. 24(a) read as follows:

(a) ALLOWANCE OF CREDIT.—

(1) IN GENERAL.—There shall be allowed as a credit against the tax imposed by this chapter for the taxable year with respect to each qualifying child of the taxpayer an amount equal to the per child amount.

(2) PER CHILD AMOUNT.—For purposes of paragraph (1), the per child amount shall be determined as follows:

In the case of any taxable year beginning in—	The per child amount is—
2003 or 2004	$1,000
2005, 2006, 2007, or 2008	700
2009	800
2010 or thereafter	1,000.

H.R. 1308, §105, provides:

SEC. 105. APPLICATION OF EGTRRA SUNSET TO THIS TITLE.

Each amendment made by this title shall be subject to title IX of the Economic Growth and Tax Relief Reconciliation Act of 2001 to the same extent and in the same manner as the provision of such Act to which such amendment relates.

(c) QUALIFYING CHILD.—For purposes of this section—

(1) IN GENERAL.—The term "qualifying child" means a qualifying child of the taxpayer (as defined in section 152(c)) who has not attained age 17.

(2) EXCEPTION FOR CERTAIN NONCITIZENS.—The term "qualifying child" shall not include any individual who would not be a dependent if *subparagraph (A) of section 152(b)(3)* were applied without regard to all that follows "resident of the United States".

[CCH Explanation at ¶160. Committee Reports at ¶10,140.]

Amendments

- **2004, Working Families Tax Relief Act of 2004 (H.R. 1308)**

H.R. 1308, §204(a):

Amended Code Sec. 24(c)(1). **Effective** for tax years beginning after 12-31-2004. Prior to amendment, Code Sec. 24(c)(1) read as follows:

(1) IN GENERAL.—The term "qualifying child" means any individual if—

(A) the taxpayer is allowed a deduction under section 151 with respect to such individual for the taxable year,

(B) such individual has not attained the age of 17 as of the close of the calendar year in which the taxable year of the taxpayer begins, and

(C) such individual bears a relationship to the taxpayer described in section 32(c)(3)(B).

H.R. 1308, §204(b):

Amended Code Sec. 24(c)(2) by striking "the first sentence of section 152(b)(3)" and inserting "subparagraph (A) of section 152(b)(3)". **Effective** for tax years beginning after 12-31-2004.

(d) PORTION OF CREDIT REFUNDABLE.—

⇛→ Caution: *Code Sec. 24(d)(1), below, was amended by §102(a) and §104(a). For sunset provision, see H.R. 1308, §105, in the amendment notes.*

(1) IN GENERAL.—The aggregate credits allowed to a taxpayer under subpart C shall be increased by the lesser of—

(A) the credit which would be allowed under this section without regard to this subsection and the limitation under subsection (b)(3), or

(B) the amount by which the aggregate amount of credits allowed by this subpart (determined without regard to this subsection) would increase if the limitation imposed by subsection (b)(3) were increased by the greater of—

(i) 15 percent of so much of the taxpayer's earned income (within the meaning of section 32) which is taken into account in computing taxable income for the taxable year as exceeds $10,000, or

(ii) in the case of a taxpayer with 3 or more qualifying children, the excess (if any) of—

(I) the taxpayer's social security taxes for the taxable year, over

(II) the credit allowed under section 32 for the taxable year.

The amount of the credit allowed under this subsection shall not be treated as a credit allowed under this subpart and shall reduce the amount of credit otherwise allowable under subsection (a) without regard to subsection (b)(3). *For purposes of subparagraph (B), any amount excluded from gross income by reason of section 112 shall be treated as earned income which is taken into account in computing taxable income for the taxable year.*

* * *

[CCH Explanation at ¶ 125 and ¶ 180. Committee Reports at ¶ 10,050, ¶ 10,070 and ¶ 10,320.]

Amendments
• 2004, Working Families Tax Relief Act of 2004 (H.R. 1308)

H.R. 1308, § 102(a):

Amended Code Sec. 24(d)(1)(B)(i) by striking "(10 percent in the case of taxable years beginning before January 1, 2005)" following "15 percent". **Effective** for tax years beginning after 12-31-2003.

H.R. 1308, § 104(a):

Amended Code Sec. 24(d)(1) by adding at the end a new sentence. **Effective** for tax years beginning after 12-31-2003.

H.R. 1308, § 105, provides:

SEC. 105. APPLICATION OF EGTRRA SUNSET TO THIS TITLE.

Each amendment made by this title shall be subject to title IX of the Economic Growth and Tax Relief Reconciliation Act of 2001 to the same extent and in the same manner as the provision of such Act to which such amendment relates.

[¶ 5025] CODE SEC. 25B. ELECTIVE DEFERRALS AND IRA CONTRIBUTIONS BY CERTAIN INDIVIDUALS.

* * *

(c) ELIGIBLE INDIVIDUAL.—For purposes of this section—

* * *

(2) DEPENDENTS AND FULL-TIME STUDENTS NOT ELIGIBLE.—The term "eligible individual" shall not include—

(A) any individual with respect to whom a deduction under section 151 is allowed to another taxpayer for a taxable year beginning in the calendar year in which such individual's taxable year begins, and

(B) any individual who is a student (as defined in section 152(f)(2)).

* * *

[CCH Explanation at ¶ 145.]
Amendments
• 2004, Working Families Tax Relief Act of 2004 (H.R. 1308)

H.R. 1308, § 207(4):

Amended Code Sec. 25B(c)(2)(B) by striking "151(c)(4)" and inserting "152(f)(2)". **Effective** for tax years beginning after 12-31-2004.

[¶ 5030] CODE SEC. 26. LIMITATION BASED ON TAX LIABILITY; DEFINITION OF TAX LIABILITY.

(a) LIMITATION BASED ON AMOUNT OF TAX.—

* * *

(2) SPECIAL *RULE FOR TAXABLE YEARS 2000 THROUGH 2005.*—For purposes of any taxable year beginning during 2000, 2001, 2002, *2003, 2004, or 2005,* the aggregate amount of credits allowed by this subpart for the taxable year shall not exceed the sum of—

(A) the taxpayer's regular tax liability for the taxable year reduced by the foreign tax credit allowable under section 27(a), and

(B) the tax imposed by section 55(a) for the taxable year.

[CCH Explanation at ¶ 135. Committee Reports at ¶ 10,320.]

Amendments

• **2004, Working Families Tax Relief Act of 2004 (H.R. 1308)**

H.R. 1308, § 312(a)(1)-(2):

Amended Code Sec. 26(a)(2) by striking "RULE FOR 2000, 2001, 2002, AND 2003.—"and inserting "RULE FOR TAXABLE YEARS 2000 THROUGH 2005.—", and by striking "or 2003" and

inserting "2003, 2004, or 2005". **Effective** for tax years beginning after 12-31-2003.

H.R. 1308, § 312(b)(2), provides:

(2) The amendments made by sections 201(b), 202(f), and 618(b) of the Economic Growth and Tax Relief Reconciliation Act of 2001 shall not apply to taxable years beginning during 2004 or 2005.

(b) REGULAR TAX LIABILITY.—For purposes of this part—

* * *

(2) EXCEPTION FOR CERTAIN TAXES.—For purposes of paragraph (1), any tax imposed by any of the following provisions shall not be treated as tax imposed by this chapter:

(A) section 55 (relating to minimum tax),

(B) section 59A (relating to environmental tax),

(C) subsection (m)(5)(B), (q), (t), or (v) of section 72 (relating to additional taxes on certain distributions),

(D) section 143(m) (relating to recapture of proration of Federal subsidy from use of mortgage bonds and mortgage credit certificates),

(E) section 530(d)(3) (relating to additional tax on certain distributions from Coverdell education savings accounts),

(F) section 531 (relating to accumulated earnings tax),

(G) section 541 (relating to personal holding company tax),

(H) section 1351(d)(1) (relating to recoveries of foreign expropriation losses),

(I) section 1374 (relating to tax on certain certain built-in gains of S corporations),

(J) section 1375 (relating to tax imposed when passive investment income of corporation having subchapter C earnings and profits exceeds 25 percent of gross receipts),

(K) subparagraph (A) of section 7518(g)(6) (relating to nonqualified withdrawals from capital construction funds taxed at highest marginal rate),

(L) sections 871(a) and 881 (relating to certain income of nonresident aliens and foreign corporations),

(M) section 860E(e) (relating to taxes with respect to certain residual interests),

(N) section 884 (relating to branch profits tax),

(O) sections 453(l)(3) and 453A(c) (relating to interest on certain deferred tax liabilities),

(P) section 860K (relating to treatment of transfers of high-yield interests to disqualified holders),

(Q) section 220(f)(4) (relating to additional tax on Archer MSA distributions not used for qualified medical expenses),

(R) section 138(c)(2) (relating to penalty for distributions from *Medicare Advantage MSA* not used for qualified medical expenses if minimum balance not maintained), *and*

(S) section 223(f)(4) (relating to additional tax on health savings account distributions not used for qualified medical expenses).

* * *

[CCH Explanation at ¶ 357 and ¶ 359. Committee Reports at ¶ 10,500 and ¶ 10,570.]

Amendments

• **2004, Working Families Tax Relief Act of 2004 (H.R. 1308)**

H.R. 1308, § 401(a)(1):

Amended Code Sec. 26(b)(2) by striking "and" at the end of subparagraph (Q), by striking the period at the end of subparagraph (R) and inserting ", and", and by adding at the end a new subparagraph (S). **Effective** as if included in

section 1201 of the Medicare Prescription Drug, Improvement, and Modernization Act of 2003 (P.L. 108-173) **[effective for tax years beginning after 12-31-2003.—CCH].**

H.R. 1308, § 408(a)(5)(A):

Amended Code Sec. 26(b)(2) by striking "Medicare+Choice MSA" and inserting "Medicare Advantage MSA". **Effective** on the date of the enactment of this Act.

[¶5035] CODE SEC. 30. CREDIT FOR QUALIFIED ELECTRIC VEHICLES.

* * *

(b) LIMITATIONS.—

(1) LIMITATION PER VEHICLE.—The amount of the credit allowed under subsection (a) for any vehicle shall not exceed $4,000.

(2) PHASEOUT.—*In the case of any qualified electric vehicle placed in service after December 31, 2005, the credit otherwise allowable under subsection (a) (determined after the application of paragraph (1)) shall be reduced by 75 percent.*

* * *

[CCH Explanation at ¶223. Committee Reports at ¶10,380.]

Amendments

• **2004, Working Families Tax Relief Act of 2004 (H.R. 1308)**

H.R. 1308, §318(a):

Amended Code Sec. 30(b)(2). **Effective** for property placed in service after 12-31-2003. Prior to amendment, Code Sec. 30(b)(2) read as follows:

(2) PHASEOUT.—In the case of any qualified electric vehicle placed in service after December 31, 2003, the credit other-

wise allowable under subsection (a) (determined after the application of paragraph (1)) shall be reduced by—

(A) 25 percent in the case of property placed in service in calendar year 2004,

(B) 50 percent in the case of property placed in service in calendar year 2005, and

(C) 75 percent in the case of property placed in service in calendar year 2006.

[¶5040] CODE SEC. 32. EARNED INCOME.

* * *

(c) DEFINITIONS AND SPECIAL RULES.—For purposes of this section—

(1) ELIGIBLE INDIVIDUAL.—

* * *

(C) EXCEPTION FOR INDIVIDUAL CLAIMING BENEFITS UNDER SECTION 911.—The term "eligible individual" does not include any individual who claims the benefits of section 911 (relating to citizens or residents living abroad) for the taxable year.

(D) LIMITATION ON ELIGIBILITY OF NONRESIDENT ALIENS.—The term "eligible individual" shall not include any individual who is a nonresident alien individual for any portion of the taxable year unless such individual is treated for such taxable year as a resident of the United States for purposes of this chapter by reason of an election under subsection (g) or (h) of section 6013.

(E) IDENTIFICATION NUMBER REQUIREMENT.—No credit shall be allowed under this section to an eligible individual who does not include on the return of tax for the taxable year—

(i) such individual's taxpayer identification number, and

(ii) if the individual is married (within the meaning of section 7703), the taxpayer identification number of such individual's spouse.

(F) INDIVIDUALS WHO DO NOT INCLUDE TIN, ETC., OF ANY QUALIFYING CHILD.—No credit shall be allowed under this section to any eligible individual who has one or more qualifying children if no qualifying child of such individual is taken into account under subsection (b) by reason of paragraph (3)(D).

(2) EARNED INCOME.—

* * *

⫸ *Caution: Code Sec. 32(c)(2)(B), below, was amended by §104(b)(1)-(3). For sunset provision, see H.R. 1308, §105, in the amendment notes.*

(B) For purposes of subparagraph (A)—

(i) the earned income of an individual shall be computed without regard to any community property laws,

(ii) no amount received as a pension or annuity shall be taken into account,

(iii) no amount to which section 871(a) applies (relating to income of nonresident alien individuals not connected with United States business) shall be taken into account,

(iv) no amount received for services provided by an individual while the individual is an inmate at a penal institution shall be taken into account,

(v) no amount described in subparagraph (A) received for service performed in work activities as defined in paragraph (4) or (7) of section 407(d) of the Social Security Act to which the taxpayer is assigned under any State program under part A of title IV of such Act shall be taken into account, but only to the extent such amount is subsidized under such State program, *and*

(vi) in the case of any taxable year ending—

(I) after the date of the enactment of this clause, and

(II) (II) before January 1, 2006,

a taxpayer may elect to treat amounts excluded from gross income by reason of section 112 as earned income.

(3) QUALIFYING CHILD.—

(A) IN GENERAL.—*The term "qualifying child" means a qualifying child of the taxpayer (as defined in section 152(c), determined without regard to paragraph (1)(D) thereof and section 152(e)).*

(B) MARRIED INDIVIDUAL.—*The term "qualifying child" shall not include an individual who is married as of the close of the taxpayer's taxable year unless the taxpayer is entitled to a deduction under section 151 for such taxable year with respect to such individual (or would be so entitled but for section 152(e)).*

(C) PLACE OF ABODE.—*For purposes of subparagraph (A), the requirements of section 152(c)(1)(B) shall be met only if the principal place of abode is in the United States.*

(D) IDENTIFICATION REQUIREMENTS.—

(i) IN GENERAL.—*A qualifying child shall not be taken into account under subsection (b) unless the taxpayer includes the name, age, and TIN of the qualifying child on the return of tax for the taxable year.*

(ii) OTHER METHODS.—*The Secretary may prescribe other methods for providing the information described in clause (i).*

(4) TREATMENT OF MILITARY PERSONNEL STATIONED OUTSIDE THE UNITED STATES.—For purposes of paragraphs (1)(A)(ii)(I) and (3)(C), the principal place of abode of a member of the Armed Forces of the United States shall be treated as in the United States during any period during which such member is stationed outside the United States while serving on extended active duty with the Armed Forces of the United States. For purposes of the preceding sentence, the term "extended active duty" means any period of active duty pursuant to a call or order to such duty for a period in excess of 90 days or for an indefinite period.

* * *

[CCH Explanation at ¶165 and ¶180. Committee Reports at ¶10,070 and ¶10,150.]

Amendments

• 2004, Working Families Tax Relief Act of 2004 (H.R. 1308)

H.R. 1308, §104(b)(1)-(3):

Amended Code Sec. 32(c)(2)(B) by striking "and" at the end of clause (iv), by striking the period at the end of clause (v) and inserting ", and", and by adding at the end a new clause (vi). **Effective** for tax years ending after the date of the enactment of this Act.

H.R. 1308, §105, provides:

SEC. 105. APPLICATION OF EGTRRA SUNSET TO THIS TITLE.

Each amendment made by this title shall be subject to title IX of the Economic Growth and Tax Relief Reconciliation Act of 2001 to the same extent and in the same manner as the provision of such Act to which such amendment relates.

H.R. 1308, §205(a):

Amended Code Sec. 32(c)(3). **Effective** for tax years beginning after 12-31-2004. Prior to amendment, Code Sec. 32(c)(3) read as follows:

(3) QUALIFYING CHILD.—

(A) IN GENERAL.—The term "qualifying child" means, with respect to any taxpayer for any taxable year, an individual—

(i) who bears a relationship to the taxpayer described in subparagraph (B),

(ii) who has the same principal place of abode as the taxpayer for more than one-half of such taxable year, and

(iii) who meets the age requirements of subparagraph (C).

(B) RELATIONSHIP TEST.—

(i) IN GENERAL.—An individual bears a relationship to the taxpayer described in this subparagraph if such individual is—

(I) a son, daughter, stepson, or stepdaughter, or a descendant of any such individual,

(II) a brother, sister, stepbrother, or stepsister, or a descendant of any such individual, who the taxpayer cares for as the taxpayer's own child, or

(III) an eligible foster child of the taxpayer.

(ii) MARRIED CHILDREN.—Clause (i) shall not apply to any individual who is married as of the close of the taxpayer's taxable year unless the taxpayer is entitled to a deduction under section 151 for such taxable year with respect to such individual (or would be so entitled but for paragraph (2) or (4) of section 152(e)).

(iii) ELIGIBLE FOSTER CHILD.—For purposes of clause (i), the term "eligible foster child" means an individual not described in subclause (I) or (II) of clause (i) who—

(I) is placed with the taxpayer by an authorized placement agency, and

(II) the taxpayer cares for as the taxpayer's own child.

(iv) ADOPTION.—For purposes of this subparagraph, a child who is legally adopted, or who is placed with the taxpayer by an authorized placement agency for adoption by the taxpayer, shall be treated as a child by blood.

(C) AGE REQUIREMENTS.—An individual meets the requirements of this subparagraph if such individual—

(i) has not attained the age of 19 as of the close of the calendar year in which the taxable year of the taxpayer begins,

(ii) is a student (as defined in section 151(c)(4)) who has not attained the age of 24 as of the close of such calendar year, or

(iii) is permanently and totally disabled (as defined in section 22(e)(3)) at any time during the taxable year.

(D) IDENTIFICATION REQUIREMENTS.—

(i) IN GENERAL.—A qualifying child shall not be taken into account under subsection (b) unless the taxpayer includes

the name, age, and TIN of the qualifying child on the return of tax for the taxable year.

(ii) OTHER METHODS.—The Secretary may prescribe other methods for providing the information described in clause (i).

(E) ABODE MUST BE IN THE UNITED STATES.—The requirements of subparagraph (A)(ii) shall be met only if the principal place of abode is in the United States.

H.R. 1308, § 205(b)(1):

Amended Code Sec. 32(c)(1) by striking subparagraph (C) and by redesignating subparagraphs (D), (E), (F), and (G) as subparagraphs (C), (D), (E), and (F), respectively. **Effective** for tax years beginning after 12-31-2004. Prior to being stricken, Code Sec. 32(c)(1)(C) read as follows:

(C) 2 OR MORE CLAIMING QUALIFYING CHILD.—

(i) IN GENERAL.—Except as provided in clause (ii), if (but for this paragraph) an individual may be claimed, and is claimed, as a qualifying child by 2 or more taxpayers for a taxable year beginning in the same calendar year, such individual shall be treated as the qualifying child of the taxpayer who is—

(I) a parent of the individual, or

(II) if subclause (I) does not apply, the taxpayer with the highest adjusted gross income for such taxable year.

(ii) MORE THAN 1 CLAIMING CREDIT.—If the parents claiming the credit with respect to any qualifying child do not file a joint return together, such child shall be treated as the qualifying child of—

(I) the parent with whom the child resided for the longest period of time during the taxable year, or

(II) if the child resides with both parents for the same amount of time during such taxable year, the parent with the highest adjusted gross income.

H.R. 1308, § 205(b)(2):

Amended Code Sec. 32(c)(4) by striking "(3)(E)" and inserting "(3)(C)". **Effective** for tax years beginning after 12-31-2004.

(m) IDENTIFICATION NUMBERS.—Solely for purposes of *subsections (c)(1)(E)* and (c)(3)(D), a taxpayer identification number means a social security number issued to an individual by the Social Security Administration (other than a social security number issued pursuant to clause (II) (or that portion of clause (III) that relates to clause (II)) of section 205(c)(2)(B)(i) of the Social Security Act).

[CCH Explanation at ¶ 165. Committee Reports at ¶ 10,150]
Amendments

• **2004, Working Families Tax Relief Act of 2004 (H.R. 1308)**

H.R. 1308, § 205(b)(3):

Amended Code Sec. 32(m) by striking "subsections (c)(1)(F)" and inserting "subsections (c)(1)(E)". **Effective** for tax years beginning after 12-31-2004.

[¶ 5045] CODE SEC. 35. HEALTH INSURANCE COSTS OF ELIGIBLE INDIVIDUALS.

* * *

(g) SPECIAL RULES.—

* * *

(3) *MEDICAL AND HEALTH SAVINGS ACCOUNTS.—Amounts distributed from an Archer MSA (as defined in section 220(d)) or from a health savings account (as defined in section 223(d)) shall not be taken into account under subsection (a).*

* * *

[CCH Explanation at ¶357. Committee Reports at ¶10,500.]

Amendments

• **2004, Working Families Tax Relief Act of 2004 (H.R. 1308)**

H.R. 1308, §401(a)(2):

Amended Code Sec. 35(g)(3). **Effective** as if included in section 1201 of the Medicare Prescription Drug, Improve-

ment, and Modernization Act of 2003 (P.L. 108-173) **[effective** for tax years beginning after 12-31-2003.—CCH]. Prior to amendment, Code Sec 35(g)(3) read as follows:

(3) MSA DISTRIBUTIONS.—Amounts distributed from an Archer MSA (as defined in section 220(d)) shall not be taken into account under subsection (a).

[¶5050] CODE SEC. 41. CREDIT FOR INCREASING RESEARCH ACTIVITIES.

* * *

(h) TERMINATION.—

(1) IN GENERAL.—This section shall not apply to any amount paid or incurred—

(A) after June 30, 1995, and before July 1, 1996, or

(B) after *December 31, 2005.*

* * *

[CCH Explanation at ¶205. Committee Reports at ¶10,200.]

Amendments

• **2004, Working Families Tax Relief Act of 2004 (H.R. 1308)**

H.R. 1308, §301(a)(1):

Amended Code Sec. 41(h)(1)(B) by striking "June 30, 2004" and inserting "December 31, 2005". **Effective** for amounts paid or incurred after 6-30-2004.

[¶5055] CODE SEC. 42. LOW-INCOME HOUSING CREDIT.

* * *

(d) ELIGIBLE BASIS.—For purposes of this section—

* * *

(2) EXISTING BUILDINGS.—

* * *

(D) SPECIAL RULES FOR SUBPARAGRAPH (B).—

* * *

(iii) RELATED PERSON, ETC.—

(I) APPLICATION OF SECTION 179.—For purposes of subparagraph (B)(i), section 179(d) shall be applied by substituting "10 percent" for "50 percent" in section 267(b) and 707(b) and in *section 179(d)(7).*

* * *

[CCH Explanation at ¶30,050. Committee Reports at ¶10,570.]

Amendments

• **2004, Working Families Tax Relief Act of 2004 (H.R. 1308)**

H.R. 1308, §408(a)(3):

Amended Code Sec. 42(d)(2)(D)(iii)(I) by striking "section 179(b)(7)" and inserting "section 179(d)(7)". **Effective** on the date of the enactment of this Act.

(i) DEFINITIONS AND SPECIAL RULES.—For purposes of this section—

* * *

(3) LOW-INCOME UNIT.—

* * *

(D) CERTAIN STUDENTS NOT TO DISQUALIFY UNIT.—A unit shall not fail to be treated as a low-income unit merely because it is occupied—

(i) by an individual who is—

(I) a student and receiving assistance under title IV of the Social Security Act, or

(II) enrolled in a job training program receiving assistance under the Job Training Partnership Act or under other similar Federal, State, or local laws, or

(ii) entirely by full-time students if such students are—

(I) single parents and their children and such parents and children are not dependents (as defined in section 152, *determined without regard to subsections (b)(1), (b)(2), and (d)(1)(B) thereof*) of another individual, or

(II) married and file a joint return.

* * *

[CCH Explanation at ¶ 145.]

Amendments

• 2004, Working Families Tax Relief Act of 2004 (H.R. 1308)

H.R. 1308, § 207(8):

Amended Code Sec. 42(i)(3)(D)(ii)(I) by inserting ", determined without regard to subsections (b)(1), (b)(2), and

(d)(1)(B) thereof" after "section 152". **Effective** for tax years beginning after 12-31-2004.

[¶ 5060] CODE SEC. 45. ELECTRICITY PRODUCED FROM CERTAIN RENEWABLE RESOURCES.

* * *

(c) DEFINITIONS.—For purposes of this section—

* * *

(3) QUALIFIED FACILITY.—

(A) WIND FACILITY.—In the case of a facility using wind to produce electricity, the term "qualified facility" means any facility owned by the taxpayer which is originally placed in service after December 31, 1993, and before *January 1, 2006*.

(B) CLOSED-LOOP BIOMASS FACILITY.—In the case of a facility using closed-loop biomass to produce electricity, the term "qualified facility" means any facility owned by the taxpayer which is originally placed in service after December 31, 1992, and before *January 1, 2006*.

(C) POULTRY WASTE FACILITY.—In the case of a facility using poultry waste to produce electricity, the term "qualified facility" means any facility of the taxpayer which is originally placed in service after December 31, 1999, and before *January 1, 2006*.

* * *

[CCH Explanation at ¶ 227. Committee Reports at ¶ 10,330.]

Amendments

• 2004, Working Families Tax Relief Act of 2004 (H.R. 1308)

H.R. 1308, § 313(a):

Amended Code Sec. 45(c)(3)(A)-(C) by striking "January 1, 2004" and inserting "January 1, 2006". **Effective** for facilities placed in service after 12-31-2003.

[¶ 5065] CODE SEC. 45A. INDIAN EMPLOYMENT CREDIT.

* * *

(c) QUALIFIED EMPLOYEE.—For purposes of this section—

* * *

(3) INFLATION ADJUSTMENT.—The Secretary shall adjust the $30,000 amount under paragraph (2) for years beginning after 1994 at the same time and in the same manner as under section 415(d), *except that the base period taken into account for purposes of such adjustment shall be the calendar quarter beginning October 1, 1993.*

* * *

[CCH Explanation at ¶343. Committee Reports at ¶10,530.]

Amendments

• **2004, Working Families Tax Relief Act of 2004 (H.R. 1308)**

H.R. 1308, §404(b)(1):

Amended Code Sec. 45A(c)(3) by inserting ", except that the base period taken into account for purposes of such

adjustment shall be the calendar quarter beginning October 1, 1993" before the period at the end. **Effective** as if included in the provision of the Economic Growth and Tax Relief Reconciliation Act of 2001 (P.L. 107-16) to which it relates [**effective** for years beginning after 12-31-2001.—CCH].

(f) TERMINATION.—This section shall not apply to taxable years beginning after *December 31, 2005.*

[CCH Explanation at ¶215. Committee Reports at ¶10,350.]

Amendments

• **2004, Working Families Tax Relief Act of 2004 (H.R. 1308)**

H.R. 1308, §315:

Amended Code Sec. 45A(f) by striking "December 31, 2004" and inserting "December 31, 2005". **Effective** on the date of the enactment of this Act.

[¶5070] CODE SEC. 45C. CLINICAL TESTING EXPENSES FOR CERTAIN DRUGS FOR RARE DISEASES OR CONDITIONS.

* * *

(b) QUALIFIED CLINICAL TESTING EXPENSES.—For purposes of this section—

(1) QUALIFIED CLINICAL TESTING EXPENSES.—

* * *

(D) SPECIAL RULE.—For purposes of this paragraph, section 41 shall be deemed to remain in effect for periods after June 30, 1995, and before July 1, 1996, and periods after *December 31, 2005.*

* * *

[CCH Explanation at ¶205. Committee Reports at ¶10,200.]

Amendments

• **2004, Working Families Tax Relief Act of 2004 (H.R. 1308)**

H.R. 1308, §301(a)(2):

Amended Code Sec. 45C(b)(1)(D) by striking "June 30, 2004" and inserting "December 31, 2005". **Effective** for amounts paid or incurred after 6-30-2004.

[¶5075] CODE SEC. 51. AMOUNT OF CREDIT.

* * *

(c) WAGES DEFINED.—For purposes of this subpart—

* * *

(4) TERMINATION.—The term "wages" shall not include any amount paid or incurred to an individual who begins work for the employer—

(A) after December 31, 1994, and before October 1, 1996, or

(B) after *December 31, 2005.*

[CCH Explanation at ¶211. Committee Reports at ¶10,220.]
Amendments

• 2004, Working Families Tax Relief Act of 2004
(H.R. 1308)

H.R. 1308, §303(a)(1):

Amended Code Sec. 51(c)(4) by striking "December 31, 2003" and inserting "December 31, 2005". **Effective** for individuals who begin work for the employer after 12-31-2003.

(i) CERTAIN INDIVIDUALS INELIGIBLE.—

(1) RELATED INDIVIDUALS.—No wages shall be taken into account under subsection (a) with respect to an individual who—

(A) bears any of the relationships described in *subparagraphs (A) through (G) of section 152(d)(2)* to the taxpayer, or, if the taxpayer is a corporation, to an individual who owns, directly or indirectly, more than 50 percent in value of the outstanding stock of the corporation, or, if the taxpayer is an entity other than a corporation, to any individual who owns, directly or indirectly, more than 50 percent of the capital and profits interests in the entity (determined with the application of section 267(c)),

(B) if the taxpayer is an estate or trust, is a grantor, beneficiary, or fiduciary of the estate or trust, or is an individual who bears any of the relationships described in *subparagraphs (A) through (G) of section 152(d)(2)* to a grantor, beneficiary, or fiduciary of the estate or trust, or

(C) is a dependent (described in section *152(d)(2)(H)*) of the taxpayer, or, if the taxpayer is a corporation, of an individual described in subparagraph (A), or, if the taxpayer is an estate or trust, of a grantor, beneficiary, or fiduciary of the estate or trust.

* * *

[CCH Explanation at ¶145.]
Amendments

• 2004, Working Families Tax Relief Act of 2004
(H.R. 1308)

H.R. 1308, §207(5)(A):

Amended Code Sec. 51(i)(1)(A) and (B) by striking "paragraphs (1) through (8) of section 152(a)" both places it appears and inserting "subparagraphs (A) through (G) of section 152(d)(2)". **Effective** for tax years beginning after 12-31-2004.

H.R. 1308, §207(5)(B):

Amended Code Sec. 51(i)(1)(C) by striking "152(a)(9)" and inserting "152(d)(2)(H)". **Effective** for tax years beginning after 12-31-2004.

[¶5080] CODE SEC. 51A. TEMPORARY INCENTIVES FOR EMPLOYING LONG-TERM FAMILY ASSISTANCE RECIPIENTS.

* * *

(f) TERMINATION.—This section shall not apply to individuals who begin work for the employer after *December 31, 2005.*

[CCH Explanation at ¶213. Committee Reports at ¶10,230.]
Amendments

• 2004, Working Families Tax Relief Act of 2004
(H.R. 1308)

H.R. 1308, §303(a)(2):

Amended Code Sec. 51A(f) by striking "December 31, 2003" and inserting "December 31, 2005". **Effective** for individuals who begin work for the employer after 12-31-2003.

[¶5085] CODE SEC. 55. ALTERNATIVE MINIMUM TAX IMPOSED.

* * *

(b) TENTATIVE MINIMUM TAX.—For purposes of this part—

* * *

(3) MAXIMUM RATE OF TAX ON NET CAPITAL GAIN OF NONCORPORATE TAXPAYERS.—The amount determined under the first sentence of paragraph (1)(A)(i) shall not exceed the sum of—

(A) the amount determined under such first sentence computed at the rates and in the same manner as if this paragraph had not been enacted on the taxable excess reduced by the lesser of—

(i) the net capital gain; or

(ii) the sum of—

(I) the adjusted net capital gain, plus

(II) the unrecaptured section 1250 gain, plus

(B) 5 percent (0 percent in the case of taxable years beginning after 2007) of so much of the adjusted net capital gain (or, if less, taxable excess) as does not exceed *an amount equal to the excess described in* section 1(h)(1)(B), plus

(C) 15 percent of the adjusted net capital gain (or, if less, taxable excess) in excess of the amount on which tax is determined under subparagraph (B), plus

(D) 25 percent of the amount of taxable excess in excess of the sum of the amounts on which tax is determined under the preceding subparagraphs of this paragraph.

Terms used in this paragraph which are also used in section 1(h) shall have the respective meanings given such terms by section 1(h) but computed with the adjustments under this part.

[CCH Explanation at ¶315. Committee Reports at ¶10,550.]

Amendments

• 2004, Working Families Tax Relief Act of 2004 (H.R. 1308)

H.R. 1308, §406(d):

Amended Code Sec. 55(b)(3)(B) by striking "the amount on which a tax is determined under" and inserting "an amount equal to the excess described in". **Effective** as if included in the provision of the Taxpayer Relief Act of 1997 (P.L. 105-34) to which it relates [effective for tax years ending after 5-6-1997.—CCH].

(d) EXEMPTION AMOUNT.—For purposes of this section—

»»→ Caution: Code Sec. 55(d)(1)(A)-(B), below, was amended by §103(a). For sunset provision, see H.R. 1308, §105, in the amendment notes.

(1) EXEMPTION AMOUNT FOR TAXPAYERS OTHER THAN CORPORATIONS.—In the case of a taxpayer other than a corporation, the term "exemption amount" means—

(A) $45,000 ($58,000 in the case of taxable years beginning in *2003, 2004, and 2005*) in the case of—

(i) a joint return, or

(ii) a surviving spouse,

(B) $33,750 ($40,250 in the case of taxable years beginning in *2003, 2004, and 2005*) in the case of an individual who—

(i) is not a married individual, and

(ii) is not a surviving spouse,

(C) 50 percent of the dollar amount applicable under paragraph (1)(A) in the case of a married individual who files a separate return, and

(D) $22,500 in the case of an estate or trust.

For purposes of this paragraph, the term "surviving spouse" has the meaning given to such term by section 2(a), and marital status shall be determined under section 7703.

* * *

[CCH Explanation at ¶130. Committee Reports at ¶10,060.]

Amendments

• 2004, Working Families Tax Relief Act of 2004 (H.R. 1308)

H.R. 1308, §103(a):

Amended Code Sec. 55(d)(1)(A)-(B) by striking "2003 and 2004" and inserting "2003, 2004, and 2005". **Effective** for tax years beginning after 12-31-2004.

H.R. 1308, §105, provides:

SEC. 105. APPLICATION OF EGTRRA SUNSET TO THIS TITLE.

Each amendment made by this title shall be subject to title IX of the Economic Growth and Tax Relief Reconciliation Act of 2001 to the same extent and in the same manner as the provision of such Act to which such amendment relates.

[¶5090] CODE SEC. 56. ADJUSTMENTS IN COMPUTING ALTERNATIVE MINIMUM TAXABLE INCOME.

* * *

(d) ALTERNATIVE TAX NET OPERATING LOSS DEDUCTION DEFINED.—

(1) IN GENERAL.—For purposes of subsection (a)(4), the term "alternative tax net operating loss deduction" means the net operating loss deduction allowable for the taxable year under section 172, except that—

(A) the amount of such deduction shall not exceed the sum of—

(i) the lesser of—

(I) the amount of such deduction attributable to net operating losses (other than the deduction described in clause (ii)(I)), or

(II) 90 percent of alternative minimum taxable income determined without regard to such deduction, plus

(ii) the lesser of—

(I) the amount of such deduction attributable to the sum of carrybacks of net operating losses *from taxable years* ending during 2001 or 2002 and *carryovers* of net operating losses to taxable years ending during 2001 and 2002, or

(II) alternative minimum taxable income determined without regard to such deduction reduced by the amount determined under clause (i), and

(B) in determining the amount of such deduction—

(i) the net operating loss (within the meaning of section 172(c)) for any loss year shall be adjusted as provided in paragraph (2), and

(ii) appropriate adjustments in the application of section 172(b)(2) shall be made to take into account the limitation of subparagraph (A).

* * *

[CCH Explanation at ¶321. Committee Reports at ¶10,520.]

Amendments

• 2004, Working Families Tax Relief Act of 2004 (H.R. 1308)

H.R. 1308, §403(b)(4)(A):

Amended Code Sec. 56(d)(1)(A)(i)(I) by striking "attributable to carryovers" following "(other than the deduction". **Effective** as if included in the provision of the Job Creation and Worker Assistance Act of 2002 (P.L. 107-147) to which it relates [**effective** for tax years after 12-31-1990.—CCH].

H.R. 1308, §403(b)(4)(B)(i)-(ii):

Amended Code Sec. 56(d)(1)(A)(ii)(I) by striking "for taxable years" and inserting "from taxable years", and by striking "carryforwards" and inserting "carryovers". **Effective** as if included in the provision of the Job Creation and Worker Assistance Act of 2002 (P.L. 107-147) to which it relates [**effective** for tax years after 12-31-1990.—CCH].

[¶5095] CODE SEC. 62. ADJUSTED GROSS INCOME DEFINED.

(a) GENERAL RULE.—For purposes of this subtitle, the term "adjusted gross income" means, in the case of an individual, gross income minus the following deductions:

* * *

(2) CERTAIN TRADE AND BUSINESS DEDUCTIONS OF EMPLOYEES.—

* * *

(D) CERTAIN EXPENSES OF ELEMENTARY AND SECONDARY SCHOOL TEACHERS.—In the case of taxable years beginning during 2002 , *2003, 2004, or 2005*, the deductions allowed by section 162 which consist of expenses, not in excess of $250, paid or incurred by an eligible educator in connection with books, supplies (other than nonathletic supplies for courses of instruction in health or physical education), computer equipment (including related software and services) and other equipment, and supplementary materials used by the eligible educator in the classroom.

* * *

[CCH Explanation at ¶185. Committee Reports at ¶10,270.]

Amendments

• **2004, Working Families Tax Relief Act of 2004 (H.R. 1308)**

H.R. 1308, §307(a):

Amended Code Sec. 62(a)(2)(D) by striking "or 2003" and inserting ", 2003, 2004, or 2005". **Effective** for expenses paid or incurred in tax years beginning after 12-31-2003.

[¶5100] CODE SEC. 63. TAXABLE INCOME DEFINED.

* * *

(c) STANDARD DEDUCTION.—For purposes of this subtitle—

* * *

⋙→ Caution: *Code Sec. 63(c)(2), below, was amended by §101(b)(1). For sunset provision, see H.R. 1308, §105, in the amendment notes.*

(2) BASIC STANDARD DEDUCTION.—*For purposes of paragraph (1), the basic standard deduction is—*

(A) *200 percent of the dollar amount in effect under subparagraph (C) for the taxable year in the case of—*

(i) *a joint return, or*

(ii) *a surviving spouse (as defined in section 2(a)),*

(B) *$4,400 in the case of a head of household (as defined in section 2(b)), or*

(C) *$3,000 in any other case.*

* * *

⋙→ Caution: *Code Sec. 63(c)(4), below, was amended by §101(b)(2)(A). For sunset provision, see H.R. 1308, §105, in the amendment notes.*

(4) ADJUSTMENTS FOR INFLATION.—In the case of any taxable year beginning in a calendar year after 1988, each dollar amount contained in paragraph (2)(B), (2)(C), or (5) or subsection (f) shall be increased by an amount equal to—

(A) such dollar amount, multiplied by

(B) the cost-of-living adjustment determined under section 1(f)(3) for the calendar year in which the taxable year begins, by substituting for "calendar year 1992" in subparagraph (B) thereof—

(i) "calendar year 1987" in the case of the dollar amounts contained in paragraph (2)(B), (2)(C), or (5)(A) or subsection (f), and

(ii) "calendar year 1997" in the case of the dollar amount contained in paragraph (5)(B).

* * *

⋙→ Caution: *Code Sec. 63(c)(7), below, was stricken by §101(b)(2)(B). For sunset provision, see H.R. 1308, §105, in the amendment notes.*

(7) [*Stricken.*]

* * *

[CCH Explanation at ¶110. Committee Reports at ¶10,020.]

Amendments

• **2004, Working Families Tax Relief Act of 2004 (H.R. 1308)**

H.R. 1308, §101(b)(1):

Amended Code Sec. 63(c)(2). **Effective** for tax years beginning after 12-31-2003. Prior to amendment, Code Sec. 63(c)(2) read as follows:

(2) BASIC STANDARD DEDUCTION.—For purposes of paragraph (1), the basic standard deduction is—

(A) the applicable percentage of the dollar amount in effect under subparagraph (D) for the taxable year in the case of—

(i) a joint return, or

(ii) a surviving spouse (as defined in section 2(a)),

(B) $4,400 in the case of a head of household (as defined in section 2(b)),

(C) one-half of the amount in effect under subparagraph (A) in the case of a married individual filing a separate return, or

(D) $3,000 in any other case.

If any amount determined under subparagraph (A) is not a multiple of $50, such amount shall be rounded to the next lowest multiple of $50.

H.R. 1308, §101(b)(2)(A):

Amended Code Sec. 63(c)(4) by striking "(2)(D)" each place it occurs and inserting "(2)(C)". **Effective** for tax years beginning after 12-31-2003.

H.R. 1308, §101(b)(2)(B):

Amended Code Sec. 63(c) by striking paragraph (7). **Effective** for tax years beginning after 12-31-2003. Prior to being stricken, Code Sec. 63(c)(7) read as follows:

(7) APPLICABLE PERCENTAGE.—For purposes of paragraph (2), the applicable percentage shall be determined in accordance with the following table:

For taxable years beginning in calendar year—	The applicable percentage is—
2003 and 2004	200
2005	174
2006	184
2007	187
2008	190
2009 and thereafter	200.

H.R. 1308, §105, provides:

SEC. 105. APPLICATION OF EGTRRA SUNSET TO THIS TITLE.

Each amendment made by this title shall be subject to title IX of the Economic Growth and Tax Relief Reconciliation Act of 2001 to the same extent and in the same manner as the provision of such Act to which such amendment relates.

[¶5105] CODE SEC. 72. ANNUITIES; CERTAIN PROCEEDS OF ENDOWMENT AND LIFE INSURANCE CONTRACTS.

* * *

(f) SPECIAL RULES FOR COMPUTING EMPLOYEES' CONTRIBUTIONS.—In computing, for purposes of subsection (c)(1)(A), the aggregate amount of premiums or other consideration paid for the contract, and for purposes of subsection (e)(6), the aggregate premiums or other consideration paid, amounts contributed by the employer shall be included, but only to the extent that—

(1) such amounts were includible in the gross income of the employee under this subtitle or prior income tax laws; or

(2) if such amounts had been paid directly to the employee at the time they were contributed, they would not have been includible in the gross income of the employee under the law applicable at the time of such contribution.

Paragraph (2) shall not apply to amounts which were contributed by the employer after December 31, 1962, and which would not have been includible in the gross income of the employee by reason of the application of section 911 if such amounts had been paid directly to the employee at the time of contribution. The preceding sentence shall not apply to amounts which were contributed by the employer, as determined under regulations prescribed by the Secretary, to provide pension or annuity credits, to the extent such credits are attributable to services performed before January 1, 1963, and are provided pursuant to pension or annuity plan provisions in existence on March 12, 1962, and on that date applicable to such services, or to the extent such credits are attributable to services performed as a foreign missionary (within the meaning of section 403(b)(2)(D)(iii), as in effect before the enactment of the *Economic Growth and Tax Relief Reconciliation Act of 2001).*

* * *

[CCH Explanation at ¶30,050. Committee Reports at ¶10,570.]

Amendments

• **2004, Working Families Tax Relief Act of 2004 (H.R. 1308)**

H.R. 1308, §408(a)(4):

Amended Code Sec. 72(f) by striking "Economic Growth and Tax Relief Reconciliation Act of 2001" and inserting

"Economic Growth and Tax Relief Reconciliation Act of 2001)". **Effective** on the date of the enactment of this Act.

(t) 10-PERCENT ADDITIONAL TAX ON EARLY DISTRIBUTIONS FROM QUALIFIED RETIREMENT PLANS.—

* * *

(2) SUBSECTION NOT TO APPLY TO CERTAIN DISTRIBUTIONS.—Except as provided in paragraphs (3) and (4), paragraph (1) shall not apply to any of the following distributions:

* * *

(D) Distributions to Unemployed Individuals for Health Insurance Premiums.—

(i) In General.—Distributions from an individual retirement plan to an individual after separation from employment—

(I) if such individual has received unemployment compensation for 12 consecutive weeks under any Federal or State unemployment compensation law by reason of such separation,

(II) if such distributions are made during any taxable year during which such unemployment compensation is paid or the succeeding taxable year, and

(III) to the extent such distributions do not exceed the amount paid during the taxable year for insurance described in section 213(d)(1)(D) with respect to the individual and the individual's spouse and dependents (as defined in section 152, *determined without regard to subsections (b)(1), (b)(2), and (d)(1)(B) thereof*).

(ii) Distributions After Reemployment.—Clause (i) shall not apply to any distribution made after the individual has been employed for at least 60 days after the separation from employment to which clause (i) applies.

(iii) Self-Employed Individuals.—To the extent provided in regulations, a self-employed individual shall be treated as meeting the requirements of clause (i)(I) if, under Federal or State law, the individual would have received unemployment compensation but for the fact the individual was self-employed.

* * *

(7) Qualified Higher Education Expenses.—For purposes of paragraph (2)(E)—

(A) In General.—The term "qualified higher education expenses" means qualified higher education expenses (as defined in section 529(e)(3)) for education furnished to—

* * *

(iii) any child (as defined in section *152(f)(1)*) or grandchild of the taxpayer or the taxpayer's spouse, at an eligible educational institution (as defined in section 529(e)(5)).

* * *

[CCH Explanation at ¶145.]

Amendments

• **2004, Working Families Tax Relief Act of 2004 (H.R. 1308)**

H.R. 1308, §207(6):

Amended Code Sec. 72(t)(2)(D)(i)(III) by inserting ", determined without regard to subsections (b)(1), (b)(2), and (d)(1)(B) thereof" after "section 152". **Effective** for tax years beginning after 12-31-2004.

H.R. 1308, §207(7):

Amended Code Sec. 72(t)(7)(A)(iii) by striking "151(c)(3)" and inserting "152(f)(1)". **Effective** for tax years beginning after 12-31-2004.

[¶5110] CODE SEC. 105. AMOUNTS RECEIVED UNDER ACCIDENT AND HEALTH PLANS.

* * *

(b) Amounts Expended for Medical Care.—Except in the case of amounts attributable to (and not in excess of) deductions allowed under section 213 (relating to medical, etc., expenses) for any prior taxable year, gross income does not include amounts referred to in subsection (a) if such amounts are paid, directly or indirectly, to the taxpayer to reimburse the taxpayer for expenses incurred by him for the medical care (as defined in section 213(d)) of the taxpayer, his spouse, and his dependents (as defined in section 152, *determined without regard to subsections (b)(1), (b)(2), and (d)(1)(B) thereof*). Any child to whom section 152(e) applies shall be treated as a dependent of both parents for purposes of this subsection.

[CCH Explanation at ¶ 145.]
Amendments
• **2004, Working Families Tax Relief Act of 2004**
(H.R. 1308)

[CCH Explanation at ¶ 145.]

Amendments

• **2004, Working Families Tax Relief Act of 2004 (H.R. 1308)**

therof" after "section 152". **Effective** for tax years beginning after 12-31-2004.

H.R. 1308, § 207(9):

Amended Code Sec. 105(b) by inserting ", determined without regard to subsections (b)(1), (b)(2), and (d)(1)(B)

(c) PAYMENTS UNRELATED TO ABSENCE FROM WORK.—Gross income does not include amounts referred to in subsection (a) to the extent such amounts—

(1) constitute payment for the permanent loss or loss of use of a member or function of the body, or the permanent disfigurement, of the taxpayer, his spouse, or a dependent (as defined in section 152, *determined without regard to subsections (b)(1), (b)(2), and (d)(1)(B) thereof*), and

(2) are computed with reference to the nature of the injury without regard to the period the employee is absent from work.

* * *

[CCH Explanation at ¶ 145.]

Amendments

• **2004, Working Families Tax Relief Act of 2004 (H.R. 1308)**

therof" after "section 152". **Effective** for tax years beginning after 12-31-2004.

H.R. 1308, § 207(9):

Amended Code Sec. 105(c)(1) by inserting ", determined without regard to subsections (b)(1), (b)(2), and (d)(1)(B)

[¶ 5115] CODE SEC. 120. AMOUNTS RECEIVED UNDER QUALIFIED GROUP LEGAL SERVICES PLANS.

* * *

(d) OTHER DEFINITIONS AND SPECIAL RULES.—For purposes of this section—

* * *

(4) DEPENDENT.—The term "dependent" has the meaning given to it by section 152(*determined without regard to subsections (b)(1), (b)(2), and (d)(1)(B) thereof*).

* * *

[CCH Explanation at ¶ 145.]

Amendments

• **2004, Working Families Tax Relief Act of 2004 (H.R. 1308)**

therof)" after "section 152". **Effective** for tax years beginning after 12-31-2004.

H.R. 1308, § 207(10):

Amended Code Sec. 120(d)(4) by inserting "(determined without regard to subsections (b)(1), (b)(2), and (d)(1)(B)

[¶ 5120] CODE SEC. 125. CAFETERIA PLANS.

* * *

(e) HIGHLY COMPENSATED PARTICIPANT AND INDIVIDUAL DEFINED.—For purposes of this section—

(1) HIGHLY COMPENSATED PARTICIPANT.—The term "highly compensated participant" means a participant who is—

* * *

(D) a spouse or dependent (within the meaning of section 152, *determined without regard to subsections (b)(1), (b)(2), and (d)(1)(B) thereof*) of an individual described in subparagraph (A), (B), or (C).

* * *

[CCH Explanation at ¶145.]

Amendments

• **2004, Working Families Tax Relief Act of 2004 (H.R. 1308)**

H.R. 1308, §207(11):

Amended Code Sec. 125(e)(1)(D) by inserting ", determined without regard to subsections (b)(1), (b)(2), and

(d)(1)(B) therof" after "section 152". **Effective** for tax years beginning after 12-31-2004.

[¶5125] CODE SEC. 129. DEPENDENT CARE ASSISTANCE PROGRAMS.

* * *

(c) PAYMENTS TO RELATED INDIVIDUALS.—No amount paid or incurred during the taxable year of an employee by an employer in providing dependent care assistance to such employee shall be excluded under subsection (a) if such amount was paid or incurred to an individual—

(1) with respect to whom, for such taxable year, a deduction is allowable under section 151(c) (relating to personal exemptions for dependents) to such employee or the spouse of such employee, or

(2) who is a child of such employee (within the meaning of section *152(f)(1)*) under the age of 19 at the close of such taxable year.

* * *

[CCH Explanation at ¶145.]

Amendments

• **2004, Working Families Tax Relief Act of 2004 (H.R. 1308)**

H.R. 1308, §207(12):

Amended Code Sec. 129(c)(2) by striking "151(c)(3)" and inserting "152(f)(1)". **Effective** for tax years beginning after 12-31-2004.

[¶5130] CODE SEC. 132. CERTAIN FRINGE BENEFITS.

* * *

(h) CERTAIN INDIVIDUALS TREATED AS EMPLOYEES FOR PURPOSES OF SUBSECTIONS (a)(1) AND (2).—For purposes of paragraphs (1) and (2) of subsection (a)—

* * *

(2) SPOUSE AND DEPENDENT CHILDREN.—

* * *

(B) DEPENDENT CHILD.—For purposes of subparagraph (A), the term "dependent child" means any child (as defined in section *152(f)(1)*) of the employee—

(i) who is a dependent of the employee, or

(ii) both of whose parents are deceased and who has not attained age 25.

For purposes of the preceding sentence, any child to whom section 152(e) applies shall be treated as the dependent of both parents.

* * *

[CCH Explanation at ¶145.]

Amendments

• **2004, Working Families Tax Relief Act of 2004 (H.R. 1308)**

H.R. 1308, §207(13):

Amended the first sentence of Code Sec. 132(h)(2)(B) by striking "151(c)(3)" and inserting "152(f)(1)". **Effective** for tax years beginning after 12-31-2004.

[¶5135] *CODE SEC. 138. MEDICARE ADVANTAGE MSA.*

(a) EXCLUSION.—Gross income shall not include any payment to the *Medicare Advantage MSA* of an individual by the Secretary of Health and Human Services under part C of title XVIII of the Social Security Act.

[CCH Explanation at ¶359. Committee Reports at ¶10,570.]

<table>
<tr><td>

Amendments

• **2004, Working Families Tax Relief Act of 2004** **(H.R. 1308)**

H.R. 1308, §408(a)(5)(A):

Amended Code Sec. 138 by striking "Medicare+Choice MSA" each place it appears in the text and inserting "Medicare Advantage MSA". **Effective** on the date of the enactment of this Act.

</td><td>

H.R. 1308, §408(a)(5)(B):

Amended the heading for Code Sec. 138. **Effective** on the date of the enactment of this Act. Prior to amendment, the heading for Code Sec. 138 read as follows:

SEC. 138. MEDICARE+CHOICE MSA.

</td></tr>
</table>

(b) *MEDICARE ADVANTAGE MSA.*—For purposes of this section, the term *"Medicare Advantage MSA"* means an Archer MSA (as defined in section 220(d))—

    (1) which is designated as a *Medicare Advantage MSA*,

    (2) with respect to which no contribution may be made other than—

        (A) a contribution made by the Secretary of Health and Human Services pursuant to part C of title XVIII of the Social Security Act, or

        (B) a trustee-to-trustee transfer described in subsection (c)(4),

    (3) the governing instrument of which provides that trustee-to-trustee transfers described in subsection (c)(4) may be made to and from such account, and

    (4) which is established in connection with an MSA plan described in section 1859(b)(3) of the Social Security Act.

[CCH Explanation at ¶359. Committee Reports at ¶10,570.]

<table>
<tr><td>

Amendments

• **2004, Working Families Tax Relief Act of 2004** **(H.R. 1308)**

H.R. 1308, §408(a)(5)(A):

Amended Code Sec. 138 by striking "Medicare+Choice MSA" each place it appears in the text and inserting "Medicare Advantage MSA". **Effective** on the date of the enactment of this Act.

</td><td>

H.R. 1308, §408(a)(5)(C):

Amended the heading for Code Sec. 138(b) by striking "MEDICARE+CHOICE MSA" and inserting "MEDICARE ADVANTAGE MSA". **Effective** on the date of the enactment of this Act.

</td></tr>
</table>

(c) SPECIAL RULES FOR DISTRIBUTIONS.—

    (1) DISTRIBUTIONS FOR QUALIFIED MEDICAL EXPENSES.—In applying section 220 to a *Medicare Advantage MSA*—

        (A) qualified medical expenses shall not include amounts paid for medical care for any individual other than the account holder, and

        (B) section 220(d)(2)(C) shall not apply.

    (2) PENALTY FOR DISTRIBUTIONS FROM *MEDICARE ADVANTAGE MSA* NOT USED FOR QUALIFIED MEDICAL EXPENSES IF MINIMUM BALANCE NOT MAINTAINED.—

        (A) IN GENERAL.—The tax imposed by this chapter for any taxable year in which there is a payment or distribution from a *Medicare Advantage MSA* which is not used exclusively to pay the qualified medical expenses of the account holder shall be increased by 50 percent of the excess (if any) of—

            (i) the amount of such payment or distribution, over

            (ii) the excess (if any) of—

                (I) the fair market value of the assets in such MSA as of the close of the calendar year preceding the calendar year in which the taxable year begins, over

                (II) an amount equal to 60 percent of the deductible under the *Medicare Advantage MSA* plan covering the account holder as of January 1 of the calendar year in which the taxable year begins.

Section 220(f)(4) shall not apply to any payment or distribution from a *Medicare Advantage MSA.*

* * *

(C) SPECIAL RULES.—For purposes of subparagraph (A)—

(i) all *Medicare Advantage MSAs* of the account holder shall be treated as 1 account,

(ii) all payments and distributions not used exclusively to pay the qualified medical expenses of the account holder during any taxable year shall be treated as 1 distribution, and

(iii) any distribution of property shall be taken into account at its fair market value on the date of the distribution.

(3) WITHDRAWAL OF ERRONEOUS CONTRIBUTIONS.—Section 220(f)(2) and paragraph (2) of this subsection shall not apply to any payment or distribution from a *Medicare Advantage MSA* to the Secretary of Health and Human Services of an erroneous contribution to such MSA and of the net income attributable to such contribution.

(4) TRUSTEE-TO-TRUSTEE TRANSFERS.—Section 220(f)(2) and paragraph (2) of this subsection shall not apply to any trustee-to-trustee transfer from a *Medicare Advantage MSA* of an account holder to another *Medicare Advantage MSA* of such account holder.

[CCH Explanation at ¶359. Committee Reports at ¶10,570.]

Amendments

• **2004, Working Families Tax Relief Act of 2004 (H.R. 1308)**

H.R. 1308, §408(a)(5)(A):

Amended Code Sec. 138 by striking "Medicare+Choice MSA" each place it appears in the text and inserting "Medicare Advantage MSA". **Effective** on the date of the enactment of this Act.

H.R. 1308, §408(a)(5)(D):

Amended the heading for Code Sec. 138(c)(2) by striking "MEDICARE+CHOICE MSA" and inserting "MEDICARE ADVANTAGE MSA". **Effective** on the date of the enactment of this Act.

H.R. 1308, §408(a)(5)(E):

Amended Code Sec. 138(c)(2)(C)(i) by striking "Medicare+Choice MSAs" and inserting "Medicare Advantage MSAs". **Effective** on the date of the enactment of this Act.

(d) SPECIAL RULES FOR TREATMENT OF ACCOUNT AFTER DEATH OF ACCOUNT HOLDER.—In applying section 220(f)(8)(A) to an account which was a *Medicare Advantage MSA* of a decedent, the rules of section 220(f) shall apply in lieu of the rules of subsection (c) of this section with respect to the spouse as the account holder of such *Medicare Advantage MSA.*

[CCH Explanation at ¶359. Committee Reports at ¶10,570.]

Amendments

• **2004, Working Families Tax Relief Act of 2004 (H.R. 1308)**

H.R. 1308, §408(a)(5)(A):

Amended Code Sec. 138 by striking "Medicare+Choice MSA" each place it appears in the text and inserting "Medi-

care Advantage MSA". **Effective** on the date of the enactment of this Act.

(e) REPORTS.—In the case of a *Medicare Advantage MSA*, the report under section 220(h)—

(1) shall include the fair market value of the assets in such *Medicare Advantage MSA* as of the close of each calendar year, and

(2) shall be furnished to the account holder—

(A) not later than January 31 of the calendar year following the calendar year to which such reports relate, and

(B) in such manner as the Secretary prescribes in such regulations.

[CCH Explanation at ¶359. Committee Reports at ¶10,570.]

• **2004, Working Families Tax Relief Act of 2004 (H.R. 1308)**

H.R. 1308, §408(a)(5)(A):

Amended Code Sec. 138 by striking "Medicare+Choice MSA" each place it appears in the text and inserting "Medi-

care Advantage MSA". **Effective** on the date of the enactment of this Act.

(f) COORDINATION WITH LIMITATION ON NUMBER OF TAXPAYERS HAVING ARCHER MSAs.—Subsection (i) of section 220 shall not apply to an individual with respect to a *Medicare Advantage MSA*, and

Medicare Advantage MSAs shall not be taken into account in determining whether the numerical limitations under section 220(j) are exceeded.

[CCH Explanation at ¶359. Committee Reports at ¶10,570.]

Amendments

• 2004, Working Families Tax Relief Act of 2004 (H.R. 1308)

H.R. 1308, §408(a)(5)(A):

Amended Code Sec. 138 by striking "Medicare+Choice MSA" each place it appears in the text and inserting "Medi-

care Advantage MSA". **Effective** on the date of the enactment of this Act.

H.R. 1308, §408(a)(5)(F):

Amended Code Sec. 138(f) by striking "Medicare+Choice MSA's" and inserting "Medicare Advantage MSAs". **Effective** on the date of the enactment of this Act.

[¶5140] CODE SEC. 151. ALLOWANCE OF DEDUCTIONS FOR PERSONAL EXEMPTIONS.

* * *

     (c) ADDITIONAL EXEMPTION FOR DEPENDENTS.—An exemption of the exemption amount for each individual who is a dependent (as defined in section 152) of the taxpayer for the taxable year.

* * *

[CCH Explanation at ¶170. Committee Reports at ¶10,100.]

Amendments

• 2004, Working Families Tax Relief Act of 2004 (H.R. 1308)

H.R. 1308, §206:

Amended Code Sec. 151(c). **Effective** for tax years beginning after 12-31-2004. Prior to amendment, Code Sec. 151(c) read as follows:

     (c) ADDITIONAL EXEMPTION FOR DEPENDENTS.—

     (1) IN GENERAL.—An exemption of the exemption amount for each dependent (as defined in section 152)—

     (A) whose gross income for the calendar year in which the taxable year of the taxpayer begins is less than the exemption amount, or

     (B) who is a child of the taxpayer and who (i) has not attained the age of 19 at the close of the calendar year in which the taxable year of the taxpayer begins, or (ii) is a student who has not attained the age of 24 at the close of such calendar year.

     (2) EXEMPTION DENIED IN CASE OF CERTAIN MARRIED DEPENDENTS.—No exemption shall be allowed under this subsection for any dependent who has made a joint return with his spouse under section 6013 for the taxable year beginning in the calendar year in which the taxable year of the taxpayer begins.

     (3) CHILD DEFINED.—For purposes of paragraph (1) (B), the term "child" means an individual who (within the meaning of section 152) is a son, stepson, daughter, or stepdaughter of the taxpayer.

     (4) STUDENT DEFINED.—For purposes of paragraph (1) (B) (ii), the term "student" means an individual who during each of 5 calendar months during the calendar year in which the taxable year of the taxpayer begins—

     (A) is a full-time student at an educational organization described in section 170(b)(1)(A)(ii); or

     (B) is pursuing a full-time course of institutional on-farm training under the supervision of an accredited agent of an educational organization described in section 170(b)(1)(A)(ii) or of a State or political subdivision of a State.

     (5) CERTAIN INCOME OF HANDICAPPED DEPENDENTS NOT TAKEN INTO ACCOUNT.—

     (A) IN GENERAL.—For purposes of paragraph (1)(A), the gross income of an individual who is permanently and totally disabled shall not include income attributable to services performed by the individual at a sheltered workshop if—

     (i) the availability of medical care at such workshop is the principal reason for his presence there, and

     (ii) the income arises solely from activities at such workshop which are incident to such medical care.

     (B) SHELTERED WORKSHOP DEFINED.—For purposes of subparagraph (A), the term "sheltered workshop" means a school—

     (i) which provides special instruction or training designed to alleviate the disability of the individual, and

     (ii) which is operated by—

     (I) an organization described in section 501(c)(3) and exempt from tax under section 501(a), or

     (II) a State, a possession of the United States, any political subdivision of any of the foregoing, the United States, or the District of Columbia.

     (C) PERMANENT AND TOTAL DISABILITY DEFINED.—An individual shall be treated as permanently and totally disabled for purposes of this paragraph if such individual would be so treated under paragraph (3) of section 22(e).

     (6) TREATMENT OF MISSING CHILDREN.—

     (A) IN GENERAL.—Solely for the purposes referred to in subparagraph (B), a child of the taxpayer—

     (i) who is presumed by law enforcement authorities to have been kidnapped by someone who is not a member of the family of such child or the taxpayer, and

     (ii) who was (without regard to this paragraph) the dependent of the taxpayer for the portion of the taxable year before the date of the kidnapping,

shall be treated as a dependent of the taxpayer for all taxable years ending during the period that the child is kidnapped.

     (B) PURPOSES.—Subparagraph (A) shall apply solely for purposes of determining—

     (i) the deduction under this section,

     (ii) the credit under section 24 (relating to child tax credit), and

     (iii) whether an individual is a surviving spouse or a head of a household (as such terms are defined in section 2).

     (C) COMPARABLE TREATMENT FOR PRINCIPAL PLACE OF ABODE REQUIREMENTS.—An individual—

     (i) who is presumed by law enforcement authorities to have been kidnapped by someone who is not a member of the family of such individual or the taxpayer, and *(ii)* who had, for the taxable year in which the kidnapping occurred, the same principal place of abode as the taxpayer for more than one-half of the portion of such year before the date of the kidnapping,

shall be treated as meeting the principal place of abode requirements of section 2(a)(1)(B), section 2(b)(1)(A), and section 32(c)(3)(A)(ii) with respect to a taxpayer for all taxable years ending during the period that the individual is kidnapped.

(D) TERMINATION OF TREATMENT.—Subparagraphs (A) and (C) shall cease to apply as of the first taxable year of the taxpayer beginning after the calendar year in which there is a determination that the child is dead (or, if earlier, in which the child would have attained age 18).

[¶ 5145] CODE SEC. 152. DEPENDENT DEFINED.

(a) IN GENERAL.—*For purposes of this subtitle, the term "dependent" means—*

(1) a qualifying child, or

(2) a qualifying relative.

(b) EXCEPTIONS.—*For purposes of this section—*

(1) DEPENDENTS INELIGIBLE.—*If an individual is a dependent of a taxpayer for any taxable year of such taxpayer beginning in a calendar year, such individual shall be treated as having no dependents for any taxable year of such individual beginning in such calendar year.*

(2) MARRIED DEPENDENTS.—*An individual shall not be treated as a dependent of a taxpayer under subsection (a) if such individual has made a joint return with the individual's spouse under section 6013 for the taxable year beginning in the calendar year in which the taxable year of the taxpayer begins.*

(3) CITIZENS OR NATIONALS OF OTHER COUNTRIES.—

(A) IN GENERAL.—*The term "dependent" does not include an individual who is not a citizen or national of the United States unless such individual is a resident of the United States or a country contiguous to the United States.*

(B) EXCEPTION FOR ADOPTED CHILD.—*Subparagraph (A) shall not exclude any child of a taxpayer (within the meaning of subsection (f)(1)(B)) from the definition of "dependent" if—*

(i) for the taxable year of the taxpayer, the child has the same principal place of abode as the taxpayer and is a member of the taxpayer's household, and

(ii) the taxpayer is a citizen or national of the United States.

(c) QUALIFYING CHILD.—*For purposes of this section—*

(1) IN GENERAL.—*The term "qualifying child" means, with respect to any taxpayer for any taxable year, an individual—*

(A) who bears a relationship to the taxpayer described in paragraph (2),

(B) who has the same principal place of abode as the taxpayer for more than one-half of such taxable year,

(C) who meets the age requirements of paragraph (3), and

(D) who has not provided over one-half of such individual's own support for the calendar year in which the taxable year of the taxpayer begins.

(2) RELATIONSHIP.—*For purposes of paragraph (1)(A), an individual bears a relationship to the taxpayer described in this paragraph if such individual is—*

(A) a child of the taxpayer or a descendant of such a child, or

(B) a brother, sister, stepbrother, or stepsister of the taxpayer or a descendant of any such relative.

(3) AGE REQUIREMENTS.—

(A) IN GENERAL.—*For purposes of paragraph (1)(C), an individual meets the requirements of this paragraph if such individual—*

(i) has not attained the age of 19 as of the close of the calendar year in which the taxable year of the taxpayer begins, or

(ii) is a student who has not attained the age of 24 as of the close of such calendar year.

(B) SPECIAL RULE FOR DISABLED.—*In the case of an individual who is permanently and totally disabled (as defined in section 22(e)(3)) at any time during such calendar year, the requirements of subparagraph (A) shall be treated as met with respect to such individual.*

(4) SPECIAL RULE RELATING TO 2 OR MORE CLAIMING QUALIFYING CHILD.—

(A) IN GENERAL.—*Except as provided in subparagraph (B), if (but for this paragraph) an individual may be and is claimed as a qualifying child by 2 or more taxpayers for a taxable year beginning in the same calendar year, such individual shall be treated as the qualifying child of the taxpayer who is—*

(i) a parent of the individual, or

(ii) if clause (i) does not apply, the taxpayer with the highest adjusted gross income for such taxable year.

(B) MORE THAN 1 PARENT CLAIMING QUALIFYING CHILD.—*If the parents claiming any qualifying child do not file a joint return together, such child shall be treated as the qualifying child of—*

(i) the parent with whom the child resided for the longest period of time during the taxable year, or

(ii) if the child resides with both parents for the same amount of time during such taxable year, the parent with the highest adjusted gross income.

(d) QUALIFYING RELATIVE.—*For purposes of this section—*

(1) IN GENERAL.—*The term "qualifying relative" means, with respect to any taxpayer for any taxable year, an individual—*

(A) who bears a relationship to the taxpayer described in paragraph (2),

(B) whose gross income for the calendar year in which such taxable year begins is less than the exemption amount (as defined in section 151(d)),

(C) with respect to whom the taxpayer provides over one-half of the individual's support for the calendar year in which such taxable year begins, and

(D) who is not a qualifying child of such taxpayer or of any other taxpayer for any taxable year beginning in the calendar year in which such taxable year begins.

(2) RELATIONSHIP.—*For purposes of paragraph (1)(A), an individual bears a relationship to the taxpayer described in this paragraph if the individual is any of the following with respect to the taxpayer:*

(A) A child or a descendant of a child.

(B) A brother, sister, stepbrother, or stepsister.

(C) The father or mother, or an ancestor of either.

(D) A stepfather or stepmother.

(E) A son or daughter of a brother or sister of the taxpayer.

(F) A brother or sister of the father or mother of the taxpayer.

(G) A son-in-law, daughter-in-law, father-in-law, mother-in-law, brother-in-law, or sister-in-law.

(H) An individual (other than an individual who at any time during the taxable year was the spouse, determined without regard to section 7703, of the taxpayer) who, for the taxable year of the taxpayer, has the same principal place of abode as the taxpayer and is a member of the taxpayer's household.

(3) SPECIAL RULE RELATING TO MULTIPLE SUPPORT AGREEMENTS.—*For purposes of paragraph (1)(C), over one-half of the support of an individual for a calendar year shall be treated as received from the taxpayer if—*

(A) no one person contributed over one-half of such support,

(B) over one-half of such support was received from 2 or more persons each of whom, but for the fact that any such person alone did not contribute over one-half of such support, would have been entitled to claim such individual as a dependent for a taxable year beginning in such calendar year,

(C) the taxpayer contributed over 10 percent of such support, and

(D) each person described in subparagraph (B) (other than the taxpayer) who contributed over 10 percent of such support files a written declaration (in such manner and form as the Secretary may by regulations prescribe) that such person will not claim such individual as a dependent for any taxable year beginning in such calendar year.

(4) SPECIAL RULE RELATING TO INCOME OF HANDICAPPED DEPENDENTS.—

(A) IN GENERAL.—*For purposes of paragraph (1)(B), the gross income of an individual who is permanently and totally disabled (as defined in section 22(e)(3)) at any time during the taxable year shall not include income attributable to services performed by the individual at a sheltered workshop if—*

(i) the availability of medical care at such workshop is the principal reason for the individual's presence there, and

(ii) the income arises solely from activities at such workshop which are incident to such medical care.

(B) SHELTERED WORKSHOP DEFINED.—*For purposes of subparagraph (A), the term "sheltered workshop" means a school—*

(i) which provides special instruction or training designed to alleviate the disability of the individual, and

(ii) which is operated by an organization described in section 501(c)(3) and exempt from tax under section 501(a), or by a State, a possession of the United States, any political subdivision of any of the foregoing, the United States, or the District of Columbia.

(5) SPECIAL RULES FOR SUPPORT.—*For purposes of this subsection—*

(A) payments to a spouse which are includible in the gross income of such spouse under section 71 or 682 shall not be treated as a payment by the payor spouse for the support of any dependent, and

(B) in the case of the remarriage of a parent, support of a child received from the parent's spouse shall be treated as received from the parent.

(e) SPECIAL RULE FOR DIVORCED PARENTS.—

(1) IN GENERAL.—*Notwithstanding subsection (c)(1)(B), (c)(4), or (d)(1)(C), if—*

(A) a child receives over one-half of the child's support during the calendar year from the child's parents—

(i) who are divorced or legally separated under a decree of divorce or separate maintenance,

(ii) who are separated under a written separation agreement, or

(iii) who live apart at all times during the last 6 months of the calendar year, and

(B) such child is in the custody of 1 or both of the child's parents for more than one-half of the calendar year,

such child shall be treated as being the qualifying child or qualifying relative of the noncustodial parent for a calendar year if the requirements described in paragraph (2) are met.

(2) REQUIREMENTS.—*For purposes of paragraph (1), the requirements described in this paragraph are met if—*

(A) a decree of divorce or separate maintenance or written separation agreement between the parents applicable to the taxable year beginning in such calendar year provides that—

(i) the noncustodial parent shall be entitled to any deduction allowable under section 151 for such child, or

(ii) the custodial parent will sign a written declaration (in such manner and form as the Secretary may prescribe) that such parent will not claim such child as a dependent for such taxable year, or

(B) in the case of such an agreement executed before January 1, 1985, the noncustodial parent provides at least $600 for the support of such child during such calendar year.

For purposes of subparagraph (B), amounts expended for the support of a child or children shall be treated as received from the noncustodial parent to the extent that such parent provided amounts for such support.

(3) CUSTODIAL PARENT AND NONCUSTODIAL PARENT.—*For purposes of this subsection—*

(A) CUSTODIAL PARENT.—*The term "custodial parent" means the parent with whom a child shared the same principal place of abode for the greater portion of the calendar year.*

(B) NONCUSTODIAL PARENT.—*The term "noncustodial parent" means the parent who is not the custodial parent.*

(4) EXCEPTION FOR MULTIPLE-SUPPORT AGREEMENTS.—*This subsection shall not apply in any case where over one-half of the support of the child is treated as having been received from a taxpayer under the provision of subsection (d)(3).*

(f) OTHER DEFINITIONS AND RULES.—*For purposes of this section—*

   (1) CHILD DEFINED.—

      (A) IN GENERAL.—*The term "child" means an individual who is—*

         (i) a son, daughter, stepson, or stepdaughter of the taxpayer, or

         (ii) an eligible foster child of the taxpayer.

      (B) ADOPTED CHILD.—*In determining whether any of the relationships specified in subparagraph (A)(i) or paragraph (4) exists, a legally adopted individual of the taxpayer, or an individual who is lawfully placed with the taxpayer for legal adoption by the taxpayer, shall be treated as a child of such individual by blood.*

      (C) ELIGIBLE FOSTER CHILD.—*For purposes of subparagraph (A)(ii), the term "eligible foster child" means an individual who is placed with the taxpayer by an authorized placement agency or by judgment, decree, or other order of any court of competent jurisdiction.*

   (2) STUDENT DEFINED.—*The term "student" means an individual who during each of 5 calendar months during the calendar year in which the taxable year of the taxpayer begins—*

      (A) is a full-time student at an educational organization described in section 170(b)(1)(A)(ii), or

      (B) is pursuing a full-time course of institutional on-farm training under the supervision of an accredited agent of an educational organization described in section 170(b)(1)(A)(ii) or of a State or political subdivision of a State.

   (3) DETERMINATION OF HOUSEHOLD STATUS.—*An individual shall not be treated as a member of the taxpayer's household if at any time during the taxable year of the taxpayer the relationship between such individual and the taxpayer is in violation of local law.*

   (4) BROTHER AND SISTER.—*The terms "brother" and "sister" include a brother or sister by the half blood.*

   (5) SPECIAL SUPPORT TEST IN CASE OF STUDENTS.—*For purposes of subsections (c)(1)(D) and (d)(1)(C), in the case of an individual who is—*

      (A) a child of the taxpayer, and

      (B) a student,

amounts received as scholarships for study at an educational organization described in section 170(b)(1)(A)(ii) shall not be taken into account.

   (6) TREATMENT OF MISSING CHILDREN.—

      (A) IN GENERAL.—*Solely for the purposes referred to in subparagraph (B), a child of the taxpayer—*

         (i) who is presumed by law enforcement authorities to have been kidnapped by someone who is not a member of the family of such child or the taxpayer, and

         (ii) who had, for the taxable year in which the kidnapping occurred, the same principal place of abode as the taxpayer for more than one-half of the portion of such year before the date of the kidnapping,

shall be treated as meeting the requirement of subsection (c)(1)(B) with respect to a taxpayer for all taxable years ending during the period that the child is kidnapped.

      (B) PURPOSES.—*Subparagraph (A) shall apply solely for purposes of determining—*

         (i) the deduction under section 151(c),

         (ii) the credit under section 24 (relating to child tax credit),

         (iii) whether an individual is a surviving spouse or a head of a household (as such terms are defined in section 2), and

         (iv) the earned income credit under section 32.

(C) COMPARABLE TREATMENT OF CERTAIN QUALIFYING RELATIVES.—*For purposes of this section, a child of the taxpayer—*

(i) *who is presumed by law enforcement authorities to have been kidnapped by someone who is not a member of the family of such child or the taxpayer, and*

(ii) *who was (without regard to this paragraph) a qualifying relative of the taxpayer for the portion of the taxable year before the date of the kidnapping,*

shall be treated as a qualifying relative of the taxpayer for all taxable years ending during the period that the child is kidnapped.

(D) TERMINATION OF TREATMENT.—*Subparagraphs (A) and (C) shall cease to apply as of the first taxable year of the taxpayer beginning after the calendar year in which there is a determination that the child is dead (or, if earlier, in which the child would have attained age 18).*

(7) CROSS REFERENCES.—

For provision treating child as dependent of both parents for purposes of certain provisions, see sections 105(b), 132(h)(2)(B), and 213(d)(5).

[CCH Explanation at ¶145. Committee Reports at ¶10,100.]

Amendments

- **2004, Working Families Tax Relief Act of 2004 (H.R. 1308)**

H.R. 1308, § 201:

Amended Code Sec. 152. **Effective** for tax years beginning after 12-31-2004. Prior to amendment, Code Sec. 152 read as follows:

SEC. 152. DEPENDENT DEFINED.

(a) GENERAL DEFINITION.—For purposes of this subtitle, the term "dependent" means any of the following individuals over half of whose support, for the calendar year in which the taxable year of the taxpayer begins, was received from the taxpayer (or is treated under subsection (c) or (e) as received from the taxpayer):

(1) A son or daughter of the taxpayer, or a descendant of either,

(2) A stepson or stepdaughter of the taxpayer,

(3) A brother, sister, stepbrother, or stepsister of the taxpayer,

(4) The father or mother of the taxpayer, or an ancestor of either,

(5) A stepfather or stepmother of the taxpayer,

(6) A son or daughter of a brother or sister of the taxpayer,

(7) A brother or sister of the father or mother of the taxpayer,

(8) A son-in-law, daughter-in-law, father-in-law, mother-in-law, brother-in-law, or sister-in-law of the taxpayer, or

(9) An individual (other than an individual who at any time during the taxable year was the spouse, determined without regard to section 7703, of the taxpayer) who, for the taxable year of the taxpayer, has as his principal place of abode the home of the taxpayer and is a member of the taxpayer's household.

(b) RULES RELATING TO GENERAL DEFINITION.—For purposes of this section—

(1) The terms "brother" and "sister" include a brother or sister by the halfblood.

(2) In determining whether any of the relationships specified in subsection (a) or paragraph (1) of this subsection exists, a legally adopted child of an individual (and a child who is a member of an individual's household, if placed with such individual by an authorized placement agency for legal adoption by such individual), or a foster child of an individual (if such child satisfies the requirements of subsection (a)(9) with respect to such individual), shall be treated as a child of such individual by blood.

(3) The term "dependent" does not include any individual who is not a citizen or national of the United States unless such individual is a resident of the United States or of a country contiguous to the United States. The preceding sentence shall not exclude from the definition of "dependent" any child of the taxpayer legally adopted by him, if, for the taxable year of the taxpayer, the child has as his principal place of abode the home of the taxpayer and is a member of the taxpayer's household, and if the taxpayer is a citizen or national of the United States.

(4) A payment to a wife which is includible in the gross income of the wife under section 71 or 682 shall not be treated as a payment by her husband for the support of any dependent.

(5) An individual is not a member of the taxpayer's household if at any time during the taxable year of the taxpayer the relationship between such individual and the taxpayer is in violation of local law.

(c) MULTIPLE SUPPORT AGREEMENTS.—For purposes of subsection (a), over half of the support of an individual for a calendar year shall be treated as received from the taxpayer if—

(1) no one person contributed over half of such support;

(2) over half of such support was received from persons each of whom, but for the fact that he did not contribute over half of such support, would have been entitled to claim such individual as a dependent for a taxable year beginning in such calendar year;

(3) the taxpayer contributed over 10 percent of such support; and

(4) each person described in paragraph (2) (other than the taxpayer) who contributed over 10 percent of such support files a written declaration (in such manner and form as the Secretary may by regulations prescribe) that he will not claim such individual as a dependent for any taxable year beginning in such calendar year.

(d) SPECIAL SUPPORT TEST IN CASE OF STUDENTS.—For purposes of subsection (a), in the case of any individual who is—

(1) a son, stepson, daughter, or stepdaughter of the taxpayer (within the meaning of this section), and

(2) a student (within the meaning of section 151(c)(4)),

amounts received as scholarships for study at an educational organization described in section 170(b)(1)(A)(ii) shall not be taken into account in determining whether such individual received more than half of his support from the taxpayer.

(e) SUPPORT TEST IN CASE OF CHILD OF DIVORCED PARENTS, ETC.—

(1) CUSTODIAL PARENT GETS EXEMPTION.—Except as otherwise provided in this subsection, if—

(A) a child (as defined in section 151(c)(3)) receives over half of his support during the calendar year from his parents—

(i) who are divorced or legally separated under a decree of divorce or separate maintenance,

(ii) who are separated under a written separation agreement, or

(iii) who live apart at all times during the last 6 months of the calendar year, and

(B) such child is in the custody of one or both of his parents for more than one-half of the calendar year,

such child shall be treated, for purposes of subsection (a), as receiving over half of his support during the calendar year from the parent having custody for a greater portion of the calendar year (hereinafter in this subsection referred to as the "custodial parent").

(2) EXCEPTION WHERE CUSTODIAL PARENT RELEASES CLAIM TO EXEMPTION FOR THE YEAR.—A child of parents described in paragraph (1) shall be treated as having received over half of his support during a calendar year from the noncustodial parent if—

(A) the custodial parent signs a written declaration (in such manner and form as the Secretary may by regulations prescribe) that such custodial parent will not claim such child as a dependent for any taxable year beginning in such calendar year, and

(B) the noncustodial parent attaches such written declaration to the noncustodial parent's return for the taxable year beginning during such calendar year.

For purposes of this subsection, the term "noncustodial parent" means the parent who is not the custodial parent.

(3) EXCEPTION FOR MULTIPLE-SUPPORT AGREEMENT.—This subsection shall not apply in any case where over half of the support of the child is treated as having been received from a taxpayer under the provisions of subsection (c).

(4) EXCEPTION FOR CERTAIN PRE-1985 INSTRUMENTS.—

(A) IN GENERAL.—A child of parents described in paragraph (1) shall be treated as having received over half his support during a calendar year from the noncustodial parent if—

(i) a qualified pre-1985 instrument between the parents applicable to the taxable year beginning in such calendar year provides that the noncustodial parent shall be entitled to any deduction allowable under section 151 for such child, and

(ii) the noncustodial parent provides at least $600 for the support of such child during such calendar year.

For purposes of this subparagraph, amounts expended for the support of a child or children shall be treated as received from the noncustodial parent to the extent that such parent provided amounts for such support.

(B) QUALIFIED PRE-1985 INSTRUMENT.—For purposes of this paragraph, the term "qualified pre-1985 instrument" means any decree of divorce or separate maintenance or written agreement—

(i) which is executed before January 1, 1985,

(ii) which on such date contains the provision described in subparagraph (A)(i), and

(iii) which is not modified on or after such date in a modification which expressly provides that this paragraph shall not apply to such decree or agreement.

(5) SPECIAL RULE FOR SUPPORT RECEIVED FROM NEW SPOUSE OF PARENT.—For purposes of this subsection, in the case of the remarriage of a parent, support of a child received from the parent's spouse shall be treated as received from the parent.

(6) CROSS REFERENCE.—

For provision treating child as dependent of both parents for purposes of medical expense deduction, see section 213(d)(5).

[¶ 5150] CODE SEC. 153. CROSS REFERENCES.

(1) For deductions of estates and trusts, in lieu of the exemptions under section 151, see section 642(b).

(2) For exemptions of nonresident aliens, see section 873(b)(3).

(3) For determination of marital status, see section 7703.

[CCH Explanation at ¶ 145.]

Amendments

• **2004, Working Families Tax Relief Act of 2004 (H.R. 1308)**

H.R. 1308, § 207(14):

Amended Code Sec. 153 by striking paragraph (1) and by redesignating paragraphs (2), (3), and (4) as paragraphs (1),

(2), and (3), respectively. **Effective** for tax years beginning after 12-31-2004. Prior to being stricken, Code Sec. 153(1), read as follows:

(1) For definitions of "husband" and "wife", as used in section 152(b)(4), see section 7701(a)(17).

[¶ 5155] CODE SEC. 165. LOSSES.

* * *

(i) DISASTER LOSSES.—

(1) ELECTION TO TAKE DEDUCTION FOR PRECEDING YEAR.—Notwithstanding the provisions of subsection (a), any loss attributable to a disaster occurring in an area subsequently determined by the President of the United States to warrant assistance by the Federal Government under the *Robert T. Stafford* Disaster Relief and Emergency Assistance Act may, at the election of the taxpayer, be taken into account for the taxable year immediately preceding the taxable year in which the disaster occurred.

* * *

[CCH Explanation at ¶ 30,050. Committee Reports at ¶ 10,570.]
Amendments
• **2004, Working Families Tax Relief Act of 2004 (H.R. 1308)**

H.R. 1308, § 408(a)(7)(A):

Amended Code Sec. 165(i)(1) by inserting "Robert T. Stafford" before "Disaster Relief and Emergency Assistance Act". **Effective** on the date of the enactment of this Act.

(k) TREATMENT AS DISASTER LOSS WHERE TAXPAYER ORDERED TO DEMOLISH OR RELOCATE RESIDENCE IN DISASTER AREA BECAUSE OF DISASTER.—In the case of a taxpayer whose residence is located in an area which has been determined by the President of the United States to warrant assistance by the Federal Government under the *Robert T. Strafford* Disaster Relief and Emergency Assistance Act, if—

    (1) not later than the 120th day after the date of such determination, the taxpayer is ordered, by the government of the State or any political subdivision thereof in which such residence is located, to demolish or relocate such residence, and

    (2) the residence has been rendered unsafe for use as a residence by reason of the disaster,

any loss attributable to such disaster shall be treated as a loss which arises from a casualty and which is described in subsection (i).

[CCH Explanation at ¶ 30,050. Committee Reports at ¶ 10,570.]
Amendments
• **2004, Working Families Tax Relief Act of 2004 (H.R. 1308)**

H.R. 1308, § 408(a)(7)(B):

Amended Code Sec. 165(k) by inserting "Robert T. Stafford" before "Disaster Relief and Emergency Assistance Act". **Effective** on the date of the enactment of this Act.

[¶ 5160] CODE SEC. 168. ACCELERATED COST RECOVERY SYSTEM.

* * *

(j) PROPERTY ON INDIAN RESERVATIONS.—

* * *

    (8) TERMINATION.—This subsection shall not apply to property placed in service after *December 31, 2005.*

[CCH Explanation at ¶ 217. Committee Reports at ¶ 10,360.]
Amendments
• **2004, Working Families Tax Relief Act of 2004 (H.R. 1308)**

H.R. 1308, § 316:

Amended Code Sec. 168(j)(8) by striking "December 31, 2004" and inserting "December 31, 2005". **Effective** on the date of the enactment of this Act.

(k) SPECIAL ALLOWANCE FOR CERTAIN PROPERTY ACQUIRED AFTER SEPTEMBER 10, 2001, AND BEFORE JANUARY 1, 2005.—

* * *

    (2) QUALIFIED PROPERTY.—For purposes of this subsection—

* * *

        (B) CERTAIN PROPERTY HAVING LONGER PRODUCTION PERIODS TREATED AS QUALIFIED PROPERTY.—

            (i) IN GENERAL.—*The term "qualified property" includes any property if such property—*

                (I) *meets the requirements of clauses (i), (ii), and (iii) of subparagraph (A),*

                (II) *has a recovery period of at least 10 years or is transportation property,*

                (III) *is subject to section 263A, and*

(IV) meets the requirements of clause (ii) or (iii) of section 263A(f)(1)(B) (determined as if such clauses also apply to property which has a long useful life (within the meaning of section 263A(f))).

(ii) ONLY PRE-JANUARY 1, 2005, BASIS ELIGIBLE FOR ADDITIONAL ALLOWANCE.—In the case of property which is qualified property solely by reason of clause (i), paragraph (1) shall apply only to the extent of the adjusted basis thereof attributable to manufacture, construction, or production before January 1, 2005.

(iii) TRANSPORTATION PROPERTY.—For purposes of this subparagraph, the term "transportation property" means tangible personal property used in the trade or business of transporting persons or property.

* * *

(D) SPECIAL RULES.—

* * *

(ii) SALE-LEASEBACKS.—For purposes of *clause (iii) and* subparagraph (A)(ii), if property *is* —

(I) originally placed in service after September 10, 2001, by a person, and

(II) sold and leased back by such person within 3 months after the date such property was originally placed in service,

such property shall be treated as originally placed in service not earlier than the date on which such property is used under the leaseback referred to in subclause (II).

(iii) SYNDICATION.—For purposes of subparagraph (A)(ii), if—

(I) property is originally placed in service after September 10, 2001, by the lessor of such property, •

(II) such property is sold by such lessor or any subsequent purchaser within 3 months after the date such property was originally placed in service, and

(III) the user of such property after the last sale during such 3-month period remains the same as when such property was originally placed in service,

such property shall be treated as originally placed in service not earlier than the date of such last sale.

(iv) LIMITATIONS RELATED TO USERS AND RELATED PARTIES.—The term "qualified property" shall not include any property if—

(I) the user of such property (as of the date on which such property is originally placed in service) or a person which is related (within the meaning of section 267(b) or 707(b)) to such user or to the taxpayer had a written binding contract in effect for the acquisition of such property at any time on or before September 10, 2001, or

(II) in the case of property manufactured, constructed, or produced for such user's or person's own use, the manufacture, construction, or production of such property began at any time on or before September 10, 2001.

* * *

(F) DEDUCTION ALLOWED IN COMPUTING *MINIMUM* TAX.—For purposes of determining alternative minimum taxable income under section 55, the deduction under subsection (a) for qualified property shall be determined under this section without regard to any adjustment under section 56.

* * *

[CCH Explanation at ¶ 327 and ¶ 30,050. Committee Reports at ¶ 10,520 and ¶ 10,570.]

Amendments

• **2004, Working Families Tax Relief Act of 2004 (H.R. 1308)**

H.R. 1308, § 403(a)(1):

Amended Code Sec. 168(k)(2)(B)(i). **Effective** as if included in the provision of the Job Creation and Worker Assistance Act of 2002 (P.L. 107-147) to which it relates

[effective for property placed in service after 9-10-2001, in tax years ending after that date.—CCH]. Prior to amendment, Code Sec. 168(k)(2)(B)(i) read as follows:

(i) IN GENERAL.—The term "qualified property" includes property—

(I) which meets the requirements of clauses (i), (ii), and (iii) of subparagraph (A),

(II) which has a recovery period of at least 10 years or is transportation property, and

(III) which is subject to section 263A by reason of clause (ii) or (iii) of subsection (f)(1)(B) thereof.

H.R. 1308, §403(a)(2)(A):

Amended Code Sec. 168(k)(2)(D) by adding at the end new clauses (iii) and (iv). **Effective** as if included in the provision of the Job Creation and Worker Assistance Act of 2002 (P.L. 107-147) to which it relates [effective for property placed in service after 9-10-2001, in tax years ending after that date.—CCH].

H.R. 1308, §403(a)(2)(B):

Amended Code Sec. 168(k)(2)(D)(ii) by inserting "clause (iii) and" before "subparagraph (A)(ii)". **Effective** as if in-

cluded in the provision of the Job Creation and Worker Assistance Act of 2002 (P.L. 107-147) to which it relates [effective for property placed in service after 9-10-2001, in tax years ending after that date.—CCH].

H.R. 1308, §408(a)(6)(A)-(B):

Amended Code Sec. 168(k)(2)(D)(ii) by inserting "is" after "if property", and by striking "is" in subclause (I) before "originally placed in service". **Effective** on the date of the enactment of this Act.

H.R. 1308, §408(a)(8):

Amended the heading for Code Sec. 168(k)(2)(F) by striking "MINIUMUM" and inserting "MINIMUM". **Effective** on the date of the enactment of this Act.

[¶5165] CODE SEC. 170. CHARITABLE, ETC., CONTRIBUTIONS AND GIFTS.

* * *

(e) CERTAIN CONTRIBUTIONS OF ORDINARY INCOME AND CAPITAL GAIN PROPERTY.—

* * *

(6) SPECIAL RULE FOR CONTRIBUTIONS OF COMPUTER TECHNOLOGY AND EQUIPMENT FOR EDUCATIONAL PURPOSES.—

* * *

(G) TERMINATION.—This paragraph shall not apply to any contribution made during any taxable year beginning after December 31, *2005.*

* * *

[CCH Explanation at ¶207. Committee Reports at ¶10,260.]

Amendments

• **2004, Working Families Tax Relief Act of 2004 (H.R. 1308)**

H.R. 1308, §306(a):

Amended Code Sec. 170(e)(6)(G) by striking "2003" and inserting "2005". **Effective** for contributions made in tax years beginning after 12-31-2003.

(g) AMOUNTS PAID TO MAINTAIN CERTAIN STUDENTS AS MEMBERS OF TAXPAYER'S HOUSEHOLD.—

(1) IN GENERAL.—Subject to the limitations provided by paragraph (2), amounts paid by the taxpayer to maintain an individual (other than a dependent, as defined in section 152*(determined without regard to subsections (b)(1), (b)(2), and (d)(1)(B) thereof)*, or a relative of the taxpayer) as a member of his household during the period that such individual is—

(A) a member of the taxpayer's household under a written agreement between the taxpayer and an organization described in paragraph (2), (3), or (4) of subsection (c) to implement a program of the organization to provide educational opportunities for pupils or students in private homes, and

(B) a full-time pupil or student in the twelfth or any lower grade at an educational organization described in section 170(b)(1)(A)(ii) located in the United States,

shall be treated as amounts paid for the use of the organization.

* * *

(3) RELATIVE DEFINED.—For purposes of paragraph (1), the term "relative of the taxpayer" means an individual who, with respect to the taxpayer, bears any of the relationships described in *subparagraphs (A) through (G) of section 152(d)(2).*

* * *

[CCH Explanation at ¶ 145.]

Amendments

• 2004, Working Families Tax Relief Act of 2004 (H.R. 1308)

H.R. 1308, § 207(15):

Amended Code Sec. 170(g)(1) by inserting "(determined without regard to subsections (b)(1), (b)(2), and (d)(1)(B) thereof)" after "section 152". **Effective** for tax years beginning after 12-31-2004.

H.R. 1308, § 207(16):

Amended Code Sec. 170(g)(3) by striking "paragraphs (1) through (8) of section 152(a)" and inserting "subparagraphs (A) through (G) of section 152(d)(2)". **Effective** for tax years beginning after 12-31-2004.

[¶ 5170] CODE SEC. 172. NET OPERATING LOSS DEDUCTION.

* * *

(b) NET OPERATING LOSS CARRYBACKS AND CARRYOVERS.—

(1) YEARS TO WHICH LOSS MAY BE CARRIED.—

* * *

(H) In the case of a net operating loss for any taxable year ending during 2001 or 2002, subparagraph (A)(i) shall be applied by substituting "5" for "2" and subparagraph (F) shall not apply.

* * *

[CCH Explanation at ¶ 321. Committee Reports at ¶ 10,520.]

Amendments

• 2004, Working Families Tax Relief Act of 2004 (H.R. 1308)

H.R. 1308, § 403(b)(1):

Amended Code Sec. 172(b)(1)(H) by striking "a taxpayer which has" following "In the case of". **Effective** as if included in the provision of the Job Creation and Worker Assistance Act of 2002 (P.L. 107-147) to which it relates [effective for net operating losses for tax years ending after 12-31-2000.—CCH].

H.R. 1308, § 403(b)(2), provides:

(2) In the case of a net operating loss for a taxable year ending during 2001 or 2002—

(A) an application under section 6411(a) of the Internal Revenue Code of 1986 with respect to such loss shall not fail to be treated as timely filed if filed before November 1, 2002,

(B) any election made under section 172(b)(3) of such Code may (notwithstanding such section) be revoked before November 1, 2002, and

(C) any election made under section 172(j) of such Code shall (notwithstanding such section) be treated as timely made if made before November 1, 2002.

[¶ 5175] CODE SEC. 179A. DEDUCTION FOR CLEAN-FUEL VEHICLES AND CERTAIN REFUELING PROPERTY.

* * *

(b) LIMITATIONS.—

(1) QUALIFIED CLEAN-FUEL VEHICLE PROPERTY.—

* * *

(B) PHASEOUT.—*In the case of any qualified clean-fuel vehicle property placed in service after December 31, 2005, the limit otherwise allowable under subparagraph (A) shall be reduced by 75 percent.*

* * *

[CCH Explanation at ¶ 225. Committee Reports at ¶ 10,390.]

Amendments

• 2004, Working Families Tax Relief Act of 2004 (H.R. 1308)

H.R. 1308, § 319(a):

Amended Code Sec. 179A(b)(1)(B). **Effective** for property placed in service after 12-31-2003. Prior to amendment, Code Sec. 179A(b)(1)(B) read as follows:

(B) PHASEOUT.—In the case of any qualified clean-fuel vehicle property placed in service after December 31, 2003, the limit otherwise applicable under subparagraph (A) shall be reduced by—

(i) 25 percent in the case of property placed in service in calendar year 2004,

(ii) 50 percent in the case of property placed in sevice in calendar year 2005, and

(iii) 75 percent in the case of property placed in service in calendar year 2006.

[¶5180] CODE SEC. 198. EXPENSING OF ENVIRONMENTAL REMEDIATION COSTS.

* * *

(h) Termination.—This section shall not apply to expenditures paid or incurred after *December 31, 2005.*

[CCH Explanation at ¶209. Committee Reports at ¶10,280.]

Amendments

• **2004, Working Families Tax Relief Act of 2004 (H.R. 1308)**

H.R. 1308, §308(a):

Amended Code Sec. 198(h) by striking "December 31, 2003" and inserting "December 31, 2005". **Effective** for expenditures paid or incurred after 12-31-2003.

[¶5185] CODE SEC. 213. MEDICAL, DENTAL, ETC., EXPENSES.

(a) Allowance of Deduction.—There shall be allowed as a deduction the expenses paid during the taxable year, not compensated for by insurance or otherwise, for medical care of the taxpayer, his spouse, or a dependent (as defined in section 152, *determined without regard to subsections (b)(1), (b)(2), and (d)(1)(B) thereof*), to the extent that such expenses exceed 7.5 percent of adjusted gross income.

* * *

[CCH Explanation at ¶145.]

Amendments

• **2004, Working Families Tax Relief Act of 2004 (H.R. 1308)**

H.R. 1308, §207(17):

Amended Code Sec. 213(a) by inserting ", determined without regard to subsections (b)(1), (b)(2), and (d)(1)(B) thereof" after "section 152". **Effective** for tax years beginning after 12-31-2004.

(d) Definitions.—For purposes of this section—

* * *

(11) Certain Payments to Relatives Treated as Not Paid for Medical Care.—An amount paid for a qualified long-term care service (as defined in section 7702B(c)) provided to an individual shall be treated as not paid for medical care if such service is provided—

(A) by the spouse of the individual or by a relative (directly or through a partnership, corporation, or other entity) unless the service is provided by a licensed professional with respect to such service, or

(B) by a corporation or partnership which is related (within the meaning of section 267(b) or 707(b)) to the individual.

For purposes of this paragraph, the term "relative" means an individual bearing a relationship to the individual which is described in any of *subparagraphs (A) through (G) of section 152(d)(2)*. This paragraph shall not apply for purposes of section 105(b) with respect to reimbursements through insurance.

* * *

[CCH Explanation at ¶145.]

Amendments

• **2004, Working Families Tax Relief Act of 2004 (H.R. 1308)**

H.R. 1308, §207(18):

Amended the second sentence of Code Sec. 213(d)(11) by striking "paragraphs (1) through (8) of section 152(a)" and inserting "subparagraphs (A) through (G) of section 152(d)(2)". **Effective** for tax years beginning after 12-31-2004.

[¶ 5190] CODE SEC. 220. ARCHER MSAs.

* * *

(d) ARCHER MSA.—For purposes of this section—

* * *

(2) QUALIFIED MEDICAL EXPENSES.—

(A) IN GENERAL.—The term "qualified medical expenses" means, with respect to an account holder, amounts paid by such holder for medical care (as defined in section 213(d)) for such individual, the spouse of such individual, and any dependent (as defined in section 152, *determined without regard to subsections (b)(1), (b)(2), and (d)(1)(B) thereof*) of such individual, but only to the extent such amounts are not compensated for by insurance or otherwise.

* * *

[CCH Explanation at ¶ 145.]

Amendments

• **2004, Working Families Tax Relief Act of 2004 (H.R. 1308)**

H.R. 1308, § 207(19):

Amended Code Sec. 220(d)(2)(A) by inserting ", determined without regard to subsections (b)(1), (b)(2), and

(d)(1)(B) thereof" after "section 152". **Effective** for tax years beginning after 12-31-2004.

(i) LIMITATION ON NUMBER OF TAXPAYERS HAVING ARCHER MSAs.—

* * *

(2) CUT-OFF YEAR.—For purposes of paragraph (1), the term "cut-off year" means the earlier of—

(A) calendar year *2005*, or

(B) the first calendar year before *2005* for which the Secretary determines under subsection (j) that the numerical limitation for such year has been exceeded.

(3) ACTIVE MSA PARTICIPANT.—For purposes of this subsection—

* * *

(B) SPECIAL RULE FOR CUT-OFF YEARS BEFORE *2005*.—In the case of a cut-off year before *2005*—

(i) an individual shall not be treated as an eligible individual for any month of such year or an active MSA participant under paragraph (1)(A) unless such individual is, on or before the cut-off date, covered under a high deductible health plan, and

(ii) an employer shall not be treated as an MSA-participating employer unless the employer, on or before the cut-off date, offered coverage under a high deductible health plan to any employee.

* * *

[CCH Explanation at ¶ 245. Committee Reports at ¶ 10,420.]

Amendments

• **2004, Working Families Tax Relief Act of 2004 (H.R. 1308)**

H.R. 1308, § 322(a):

Amended Code Sec. 220(i)(2) and (3)(B) by striking "2003" each place it appears in the text and headings [sic] and inserting "2005". **Effective** 1-1-2004.

(j) DETERMINATION OF WHETHER NUMERICAL LIMITS ARE EXCEEDED.—

* * *

(2) DETERMINATION OF WHETHER LIMIT EXCEEDED FOR 1998, 1999, 2001, 2002, OR *2004*.—

(A) IN GENERAL.—The numerical limitation for 1998, 1999, 2001, 2002, *or 2004* is exceeded if the sum of—

(i) the number of MSA returns filed on or before April 15 of such calendar year for taxable years ending with or within the preceding calendar year, plus

(ii) the Secretary's estimate (determined on the basis of the returns described in clause (i)) of the number of MSA returns for such taxable years which will be filed after such date,

exceeds 750,000 (600,000 in the case of 1998). For purposes of the preceding sentence, the term "MSA return" means any return on which any exclusion is claimed under section 106(b) or any deduction is claimed under this section.

(B) ALTERNATIVE COMPUTATION OF LIMITATION.—The numerical limitation for 1998, 1999, *2001, 2002, or 2004* is also exceeded if the sum of—

(i) 90 percent of the sum determined under subparagraph (A) for such calendar year, plus

(ii) the product of 2.5 and the number of Archer MSAs established during the portion of such year preceding July 1 (based on the reports required under paragraph (4)) for taxable years beginning in such year,

exceeds 750,000.

(C) *No LIMITATION FOR 2000 OR 2003.—The numerical limitation shall not apply for 2000 or 2003.*

* * *

(4) REPORTING BY MSA TRUSTEES.—

(A) IN GENERAL.—Not later than August 1 of 1997, 1998, 1999, 2001, *2002, and 2004,* each person who is the trustee of an Archer MSA established before July 1 of such calendar year shall make a report to the Secretary (in such form and manner as the Secretary shall specify) which specifies—

(i) the number of Archer MSAs established before such July 1 (for taxable years beginning in such calendar year) of which such person is the trustee,

(ii) the name and TIN of the account holder of each such account, and

(iii) the number of such accounts which are accounts of previously uninsured individuals.

* * *

[CCH Explanation at ¶245. Committee Reports at ¶10,420.]

Amendments

• **2004, Working Families Tax Relief Act of 2004 (H.R. 1308)**

H.R. 1308, §322(b)(1)(A)-(B):

Amended Code Sec. 220(j)(2) in the text by striking "or 2002" each place it appears and inserting "2002, or 2004", and in the heading by striking "OR 2002" and inserting "2002, OR 2004". **Effective 1-1-2004.**

H.R. 1308, §322(b)(2):

Amended Code Sec. 220(j)(4)(A) by striking "and 2002" and inserting "2002, and 2004". **Effective 1-1-2004.**

H.R. 1308, §322(b)(3):

Amended Code Sec. 220(j)(2)(C). **Effective 1-1-2004.** Prior to amendment, Code Sec. 220(j)(2)(C) read as follows:

(C) NO LIMITATION FOR 2000.—The numerical limitation shall not apply for 2000.

[¶5195] CODE SEC. 221. INTEREST ON EDUCATION LOANS.

* * *

(d) DEFINITIONS.—For purposes of this section—

* * *

(4) DEPENDENT.—The term "dependent" has the meaning given such term by section 152*(determined without regard to subsections (b)(1), (b)(2), and (d)(1)(B) therof).*

[CCH Explanation at ¶145.]

Amendments

• 2004, Working Families Tax Relief Act of 2004 (H.R. 1308)

H.R. 1308, §207(20):

Amended Code Sec. 221(d)(4) by inserting "(determined without regard to subsections (b)(1), (b)(2), and (d)(1)(B)

therof)" after "section 152". **Effective** for tax years beginning after 12-31-2004.

[¶5200] CODE SEC. 246. RULES APPLYING TO DEDUCTIONS FOR DIVIDENDS RECEIVED.

* * *

(c) EXCLUSION OF CERTAIN DIVIDENDS.—

(1) IN GENERAL.—No deduction shall be allowed under section 243, 244, or 245, in respect of any dividend on any share of stock—

(A) which is held by the taxpayer for 45 days or less during the *91-day period* beginning on the date which is 45 days before the date on which such share becomes ex-dividend with respect to such dividend, or

(B) to the extent that the taxpayer is under an obligation (whether pursuant to a short sale or otherwise) to make related payments with respect to positions in substantially similar or related property.

(2) 90-DAY RULE IN THE CASE OF CERTAIN PREFERENCE DIVIDENDS.—In the case of stock having preference in dividends, if the taxpayer receives dividends with respect to such stock which are attributable to a period or periods aggregating in excess of 366 days, paragraph (1)(A) shall be applied—

(A) by substituting "90 days" for "45 days" each place it appears, and

(B) by substituting *"181-day period"* for *"91-day period"*.

* * *

[CCH Explanation at ¶305. Committee Reports at ¶10,550.]

Amendments

• 2004, Working Families Tax Relief Act of 2004 (H.R. 1308)

H.R. 1308, §406(f)(1):

Amended Code Sec. 246(c)(1)(A) by striking "90-day period", and inserting "91-day period". **Effective** as if included in the provision of the Taxpayer Relief Act of 1997 (P.L. 105-34) to which it relates [effective generally for dividends received or accrued after 9-4-97.—CCH].

H.R. 1308, §406(f)(2)(A)-(B):

Amended Code Sec. 246(c)(2)(B) by striking "180-day period" and inserting "181-day period", and by striking "90-day period" and inserting "91-day period". **Effective** as if included in the provision of the Taxpayer Relief Act of 1997 (P.L. 105-34) to which it relates [effective generally for dividends received or accrued after 9-4-97.—CCH].

[¶5205] CODE SEC. 246A. DIVIDENDS RECEIVED DEDUCTION REDUCED WHERE PORTFOLIO STOCK IS DEBT FINANCED.

* * *

(b) SECTION NOT TO APPLY TO DIVIDENDS FOR WHICH 100 PERCENT DIVIDENDS RECEIVED DEDUCTION ALLOWABLE.—Subsection (a) shall not apply to—

(1) qualifying dividends (as defined in section 243(b) without regard to *section 243(d)(4)*), and

(2) dividends received by a small business investment company operating under the Small Business Investment Act of 1958.

* * *

[CCH Explanation at ¶30,050. Committee Reports at ¶10,570.]
Amendments
• **2004, Working Families Tax Relief Act of 2004**
(H.R. 1308)

H.R. 1308, § 408(a)(9):

Amended Code Sec. 246A(b)(1) by striking "section 243(c)(4)" and inserting "section 243(d)(4)". **Effective** on the date of the enactment of this Act.

[¶5210] CODE SEC. 263. CAPITAL EXPENDITURES.

* * *

(g) CERTAIN INTEREST AND CARRYING COSTS IN THE CASE OF STRADDLES.—

* * *

(2) INTEREST AND CARRYING CHARGES DEFINED.—For purposes of paragraph (1), the term "interest and carrying charges" means the excess of—

(A) the sum of—

(i) interest on indebtedness incurred or continued to purchase or carry the personal property, and

(ii) all other amounts (including charges to insure, store, or transport the personal property) paid or incurred to carry the personal property, over

(B) the sum of—

(i) the amount of interest (including original issue discount) includible in gross income for the taxable year with respect to the property described in subparagraph (A),

(ii) any amount treated as ordinary income under section 1271(a)(3)(A), *1276*, or 1281(a) with respect to such property for the taxable year,

(iii) the excess of any dividends includible in gross income with respect to such property for the taxable year over the amount of any deduction allowable with respect to such dividends under section 243, 244, or 245, and

(iv) any amount which is a payment with respect to a security loan (within the meaning of section 512(a)(5)) includible in gross income with respect to such property for the taxable year.

For purposes of subparagraph (A), the term "interest" includes any amount paid or incurred in connection with personal property used in a short sale.

* * *

[CCH Explanation at ¶30,050. Committee Reports at ¶10,570.]
Amendments
• **2004, Working Families Tax Relief Act of 2004**
(H.R. 1308)

H.R. 1308, § 408(a)(10):

Amended Code Sec. 263(g)(2)(B)(ii) by striking "1278" and inserting "1276". **Effective** on the date of the enactment of this Act.

[¶5215] CODE SEC. 401. QUALIFIED PENSION, PROFIT-SHARING, AND STOCK BONUS PLANS.

(a) REQUIREMENTS FOR QUALIFICATION.—A trust created or organized in the United States and forming part of a stock bonus, pension, or profit-sharing plan of an employer for the exclusive benefit of his employees or their beneficiaries shall constitute a qualified trust under this section—

* * *

(26) ADDITIONAL PARTICIPATION REQUIREMENTS.—

* * *

(C) SPECIAL RULE FOR COLLECTIVE BARGAINING UNITS.—Except to the extent provided in regulations, a plan covering only employees described in section 410(b)(3)(A) may exclude from consideration any employees who are not included in the unit or units in which the covered employees are included.

(D) PARAGRAPH NOT TO APPLY TO MULTIEMPLOYER PLANS.—Except to the extent provided in regulations, this paragraph shall not apply to employees in a multiemployer plan (within the meaning of section 414(f)) who are covered by collective bargaining agreements.

(E) SPECIAL RULE FOR CERTAIN DISPOSITIONS OR ACQUISITIONS.—Rules similar to the rules of section 410(b)(6)(C) shall apply for purposes of this paragraph.

(F) SEPARATE LINES OF BUSINESS.—At the election of the employer and with the consent of the Secretary, this paragraph may be applied separately with respect to each separate line of business of the employer. For purposes of this paragraph, the term "separate line of business" has the meaning given such term by section 414(r) (without regard to paragraph (2)(A) or (7) thereof).

(G) EXCEPTION FOR STATE AND LOCAL GOVERNMENTAL PLANS.—This paragraph shall not apply to a governmental plan (within the meaning of section 414(d)) maintained by a State or local government or political subdivision thereof (or agency or instrumentality thereof).

(H) REGULATIONS.—The Secretary may by regulation provide that any separate benefit structure, any separate trust, or any other separate arrangement is to be treated as a separate plan for purposes of applying this paragraph.

* * *

[CCH Explanation at ¶351. Committee Reports at ¶10,560.]

Amendments

• **2004, Working Families Tax Relief Act of 2004 (H.R. 1308)**

H.R. 1308, §407(b):

Amended Code Sec. 401(a)(26) by striking subparagraph (C) and by resdesignating subparagraphs (D) through (I) as subparagraphs (C) through (H), respectively. **Effective** as if included in the provision of the Small Business Job Protec-

tion Act of 1996 (P.L. 104-188) to which it relates [**effective for years beginning after 12-31-96.—CCH**]. Prior to being stricken, Code Sec. 401(a)(26)(C) read as follows:

(C) ELIGIBILITY TO PARTICIPATE.—In the case of contributions under section 401(k) or 401(m), employees who are eligible to contribute (or may elect to have contributions made on their behalf) shall be treated as benefiting under the plan.

[¶5220] CODE SEC. 403. TAXATION OF EMPLOYEE ANNUITIES.

(a) TAXABILITY OF BENEFICIARY UNDER A QUALIFIED ANNUITY PLAN.—

* * *

(4) ROLLOVER AMOUNTS.—

* * *

(B) CERTAIN RULES MADE APPLICABLE.—*The rules of paragraphs (2) through (7) and (9) of section 402(c) and section 402(f) shall apply for purposes of subparagraph (A).*

* * *

[CCH Explanation at ¶347. Committee Reports at ¶10,530.]

Amendments

• **2004, Working Families Tax Relief Act of 2004 (H.R. 1308)**

H.R. 1308, §404(e):

Amended Code Sec. 403(a)(4)(B). **Effective** as if included in the provision of the Economic Growth and Tax Relief

Reconciliation Act of 2001 (P.L. 107-16) to which it relates [**effective for distributions after 12-31-2001.—CCH**]. Prior to amendment, Code Sec. 403(a)(4)(B) read as follows:

(B) CERTAIN RULES MADE APPLICABLE.—Rules similar to the rules of paragraphs (2) through (7) of section 402(c) shall apply for purposes of subparagraph (A).

(b) TAXABILITY OF BENEFICIARY UNDER ANNUITY PURCHASED BY SECTION 501(c)(3) ORGANIZATION OR PUBLIC SCHOOL.—

* * *

(7) CUSTODIAL ACCOUNTS FOR REGULATED INVESTMENT COMPANY STOCK.—

(A) AMOUNTS PAID TREATED AS CONTRIBUTIONS.—For purposes of this title, amounts paid by an employer described in paragraph (1)(A) to a custodial account which satisfies the requirements of section 401(f)(2) shall be treated as amounts contributed by him for an annuity contract for his employee if—

(i) the amounts are to be invested in regulated investment company stock to be held in that custodial account, and

(ii) under the custodial account no such amounts may be paid or made available to any distributee before the employee dies, attains age 59½, has a severance from employment, becomes disabled (within the meaning of section 72(m)(7)), or in the case of contributions made pursuant to a salary reduction agreement (within the meaning of *section 3121(a)(5)(D)*), encounters financial hardship.

* * *

[CCH Explanation at ¶ 30,050. Committee Reports at ¶ 10,570.]
Amendments
• **2004, Working Families Tax Relief Act of 2004 (H.R. 1308)**

H.R. 1308, § 408(a)(11):

Amended Code Sec. 403(b)(7)(A)(ii) by striking "section 3121(a)(1)(D)" and inserting "section 3121(a)(5)(D)". **Effective** on the date of the enactment of this Act.

[¶ 5225] CODE SEC. 408. INDIVIDUAL RETIREMENT ACCOUNTS.

(a) INDIVIDUAL RETIREMENT ACCOUNT.—For purposes of this section, the term "individual retirement account" means a trust created or organized in the United States for the exclusive benefit of an individual or his beneficiaries, but only if the written governing instrument creating the trust meets the following requirements:

(1) Except in the case of a rollover contribution described in subsection (d)(3), in section 402(c), 403(a)(4), 403(b)(8), or *457(e)(16)*, no contribution will be accepted unless it is in cash, and contributions will not be accepted for the taxable year on behalf of any individual in excess of the amount in effect for such taxable year under section 219(b)(1)(A).

* * *

[CCH Explanation at ¶ 30,050. Committee Reports at ¶ 10,570.]
Amendments
• **2004, Working Families Tax Relief Act of 2004 (H.R. 1308)**

H.R. 1308, § 408(a)(12):

Amended Code Sec. 408(a)(1) by striking "457(e)(16)" and inserting "457(e)(16),". **Effective** on the date of the enactment of this Act.

(n) BANK.—For purposes of subsection (a)(2), the term "bank" means—

(1) any bank (as defined in section 581),

(2) an insured credit union (within the meaning of *paragraph (6) or (7) of section 101* of the Federal Credit Union Act), and

(3) a corporation which, under the laws of the State of its incorporation, is subject to supervision and examination by the Commissioner of Banking or other officer of such State in charge of the administration of the banking laws of such State.

* * *

[CCH Explanation at ¶ 30,050. Committee Reports at ¶ 10,570.]
Amendments
• **2004, Working Families Tax Relief Act of 2004 (H.R. 1308)**

H.R. 1308, § 408(a)(13):

Amended Code Sec. 408(n)(2) by striking "section 101(6)" and inserting "paragraph (6) or (7) of section 101". **Effective** on the date of the enactment of this Act.

(p) Simple Retirement Accounts.—

* * *

(6) Definitions.—For purposes of this subsection—

(A) Compensation.—

(i) In general.—The term "compensation" means amounts described in paragraphs (3) and (8) of section 6051(a). *For purposes of the preceding sentence, amounts described in section 6051(a)(3) shall be determined without regard to section 3401(a)(3).*

* * *

[CCH Explanation at ¶ 347. Committee Reports at ¶ 10,530.]

Amendments

• **2004, Working Families Tax Relief Act of 2004 (H.R. 1308)**

H.R. 1308, §404(d):

Amended Code Sec. 408(p)(6)(A)(i) by adding at the end a new sentence. **Effective** as if included in the provision of the

Economic Growth and Tax Relief Reconciliation Act of 2001 (P.L. 107-16) to which it relates [**effective for tax years** beginning after 12-31-2001.—CCH].

[¶ 5230] CODE SEC. 411. MINIMUM VESTING STANDARDS.

(a) General Rule.—A trust shall not constitute a qualified trust under section 401(a) unless the plan of which such trust is a part provides that an employee's right to his normal retirement benefit is nonforfeitable upon the attainment of normal retirement age (as defined in paragraph (8)) and in addition satisfies the requirements of paragraphs (1), (2), and (11) of this subsection and the requirements of subsection (b)(3), and also satisfies, in the case of a defined benefit plan, the requirements of subsection (b)(1) and, in the case of a defined contribution plan, the requirements of subsection (b)(2).

* * *

(12) Faster Vesting for Matching Contributions.—In the case of matching contributions (as defined in section 401(m)(4)(A)), paragraph (2) shall be applied—

(A) by substituting "3 years" for "5 years" in subparagraph (A), and

(B) by substituting the following table for the table contained in subparagraph (B):

Years of service:	The nonforfeitable percentage is:
2	20
3	40
4	60
5	80
6 or more	100.

* * *

[CCH Explanation at ¶ 30,050. Committee Reports at ¶ 10,570.]

Amendments

• **2004, Working Families Tax Relief Act of 2004 (H.R. 1308)**

H.R. 1308, §408(a)(14):

Amended the table contained in Code Sec. 411(a)(12)(B) by striking the last line and inserting a new line. **Effective**

on the date of the enactment of this Act. Prior to being stricken, the last line of the table contained in Code Sec. 411(a)(12)(B) read as follows:

6	100.

[¶ 5235] CODE SEC. 414. DEFINITIONS AND SPECIAL RULES.

* * *

(q) Highly Compensated Employee.—

* * *

(7) Coordination with Other Provisions.—Subsections (b), (c), (m), (n), and (o) shall be applied before the application of this *subsection.*

* * *

[CCH Explanation at ¶30,050. Committee Reports at ¶10,570.]
Amendments
• 2004, Working Families Tax Relief Act of 2004 (H.R. 1308)

H.R. 1308, §408(a)(15):

Amended Code Sec. 414(q)(7) by striking "section" and inserting "subsection". **Effective** on the date of the enactment of this Act.

[¶5240] CODE SEC. 415. LIMITATIONS ON BENEFITS AND CONTRIBUTION UNDER QUALIFIED PLANS.

* * *

(c) LIMITATION FOR DEFINED CONTRIBUTION PLANS.—

* * *

(7) SPECIAL RULES RELATING TO CHURCH PLANS.—

* * *

(C) FOREIGN MISSIONARIES.—In the case of any individual described in *subparagraph (B)* performing services outside the United States, contributions and other additions for an annuity contract or retirement income account described in section 403(b) with respect to such employee, when expressed as an annual addition to such employee's account, shall not be treated as exceeding the limitation of paragraph (1) if such annual addition is not in excess of the greater of $3,000 or the employee's includible compensation determined under section 403(b)(3).

* * *

[CCH Explanation at ¶30,050. Committee Reports at ¶10,570.]
Amendments
• 2004, Working Families Tax Relief Act of 2004 (H.R. 1308)

H.R. 1308, §408(a)(17):

Amended Code Sec. 415(c)(7)(C) by striking "subparagraph (D)" and inserting "subparagraph (B)". **Effective** on the date of the enactment of this Act.

(d) COST-OF-LIVING ADJUSTMENTS.—

* * *

(4) ROUNDING.—

(A) $160,000 AMOUNT.—Any increase under subparagraph (A) of paragraph (1) which is not a multiple of $5,000 shall be rounded to the next lowest multiple of $5,000. *This subparagraph shall also apply for purposes of any provision of this title that provides for adjustments in accordance with the method contained in this subsection, except to the extent provided in such provision.*

* * *

[CCH Explanation at ¶343. Committee Reports at ¶10,530.]
Amendments
• 2004, Working Families Tax Relief Act of 2004 (H.R. 1308)

Economic Growth and Tax Relief Reconciliation Act of 2001 (P.L. 107-16) to which it relates [**effective** for years beginning after 12-31-2001.—CCH].

H.R. 1308, §404(b)(2):

Amended Code Sec. 415(d)(4)(A) by adding at the end a new sentence. **Effective** as if included in the provision of the

[¶5245] CODE SEC. 416. SPECIAL RULES FOR TOP-HEAVY PLANS.

* * *

(i) DEFINITIONS.—For purposes of this section—

(1) KEY EMPLOYEE.—

(A) IN GENERAL.—The term "key employee" means an employee who, at any time during the plan year, is—

(i) an officer of the employer having an annual compensation greater than $130,000,

(ii) a 5-percent owner of the employer, or

(iii) a 1-percent owner of the employer having an annual compensation from the employer of more than $150,000.

For purposes of clause (i), no more than 50 employees (or, if lesser, the greater of 3 or 10 percent of the employees) shall be treated as officers. *In the case of plan years* beginning after December 31, 2002, the $130,000 amount in clause (i) shall be adjusted at the same time and in the same manner as under section 415(d), except that the base period shall be the calendar quarter beginning July 1, 2001, and any increase under this sentence which is not a multiple of $5,000 shall be rounded to the next lower multiple of $5,000. Such term shall not include any officer or employee of an entity referred to in section 414(d) (relating to governmental plans). For purposes of determining the number of officers taken into account under clause (i), employees described in section 414(q)(5) shall be excluded.

* * *

[CCH Explanation at ¶30,050. Committee Reports at ¶10,570.]

Amendments

• 2004, Working Families Tax Relief Act of 2004 (H.R. 1308)

H.R. 1308, §408(a)(16):

Amended Code Sec. 416(i)(1)(A) by striking "in the case of plan years" and inserting "In the case of plan years" in the matter following clause (iii). **Effective** on the date of the enactment of this Act.

[¶5250] CODE SEC. 529. QUALIFIED TUITION PROGRAMS.

* * *

(c) TAX TREATMENT OF DESIGNATED BENEFICIARIES AND CONTRIBUTORS.—

* * *

(5) OTHER GIFT TAX RULES.—For purposes of chapters 12 and 13—

(A) TREATMENT OF DISTRIBUTIONS.—Except as provided in subparagraph (B), in no event shall a distribution from a qualified tuition program be treated as a taxable gift.

(B) TREATMENT OF DESIGNATION OF NEW BENEFICIARY.—*The taxes imposed by chapters 12 and 13 shall apply to a transfer by reason of a change in the designated beneficiary under the program (or a rollover to the account of a new beneficiary) unless the new beneficiary is—*

(i) assigned to the same generation as (or a higher generation than) the old beneficiary (determined in accordance with section 2651), and

(ii) a member of the family of the old beneficiary.

* * *

[CCH Explanation at ¶369. Committee Reports at ¶10,550.]

Amendments

• 2004, Working Families Tax Relief Act of 2004 (H.R. 1308)

H.R. 1308, §406(a):

Amended Code Sec. 529(c)(5)(B). **Effective** as if included in the provision of the Taxpayer Relief Act of 1997 (P.L. 105-34) to which it relates [**effective** for transfers made after 8-5-97.—CCH]. Prior to amendment, Code Sec. 529(c)(5)(B) read as follows:

(B) TREATMENT OF DESIGNATION OF NEW BENEFICIARY.—The taxes imposed by chapters 12 and 13 shall apply to a transfer by reason of a change in the designated beneficiary under the program (or a rollover to the account of a new beneficiary) only if the new beneficiary is a generation below the generation of the old beneficiary (determined in accordance with section 2651).

(e) OTHER DEFINITIONS AND SPECIAL RULES.—For purposes of this section—

* * *

(2) MEMBER OF FAMILY.—The term "member of the family" means, with respect to any designated beneficiary—

(A) the spouse of such beneficiary;

(B) an individual who bears a relationship to such beneficiary which is described in *subparagraphs (A) through (G) of section 152(d)(2);*

(C) the spouse of any individual described in subparagraph (B); and

(D) any first cousin of such beneficiary.

* * *

[CCH Explanation at ¶145.]

Amendments

• **2004, Working Families Tax Relief Act of 2004 (H.R. 1308)**

H.R. 1308, §207(21):

Amended Code Sec. 529(e)(2)(B) by striking "paragraphs (1) through (8) of section 152(a)" and inserting "subpara-

graphs (A) through (G) of section 152(d)(2)". **Effective for** tax years beginning after 12-31-2004.

[¶5255] CODE SEC. 530. COVERDELL EDUCATION SAVINGS ACCOUNTS.

* * *

(d) TAX TREATMENT OF DISTRIBUTIONS.—

* * *

(2) DISTRIBUTIONS FOR QUALIFIED EDUCATION EXPENSES.—

* * *

(C) COORDINATION WITH HOPE AND LIFETIME LEARNING CREDITS AND QUALIFIED TUITION PROGRAMS.—For purposes of subparagraph (A)—

(i) CREDIT COORDINATION.—The total amount of qualified education expenses with respect to an individual for the taxable year shall be reduced—

(I) as provided in section 25A(g)(2), and

(II) by the amount of such expenses which were taken into account in determining the credit allowed to the taxpayer or any other person under section 25A.

* * *

(4) ADDITIONAL TAX FOR DISTRIBUTIONS NOT USED FOR EDUCATIONAL EXPENSES.—

* * *

(B) EXCEPTIONS.—Subparagraph (A) shall not apply if the payment or distribution is—

(i) made to a beneficiary (or to the estate of the designated beneficiary) on or after the death of the designated beneficiary,

(ii) attributable to the designated beneficiary's being disabled (within the meaning of section 72(m)(7)),

(iii) made on account of a scholarship, allowance, or payment described in section 25A(g)(2) received by the *designated beneficiary* to the extent the amount of the payment or distribution does not exceed the amount of the scholarship, allowance, or payment,

(iv) made on account of the attendance of the designated beneficiary at the United States Military Academy, the United States Naval Academy, the United States Air Force Academy, the United States Coast Guard Academy, or the United States Merchant Marine Academy, to the extent that the amount of the payment or distribution does not exceed the costs of advanced education (as defined by section 2005(e)(3) of title 10, United States Code, as in effect on the date of the enactment of this section) attributable to such attendance, or

(v) an amount which is includible in gross income solely by application of paragraph (2)(C)(i)(II) for the taxable year.

* * *

[CCH Explanation at ¶347, ¶365 and ¶367. Committee Reports at ¶10,530 and ¶10,550.]

Amendments

• 2004, Working Families Tax Relief Act of 2004 (H.R. 1308)

H.R. 1308, §404(a):

Amended Code Sec. 530(d)(2)(C)(i) by striking "higher" after "qualified". **Effective** as if included in the provision of the Economic Growth and Tax Relief Reconciliation Act of 2001 (P.L. 107-16) to which it relates [**effective** for tax years beginning after 12-31-2001.—CCH].

H.R. 1308, §406(b):

Amended Code Sec. 530(d)(4)(B)(iii) by striking "account holder" and inserting "designated beneficiary". **Effective** as if included in the provision of the Taxpayer Relief Act of 1997 (P.L. 105-34) to which it relates [**effective** for tax years beginning after 12-31-1997.—CCH].

[¶5260] CODE SEC. 613A. LIMITATIONS ON PERCENTAGE DEPLETION IN CASE OF OIL AND GAS WELLS.

* * *

(c) EXEMPTION FOR INDEPENDENT PRODUCERS AND ROYALTY OWNERS.—

* * *

(6) OIL AND NATURAL GAS PRODUCED FROM MARGINAL PROPERTIES.—

* * *

(H) TEMPORARY SUSPENSION OF TAXABLE INCOME LIMIT WITH RESPECT TO MARGINAL PRODUCTION.—The second sentence of subsection (a) of section 613 shall not apply to so much of the allowance for depletion as is determined under subparagraph (A) for any taxable year beginning after December 31, 1997, and before *January 1, 2006.*

* * *

[CCH Explanation at ¶229. Committee Reports at ¶10,340.]

Amendments

• 2004, Working Families Tax Relief Act of 2004 (H.R. 1308)

H.R. 1308, §314(a):

Amended Code Sec. 613A(c)(6)(H) by striking "January 1, 2004" and inserting "January 1, 2006". **Effective** for tax years beginning after 12-31-2003.

[¶5265] CODE SEC. 691. RECIPIENTS OF INCOME IN RESPECT OF DECEDENTS.

* * *

(c) DEDUCTION FOR ESTATE TAX.—

* * *

(4) COORDINATION WITH CAPITAL GAIN PROVISIONS.—For purposes of sections 1(h), 1201, 1202, and 1211, the amount taken into account with respect to any item described in subsection (a)(1) shall be reduced (but not below zero) by the amount of the deduction allowable under paragraph (1) of this subsection with respect to such item.

* * *

[CCH Explanation at ¶309. Committee Reports at ¶10,510.]

Amendments

• 2004, Working Families Tax Relief Act of 2004 (H.R. 1308)

H.R. 1308, §402(a)(4):

Amended Code Sec. 691(c)(4) by striking "of any gain" following "1211, the amount". **Effective** as if included in section 302 of the Jobs and Growth Tax Relief Reconciliation Act of 2003 (P.L. 108-27) [**effective** generally for tax years beginning after 12-31-2002.—CCH].

[¶5270] CODE SEC. 854. LIMITATIONS APPLICABLE TO DIVIDENDS RECEIVED FROM REGULATED INVESTMENT COMPANY.

* * *

(b) Other Dividends.—

(1) Amount Treated as Dividend.—

* * *

(B) Maximum Rate Under Section 1(h).—

(i) In General.—*In any case in which—*

(I) a dividend is received from a regulated investment company (other than a dividend to which subsection (a) applies),

(II) such investment company meets the requirements of section 852(a) for the taxable year during which it paid such dividend, and

(III) the qualified dividend income of such investment company for such taxable year is less than 95 percent of its gross income,

then, in computing qualified dividend income, there shall be taken into account only that portion of such dividend designated by the regulated investment company.

(ii) Gross Income.—For purposes of clause (i), in the case of 1 or more sales or other dispositions of stock or securities, the term "gross income" includes only the excess of—

(I) the net short-term capital gain from such sales or dispositions, over

(II) the net long-term capital loss from such sales or dispositions.

(C) Limitations.—

(i) Subparagraph (A).—*The aggregate amount which may be designated as dividends under subparagraph (A) shall not exceed the aggregate dividends received by the company for the taxable year.*

(ii) Subparagraph (B).—*The aggregate amount which may be designated as qualified dividend income under subparagraph (B) shall not exceed the sum of—*

(I) the qualified dividend income of the company for the taxable year, and

(II) the amount of any earnings and profits which were distributed by the company for such taxable year and accumulated in a taxable year with respect to which this part did not apply.

(2) Notice to Shareholders.—The amount of any distribution by a regulated investment company which may be taken into account *as qualified dividend income for purposes of section 1(h)(11) and as dividends for purposes of* the deduction under section 243 shall not exceed the amount so designated by the company in a written notice to its shareholders mailed not later than 60 days after the close of its taxable year.

* * *

(5) Qualified Dividend Income.—For purposes of this subsection, the term "qualified dividend income" has the meaning given such term by section 1(h)(11)(B).

[CCH Explanation at ¶307. Committee Reports at ¶10,510.]

Amendments

• **2004, Working Families Tax Relief Act of 2004 (H.R. 1308)**

H.R. 1308, §402(a)(5)(A)(i):

Amended Code Sec. 854(b)(1)(B) by striking clauses (iii) and (iv). **Effective** as if included in section 302 of the Jobs and Growth Tax Relief Reconciliation Act of 2003 (P.L. 108-27) [**effective** generally for tax years ending after 12-31-2002.—CCH]. Prior to being stricken, Code Sec. 854(b)(1)(B)(iii) and (iv) read as follows:

(iii) Dividends from real estate investment trusts.—For purposes of clause (i)—

(I) paragraph (3)(B)(ii) shall not apply, and

(II) in the case of a distribution from a trust described in such paragraph, the amount of such distribution which is a dividend shall be subject to the limitations under section 857(c).

(iv) Dividends from qualified foreign corporations.—For purposes of clause (i), dividends received from qualified foreign corporations (as defined in section 1(h)(11)) shall also be taken into account in computing aggregate dividends received.

H.R. 1308, §402(a)(5)(A)(ii):

Amended Code Sec. 854(b)(1)(B)(i). **Effective** as if included in section 302 of the Jobs and Growth Tax Relief Reconciliation Act of 2003 (P.L. 108-27) [**effective** generally for tax years ending after 12-31-2002.—CCH]. Prior to amendment, Code Sec. 854(b)(1)(B)(i) read as follows:

(i) In general.—If the aggregate dividends received by a regulated investment company during any taxable year are less than 95 percent of its gross income, then, in computing the maximum rate under section 1(h)(11), rules similar to the rules of subparagraph (A) shall apply.

H.R. 1308, §402(a)(5)(B):

Amended Code Sec. 854(b)(1)(C). **Effective** as if included in section 302 of the Jobs and Growth Tax Relief Reconciliation Act of 2003 (P.L. 108-27) [**effective** generally for tax years ending after 12-31-2002.—CCH]. Prior to amendment, Code Sec. 854(b)(1)(C) read as follows:

(C) LIMITATION.—The aggregate amount which may be designated as dividends under subparagraph (A) or (B) shall not exceed the aggregate dividends received by the company for the taxable year.

H.R. 1308, §402(a)(5)(C):

Amended Code Sec. 854(b)(2) by striking "as a dividend for purposes of the maximum rate under section 1(h)(11) and" and inserting "as qualified dividend income for purposes of section 1(h)(11) and as dividends for purposes of". **Effective** as if included in section 302 of the Jobs and Growth Tax Relief Reconciliation Act of 2003 (P.L. 108-27) [**effective** generally for tax years ending after 12-31-2002.— CCH]. For a special rule, see Act. Sec. 402(a)(5)(F), below.

H.R. 1308, §402(a)(5)(D):

Amended Code Sec. 854(b)(5). **Effective** as if included in section 302 of the Jobs and Growth Tax Relief Reconciliation Act of 2003 (P.L. 108-27) [**effective** generally for tax years ending after 12-31-2002.—CCH]. Prior to amendment, Code Sec. 854(b)(5) read as follows:

(5) COORDINATION WITH SECTION 1(h)(11).—For purposes of paragraph (1)(B), an amount shall be treated as a dividend only if the amount is qualified dividend income (within the meaning of section 1(h)(11)(B)).

H.R. 1308, §402(a)(5)(F), provides:

(F) With respect to any taxable year of a regulated investment company or real estate investment trust ending on or before November 30, 2003, the period for providing notice of the qualified dividend amount to shareholders under sections 854(b)(2) and 857(c)(2)(C) of the Internal Revenue Code of 1986, as amended by this section, shall not expire before the date on which the statement under section 6042(c) of such Code is required to be furnished with respect to the last calendar year beginning in such taxable year.

[¶5275] CODE SEC. 857. TAXATION OF REAL ESTATE INVESTMENT TRUSTS AND THEIR BENEFICIARIES.

* * *

(c) RESTRICTIONS APPLICABLE TO DIVIDENDS RECEIVED FROM REAL ESTATE INVESTMENT TRUSTS.—

(1) SECTION 243.—For purposes of section 243 (relating to deductions for dividends received by corporations), a dividend received from a real estate investment trust which meets the requirements of this part shall not be considered a dividend.

(2) SECTION (1)(h)(11).—

(A) IN GENERAL.—In any case in which—

(i) a dividend is received from a real estate investment trust (other than a capital gain dividend), and

(ii) such trust meets the requirements of section 856(a) for the taxable year during which it paid such dividend,

then, in computing qualified dividend income, there shall be taken into account only that portion of such dividend designated by the real estate investment trust.

(B) LIMITATION.—The aggregate amount which may be designated as qualified dividend income under subparagraph (A) shall not exceed the sum of—

(i) the qualified dividend income of the trust for the taxable year,

(ii) the excess of—

(I) the sum of the real estate investment trust taxable income computed under section 857(b)(2) for the preceding taxable year and the income subject to tax by reason of the application of the regulations under section 337(d) for such preceding taxable year, over

(II) the sum of the taxes imposed on the trust for such preceding taxable year under section 857(b)(1) and by reason of the application of such regulations, and

(iii) the amount of any earnings and profits which were distributed by the trust for such taxable year and accumulated in a taxable year with respect to which this part did not apply.

(C) NOTICE TO SHAREHOLDERS.—The amount of any distribution by a real estate investment trust which may be taken into account as qualified dividend income shall not exceed the amount so designated by the trust in a written notice to its shareholders mailed not later than 60 days after the close of its taxable year.

(D) QUALIFIED DIVIDEND INCOME.—For purposes of this paragraph, the term "qualified dividend income" has the meaning given such term by section 1(h)(11)(B).

* * *

[CCH Explanation at ¶307. Committee Reports at ¶10,510.]

Amendments

• **2004, Working Families Tax Relief Act of 2004 (H.R. 1308)**

H.R. 1308, §402(a)(5)(E):

Amended Code Sec. 857(c)(2). **Effective** as if included in section 302 of the Jobs and Growth Tax Relief Reconciliation Act of 2003 (P.L. 108-27) [**effective** generally for tax years ending after 12-31-2002.—CCH]. For a special rule, see Act Sec. 402(a)(5)(F), below. Prior to amendment, Code Sec. 857(c)(2) read as follows:

(2) SECTION 1(h)(11).—For purposes of section 1(h)(11) (relating to maximum rate of tax on dividends)—

(A) rules similar to the rules of subparagraphs (B) and (C) of section 854(b)(1) shall apply to dividends received from a real estate investment trust which meets the requirements of this part, and

(B) for purposes of such rules, such a trust shall be treated as receiving qualified dividend income during any taxable year in an amount equal to the sum of—

(i) the excess of real estate investment trust taxable income computed under section 857(b)(2) for the preceding taxable year over the tax payable by the trust under section 857(b)(1) for such preceding taxable year, and

(ii) the excess of the income subject to tax by reason of the application of the regulations under section 337(d) for the preceding taxable year over the tax payable by the trust on such income for such preceding taxable year.

H.R. 1308, §402(a)(5)(F), provides:

(F) With respect to any taxable year of a regulated investment company or real estate investment trust ending on or before November 30, 2003, the period for providing notice of the qualified dividend amount to shareholders under sections 854(b)(2) and 857(c)(2)(C) of the Internal Revenue Code of 1986, as amended by this section, shall not expire before the date on which the statement under section 6042(c) of such Code is required to be furnished with respect to the last calendar year beginning in such taxable year.

[¶5280] CODE SEC. 901. TAXES OF FOREIGN COUNTRIES AND OF POSSESSIONS OF UNITED STATES.

* * *

(k) MINIMUM HOLDING PERIOD FOR CERTAIN TAXES.—

(1) WITHHOLDING TAXES.—

(A) IN GENERAL.—In no event shall a credit be allowed under subsection (a) for any withholding tax on a dividend with respect to stock in a corporation if—

(i) such stock is held by the recipient of the dividend for 15 days or less during the *31-day period* beginning on the date which is 15 days before the date on which such share becomes ex-dividend with respect to such dividend, or

(ii) to the extent that the recipient of the dividend is under an obligation (whether pursuant to a short sale or otherwise) to make related payments with respect to positions in substantially similar or related property.

* * *

(3) 45-DAY RULE IN THE CASE OF CERTAIN PREFERENCE DIVIDENDS.—In the case of stock having preference in dividends and dividends with respect to such stock which are attributable to a period or periods aggregating in excess of 366 days, paragraph (1)(A)(i) shall be applied—

(A) by substituting "45 days" for "15 days" each place it appears, and

(B) by substituting *"91-day period"* for *"31-day period"*.

* * *

[CCH Explanation at ¶305. Committee Reports at ¶10,550.]

Amendments

• **2004, Working Families Tax Relief Act of 2004 (H.R. 1308)**

H.R. 1308, §406(g)(1):

Amended Code Sec. 901(k)(1)(A)(i) by striking "30-day period" and inserting "31-day period". **Effective** as if included in the provision of the Taxpayer Relief Act of 1997 (P.L. 105-34) to which it relates [**effective** for dividends paid or accrued after 9-4-97.—CCH].

H.R. 1308, §406(g)(2)(A)-(B):

Amended Code Sec. 901(k)(3)(B) by striking "90-day period" and inserting "91-day period", and by striking "30-day period" and inserting "31-day period". **Effective** as if included in the provision of the Taxpayer Relief Act of 1997 (P.L. 105-34) to which it relates [**effective** for dividends paid or accrued after 9-4-97.—CCH].

[¶5285] CODE SEC. 904. LIMITATION ON CREDIT.

* * *

(h) COORDINATION WITH NONREFUNDABLE PERSONAL CREDITS.—In the case of an individual, for purposes of subsection (a), the tax against which the credit is taken is such tax reduced by the sum of the credits allowable under subpart A of part IV of subchapter A of this chapter (other than sections

23, 24, and 25B). This subsection shall not apply to taxable years beginning during 2000, 2001, 2002, 2003, 2004, or 2005.

* * *

[CCH Explanation at ¶ 135. Committee Reports at ¶ 10,320.]

Amendments

• **2004, Working Families Tax Relief Act of 2004 (H.R. 1308)**

H.R. 1308, § 312(b)(1):

Amended Code Sec. 904(h) by striking "or 2003" and inserting "2003, 2004, or 2005". **Effective** for tax years beginning after 12-31-2003.

H.R. 1308, § 312(b)(2), provides:

(2) The amendments made by sections 201(b), 202(f), and 618(b) of the Economic Growth and Tax Relief Reconciliation Act of 2001 shall not apply to taxable years beginning during 2004 or 2005.

[¶ 5290] CODE SEC. 1033. INVOLUNTARY CONVERSIONS.

* * *

(h) SPECIAL RULES FOR PROPERTY DAMAGED BY PRESIDENTIALLY DECLARED DISASTERS.—

* * *

(3) PRESIDENTIALLY DECLARED DISASTER.—For purposes of this subsection, the term "Presidentially declared disaster" means any disaster which, with respect to the area in which the property is located, resulted in a subsequent determination by the President that such area warrants assistance by the Federal Government under the *Robert T. Stafford* Disaster Relief and Emergency Assistance Act.

* * *

[CCH Explanation at ¶ 30,050. Committee Reports at ¶ 10,570.]

Amendments

• **2004, Working Families Tax Relief Act of 2004 (H.R. 1308)**

H.R. 1308, § 408(a)(7)(C):

Amended Code Sec. 1033(h)(3) by inserting "Robert T. Stafford" before "Disaster Relief and Emergency Assistance Act". **Effective** on the date of the enactment of this Act.

[¶ 5295] CODE SEC. 1234B. GAINS OR LOSSES FROM SECURITIES FUTURES CONTRACTS.

* * *

(c) SECURITIES FUTURES CONTRACT.—For purposes of this section, the term "securities futures contract" means any security future (as defined in section 3(a)(55)(A) of the Securities Exchange Act of 1934, as in effect on the date of the enactment of this section). *The Secretary may prescribe regulations regarding the status of contracts the values of which are determined directly or indirectly by reference to any index which becomes (or ceases to be) a narrow-based security index (as defined for purposes of section 1256(g)(6)).*

* * *

[CCH Explanation at ¶ 311. Committee Reports at ¶ 10,540.]

Amendments

• **2004, Working Families Tax Relief Act of 2004 (H.R. 1308)**

H.R. 1308, § 405(a)(1):

Amended Code Sec. 1234B(c) by adding at the end a new sentence. **Effective** as if included in section 401 of the Community Renewal Tax Relief Act of 2000 (P.L. 106-554) [effective 12-21-2000.—CCH].

[¶ 5300] CODE SEC. 1256. SECTION 1256 CONTRACTS MARKED TO MARKET.

* * *

(g) DEFINITIONS.—For purposes of this section—

* * *

(6) EQUITY OPTION.—The term "equity option" means any option—

(A) to buy or sell stock, or

(B) the value of which is determined directly or indirectly by reference to any stock or any narrow-based security index (as defined in section 3(a)(55) of the Securities Exchange Act of 1934, as in effect on the date of the enactment of this paragraph).

The term "equity option" includes such an option on a group of stocks only if such group meets the requirements for a narrow-based security index (as so defined). *The Secretary may prescribe regulations regarding the status of options the values of which are determined directly or indirectly by reference to any index which becomes (or ceases to be) a narrow-based security index (as so defined).*

* * *

[CCH Explanation at ¶311. Committee Reports at ¶10,540.]

Amendments

• **2004, Working Families Tax Relief Act of 2004 (H.R. 1308)**

Community Renewal Tax Relief Act of 2000 (P.L. 106-554) [effective 12-21-2000.—CCH].

H.R. 1308, §405(a)(2):

Amended Code Sec. 1256(g)(6) by adding at the end a new sentence. **Effective** as if included in section 401 of the

[¶5305] CODE SEC. 1259. CONSTRUCTIVE SALES TREATMENT FOR APPRECIATED FINANCIAL POSITIONS.

* * *

(c) CONSTRUCTIVE SALE.—For purposes of this section—

* * *

(2) EXCEPTION FOR SALES OF NONPUBLICLY TRADED PROPERTY.—*A taxpayer shall not be treated as having made a constructive sale soley because the taxpayer enters into a contract* for sale of any stock, debt instrument, or partnership interest which is not a marketable security (as defined in section 453(f)) if the contract settles within 1 year after the date such contract is entered into.

(3) EXCEPTION FOR CERTAIN CLOSED TRANSACTIONS.—

(A) IN GENERAL.—In applying this section, there shall be disregarded any transaction (which would otherwise *cause a constructive sale*) during the taxable year if—

(i) such transaction is closed *on or before* the 30th day after the close of such taxable year,

(ii) the taxpayer holds the appreciated financial position throughout the 60-day period beginning on the date such transaction is closed, and

(iii) at no time during such 60-day period is the taxpayer's risk of loss with respect to such position reduced by reason of a circumstance which would be described in section 246(c)(4) if references to stock included references to such position.

(B) TREATMENT OF *CERTAIN CLOSED TRANSACTIONS WHERE RISK OF LOSS ON APPRECIATED FINANCIAL POSITION DIMINISHED.*—If—

(i) a transaction, which would otherwise *cause a constructive sale* of an appreciated financial position, is closed during the taxable year or during the 30 days thereafter, and

(ii) another transaction is entered into during the 60-day period beginning on the date the transaction referred to in clause (i) is closed—

(I) *which would (but for this subparagraph) cause the requirement of subparagraph (A)(iii) not to be met with respect to the transaction described in clause (i) of this subparagraph,*

(II) which is closed *on or* before the 30th day after the close of the taxable year in which the transaction referred to in clause (i) occurs, and

(III) which meets the requirements of clauses (ii) and (iii) of subparagraph (A),

the transaction referred to in clause (ii) shall be disregarded for purposes of determining whether the requirements of subparagraph (A)(iii) are met with respect to the transaction described in clause (i).

* * *

[CCH Explanation at ¶ 313. Committee Reports at ¶ 10,550.]

Amendments

• **2004, Working Families Tax Relief Act of 2004 (H.R. 1308)**

H.R. 1308, § 406(e)(1):

Amended Code Sec. 1259(c)(2) by striking "The term 'constructive sale' shall not include any contract" and inserting "A taxpayer shall not be treated as having made a constructive sale solely because the taxpayer enters into a contract". **Effective** as if included in the provision of the Taxpayer Relief Act of 1997 (P.L. 105-34) to which it relates [**effective** for constructive sales after 6-8-97, generally.—CCH].

H.R. 1308, § 406(e)(2):

Amended Code Sec. 1259(c)(3)(A) and (B)(i) by striking "be treated as a constructive sale" and inserting "cause a constructive sale". **Effective** as if included in the provision of the Taxpayer Relief Act of 1997 (P.L. 105-34) to which it relates [**effective** for constructive sales after 6-8-97, generally.—CCH].

H.R. 1308, § 406(e)(3):

Amended Code Sec. 1259(c)(3)(A)(i) by striking "before the end of" and inserting "on or before". **Effective** as if included in the provision of the Taxpayer Relief Act of 1997 (P.L. 105-34) to which it relates [**effective** for constructive sales after 6-8-97, generally.—CCH].

H.R. 1308, § 406(e)(4):

Amended Code Sec. 1259(c)(3)(B)(ii) by striking "substantially similar" following "(ii) another". **Effective** as if in-

cluded in the provision of the Taxpayer Relief Act of 1997 (P.L. 105-34) to which it relates [**effective** for constructive sales after 6-8-97, generally.—CCH].

H.R. 1308, § 406(e)(5):

Amended Code Sec. 1259(c)(3)(B)(ii)(I). **Effective** as if included in the provision of the Taxpayer Relief Act of 1997 (P.L. 105-34) to which it relates [**effective** for constructive sales after 6-8-97, generally.—CCH]. Prior to amendment, Code Sec. 1259(c)(3)(B)(ii)(I) read as follows:

(I) which also would otherwise be treated as a constructive sale of such position,

H.R. 1308, § 406(e)(6):

Amended Code Sec. 1259(c)(3)(B)(ii)(II) by inserting "on or" before "before the 30th day". **Effective** as if included in the provision of the Taxpayer Relief Act of 1997 (P.L. 105-34) to which it relates [**effective** for constructive sales after 6-8-97, generally.—CCH].

H.R. 1308, § 406(e)(7):

Amended the heading for Code Sec. 1259(c)(3)(B) by striking "POSITIONS WHICH ARE REESTABLISHED" and inserting "CERTAIN CLOSED TRANSACTIONS WHERE RISK OF LOSS ON APPRECIATED FINANCIAL POSITION DIMINISHED". **Effective** as if included in the provision of the Taxpayer Relief Act of 1997 (P.L. 105-34) to which it relates [**effective** for constructive sales after 6-8-97, generally.—CCH].

[¶ 5310] CODE SEC. 1296. ELECTION OF MARK TO MARKET FOR MARKETABLE STOCK.

* * *

(h) COORDINATION WITH SECTION 851(b).—For purposes of *section 851(b)(2)*, any amount included in gross income under subsection (a) shall be treated as a dividend.

* * *

[CCH Explanation at ¶ 30,050. Committee Reports at ¶ 10,570.]

Amendments

• **2004, Working Families Tax Relief Act of 2004 (H.R. 1308)**

H.R. 1308, § 408(a)(19):

Amended Code Sec. 1296(h) by striking "paragraphs (2) and (3) of section 851(b)" and inserting "section 851(b)(2)". **Effective** on the date of the enactment of this Act.

[¶ 5315] CODE SEC. 1377. DEFINITIONS AND SPECIAL RULE.

* * *

(b) POST-TERMINATION TRANSITION PERIOD.—

* * *

(2) DETERMINATION DEFINED.—For purposes of paragraph (1), the term "determination" means—

(A) a determination as defined in section 1313(a), or

(B) an agreement between the corporation and the Secretary that the corporation failed to qualify as an S corporation.

(3) SPECIAL RULES FOR AUDIT RELATED POST-TERMINATION TRANSITION PERIODS.—

(A) NO APPLICATION TO CARRYOVERS.—Paragraph (1)(B) shall not apply for purposes of section 1366(d)(3).

(B) LIMITATION ON APPLICATION TO DISTRIBUTIONS.—Paragraph (1)(B) shall apply to a distribution described in section 1371(e) only to the extent that the amount of such distribution does not exceed the aggregate increase (if any) in the accumulated adjustments account (within the meaning of section 1368(e)) by reason of the adjustments referred to in such paragraph.

[CCH Explanation at ¶377. Committee Reports at ¶10,560.]

Amendments

• **2004, Working Families Tax Relief Act of 2004 (H.R. 1308)**

H.R. 1308, §407(a):

Amended Code Sec. 1377(b) by adding at the end a new paragraph (3). **Effective** as if included in the provision of the Small Business Job Protection Act of 1996 (P.L. 104-188) to which it relates [**effective** for determinations after 12-31-96.—CCH].

[¶5320] CODE SEC. 1397E. CREDIT TO HOLDERS OF QUALIFIED ZONE ACADEMY BONDS.

* * *

(e) LIMITATION ON AMOUNT OF BONDS DESIGNATED.—

(1) NATIONAL LIMITATION.—There is a national zone academy bond limitation for each calendar year. Such limitation is $400,000,000 for 1998, 1999, 2000, 2001, 2002, *2003, 2004, and 2005,* and, except as provided in paragraph (4), zero thereafter.

* * *

[CCH Explanation at ¶239. Committee Reports at ¶10,240.]

Amendments

• **2004, Working Families Tax Relief Act of 2004 (H.R. 1308)**

H.R. 1308, §304(a):

Amended Code Sec. 1397E(e)(1) by striking "and 2003" and inserting "2003, 2004, and 2005". **Effective** for obligations issued after 12-31-2003.

(i) S CORPORATIONS.—In the case of a qualified zone academy bond held by an S corporation which is an eligible taxpayer—

(1) each shareholder shall take into account such shareholder's pro rata share of the credit, and

(2) no basis adjustments to the stock of the corporation shall be made under section 1367 on account of this section.

[CCH Explanation at ¶375. Committee Reports at ¶10,550.]

Amendments

• **2004, Working Families Tax Relief Act of 2004 (H.R. 1308)**

H.R. 1308, §406(c):

Amended Code Sec. 1397E by adding at the end a new subsection (i). **Effective** as if included in the provision of the Taxpayer Relief Act of 1997 (P.L. 105-34) to which it relates [**effective** for obligations issued after 12-31-1997.—CCH].

[¶5325] CODE SEC. 1400. ESTABLISHMENT OF DC ZONE.

* * *

(f) TIME FOR WHICH DESIGNATION APPLICABLE.—

(1) IN GENERAL.—The designation made by subsection (a) shall apply for the period beginning on January 1, 1998, and ending on *December 31, 2005.*

(2) C\ *OORDINATION WITH* DC ENTERPRISE COMMUNITY DESIGNATED UNDER SUBCHAPTER U.—The designation under subchapter U of the census tracts referred to in subsection (b)(1) as an enterprise community shall terminate on *December 31, 2005.*

[CCH Explanation at ¶237. Committee Reports at ¶10,300.]
Amendments
• **2004, Working Families Tax Relief Act of 2004 (H.R. 1308)**

H.R. 1308, §310(a):

Amended Code Sec. 1400(f) by striking "December 31, 2003" both places it appears and inserting "December 31, 2005". **Effective** on 1-1-2004.

[¶5330] CODE SEC. 1400A. TAX-EXEMPT ECONOMIC DEVELOPMENT BONDS.
* * *

(b) PERIOD OF APPLICABILITY.—This section shall apply to bonds issued during the period beginning on January 1, 1998, and ending on *December 31, 2005.*

[CCH Explanation at ¶237. Committee Reports at ¶10,300.]
Amendments
• **2004, Working Families Tax Relief Act of 2004 (H.R. 1308)**

H.R. 1308, §310(b):

Amended Code Sec. 1400A(b) by striking "December 31, 2003" and inserting "December 31, 2005". **Effective** for obligations issued after the date of the enactment of this Act.

[¶5335] CODE SEC. 1400B. ZERO PERCENT CAPITAL GAINS RATE.
* * *

(b) DC ZONE ASSET.—For purposes of this section—
* * *

(2) DC ZONE BUSINESS STOCK.—

(A) IN GENERAL.—The term "DC Zone business stock" means any stock in a domestic corporation which is originally issued after December 31, 1997, if—

(i) such stock is acquired by the taxpayer, before *January 1, 2006,* at its original issue (directly or through an underwriter) solely in exchange for cash,

(ii) as of the time such stock was issued, such corporation was a DC Zone business (or, in the case of a new corporation, such corporation was being organized for purposes of being a DC Zone business), and

(iii) during substantially all of the taxpayer's holding period for such stock, such corporation qualified as a DC Zone business.

(3) DC ZONE PARTNERSHIP INTEREST.—The term "DC Zone partnership interest" means any capital or profits interest in a domestic partnership which is originally issued after December 31, 1997, if—

(A) such interest is acquired by the taxpayer, before *January 1, 2006,* from the partnership solely in exchange for cash,

(B) as of the time such interest was acquired, such partnership was a DC Zone business (or, in the case of a new partnership, such partnership was being organized for purposes of being a DC Zone business), and

(C) during substantially all of the taxpayer's holding period for such interest, such partnership qualified as a DC Zone business.

A rule similar to the rule of paragraph (2)(B) shall apply for purposes of this paragraph.

(4) DC ZONE BUSINESS PROPERTY.—

(A) IN GENERAL.—The term "DC Zone business property" means tangible property if—

(i) such property was acquired by the taxpayer by purchase (as defined in section 179(d)(2)) after December 31, 1997, and before *January 1, 2006,*

(ii) the original use of such property in the DC Zone commences with the taxpayer, and

(iii) during substantially all of the taxpayer's holding period for such property, substantially all of the use of such property was in a DC Zone business of the taxpayer.

(B) SPECIAL RULE FOR BUILDINGS WHICH ARE SUBSTANTIALLY IMPROVED.—

(i) IN GENERAL.—The requirements of clauses (i) and (ii) of subparagraph (A) shall be treated as met with respect to—

(I) property which is substantially improved by the taxpayer before *January 1, 2006,* and

(II) any land on which such property is located.

* * *

[CCH Explanation at ¶237. Committee Reports at ¶10,300.]

Amendments
• **2004, Working Families Tax Relief Act of 2004 (H.R. 1308)**

H.R. 1308, §310(c)(1):

Amended Code Sec. 1400B(b) by striking "January 1, 2004" each place it appears and inserting "January 1, 2006". **Effective** on 1-1-2004.

(e) OTHER DEFINITIONS AND SPECIAL RULES.—For purposes of this section—

* * *

(2) GAIN BEFORE 1998 OR AFTER *2010* NOT QUALIFIED.—The term "qualified capital gain" shall not include any gain attributable to periods before January 1, 1998, or after *December 31, 2010.*

* * *

[CCH Explanation at ¶237. Committee Reports at ¶10,300.]

Amendments
• **2004, Working Families Tax Relief Act of 2004 (H.R. 1308)**

H.R. 1308, §310(c)(2)(A)(i)-(ii):

Amended Code Sec. 1400B(e)(2) by striking "December 31, 2008" and inserting "December 31, 2010", and by strik-ing "2008" in the heading and inserting "2010". **Effective** on 1-1-2004.

(g) SALES AND EXCHANGES OF INTERESTS IN PARTNERSHIPS AND S CORPORATIONS WHICH ARE DC ZONE BUSINESSES.—In the case of the sale or exchange of an interest in a partnership, or of stock in an S corporation, which was a DC Zone business during substantially all of the period the taxpayer held such interest or stock, the amount of qualified capital gain shall be determined without regard to—

(1) any gain which is attributable to real property, or an intangible asset, which is not an integral part of a DC Zone business, and

(2) any gain attributable to periods before January 1, 1998, or after *December 31, 2010.*

[CCH Explanation at ¶237. Committee Reports at ¶10,300.]
Amendments
• **2004, Working Families Tax Relief Act of 2004 (H.R. 1308)**

H.R. 1308, §310(c)(2)(B):

Amended Code Sec. 1400B(g)(2) by striking "December 31, 2008" and inserting "December 31, 2010". **Effective** on 1-1-2004.

[¶ 5340] CODE SEC. 1400C. FIRST-TIME HOMEBUYER CREDIT FOR DISTRICT OF COLUMBIA.

* * *

(i) Application of Section.—This section shall apply to property purchased after August 4, 1997, and before *January 1, 2006.*

[CCH Explanation at ¶ 237. Committee Reports at ¶ 10,300.]

Amendments

• **2004, Working Families Tax Relief Act of 2004 (H.R. 1308)**

H.R. 1308, § 310(d):

Amended Code Sec. 1400C(i) by striking "January 1, 2004" and inserting "January 1, 2006". **Effective** on 1-1-2004.

[¶ 5345] CODE SEC. 1400F. RENEWAL COMMUNITY CAPITAL GAIN.

* * *

(d) Certain Rules to Apply.—For purposes of this section, rules similar to the rules of paragraphs (5), (6), and (7) of subsection (b), and subsections (f) and (g), of section 1400B shall apply; except that for such purposes section 1400B(g)(2) shall be applied by substituting "January 1, 2002" for "January 1, 1998" and "December 31, 2014" for *"December 31, 2010".*

* * *

[CCH Explanation at ¶ 237. Committee Reports at ¶ 10,300.]

Amendments

• **2004, Working Families Tax Relief Act of 2004 (H.R. 1308)**

H.R. 1308, § 310(c)(2)(C):

Amended Code Sec. 1400F(d) by striking "December 31, 2008" and inserting "December 31, 2010". **Effective** on 1-1-2004.

[¶ 5350] CODE SEC. 1400L. TAX BENEFITS FOR NEW YORK LIBERTY ZONE.

(a) Expansion of Work Opportunity Tax Credit.—

* * *

(2) New York Liberty Zone Business Employee.—For purposes of this subsection—

(A) In General.—The term "New York Liberty Zone business employee" means, with respect to any period, any employee of a New York Liberty Zone business if substantially all the services performed during such period by such employee for such business are performed in the New York Liberty Zone.

(B) Inclusion of Certain Employees Outside the New York Liberty Zone.—

(i) In General.—In the case of a New York Liberty Zone business described in subclause (II) of subparagraph (C)(i), the term "New York Liberty Zone business employee" includes any employee of such business (not described in subparagraph (A)) if substantially all the services performed during such period by such employee for such business are performed in the City of New York, New York.

(ii) Limitation.—The number of employees of such a business that are treated as New York Liberty Zone business employees on any day by reason of clause (i) shall not exceed the excess of—

(I) the number of employees of such business on September 11, 2001, in the New York Liberty Zone, over

(II) the number of New York Liberty Zone business employees (determined without regard to this subparagraph) of such business on the day to which the limitation is being applied.

The Secretary may require any trade or business to have the number determined under subclause (I) verified by the New York State Department of Labor.

(C) New York Liberty Zone Business.—

(i) In general.—The term "New York Liberty Zone business" means any trade or business which is—

(I) located in the New York Liberty Zone, or

(II) located in the City of New York, New York, outside the New York Liberty Zone, as a result of the physical destruction or damage of such place of business by the September 11, 2001, terrorist attack.

(ii) Credit not allowed for large businesses.—The term "New York Liberty Zone business" shall not include any trade or business for any taxable year if such trade or business employed an average of more than 200 employees on business days during the taxable year.

(D) Special rules for determining amount of credit.—For purposes of applying subpart F of part IV of *subchapter A* of this chapter to wages paid or incurred to any New York Liberty Zone business employee—

(i) section 51(a) shall be applied by substituting "qualified wages" for "qualified first-year wages",

(ii) the rules of section 52 shall apply for purposes of determining the number of employees under *this paragraph,*

(iii) subsections (c)(4) and (i)(2) of section 51shall not apply, and

(iv) in determining qualified wages, the following shall apply in lieu of section 51(b):

(I) Qualified wages.—The term "qualified wages" means wages paid or incurred by the employer to individuals who are New York Liberty Zone business employees of such employer for work performed during calendar year 2002 or 2003.

(II) Only first $6,000 of wages per calendar year taken into account.—The amount of the qualified wages which may be taken into account with respect to any individual shall not exceed $6,000 per calendar year.

[CCH Explanation at ¶337. Committee Reports at ¶10,520.]

Amendments

• **2004, Working Families Tax Relief Act of 2004 (H.R. 1308)**

H.R. 1308, §403(c)(1)(A)-(B):

Amended Code Sec. 1400L(a)(2)(D) by striking "subchapter B" and inserting "subchapter A", and by striking

"subparagraph (B)" and inserting "this paragraph" in clause (ii). **Effective** as if included in the provision of the Job Creation and Worker Assistance Act of 2002 (P.L. 107-147) to which it relates [**effective 3-9-2002.**—CCH].

(b) Special Allowance for Certain Property Acquired after September 10, 2001.—

* * *

(2) Qualified New York Liberty Zone Property.—For purposes of this subsection—

* * *

(D) Special rules.—For purposes of this subsection, rules similar to the rules of section 168(k)(2)(D) shall apply, except that clause (i) thereof shall be applied without regard to "and before September 11, 2004", *and clause (iv) thereof shall be applied by substituting "qualified New York Liberty Zone property" for "qualified property".*

* * *

[CCH Explanation at ¶331. Committee Reports at ¶10,520.]

Amendments

• **2004, Working Families Tax Relief Act of 2004 (H.R. 1308)**

H.R. 1308, §403(c)(2):

Amended Code Sec. 1400L(b)(2)(D) by inserting ", and clause (iv) thereof shall be applied by substituting 'qualified

New York Liberty Zone property' for 'qualified property'" before the period at the end. **Effective** as if included in the provision of the Job Creation and Worker Assistance Act of 2002 (P.L. 107-147) to which it relates [**effective 3-9-2002.**—CCH].

(c) 5-Year Recovery Period for Depreciation of Certain Leasehold Improvements.—

* * *

(5) Election Out.—*For purposes of this subsection, rules similar to the rules of section 168(k)(2)(C)(iii) shall apply.*

[CCH Explanation at ¶335. Committee Reports at ¶10,520.]

Amendments

• **2004, Working Families Tax Relief Act of 2004 (H.R. 1308)**

H.R. 1308, §403(c)(3):

Amended Code Sec. 1400L(c) by adding at the end a new paragraph (5). **Effective** as if included in the provision of the Job Creation and Worker Assistance Act of 2002 (P.L. 107-147) to which it relates [**effective** 3-9-2002.—CCH].

(d) Tax-Exempt Bond Financing.—

* * *

(2) Qualified New York Liberty Bond.—For purposes of this subsection, the term "qualified New York Liberty Bond" means any bond issued as part of an issue if—

* * *

(D) such bond is issued after the the date of the enactment of this section and before January 1, *2010*.

* * *

[CCH Explanation at ¶235. Committee Reports at ¶10,290.]

Amendments

• **2004, Working Families Tax Relief Act of 2004 (H.R. 1308)**

H.R. 1308, §309(a):

Amended Code Sec. 1400L(d)(2)(D) by striking "2005" and inserting "2010". **Effective** on the date of the enactment of this Act.

(e) Advance Refundings of Certain Tax-Exempt Bonds.—

(1) In general.—With respect to a bond described in paragraph (2) issued as part of an issue 90 percent (95 percent in the case of a bond described in paragraph (2)(C)) or more of the net proceeds (as defined in section 150(a)(3)) of which were used to finance facilities located within the City of New York, New York (or property which is functionally related and subordinate to facilities located within the City of New York for the furnishing of water), one additional advanced refunding after the date of the enactment of this section and before January 1, *2006*, shall be allowed under the applicable rules of section 149(d) if—

(A) the Governor or the Mayor designates the advance refunding bond for purposes of this subsection, and

(B) the requirements of paragraph (4) are met.

(2) Bonds described.—A bond is described in this paragraph if such bond was outstanding on September 11, 2001, and is—

* * *

(B) a State or local bond (as so defined) other than a private activity bond (as defined in section 141(a)) issued by the New York Municipal Water Finance Authority or the Metropolitan Transportation Authority of the State of New York *or the Municipal Assistance Corporation*, or

* * *

[CCH Explanation at ¶235. Committee Reports at ¶10,290.]

Amendments

• **2004, Working Families Tax Relief Act of 2004 (H.R. 1308)**

H.R. 1308, §309(b):

Amended Code Sec. 1400L(e)(1) by striking "2005" and inserting "2006". **Effective** on the date of the enactment of this Act.

H.R. 1308, §309(c):

Amended Code Sec. 1400L(e)(2)(B) by striking ", or" and inserting "or the Municipal Assistance Corporation, or". **Effective** as if included in the amendments made by section 301 of the Job Creation and Worker Assistance Act of 2002 (P.L. 107-147) [**effective** 3-9-2002.—CCH].

(f) INCREASE IN EXPENSING UNDER SECTION 179.—

* * *

(2) QUALIFIED NEW YORK LIBERTY ZONE PROPERTY.—For purposes of this subsection, the term "qualified New York Liberty Zone property" has the meaning given such term by subsection (b)(2), *determined without regard to subparagraph (C)(i) thereof.*

* * *

[CCH Explanation at ¶333. Committee Reports at ¶10,520.]

Amendments

• **2004, Working Families Tax Relief Act of 2004 (H.R. 1308)**

H.R. 1308, §403(c)(4):

Amended Code Sec. 1400L(f)(2) by inserting before the period ", determined without regard to subparagraph (C)(i)

thereof". **Effective** as if included in the provision of the Job Creation and Worker Assistance Act of 2002 (P.L. 107-147) to which it relates [**effective** 3-9-2002.—CCH].

[¶5355] CODE SEC. 2032A. VALUATION OF CERTAIN FARM, ETC., REAL PROPERTY.

* * *

(c) TAX TREATMENT OF DISPOSITIONS AND FAILURES TO USE FOR QUALIFIED USE.—

* * *

(7) SPECIAL RULES.—

* * *

(D) STUDENT.—For purposes of subparagraph (C), an individual shall be treated as a student with respect to periods during any calendar year if (and only if) such individual is a student (within the meaning of *section 152(f)(2)*) for such calendar year.

* * *

[CCH Explanation at ¶145.]

Amendments

• **2004, Working Families Tax Relief Act of 2004 (H.R. 1308)**

H.R. 1308, §207(22):

Amended Code Sec. 2032A(c)(7)(D) by striking "section 151(c)(4)" and inserting "section 152(f)(2)". **Effective** for tax years beginning after 12-31-2004.

[¶5360] CODE SEC. 2057. FAMILY-OWNED BUSINESS INTERESTS.

* * *

(d) ADJUSTED VALUE OF THE QUALIFIED FAMILY-OWNED BUSINESS INTERESTS.—For purposes of this section, the adjusted value of any qualified family-owned business interest is the value of such interest for purposes of this chapter (determined without regard to this section), reduced by the excess of—

(1) any amount deductible under paragraph (3) or (4) of section 2053(a), over

(2) the sum of—

(A) any indebtedness on any qualified residence of the decedent the interest on which is deductible under section 163(h)(3), plus

(B) any indebtedness to the extent the taxpayer establishes that the proceeds of such indebtedness were used for the payment of educational and medical expenses of the decedent, the decedent's spouse, or the decedent's dependents (within the meaning of section 152, *determined without regard to subsections (b)(1), (b)(2), and (d)(1)(B) thereof*), plus

(C) any indebtedness not described in subparagraph (A) or (B), to the extent such indebtedness does not exceed $10,000.

* * *

[CCH Explanation at ¶145.]

Amendments

• **2004, Working Families Tax Relief Act of 2004 (H.R. 1308)**

H.R. 1308, §207(23):

Amended Code Sec. 2057(d)(2)(B) by inserting ", determined without regard to subsections (b)(1), (b)(2), and

(d)(1)(B) thereof" after "section 152". **Effective** for tax years beginning after 12-31-2004.

[¶5365] CODE SEC. 4972. TAX ON NONDEDUCTIBLE CONTRIBUTIONS TO QUALIFIED EMPLOYER PLANS.

* * *

(c) NONDEDUCTIBLE CONTRIBUTIONS.—For purposes of this section—

* * *

(6) EXCEPTIONS.—In determining the amount of nondeductible contributions for any taxable year, there shall not be taken into account—

(A) so much of the contributions to 1 or more defined contribution plans which are not deductible when contributed solely because of section 404(a)(7) as does not exceed the greater of—

(i) the amount of contributions not in excess of 6 percent of compensation (within the meaning of section 404(a) and as adjusted under section 404(a)(12)) paid or accrued (during the taxable year for which the contributions were made) to beneficiaries under the plans, or

(ii) *the amount of contributions described in section 401(m)(4)(A), or*

(B) so much of the contributions to a simple retirement account (within the meaning of section 408(p)) or a simple plan (within the meaning of section 401(k)(11)) which are not deductible when contributed solely because such contributions are not made in connection with a trade or business of the employer.

For purposes of subparagraph (A), the deductible limits under section 404(a)(7) shall first be applied to amounts contributed to a defined benefit plan and then to amounts described in subparagraph (A). Subparagraph (B) shall not apply to contributions made on behalf of the employer or a member of the employer's family (as defined in section 447(e)(1)).

* * *

[CCH Explanation at ¶345. Committee Reports at ¶10,530.]

Amendments

• **2004, Working Families Tax Relief Act of 2004 (H.R. 1308)**

H.R. 1308, §404(c):

Amended Code Sec. 4972(c)(6)(A)(ii). **Effective** as if included in the provision of the Economic Growth and Tax Relief Reconciliation Act of 2001 (P.L. 107-16) to which it relates [effective for years beginning after 12-31-2001.—

CCH]. Prior to amendment, Code Sec. 4972(c)(6)(A)(ii) read as follows:

(ii) the sum of—

(I) the amount of contributions described in section 401(m)(4)(A), plus

(II) the amount of contributions described in section 402(g)(3)(A), or

[¶5370] CODE SEC. 4973. TAX ON EXCESS CONTRIBUTIONS TO CERTAIN TAX-FAVORED ACCOUNTS AND ANNUITIES.

* * *

(c) SECTION 403(b) CONTRACTS.—For purposes of this section, in the case of a custodial account referred to in *subsection (a)(3)*, the term "excess contributions" means the sum of—

(1) the excess (if any) of the amount contributed for the taxable year to such account (other than a rollover contribution described in section 403(b)(8), or 408(d)(3)(A)(iii)), over the lesser of the amount excludable from gross income under section 403(b) or the amount permitted to be contributed under the limitations contained in section 415 (or under whichever such section is applicable, if only one is applicable), and

(2) the amount determined under this subsection for the preceding taxable year, reduced by—

(A) the excess (if any) of the lesser of (i) the amount excludable from gross income under section 403(b) or (ii) the amount permitted to be contributed under the limitations contained in section 415 over the amount contributed to the account for the taxable year (or under whichever such section is applicable, if only one is applicable), and

(B) the sum of the distributions out of the account (for all prior taxable years) which are included in gross income under section 72(e).

* * *

[CCH Explanation at ¶ 30,050. Committee Reports at ¶ 10,570.]

Amendments

• **2004, Working Families Tax Relief Act of 2004 (H.R. 1308)**

H.R. 1308, § 408(a)(22):

Amended Code Sec. 4973(c) by striking "subsection (a)(2)" and inserting "subsection (a)(3)". **Effective** on the date of the enactment of this Act.

[¶ 5375] CODE SEC. 4978. TAX ON CERTAIN DISPOSITIONS BY EMPLOYEE STOCK OWNERSHIP PLANS AND CERTAIN COOPERATIVES.

(a) TAX ON DISPOSITIONS OF SECURITIES TO WHICH SECTION 1042 APPLIES BEFORE CLOSE OF MINIMUM HOLDING PERIOD.—If, during the 3-year period after the date on which the employee stock ownership plan or eligible worker-owned cooperative acquired any qualified securities in a sale to which section 1042 applied or acquired any qualified employer securities in a qualified gratuitous transfer to which section 664(g) applied, such plan or cooperative disposes of any qualified securities and—

(1) the total number of shares held by such plan or cooperative after such disposition is less than the total number of employer securities held immediately after such sale, or

(2) except to the extent provided in regulations, the value of qualified securities held by such plan or cooperative after such disposition is less than 30 percent of the total value of all employer securities as of such disposition (*60 percent* of the total value of all employer securities as of such disposition in the case of any qualified employer securities acquired in a qualified gratuitous transfer to which section 664(g) applied),

there is hereby imposed a tax on the disposition equal to the amount determined under subsection (b).

* * *

[CCH Explanation at ¶ 30,050. Committee Reports at ¶ 10,570.]

Amendments

• **2004, Working Families Tax Relief Act of 2004 (H.R. 1308)**

H.R. 1308, § 408(a)(23):

Amended Code Sec. 4978(a)(2) by striking "60 percent" and inserting "(60 percent". **Effective** on the date of the enactment of this Act.

[¶ 5380] CODE SEC. 5064. LOSSES RESULTING FROM DISASTER, VANDALISM, OR MALICIOUS MISCHIEF.

* * *

(b) CLAIMS.—

* * *

(3) SPECIAL RULES FOR MAJOR DISASTERS.—If the President has determined under the *Robert T. Stafford* Disaster Relief and Emergency Assistance Act that a "major disaster" (as defined in such Act) has occurred in any part of the United States, and if the disaster referred to in subsection (a)(1) occurs in such part of the United States by reason of such major disaster, then—

    (A) paragraph (2) shall not apply, and

    (B) the filing period set forth in paragraph (1)(A) shall not expire before the day which is 6 months after the date on which the President makes the determination that such major disaster has occurred.

* * *

[CCH Explanation at ¶ 30,050. Committee Reports at ¶ 10,570.]
        Amendments
• **2004, Working Families Tax Relief Act of 2004 (H.R. 1308)**

H.R. 1308, § 408(a)(7)(D):

   Amended Code Sec. 5064(b)(3) by inserting "Robert T. Stafford" before "Disaster Relief and Emergency Assistance Act". **Effective** on the date of the enactment of this Act.

[¶ 5385] CODE SEC. 5708. LOSSES CAUSED BY DISASTER.

(a) AUTHORIZATION.—Where the President has determined under the *Robert T. Stafford* Disaster Relief and Emergency Assistance Act, that a "major disaster" as defined in such Act has occurred in any part of the United States, the Secretary shall pay (without interest) an amount equal to the amount of the internal revenue taxes paid or determined and customs duties paid on tobacco products and cigarette papers and tubes removed, which were lost, rendered unmarketable, or condemned by a duly authorized official by reason of such disaster occurring in such part of the United States on and after the effective date of this section, if such tobacco products or cigarette papers or tubes were held and intended for sale at the time of such disaster. The payments authorized by this section shall be made to the person holding such tobacco products or cigarette papers or tubes for sale at the time of such disaster.

* * *

[CCH Explanation at ¶ 30,050. Committee Reports at ¶ 10,570.]
        Amendments
• **2004, Working Families Tax Relief Act of 2004 (H.R. 1308)**

H.R. 1308, § 408(a)(7)(E):

   Amended Code Sec. 5708(a) by inserting "Robert T. Stafford" before "Disaster Relief and Emergency Assistance Act". **Effective** on the date of the enactment of this Act.

[¶ 5390] CODE SEC. 6103. CONFIDENTIALITY AND DISCLOSURE OF RETURNS AND RETURN INFORMATION.

* * *

(d) DISCLOSURE TO STATE TAX OFFICIALS AND STATE AND LOCAL LAW ENFORCEMENT AGENCIES.—

* * *

   (5) DISCLOSURE FOR COMBINED EMPLOYMENT TAX REPORTING.—

    (A) IN GENERAL.—The Secretary may disclose taxpayer identity information and signatures to any agency, body, or commission of any State for the purpose of carrying out with such agency, body, or commission a combined Federal and State employment tax reporting program approved by the Secretary. Subsections (a)(2) and (p)(4) and sections 7213 and 7213A shall not apply with respect to disclosures or inspections made pursuant to this paragraph.

    (B) TERMINATION.—The Secretary may not make any disclosure under this paragraph after December 31, 2005.

* * *

[CCH Explanation at ¶253. Committee Reports at ¶10,310.]

Amendments

• **2004, Working Families Tax Relief Act of 2004 (H.R. 1308)**

H.R. 1308, §311(a):

Amended Code Sec. 6103(d)(5). **Effective** on the date of the enactment of this Act. Prior to amendment, Code Sec. 6103(d)(5) read as follows:

(5) DISCLOSURE FOR CERTAIN COMBINED REPORTING PROJECT.—The Secretary shall disclose taxpayer identities and signatures for purposes of the demonstration project described in section 976 of the Taxpayer Relief Act of 1997. Subsections (a)(2) and (p)(4) and sections 7213 and 7213A shall not apply with respect to disclosures or inspections made pursuant to this paragraph.

(i) DISCLOSURE TO FEDERAL OFFICERS OR EMPLOYEES FOR ADMINISTRATION OF FEDERAL LAWS NOT RELATING TO TAX ADMINISTRATION.—

* * *

(3) DISCLOSURE OF RETURN INFORMATION TO APPRISE APPROPRIATE OFFICIALS OF CRIMINAL OR TERRORIST ACTIVITIES OR EMERGENCY CIRCUMSTANCES.—

* * *

(C) TERRORIST ACTIVITIES, ETC.—

* * *

(iv) TERMINATION.—No disclosure may be made under this subparagraph after *December 31, 2005.*

* * *

(7) DISCLOSURE UPON REQUEST OF INFORMATION RELATING TO TERRORIST ACTIVITIES, ETC.—

(A) DISCLOSURE TO LAW ENFORCEMENT AGENCIES.—

* * *

(v) TAXPAYER IDENTITY.—*For purposes of this subparagraph, a taxpayer's identity shall not be treated as taxpayer return information.*

* * *

(E) TERMINATION.—No disclosure may be made under this paragraph after *December 31, 2005.*

* * *

[CCH Explanation at ¶257. Committee Reports at ¶10,400.]

Amendments

• **2004, Working Families Tax Relief Act of 2004 (H.R. 1308)**

H.R. 1308, §320(a):

Amended Code Sec. 6103(i)(3)(C)(iv) and (7)(E) by striking "December 31, 2003" and inserting "December 31, 2005". **Effective** for disclosures on or after the date of the enactment of this Act.

H.R. 1308, §320(b):

Amended Code Sec. 6103(i)(7)(A) by adding at the end a new clause (v). **Effective** as if included in section 201 of the Victims of Terrorism Tax Relief Act of 2001 (P.L. 107-134) [effective for disclosures on or after 1-23-2002.—CCH].

(l) DISCLOSURE OF RETURNS AND RETURN INFORMATION FOR PURPOSES OTHER THAN TAX ADMINISTRATION.—

* * *

(13) DISCLOSURE OF RETURN INFORMATION TO CARRY OUT INCOME CONTINGENT REPAYMENT OF STUDENT LOANS.—

* * *

(D) TERMINATION.—This paragraph shall not apply to any request made after *December 31, 2005.*

* * *

Code Sec. 6103(l)(13)(D) **¶5390**

[CCH Explanation at ¶ 255. Committee Reports at ¶ 10,370.]

Amendments

• 2004, Working Families Tax Relief Act of 2004 (H.R. 1308)

H.R. 1308, §317:

Amended Code Sec. 6103(l)(13)(D) by striking "December 31, 2004" and inserting "December 31, 2005". Effective on the date of the enactment of this Act.

(p) PROCEDURE AND RECORDKEEPING.—

* * *

(4) SAFEGUARDS.—Any Federal agency described in subsection (h)(2), (h)(5), (i)(1), (2), (3), (5), or (7), (j)(1), (2), or (5), (k)(8), (l)(1), (2), (3), (5), (10), (11), (13), (14), or (17), or (o)(1), the General Accounting Office, the Congressional Budget Office, or any agency, body, or commission described in subsection (d), (i)(3)(B)(i) or (7)(A)(ii), or (l)(6), (7), (8), (9), (12), (15), or (16) or any other person described in subsection (l)(16), (17), (19), or (20) shall, as a condition for receiving returns or return information—

(A) establish and maintain, to the satisfaction of the Secretary, a permanent system of standardized records with respect to any request, the reason for such request, and the date of such request made by or of it and any disclosure of return or return information made by or to it;

(B) establish and maintain, to the satisfaction of the Secretary, a secure area or place in which such returns or return information shall be stored;

(C) restrict, to the satisfaction of the Secretary, access to the returns or return information only to persons whose duties or responsibilities require access and to whom disclosure may be made under the provisions of this title;

(D) provide such other safeguards which the Secretary determines (and which he prescribes in regulations) to be necessary or appropriate to protect the confidentiality of the returns or return information;

(E) furnish a report to the Secretary, at such time and containing such information as the Secretary may prescribe, which describes the procedures established and utilized by such agency, body, or commission, the General Accounting Office, or the Congressional Budget Office for ensuring the confidentiality of returns and return information required by this paragraph; and

(F) upon completion of use of such returns or return information—

(i) in the case of an agency, body, or commission described in subsection (d), (i)(3)(B)(i), or (l)(6), (7), (8), (9), or (16), or any other person described in subsection (l)(16), (17), (19), or (20) return to the Secretary such returns or return information (along with any copies made therefrom) or make such returns or return information undisclosable in any manner and furnish a written report to the Secretary describing such manner,

(ii) in the case of an agency described in subsections (h)(2), (h)(5), (i)(1), (2), (3), (5) or (7), (j)(1), (2), or (5), (k)(8), (l)(1), (2), (3), (5), (10), (11), (12), (13), (14), (15), or (17) or (o)(1), the General Accounting Office, or the Congressional Budget Office, either—

(I) return to the Secretary such returns or return information (along with any copies made therefrom),

(II) otherwise make such returns or return information undisclosable, or

(III) to the extent not so returned or made undisclosable, ensure that the conditions of subparagraphs (A), (B), (C), (D), and (E) of this paragraph continue to be met with respect to such returns or return information, and

(iii) in the case of the Department of Health and Human Services for purposes of subsection (m)(6), destroy all such return information upon completion of its use in providing the notification for which the information was obtained, so as to make such information undisclosable;

except that the conditions of subparagraphs (A), (B), (C), (D), and (E) shall cease to apply with respect to any return or return information if, and to the extent that, such return or return information is disclosed in the course of any judicial or administrative proceeding and made a part of the public record thereof. If the Secretary determines that any such agency, body, or commission, including an agency or any other person described in subsection (l)(16), (17), (19), or (20), or the General Accounting Office or the Congressional Budget Office has failed to, or does not, meet the requirements of this paragraph, he may, after any proceedings for review established under paragraph (7), take such actions as are necessary to ensure such requirements are met, including refusing to disclose returns or return information to such agency, body, or commission, including an agency or any other person described in subsection (l)(16), (17), (19), or (20), or the General Accounting Office or the Congressional Budget Office until he determines that such requirements have been or will be met. In the case of any agency which receives any mailing address under paragraph (2), (4), (6), or (7) of subsection (m) and which discloses any such mailing address to any agent or which receives any information under paragraph (6)(A), (12)(B), or (16) of subsection (l) and which discloses any such information to any agent, or any person including an agent described in subsection (l)(16), this paragraph shall apply to such agency and each such agent or other person (except that, in the case of an agent, or any person including an agent described in subsection (l)(16), any report to the Secretary or other action with respect to the Secretary shall be made or taken through such agency). For purposes of applying this paragraph in any case to which subsection (m)(6) applies, the term "return information" includes related blood donor records (as defined in section 1141(h)(2) of the Social Security Act).

* * *

[CCH Explanation at ¶30,050. Committee Reports at ¶10,570.]

Amendments

- **2004, Working Families Tax Relief Act of 2004 (H.R. 1308)**

H.R. 1308, §408(a)(24):

Amended Code Sec. 6103(p)(4) by striking "subsection (l)(16) or (17)" each place it appears and inserting "subsec-

tion (l)(16) or (18)". **Effective** on the date of the enactment of this Act. [P.L. 108-173, §105(e)(3), struck "(l)(16) or (17)" and inserted "(l)(16), (17), or (19)". Therefore, this amendment cannot be made.—CCH.]

[¶5395] CODE SEC. 7652. SHIPMENTS TO THE UNITED STATES.

* * *

(f) LIMITATION ON COVER OVER OF TAX ON DISTILLED SPIRITS.—For purposes of this section, with respect to taxes imposed under section 5001 or this section on distilled spirits, the amount covered into the treasuries of Puerto Rico and the Virgin Islands shall not exceed the lesser of the rate of—

(1) $10.50 ($13.25 in the case of distilled spirits brought into the United States after June 30, 1999, and before *January 1, 2006*), or

* * *

[CCH Explanation at ¶265. Committee Reports at ¶10,250.]

Amendments

- **2004, Working Families Tax Relief Act of 2004 (H.R. 1308)**

H.R. 1308, §305(a):

Amended Code Sec. 7652(f)(1) by striking "January 1, 2004" and inserting "January 1, 2006". **Effective** for articles brought into the United States after 12-31-2003.

[¶5400] CODE SEC. 7701. DEFINITIONS.

(a) When used in this title, where not otherwise distinctly expressed or manifestly incompatible with the intent thereof—

* * *

(17) HUSBAND AND WIFE.—As used in sections *682* and 2516, if the husband and wife therein referred to are divorced, wherever appropriate to the meaning of such sections, the term "wife" shall be read "former wife" and the term "husband" shall be read "former husband"; and, if the payments described in such sections are made by or on behalf of the wife or former wife to the husband or former husband instead of vice versa, wherever appropriate to the meaning of such sections, the term "husband" shall be read "wife" and the term "wife" shall be read "husband."

* * *

[CCH Explanation at ¶ 145.]

Amendments

• **2004, Working Families Tax Relief Act of 2004 (H.R. 1308)**

H.R. 1308, § 207(24):

Amended Code Sec. 7701(a)(17) by striking "152(b)(4), 682," and inserting "682". **Effective** for tax years beginning after 12-31-2004.

[¶ 5405] CODE SEC. 7702B. TREATMENT OF QUALIFIED LONG-TERM CARE INSURANCE.

* * *

(f) TREATMENT OF CERTAIN STATE-MAINTAINED PLANS.—

* * *

(2) STATE LONG-TERM CARE PLAN.—For purposes of paragraph (1), the term "State long-term care plan" means any plan—

* * *

(C) under which such coverage is provided only to—

* * *

(iii) individuals bearing a relationship to such employees or spouses which is described in any of *subparagraphs (A) through (G) of section 152(d)(2)*.

* * *

[CCH Explanation at ¶ 145.]

Amendments

• **2004, Working Families Tax Relief Act of 2004 (H.R. 1308)**

H.R. 1308, § 207(25):

Amended Code Sec. 7702B(f)(2)(C)(iii) by striking "paragraphs (1) through (8) of section 152(a)" and inserting

"subparagraphs (A) through (G) of section 152(d)(2)". **Effective** for tax years beginning after 12-31-2004.

[¶ 5410] CODE SEC. 7703. DETERMINATION OF MARITAL STATUS.

* * *

(b) CERTAIN MARRIED INDIVIDUALS LIVING APART.—For purposes of those provisions of this title which refer to this subsection, if—

(1) an individual who is married (within the meaning of subsection (a)) and who files a separate return maintains as his home a household which constitutes for more than one-half of the taxable year the principal place of abode of a child (within the meaning of section *152(f)(1)*) with respect to whom such individual is entitled to a deduction for the taxable year under section 151 (or would be so entitled but for section 152(e)),

(2) such individual furnishes over one-half of the cost of maintaining such household during the taxable year, and

(3) during the last 6 months of the taxable year, such individual's spouse is not a member of such household,

such individual shall not be considered as married.

[CCH Explanation at ¶ 145.]

Amendments

• **2004, Working Families Tax Relief Act of 2004 (H.R. 1308)**

H.R. 1308, § 207(26)(A)-(B):

Amended Code Sec. 7703(b)(1) by striking "151(c)(3)" and inserting "152(f)(1)" and by striking "paragraph (2) or (4)

of" after "entitled but for". **Effective** for tax years beginning after 12-31-2004.

[¶5415] CODE SEC. 8021. POWERS.

* * *

(f) RELATING TO JOINT REVIEWS.—

* * *

(2) JOINT REVIEWS.—Before June 1 of each calendar year after 1998 and before *2005*, there shall be a joint review of the strategic plans and budget for the Internal Revenue Service and such other matters as the Chairman of the Joint Committee deems appropriate. Such joint review shall be held at the call of the Chairman of the Joint Committee and shall include two members of the majority and one member of the minority from each of the Committees on Finance, Appropriations, and Governmental Affairs of the Senate, and the Committees on Ways and Means, Appropriations, and Government Reform and Oversight of the House of Representatives.

[CCH Explanation at ¶259. Committee Reports at ¶10,410.]

Amendments

● **2004, Working Families Tax Relief Act of 2004 (H.R. 1308)**

H.R. 1308, §321(a):

Amended Code Sec. 8021(f)(2) by striking "2004" and inserting "2005". **Effective** on the date of the enactment of this Act.

H.R. 1308, §321(c) provides:

(c) TIME FOR JOINT REVIEW.—The joint review required by section 8021(f)(2) of the Internal Revenue Code of 1986 to be made before June 1, 2004, shall be treated as timely if made before June 1, 2005.

[¶5420] CODE SEC. 8022. DUTIES.

It shall be the duty of the Joint Committee—

* * *

(3) REPORTS.—

* * *

(C) To report, for each calendar year after 1998 and before *2005*, to the Committees on Finance, Appropriations, and Governmental Affairs of the Senate, and to the Committees on Ways and Means, Appropriations, and Government Reform and Oversight of the House of Representatives, *with respect to the matters addressed in the joint review referred to in section 8021(f)(2).*

* * *

[CCH Explanation at ¶259. Committee Reports at ¶10,410.]

Amendments

● **2004, Working Families Tax Relief Act of 2004 (H.R. 1308)**

H.R. 1308, §321(b)(1)-(2):

Amended Code Sec. 8022(3)(C) by striking "2004" and inserting "2005", and by striking "with respect to—"and all

that follows and inserting "with respect to the matters addressed in the joint review referred to in section 8021(f)(2)". **Effective** on the date of the enactment of this Act.

[¶5425] CODE SEC. 9812. PARITY IN THE APPLICATION OF CERTAIN LIMITS TO MENTAL HEALTH BENEFITS.

* * *

(f) APPLICATION OF SECTION.—This section shall not apply to benefits for services furnished—

(1) on or after September 30, 2001, and before January 10, 2002,

(2) *on or after January 1, 2004, and before the date of the enactment of the Working Families Tax Relief Act of 2004, and*

(3) *after December 31, 2005.*

[CCH Explanation at ¶247. Committee Reports at ¶10,210.]

Amendments

• 2004, Working Families Tax Relief Act of 2004 (H.R. 1308)

H.R. 1308, §302(a)(1)-(2):

Amended Code Sec. 9812(f) by striking "and" at the end of paragraph (1), and by striking paragraph (2) and in-

serting new paragraphs (2) and (3). **Effective** on the date of the enactment of this Act. Prior to being stricken, Code Sec. 9812(f)(2) read as follows:

(2) after December 31, 2003.

ACT SECTIONS NOT AMENDING CODE SECTIONS

WORKING FAMILIES TAX RELIEF ACT OF 2004

[¶7005] ACT SEC. 1. SHORT TITLE; AMENDMENT OF 1986 CODE; TABLE OF CONTENTS.

(a) SHORT TITLE.—This Act may be cited as the "Working Families Tax Relief Act of 2004".

(b) AMENDMENT OF 1986 CODE.—Except as otherwise expressly provided, whenever in this Act an amendment or repeal is expressed in terms of an amendment to, or repeal of, a section or other provision, the reference shall be considered to be made to a section or other provision of the Internal Revenue Code of 1986.

* * *

TITLE I—EXTENSION OF FAMILY TAX PROVISIONS
* * *

[¶7010] ACT SEC. 105. APPLICATION OF EGTRRA SUNSET TO THIS TITLE.

Each amendment made by this title shall be subject to title IX of the Economic Growth and Tax Relief Reconciliation Act of 2001 to the same extent and in the same manner as the provision of such Act to which such amendment relates.

* * *

[CCH Explanation at ¶29,001.]

TITLE III—EXTENSIONS OF CERTAIN EXPIRING PROVISIONS
* * *

[¶7015] ACT SEC. 302. PARITY IN THE APPLICATION OF CERTAIN LIMITS TO MENTAL HEALTH BENEFITS.
* * *

(b) ERISA.—Section 712(f) of the Employee Retirement Income Security Act of 1974 (29 U.S.C. 1185a(f)) is amended by striking "on or after December 31, 2004" and inserting "after December 31, 2005".

(c) PHSA.—Section 2705(f) of the Public Health Service Act (42 U.S.C. 300gg-5(f)) is amended by striking "on or after December 31, 2004" and inserting "after December 31, 2005".

(d) EFFECTIVE DATES.—The amendments made by this section shall take effect on the date of the enactment of this Act.

* * *

[CCH Explanation at ¶247. Committee Reports at ¶10,210.]

[¶7020] ACT SEC. 312. ALLOWANCE OF NONREFUNDABLE PERSONAL CREDITS AGAINST REGULAR AND MINIMUM TAX LIABILITY.
* * *

(b) CONFORMING PROVISIONS.—

* * *

(2) The amendments made by sections 201(b), 202(f), and 618(b) of the Economic Growth and Tax Relief Reconciliation Act of 2001 shall not apply to taxable years beginning during 2004 or 2005.

* * *

[CCH Explanation at ¶135. Committee Reports at ¶10,320.]

[¶7022] ACT SEC. 321. JOINT REVIEW OF STRATEGIC PLANS AND BUDGET FOR THE INTERNAL REVENUE SERVICE.

* * *

(c) TIME FOR JOINT REVIEW.—The joint review required by section 8021(f)(2) of the Internal Revenue Code of 1986 to be made before June 1, 2004, shall be treated as timely if made before June 1, 2005.

[CCH Explanation at ¶259. Committee Reports at ¶10,410.]

[¶7023] ACT SEC. 322. AVAILABILITY OF MEDICAL SAVINGS ACCOUNTS.

* * *

(d) TIME FOR FILING REPORTS, ETC.—

(1) The report required by section 220(j)(4) of the Internal Revenue Code of 1986 to be made on August 1, 2004, shall be treated as timely if made before the close of the 90-day period beginning on the date of the enactment of this Act.

(2) The determination and publication required by section 220(j)(5) of such Code with respect to calendar year 2004 shall be treated as timely if made before the close of the 120-day period beginning on the date of the enactment of this Act. If the determination under the preceding sentence is that 2004 is a cut-off year under section 220(i) of such Code, the cut-off date under such section 220(i) shall be the last day of such 120-day period.

[CCH Explanation at ¶245. Committee Reports at ¶10,420.]

TITLE IV—TAX TECHNICAL CORRECTIONS

* * *

[¶7025] ACT SEC. 402. AMENDMENTS RELATED TO JOBS AND GROWTH TAX RELIEF RECONCILIATION ACT OF 2003.

(a) AMENDMENTS RELATED TO SECTION 302 OF THE ACT.—

* * *

(5) * * *

* * *

(F) With respect to any taxable year of a regulated investment company or real estate investment trust ending on or before November 30, 2003, the period for providing notice of the qualified dividend amount to shareholders under sections 854(b)(2) and 857(c)(2)(C) of the Internal Revenue Code of 1986, as amended by this section, shall not expire before the date on which the statement under section 6042(c) of such Code is required to be furnished with respect to the last calendar year beginning in such taxable year.

(6) Paragraph (2) of section 302(f) of the Jobs and Growth Tax Relief Reconciliation Act of 2003 is amended to read as follows:

"(2) PASS-THRU ENTITIES.—In the case of a pass-thru entity described in subparagraph (A), (B), (C), (D), (E), or (F) of section 1(h)(10) of the Internal Revenue Code of 1986, as amended by this Act, the amendments made by this section shall apply to taxable years ending after December 31, 2002; except that dividends received by such an entity on or before such date shall not be treated as qualified dividend income (as defined in section 1(h)(11)(B) of such Code, as added by this Act).".

ACT SEC. 302. DIVIDENDS OF INDIVIDUALS TAXED AT CAPITAL GAIN RATES.

* * *

(f) EFFECTIVE DATE.—

* * *

(2) REGULATED INVESTMENT COMPANIES AND REAL ESTATE INVESTMENT TRUSTS.—In the case of a regulated investment company or a real estate investment trust, the amendments made by this section shall apply to taxable years ending after December 31, 2002; except that dividends received by such a company or trust on or before such date shall not be treated as qualified dividend income (as defined in section 1(h)(11)(B) of the Internal Revenue Code of 1986, as added by this Act).

(b) EFFECTIVE DATE.—The amendments made by subsection (a) shall take effect as if included in section 302 of the Jobs and Growth Tax Relief Reconciliation Act of 2003.

[CCH Explanation at ¶307. Committee Reports at ¶10,510.]

[¶7030] ACT SEC. 403. AMENDMENTS RELATED TO JOB CREATION AND WORKER ASSISTANCE ACT OF 2002.

* * *

(b) AMENDMENTS RELATED TO SECTION 102 OF THE ACT.—

* * *

(2) In the case of a net operating loss for a taxable year ending during 2001 or 2002—

(A) an application under section 6411(a) of the Internal Revenue Code of 1986 with respect to such loss shall not fail to be treated as timely filed if filed before November 1, 2002,

(B) any election made under section 172(b)(3) of such Code may (notwithstanding such section) be revoked before November 1, 2002, and

(C) any election made under section 172(j) of such Code shall (notwithstanding such section) be treated as timely made if made before November 1, 2002.

(3) Section 102(c)(2) of the Job Creation and Worker Assistance Act of 2002 (Public Law 107-147) is amended by striking "before January 1, 2003" and inserting "after December 31, 1990".

ACT SEC. 102. CARRYBACK OF CERTAIN NET OPERATING LOSSES ALLOWED FOR 5 YEARS; TEMPORARY SUSPENSION OF 90 PERCENT AMT LIMIT.

* * *

(c) TEMPORARY SUSPENSION OF 90 PERCENT LIMIT ON CERTAIN NOL CARRYOVERS.—

* * *

(2) EFFECTIVE DATE.—The amendment made by this subsection shall apply to taxable years ending *after December 31, 1990.*

---

* * *

(d) AMENDMENT RELATED TO SECTION 405 OF THE ACT.—The last sentence of section 4006(a)(3)(E)(iii)(IV) of the Employee Retirement Income Security Act of 1974 (29 U.S.C. 1306(a)(3)(E)(iii)(IV)) is amended—

(1) by inserting "or this subparagraph" after "this clause" both places it appears, and

(2) by inserting "(other than sections 4005, 4010, 4011, and 4043)" after "subsections".

(e) AMENDMENT RELATED TO SECTION 411 OF THE ACT.—Subparagraph (B) of section 411(c)(2) of the Job Creation and Worker Assistance Act of 2002 is amended by striking "Paragraph (2)" and inserting "Paragraph (1)".

• • *JCWAA OF 2002 ACT SEC. 411(c)(2)(B) AS AMENDED*————————————

ACT SEC. 411. AMENDMENTS RELATED TO ECONOMIC GROWTH AND TAX RELIEF RECONCILIATION ACT OF 2001.

* * *

(c) AMENDMENTS RELATED TO SECTION 202 OF THE ACT.—

* * *

(2) CORRECTIONS TO EXCLUSION FOR EMPLOYER-PROVIDED ADOPTION ASSISTANCE.—

* * *

(B) *Paragraph (1)* of section 137(b) is amended by striking "subsection (a)(1)" and inserting "subsection (a)".

(f) EFFECTIVE DATE.—The amendments made by this section shall take effect as if included in the provisions of the Job Creation and Worker Assistance Act of 2002 to which they relate.

* * *

[CCH Explanation at ¶321, ¶339 and ¶341. Committee Reports at ¶10,520.]

[¶7035] ACT SEC. 408. CLERICAL AMENDMENTS.

* * *

(b) OTHER LAWS.—

(1) Subsection (c) of section 156 of the Community Renewal Tax Relief Act of 2000 (114 Stat. 2763A-623) is amended in the first sentence by inserting "than" after "not later".

• • *CRTRA OF 2000 ACT SEC. 156(c) AS AMENDED*————————————

ACT SEC. 156. REPORTS.

* * *

(c) FINAL REPORT.—The Advisory Council shall transmit a final report to the Secretary not later *than* September 30, 2003. The final report shall contain a detailed statement of the findings and conclusions of the Advisory Council, together with any recommendations for legislative or administrative action that the Advisory Council considers appropriate.

---

(2) Paragraph (6) of section 1(a) of Public Law 107-22 shall be applied by substituting "part VIII" for "part VII" in such paragraph.

(3) Subparagraph (A) of section 1(b)(3) of Public Law 107-22 shall be applied by substituting "EDUCATIONAL" for "EDUCATION" in the matter preceding subparagraph (A) in such section.

• • *P.L. 107-22 ACT SEC. 1(b)(3)(A) AS ENACTED*————————————

ACT SEC. 1. RENAMING EDUCATION INDIVIDUAL RETIREMENT ACCOUNTS AS COVERDELL EDUCATION SAVINGS ACCOUNTS.

* * *

(b) CONFORMING AMENDMENTS.—

* * *

(3) The headings for the following provisions of such Code are amended by striking "EDUCATION INDIVIDUAL RETIREMENT" each place it appears and inserting "COVERDELL EDUCATION SAVINGS".

(A) Section 72(e)(9).

(4) Paragraph (1) of section 204(e) of the Railroad Retirement and Survivors' Improvement Act of 2001 shall be applied by substituting "Section 24(d)(2)(A)(iii)" for "Section 24(d)(3)(A)(iii)" in such paragraph.

• • *RRSIA of 2001 ACT SEC. 204(e)(1) AS ENACTED*———————————————————

ACT SEC. 204. EMPLOYER, EMPLOYEE REPRESENTATIVE, AND EMPLOYEE TIER 2 TAX RATE ADJUSTMENTS.

* * *

(e) CONFORMING AMENDMENTS.—

(1) Section 24(d)(3)(A)(iii) is amended by striking "section 3211(a)(1)" and inserting "section 3211(a)".

___

(5) Paragraph (2) of section 412(b) of the Economic Growth and Tax Relief Reconciliation Act of 2001 shall be applied by substituting "Section 221(f)(1)" for "Section 221(g)(1)" in such paragraph.

• • *EGTRRA of 2001 ACT SEC. 412(b)(2) AS ENACTED*—————————————————

ACT SEC. 412. ELIMINATION OF 60-MONTH LIMIT AND INCREASE IN INCOME LIMITATION ON STUDENT LOAN INTEREST DEDUCTION.

* * *

(b) INCREASE IN INCOME LIMITATION.—

* * *

(2) CONFORMING AMENDMENT.—Section 221(g)(1) is amended by striking "$40,000 and $60,000 amounts" and inserting "$50,000 and $100,000 amounts".

___

(6) Subsection (b) of section 531 of the Economic Growth and Tax Relief Reconciliation Act of 2001 shall be applied by substituting "section" for "subsection" in such subsection.

• • *EGTRRA of 2001 ACT SEC. 531(b) AS ENACTED*————————————————————

ACT SEC. 531. REDUCTION OF CREDIT FOR STATE DEATH TAXES.

* * *

(b) EFFECTIVE DATE.—The amendments made by this subsection shall apply to estates of decedents dying after December 31, 2001.

___

(7) Paragraph (3) of section 619(c) of the Economic Growth and Tax Relief Reconciliation Act of 2001 shall be applied by substituting "after the item relating to section 45D" for "at the end" in such paragraph.

(8) The table contained in section 203(a)(4)(B) of the Employee Retirement Income Security Act of 1974 (29 U.S.C. 1053(a)(4)(B)) is amended by striking the last line and inserting the following:

"6 or more . . . .   100.".

(9) Paragraph (3) of section 652(b) of the Economic Growth and Tax Relief Reconciliation Act of 2001 shall be applied by inserting "each place it appears" before "in the next to last sentence" in such paragraph.

• • *EGTRRA of 2001 ACT SEC. 652(b)(3) AS ENACTED*————————

ACT SEC. 652. MAXIMUM CONTRIBUTION DEDUCTION RULES MODIFIED AND APPLIED TO ALL DEFINED BENEFIT PLANS.

* * *

(b) CONFORMING AMENDMENT.—Paragraph (6) of section 4972(c), as amended by sections 616 and 637, is amended—

* * *

(3) by striking "subparagraph (B)" in the next to last sentence and inserting "subparagraph (A)", and

---

[CCH Explanation at ¶ 30,050. Committee Reports at ¶ 10,570.]

Committee Reports
Working Familes Tax Relief Act of 2004

¶ 10,001
Introduction

The Conference Committee Report accompanying H.R. 1308, the Working Families Tax Relief Act of 2004, explains the intent of Congress regarding the provisions in the Act. At the end of the Conference Report text, references are provided to corresponding explanations and Code provisions. Subscribers to the electronic version can link from these references to the corresponding material. *The pertinent sections of the Conference Report appear in Act Section order beginning at ¶10,010.*

¶ 10,005
Background

The Working Families Tax Relief Act of 2004 (H.R. 1308) was introduced in the House of Representatives (House) on March 18, 2003, as the Tax Relief, Simplification, and Equity Act of 2003. On March 19, 2003, the House considered H.R. 1308 under suspension of the rules and passed the bill by voice vote. On June 5, 2003, H.R. 1308, as amended and renamed the Relief for Working Families Tax Act of 2003, passed the Senate by voice vote. The Senate insisted on its amendment and requested a conference the same day.

On June 12, 2003, the House, pursuant to H. RES. 270, agreed to the Senate amendment to the text with an amendment. That same day, the House also insisted upon its amendment to the Senate amendments, requested a conference, and appointed conferees. On June 18, 2003, the Senate disagreed to the House amendments, agreed to the request for a conference, and appointed conferees. From June, 2003, through September, 2004, numerous motions to instruct conferees failed in the House.

A conference on H.R. 1308 was held on September 21, 2004. Within days, the conferees agreed to file a conference report, which was filed on September 23, 2004 (H.R. CONF. REP. NO. 108-696). On the same day, pursuant to H. RES. 794, all points of order against the conference report and against its consideration were waived. In the late afternoon on September 23, 2004, the House passed the conference agreement by a vote of 339 to 65. Later that same day, the Senate passed the conference agreement by a vote of 92 to 3. As we go to press, the President has yet to sign H.R. 1308, but has indicated that he will sign it into law.

The following material is the official wording of the conference report accompanying H.R. 1308, The Working Families Tax Relief Act of 2004, as released on September 23, 2004. The report is referred to herein as Conference Committee Report (H.R. CONF. REP. NO. 108-696). Headings have been added for the reader's convenience. Omissions of text are indicated by asterisks (* * *).

[¶ 10,010] Act Sec. 101(a). Extension of the child tax credit

Conference Committee Report (H.R. CONF. REP. NO. 108-696)

[Code Sec. 24]

Present Law

In general

For 2004, an individual may claim a $1,000 tax credit for each qualifying child under the age of 17. In general, a qualifying child is an individual for whom the taxpayer can claim a dependency exemption and who is the taxpayer's son or daughter (or descendent of either), stepson or stepdaughter (or descendent of either), or eligible foster child.

The child tax credit is scheduled to revert to $700 in 2005, and then, over several years, increase to $1,000.

Table 1, below, shows the scheduled amount of the child tax credit.

Table 1.—SCHEDULED AMOUNT OF THE CHILD TAX CREDIT

Taxable Year	Credit Amount Per Child
2003-2004	$1,000
2005-2008	700
2009	800
2010 [1]	1,000

[1] The credit reverts to $500 in taxable years beginning after December 31, 2010, under the sunset provision of EGTRRA (the "Economic Growth and Tax Relief Reconciliation Act of 2001," Pub. L. No. 107-16).

The child tax credit is phased out for individuals with income over certain thresholds. Specifically, the otherwise allowable child tax credit is reduced by $50 for each $1,000 (or fraction thereof) of modified adjusted gross income over $75,000 for single individuals or heads of households, $110,000 for married individuals filing joint returns, and $55,000 for married individuals filing separate returns.[1] The length of the phase-out range depends on the number of qualifying children. For example, the phase-out range for a single individual with one qualifying child is between $75,000 and $95,000 of modified adjusted gross income. The phase-out range for a single individual with two qualifying children is between $75,000 and $115,000.

The amount of the tax credit and the phase-out ranges are not adjusted annually for inflation.

* * *

Alternative minimum tax liability

The child credit is allowed against the individual's regular income tax and alternative minimum tax. For taxable years beginning after December 31, 2010, the sunset provision of EGTRRA applies to the rules allowing the child credit against the alternative minimum tax.

House Bill

The bill increases the credit to $1,000 for taxable years 2005-2009. Therefore, the maximum child credit is $1,000 per child for taxable years 2003-2010.[3] * * * Finally, the bill provides that the beginning point of the phase-out range for the child credit is $150,000 for married individuals filing joint returns ($75,000 for unmarried individuals and married individuals filing separately) for taxable years beginning after December 31, 2002, and before January 1, 2011. All modifications to the child credit under the bill are subject to the sunset provision of EGTRRA.

Effective Date

Taxable years beginning after December 31, 2002.

Senate Amendment

* * * Also, the Senate amendment provides that the beginning point of the phase-out range for the credit for married individuals filing joint returns is increased to $115,000 in 2008 and 2009 and $150,000 in 2010. It also provides that the beginning point for such phase-out range in the case of unmarried individuals and married individuals filing separately will be one-half of the beginning point of the phase-out range for married individuals filing joint returns for taxable years beginning in 2008 through 2010. * * * All modifications to the child credit under the Senate amendment are subject to the sunset provision of EGTRRA.

---

[1] Modified adjusted gross income is the taxpayer's total gross income plus certain amounts excluded from gross income (i.e., excluded income of U.S. citizens or residents living abroad (sec. 911); residents of Guam, American Samoa, and the Northern Mariana Islands (sec. 931); and residents of Puerto Rico (sec. 933)).

[3] The credit reverts to $500 in taxable years beginning after December 31, 2010, under the sunset provision of EGTRRA.

Effective Date

The provision is effective for taxable years beginning after December 31, 2002.

Conference Agreement

In general

The conference agreement increases the child credit to $1,000 for taxable years 2005-2009. Therefore, the maximum child tax credit is $1,000 per child for taxable years 2005-2010. All modifications to the child credit under the conference agreement are subject to the sunset provision of EGTRRA.[4]

Effective Dates

The provision generally applies to taxable years beginning after December 31, 2004. The provision relating to the acceleration of the refundability of the child credit applies to taxable years beginning after December 31, 2003. The provision relating to the treatment of combat pay as earned income for purposes of the child credit is effective for taxable years beginning after December 31, 2003. The earned income credit election is effective for taxable years ending after the date of enactment and before January 1, 2006.

[Law at ¶5020. CCH Explanation at ¶105.]

* * *

[¶ 10,020] Act Sec. 101(b). Standard deduction marriage penalty relief

Conference Committee Report (H.R. CONF. REP. NO. 108-696)

[Code Sec. 63(c)]

Present Law

Marriage penalty

A married couple generally is treated as one tax unit that must pay tax on the couple's total taxable income. Although married couples may elect to file separate returns, the rate schedules and other provisions are structured so that filing separate returns usually results in a higher tax than filing a joint return. Other rate schedules apply to single persons and to single heads of households.

A "marriage penalty" exists when the combined tax liability of a married couple filing a joint return is greater than the sum of the tax liabilities of each individual computed as if they were not married. A "marriage bonus" exists when the combined tax liability of a married couple filing a joint return is less than the sum of the tax liabilities of each individual computed as if they were not married.

Basic standard deduction

Taxpayers who do not itemize deductions may choose the basic standard deduction (and additional standard deductions, if applicable),[5] which is subtracted from adjusted gross income ("AGI") in arriving at taxable income. The size of the basic standard deduction varies according to filing status and is adjusted annually for inflation.[6] In general, two unmarried individuals have standard deductions whose sum exceeds the standard deduction for a married couple filing a joint return. EGTRRA increased the basic standard deduction for a married couple filing a joint return, providing for a phase-in of the increase until the basic standard deduction for a married couple filing a joint return equaled twice the basic standard deduction for an unmarried individual filing a single return by 2009.[7] The Jobs and Growth Tax Relief Reconciliation Act of 2003 ("JGTRRA") accelerated the phase-in, providing that the basic standard deduction for a married couple filing a joint return equaled twice the basic standard deduction for an unmarried individual filing a single return for 2003 and 2004, reverting to the phase-in schedule provided by EGTRAA for 2005-2009.

Table 2, below, shows the standard deduction for married couples filing a joint return as a percentage of the standard deduction for single individuals during the phase-in period.

---

[4] The credit reverts to $500 in taxable years beginning after December 31, 2010, under the sunset provision of EGTRRA.

[5] Additional standard deductions are allowed with respect to any individual who is elderly (age 65 or over) or blind.

[6] For 2004 the basic standard deduction amounts are: (1) $4,850 for unmarried individuals; (2) $9,700 for married individuals filing a joint return; (3) $7,150 for heads of households; and (4) $4,850 for married individuals filing separately.

[7] The basic standard deduction for a married taxpayer filing separately will continue to equal one-half of the basic standard deduction for a married couple filing jointly; thus, the basic standard deduction for unmarried individuals filing a single return and for married couples filing separately will be the same after the phase-in period.

Table 2.—SCHEDULED AMOUNT OF THE BASIC STANDARD DEDUCTION FOR MARRIED COUPLES FILING JOINT RETURNS

Taxable year	Standard deduction for married couples filing joint returns as percentage of standard deduction for unmarried individuals returns
2005	174
2006	184
2007	187
2008	190
2009 and 2010 [1]	200

[1] The basic standard deduction increases are repealed for taxable years beginning after December 31, 2010, under the sunset provision of EGTRRA.

House Bill

No provision.

Senate Amendment

No provision.

Conference Agreement

The conference agreement increases the basic standard deduction amount for joint returns to twice the basic standard deduction amount for single returns effective for 2005-2008. Therefore, the basic standard deduction for joint returns is twice the basic standard deduction for single returns for taxable years 2005-2010. All modifications to the basic standard deduction under the conference agreement are subject to the sunset provision of EGTRRA.

Effective Date

The conference agreement provision is effective for taxable years beginning after December 31, 2004.

[Law at ¶5100. CCH Explanation at ¶110.]

[¶10,030] Act Sec. 101(c). Increase the size of the 15-percent rate bracket for married couples filing joint returns

Conference Committee Report (H.R. CONF. REP. NO. 108-696)

[Code Sec. 1(f)]

Present Law

In general

Under the Federal individual income tax system, an individual who is a citizen or resident of the United States generally is subject to tax on worldwide taxable income. Taxable income is total gross income less certain exclusions, exemptions, and deductions. An individual may claim either a standard deduction or itemized deductions.

An individual's income tax liability is determined by computing his or her regular income tax liability and, if applicable, alternative minimum tax liability.

Regular income tax liability

Regular income tax liability is determined by applying the regular income tax rate schedules (or tax tables) to the individual's taxable income and then is reduced by any applicable tax credits. The regular income tax rate schedules are divided into several ranges of income, known as income brackets, and the marginal tax rate increases as the individual's income increases. The income bracket amounts are ad-

justed annually for inflation. Separate rate schedules apply based on filing status: single individuals (other than heads of households and surviving spouses), heads of households, married individuals filing joint returns (including surviving spouses), married individuals filing separate returns, and estates and trusts. Lower rates may apply to capital gains.

In general, the bracket breakpoints for single individuals are approximately 60 percent of the rate bracket breakpoints for married couples filing joint returns.[8] The rate bracket breakpoints for married individuals filing separate returns are exactly one-half of the rate brackets for married individuals filing joint returns. A separate, compressed rate schedule applies to estates and trusts.

15-percent regular income tax rate bracket

EGTRRA increased the size of the 15-percent regular income tax rate bracket for a married couple filing a joint return to twice the size of the corresponding rate bracket for a single individual filing a single return, phasing in the increase over four years, beginning in 2005. JGTRRA accelerated these increases, making the size of the 15-percent regular income tax rate bracket for a

---

[8] Under present law, the rate bracket breakpoint for the 35-percent marginal tax rate is the same for single individuals and married couples filing joint returns.

married couple filing a joint return equal to twice the size of the corresponding rate bracket for a single individual filing a single return for taxable years beginning in 2003 and 2004. For taxable years beginning after 2004, the applicable percentages will revert to those provided by EGTRRA. Table 3, below, shows the size of the 15-percent bracket during the phase-in period.

Table 3.—SCHEDULED SIZE OF THE 15-PERCENT RATE BRACKET FOR MARRIED COUPLES FILING JOINT RETURNS

Taxable year	End Point of 15-Percent Rate Bracket for Married Couples Filing Joint Returns as Percentage of End Point of 15-Percent Rate Bracket for Unmarried Individuals
2005	180
2006	187
2007	193
2008 through 2010 [1]	200

[1] The increases in the 15-percent rate bracket for married couples filing a joint return are repealed for taxable years beginning after December 31, 2010, under the sunset provision of EGTRRA.

House Bill

No provision.

Senate Amendment

No provision.

Conference Agreement

The conference agreement increases the size of the 15-percent rate bracket for joint returns to twice the size of the corresponding rate bracket for single returns effective for 2005-2007. Therefore, the size of the 15-percent rate bracket for joint returns is twice the size of the corresponding rate bracket for single returns for taxable years 2005-2010. The modification to the 15-percent rate bracket under the conference agreement is subject to the sunset provision of EGTRRA.

Effective Date

The conference agreement provision is effective for taxable years beginning after December 31, 2004.

[Law at ¶5005. CCH Explanation at ¶115.]

[¶ 10,040] Act Sec. 101(d). Extend size of 10-percent rate bracket for individuals

Conference Committee Report (H.R. CONF. REP. NO. 108-696)

[Code Sec. 1(i)]

Present Law

In general

Under the Federal individual income tax system, an individual who is a citizen or a resident of the United States generally is subject to tax on worldwide taxable income. Taxable income is total gross income less certain exclusions, exemptions, and deductions. An individual may claim either a standard deduction or itemized deductions.

An individual's income tax liability is determined by computing his or her regular income tax liability and, if applicable, alternative minimum tax liability.

Regular income tax liability

Regular income tax liability is determined by applying the regular income tax rate schedules (or tax tables) to the individual's taxable income. This tax liability is then reduced by any applicable tax credits. The regular income tax rate schedules are divided into several ranges of income, known as income brackets, and the mar-

ginal tax rate increases as the individual's income increases. The income bracket amounts are adjusted annually for inflation. Separate rate schedules apply based on filing status: single individuals (other than heads of households and surviving spouses), heads of households, married individuals filing joint returns (including surviving spouses), married individuals filing separate returns, and estates and trusts. Lower rates may apply to capital gains.

Ten-percent regular income tax rate

EGTRRA created a new 10-percent rate that applied to the first $6,000 of taxable income for single individuals, $10,000 of taxable income for heads of households, and $12,000 for married couples filing joint returns, and provided a scheduled increase effective beginning in 2008 under which the $6,000 amount would increase to $7,000 and the $12,000 amount would increase to $14,000, with such amounts adjusted annually for inflation for taxable years beginning after December 31, 2008. JGTRRA accelerated the scheduled increases to 2003 and 2004 (with indexing). For 2004, the size of the 10-percent bracket for single individuals is $7,150 ($14,300 for married individuals filing a joint return). For 2005-2010, the size of the 10-percent bracket reverts to the levels provided under EGTRRA. Thus the amounts drop to $6,000 for single individuals, $10,000 for heads of households and $12,000 for married individuals filing a joint return)[sic] for 2005-2007. In 2008, the amounts will increase to $7,000 ($14,000 for married individuals filing a joint return). These amounts ($7,000 for single individuals, $10,000 for heads of households and $14,000 for married individuals) are adjusted annually for inflation for taxable years beginning after December 31, 2008. The 10-percent rate bracket will expire for taxable years beginning after December 31, 2010, under the sunset provision of EGTRRA.

House Bill

No provision.

Senate Amendment

No provision.

Conference Agreement

The conference agreement extends the size of the 10-percent rate bracket through 2010. Specifically, the size of the 10-percent rate bracket for 2005 through 2010 is set at the 2003 level ($7,000 for single individuals, $10,000 for heads of households and $14,000 for married individuals) with annual indexing from 2003. The modifications to the 10-percent rate bracket under the conference agreement are subject to the sunset provision of EGTRRA.

Effective Date

The conference agreement provision is effective for taxable years beginning after December 31, 2004.

[Law at ¶ 5005. CCH Explanation at ¶ 120.]

[¶ 10,050] Act Sec. 102. Acceleration of refundability of the child tax credit

Conference Committee Report (H.R. CONF. REP. NO. 108-696)

[Code Sec. 24]

Present Law

In general

For 2004, an individual may claim a $1,000 tax credit for each qualifying child under the age of 17. In general, a qualifying child is an individual for whom the taxpayer can claim a dependency exemption and who is the taxpayer's son or daughter (or descendent of either), stepson or stepdaughter (or descendent of either), or eligible foster child.

* * *

The child tax credit is phased out for individuals with income over certain thresholds. Specifically, the otherwise allowable child tax credit is reduced by $50 for each $1,000 (or fraction thereof) of modified adjusted gross income over $75,000 for single individuals or heads of households, $110,000 for married individuals filing joint returns, and $55,000 for married individuals filing separate returns.[1] The length of the phase-out range depends on the number of qualifying children. For example, the phase-out range for a single individual with one qualifying

child is between $75,000 and $95,000 of modified adjusted gross income. The phase-out range for a single individual with two qualifying children is between $75,000 and $115,000.

The amount of the tax credit and the phase-out ranges are not adjusted annually for inflation.

Refundability

For 2004, the child credit is refundable to the extent of 10 percent of the taxpayer's taxable earned income (which is taken into account in determining taxable income) in excess of $10,750.[2] The percentage is increased to 15 percent for taxable years 2005 and thereafter. Families with three or more children are allowed a refundable credit for the amount by which the taxpayer's social security taxes exceed the taxpayer's earned income credit, if that amount is greater than the refundable credit based on the taxpayer's taxable earned income in excess of $10,750 (for 2004). The refundable portion of the child credit does not constitute income and is not treated as resources for purposes of determining eligibility or the amount or nature of benefits or assistance under any Federal program or any

---

[1] Modified adjusted gross income is the taxpayer's total gross income plus certain amounts excluded from gross income (i.e., excluded income of U.S. citizens or residents living abroad (sec. 911); residents of Guam, American Sa-

moa, and the Northern Mariana Islands (sec. 931); and residents of Puerto Rico (sec. 933)).

[2] The $10,750 amount is indexed for inflation.

State or local program financed with Federal funds. For taxable years beginning after December 31, 2010, the sunset provision of EGTRRA applies to the 15-percent rule for allowing refundable child credits.

Alternative minimum tax liability

The child credit is allowed against the individual's regular income tax and alternative minimum tax. For taxable years beginning after December 31, 2010, the sunset provision of EGTRRA applies to the rules allowing the child credit against the alternative minimum tax.

House Bill

* * * The bill also accelerates to 2003 the increase in refundability of the child credit to 15 percent of the taxpayer's earned income in excess of $10,500 (with indexing). Finally, the bill provides that the beginning point of the phase-out range for the child credit is $150,000 for married individuals filing joint returns ($75,000 for unmarried individuals and married individuals filing separately) for taxable years beginning after December 31, 2002, and before January 1, 2011. All modifications to the child credit under the bill are subject to the sunset provision of EGTRRA.

Effective Date

Taxable years beginning after December 31, 2002.

Senate Amendment

The Senate amendment accelerates to 2003 the increase in refundability of the child credit to 15 percent of the taxpayer's earned income in excess of $10,500 (with indexing). The Senate amendment also provides that taxpayers eligible for such additional refundable child credit amount will receive this additional amount as an advance payment. No advance payments may be made after December 31, 2003. Also, the Senate amendment provides that the beginning point of the phase-out range for the credit for married

individuals filing joint returns is increased to $115,000 in 2008 and 2009 and $150,000 in 2010. It also provides that the beginning point for such phase-out range in the case of unmarried individuals and married individuals filing separately will be one-half of the beginning point of the phase-out range for married individuals filing joint returns for taxable years beginning in 2008 through 2010. * * * All modifications to the child credit under the Senate amendment are subject to the sunset provision of EGTRRA.

Effective Date

The provision is effective for taxable years beginning after December 31, 2002.

Conference Agreement

In general

* * * All modifications to the child credit under the conference agreement are subject to the sunset provision of EGTRRA.[4]

Refundability

The conference agreement accelerates to 2004 the increase in refundability of the child credit to 15 percent of the taxpayer's earned income in excess of $10,750 (with indexing).

* * *

Effective Dates

The provision generally applies to taxable years beginning after December 31, 2004. The provision relating to the acceleration of the refundability of the child credit applies to taxable years beginning after December 31, 2003. The provision relating to the treatment of combat pay as earned income for purposes of the child credit is effective for taxable years beginning after December 31, 2003. The earned income credit election is effective for taxable years ending after the date of enactment and before January 1, 2006.

[Law at ¶5020. CCH Explanation at ¶125.]

[¶ 10,060] Act Sec. 103. Extend alternative minimum tax exemption for individuals

Conference Committee Report (H.R. CONF. REP. NO. 108-696)

[Code Sec. 55]

Present Law

The alternative minimum tax is the amount by which the tentative minimum tax exceeds the

regular income tax. An individual's tentative minimum tax is the sum of (1) 26 percent of so much of the taxable excess as does not exceed $175,000 ($87,500 in the case of a married individual filing a separate return) and (2) 28 percent

---

[4] The credit reverts to $500 in taxable years beginning after December 31, 2010, under the sunset provision of EGTRRA.

of the remaining taxable excess. The taxable excess is so much of the alternative minimum taxable income ("AMTI") as exceeds the exemption amount. The maximum tax rates on net capital gain and dividends used in computing the regular tax are used in computing the tentative minimum tax. AMTI is the individual's taxable income adjusted to take account of specified preferences and adjustments.

The exemption amount is: (1) $45,000 ($58,000 for taxable years beginning before 2005) in the case of married individuals filing a joint return and surviving spouses; (2) $33,750 ($40,250 for taxable years beginning before 2005) in the case of other unmarried individuals; (3) $22,500 ($29,000 for taxable years beginning before 2005) in the case of married individuals filing a separate return; and (4) $22,500 in the case of an estate or trust. The exemption amount is phased out by an amount equal to 25 percent of the amount by which the individual's AMTI exceeds (1) $150,000 in the case of married individuals filing a joint return and surviving

spouses, (2) $112,500 in the case of other unmarried individuals, and (3) $75,000 in the case of married individuals filing separate returns, an estate, or a trust. These amounts are not indexed for inflation.

House Bill

No provision.

Senate Amendment

No provision.

Conference Agreement

The conference agreement extends the increased alternative minimum tax exemption amounts to taxable years beginning in 2005.

Effective Date

The provision applies to taxable years beginning after December 31, 2004.

[Law at ¶ 5085. CCH Explanation at ¶ 130.]

[¶ 10,070] Act Sec. 104. Treatment of combat pay as earned income for purposes of the child tax credit and earned income credit

Conference Committee Report (H.R. CONF. REP. NO. 108-696)

[Code Secs. 24 and 32]

Present Law

In general

For 2004, an individual may claim a $1,000 tax credit for each qualifying child under the age of 17. In general, a qualifying child is an individual for whom the taxpayer can claim a dependency exemption and who is the taxpayer's son or daughter (or descendent of either), stepson or stepdaughter (or descendent of either), or eligible foster child.

* * *

The child tax credit is phased out for individuals with income over certain thresholds. Specifically, the otherwise allowable child tax credit is reduced by $50 for each $1,000 (or fraction thereof) of modified adjusted gross income over $75,000 for single individuals or heads of households, $110,000 for married individuals filing joint returns, and $55,000 for married individuals filing separate returns.[1] The length of the phase-out range depends on the number of qualifying children. For example, the phase-out

range for a single individual with one qualifying child is between $75,000 and $95,000 of modified adjusted gross income. The phase-out range for a single individual with two qualifying children is between $75,000 and $115,000.

The amount of the tax credit and the phase-out ranges are not adjusted annually for inflation.

Refundability

For 2004, the child credit is refundable to the extent of 10 percent of the taxpayer's taxable earned income (which is taken into account in determining taxable income) in excess of $10,750.[2] The percentage is increased to 15 percent for taxable years 2005 and thereafter. Families with three or more children are allowed a refundable credit for the amount by which the taxpayer's social security taxes exceed the taxpayer's earned income credit, if that amount is greater than the refundable credit based on the taxpayer's taxable earned income in excess of $10,750 (for 2004). The refundable portion of the child credit does not constitute income and is not treated as resources for purposes of determining

---

[1] Modified adjusted gross income is the taxpayer's total gross income plus certain amounts excluded from gross income (i.e., excluded income of U.S. citizens or residents living abroad (sec. 911); residents of Guam, American Samoa, and the Northern Mariana Islands (sec. 931); and residents of Puerto Rico (sec. 933)).

[2] The $10,750 amount is indexed for inflation.

eligibility or the amount or nature of benefits or assistance under any Federal program or any State or local program financed with Federal funds. For taxable years beginning after December 31, 2010, the sunset provision of EGTRRA applies to the 15-percent rule for allowing refundable child credits.

Alternative minimum tax liability

The child credit is allowed against the individual's regular income tax and alternative minimum tax. For taxable years beginning after December 31, 2010, the sunset provision of EGT-RRA applies to the rules allowing the child credit against the alternative minimum tax.

House Bill

* * * The bill also accelerates to 2003 the increase in refundability of the child credit to 15 percent of the taxpayer's earned income in excess of $10,500 (with indexing). Finally, the bill provides that the beginning point of the phase-out range for the child credit is $150,000 for married individuals filing joint returns ($75,000 for unmarried individuals and married individuals filing separately) for taxable years beginning after December 31, 2002, and before January 1, 2011. All modifications to the child credit under the bill are subject to the sunset provision of EGTRRA.

Effective Date

Taxable years beginning after December 31, 2002.

Senate Amendment

The Senate amendment accelerates to 2003 the increase in refundability of the child credit to 15 percent of the taxpayer's earned income in excess of $10,500 (with indexing). The Senate amendment also provides that taxpayers eligible for such additional refundable child credit amount will receive this additional amount as an advance payment. No advance payments may be made after December 31, 2003. Also, the Senate amendment provides that the beginning point of the phase-out range for the credit for married individuals filing joint returns is increased to $115,000 in 2008 and 2009 and $150,000 in 2010. It also provides that the beginning point for such phase-out range in the case of unmarried individuals and married individuals filing separately will be one-half of the beginning point of the phase-out range for married individuals filing joint returns for taxable years beginning in 2008

through 2010. Finally, the Senate amendment provides that any amount excluded from gross income under section 112 of the Code (relating to certain combat zone compensation) is treated as earned income for purposes of the calculation of the child tax credit. All modifications to the child credit under the Senate amendment are subject to the sunset provision of EGTRRA.

Effective Date

The provision is effective for taxable years beginning after December 31, 2002.

Conference Agreement

In general

* * * All modifications to the child credit under the conference agreement are subject to the sunset provision of EGTRRA.[4]

Refundability

The conference agreement accelerates to 2004 the increase in refundability of the child credit to 15 percent of the taxpayer's earned income in excess of $10,750 (with indexing).

Combat pay treated as earned income

The conference agreement provides that combat pay that is otherwise excluded from gross income under section 112 is treated as earned income which is taken into account in computing taxable income for purposes of calculating the refundable portion of the child credit.

The conference agreement provides that any taxpayer may elect to treat combat pay that is otherwise excluded from gross income under section 112 as earned income for purposes of the earned income credit. This election is available with respect to any taxable year ending after the date of enactment and before January 1, 2006.

Effective Date

* * * The provision relating to the acceleration of the refundability of the child credit applies to taxable years beginning after December 31, 2003. The provision relating to the treatment of combat pay as earned income for purposes of the child credit is effective for taxable years beginning after December 31, 2003. The earned income credit election is effective for taxable years ending after the date of enactment and before January 1, 2006.

[Law at ¶5020 and ¶5040. CCH Explanation at ¶180.]

---

[4] The credit reverts to $500 in taxable years beginning after December 31, 2010, under the sunset provision of EGTRRA.

[¶ 10,100] Act Secs. 201, 206 and 207. Establish uniform definition of a qualifying child: Dependency exemption

Conference Committee Report (H.R. CONF. REP. NO. 108-696)

[Code Secs. 151 and 152]

Present Law

In general

Present law contains five commonly used provisions that provide benefits to taxpayers with children: (1) the dependency exemption; (2) the child credit; (3) the earned income credit; (4) the dependent care credit; and (5) head of household filing status. Each provision has separate criteria for determining whether the taxpayer qualifies for the applicable tax benefit with respect to a particular child. The separate criteria include factors such as the relationship (if any) the child must bear to the taxpayer, the age of the child, and whether the child must live with the taxpayer. Thus, with respect to the same individual, a taxpayer is required to determine eligibility for each benefit separately, and an individual who qualifies a taxpayer for one provision does not automatically qualify the taxpayer for another provision.

Dependency exemption[35]

In general

Taxpayers are entitled to a personal exemption deduction for the taxpayer, his or her spouse, and each dependent. For 2004, the amount deductible for each personal exemption is $3,100. The deduction for personal exemptions is phased out for taxpayers with incomes above certain thresholds.[36]

In general, a taxpayer is entitled to a dependency exemption for an individual if the individual: (1) satisfies a relationship test or is a member of the taxpayer's household for the entire taxable year; (2) satisfies a support test; (3) satisfies a gross income test or is a child of the taxpayer under a certain age; (4) is a citizen or resident of the U.S. or resident of Canada or Mexico;[37] and (5) did not file a joint return with his or her

spouse for the year.[38] In addition, the taxpayer identification number of the individual must be included on the taxpayer's return.

Relationship or member of household test

Relationship test.—The relationship test is satisfied if an individual is the taxpayer's (1) son or daughter or a descendant of either (e.g., grandchild or great-grandchild); (2) stepson or stepdaughter; (3) brother or sister (including half brother, half sister, stepbrother, or stepsister); (4) parent, grandparent, or other direct ancestor (but not foster parent); (5) stepfather or stepmother; (6) brother or sister of the taxpayer's father or mother; (7) son or daughter of the taxpayer's brother or sister; or (8) the taxpayer's father-in-law, mother-in-law, son-in-law, daughter-in-law, brother-in-law, or sister-in-law.

An adopted child (or a child who is a member of the taxpayer's household and who has been placed with the taxpayer for adoption) is treated as a child of the taxpayer. A foster child is treated as a child of the taxpayer if the foster child is a member of the taxpayer's household for the entire taxable year.

Member of household test.—If the relationship test is not satisfied, then the individual may be considered the dependent of the taxpayer if the individual is a member of the taxpayer's household for the entire year. Thus, a taxpayer may be eligible to claim a dependency exemption with respect to an unrelated child who lives with the taxpayer for the entire year.

For the member of household test to be satisfied, the taxpayer must both maintain the household and occupy the household with the individual.[39] A taxpayer or other individual does not fail to be considered a member of a household because of "temporary" absences due to special circumstances, including absences due to illness, education, business, vacation, and mili-

---

[35] Secs. 151 and 152. Under the statutory structure, section 151 provides for the deduction for personal exemptions with respect to "dependents." The term "dependent" is defined in section 152. Most of the requirements regarding dependents are contained in section 152; section 151 contains additional requirements that must be satisfied in order to obtain a dependency exemption with respect to a dependent (as so defined). In particular, section 151 contains the gross income test, the rules relating to married dependents filing a joint return, and the requirement for a taxpayer identification number. The other rules discussed here are contained in section 151.

[36] Sec. 151(d)(3).

[37] A legally adopted child who does not satisfy the residency or citizenship requirement may nevertheless qualify as a dependent (provided other applicable requirements are met) if (1) the child's principal place of abode is the taxpayer's home and (2) the taxpayer is a citizen or national of the United States. Sec. 152(b)(3).

[38] This restriction does not apply if the return was filed solely to obtain a refund and no tax liability would exist for either spouse if they filed separate returns. Rev. Rul. 54-567, 1954-2 C.B. 108.

[39] Treas. Reg. sec. 1.152-1(b).

tary service.[40] Similarly, an individual does not fail to be considered a member of the taxpayer's household due to a custody agreement under which the individual is absent for less than six months.[41] Indefinite absences that last for more than the taxable year may be considered "temporary." For example, the IRS has ruled that an elderly woman who was indefinitely confined to a nursing home was temporarily absent from a taxpayer's household. Under the facts of the ruling, the woman had been an occupant of the household before being confined to a nursing home, the confinement had extended for several years, and it was possible that the woman would die before becoming well enough to return to the taxpayer's household. There was no intent on the part of the taxpayer or the woman to change her principal place of abode.[42]

Support test

In general.—The support test is satisfied if the taxpayer provides over one half of the support of the individual for the taxable year. To determine whether a taxpayer has provided more than one half of an individual's support, the amount the taxpayer contributed to the individual's support is compared with the entire amount of support the individual received from all sources, including the individual's own funds.[43] Governmental payments and subsidies (e.g., Temporary Assistance to Needy Families, food stamps, and housing) generally are treated as support provided by a third party. Expenses that are not directly related to any one member of a household, such as the cost of food for the household, must be divided among the members of the household. If any person furnishes support in kind (e.g., in the form of housing), then the fair market value of that support must be determined.

Multiple support agreements.—In some cases, no one taxpayer provides more than one half of the support of an individual. Instead, two or more taxpayers, each of whom would be able to claim a dependency exemption but for the support test, together provide more than one half of the individual's support. If this occurs, the taxpayers may agree to designate that one of the taxpayers who individually provides more than 10 percent of the individual's support can claim a dependency exemption for the child. Each of the others must sign a written statement agreeing not to claim the exemption for that year. The statements must be filed with the income tax return of the taxpayer who claims the exemption.

Special rules for divorced or legally separated parents.—Special rules apply in the case of a child of divorced or legally separated parents (or parents who live apart at all times during the last six months of the year) who provide over one half the child's support during the calendar year.[44] If such a child is in the custody of one or both of the parents for more than one half of the year, then the parent having custody for the greater portion of the year is deemed to satisfy the support test; however, the custodial parent may release the dependency exemption to the noncustodial parent by filing a written declaration with the IRS.[45]

Gross income test

In general, an individual may not be claimed as a dependent of a taxpayer if the individual has gross income that is at least equal to the personal exemption amount for the taxable year.[46] If the individual is the child of the taxpayer and under age 19 (or under age 24, if a full-time student), the gross income test does not apply.[47] For purposes of this rule, a "child" means a son, daughter, stepson, or stepdaughter (including an adopted child of the taxpayer, a foster child who resides with the taxpayer for the entire year, or a child placed with the taxpayer for adoption by an authorized adoption agency).

* * *

House Bill

No provision.

---

[40] *Id.*

[41] *Id.*

[42] Rev. Rul. 66-28, 1966-1 C.B. 31.

[43] In the case of a son, daughter, stepson, or stepdaughter of the taxpayer who is a full-time student, scholarships are not taken into account for purpose of the support test. Sec. 152(d).

[44] For purposes of this rule, a "child" means a son, daughter, stepson, or stepdaughter (including an adopted child or foster child, or child placed with the taxpayer for adoption). Sec. 152(e)(1)(A).

[45] Special support rules also apply in the case of certain pre-1985 agreements between divorced or legally separated parents. Sec. 152(e)(4).

[46] Certain income from sheltered workshops is not taken into account in determining the gross income of permanently and totally disabled individuals. Sec. 151(c)(5).

[47] Sec. 151(c). The IRS has issued guidance stating that for purposes of the dependency exemption, an individual attains a specified age on the anniversary of the date that the child was born (e.g., a child born on January 1, 1987, attains the age of 17 on January 1, 2004). Rev. Rul. 2003-72, 2003-33 I.R.B. 346.

Senate Amendment

In general

In general

The Senate amendment establishes a uniform definition of qualifying child for purposes of the dependency exemption, the child credit, the earned income credit, the dependent care credit, and head of household filing status. A taxpayer generally may claim an individual who does not meet the uniform definition of qualifying child (with respect to any taxpayer) as a dependent if the present-law dependency requirements are satisfied. The Senate amendment generally does not modify other parameters of each tax benefit (e.g., the earned income requirements of the earned income credit) or the rules for determining whether individuals other than children of the taxpayer qualify for each tax benefit.

Under the uniform definition, in general, a child is a qualifying child of a taxpayer if the child satisfies each of three tests: (1) the child has the same principal place of abode as the taxpayer for more than one half the taxable year; (2) the child has a specified relationship to the taxpayer; and (3) the child has not yet attained a specified age. A tie-breaking rule applies if more than one taxpayer claims a child as a qualifying child.

Under the Senate amendment, the present-law support and gross income tests for determining whether an individual is a dependent generally do not apply to a child who meets the requirements of the uniform definition of qualifying child.

Residency test

Under the uniform definition's residency test, a child must have the same principal place of abode as the taxpayer for more than one half of the taxable year. It is intended that, as is the case under present law, temporary absences due to special circumstances, including absences due to illness, education, business, vacation, or military service, are not treated as absences.

Relationship test

In order to be a qualifying child under the Senate amendment, the child must be the taxpayer's son, daughter, stepson, stepdaughter, brother, sister, stepbrother, stepsister, or a descendant of any such individual. An individual legally adopted by the taxpayer, or an individual who is placed with the taxpayer by an author-ized placement agency for adoption by the taxpayer, is treated as a child of such taxpayer by blood. A foster child who is placed with the taxpayer by an authorized placement agency or by judgment, decree, or other order of any court of competent jurisdiction is treated as the taxpayer's child.[65]

Age test

Under the Senate amendment, the age test varies depending upon the tax benefit involved. In general, a child must be under age 19 (or under age 24 in the case of a full-time student) in order to be a qualifying child.[66] In general, no age limit applies with respect to individuals who are totally and permanently disabled within the meaning of section 22(e)(3) at any time during the calendar year. The Senate amendment retains the present-law requirements that a child must be under age 13 (if he or she is not disabled) for purposes of the dependent care credit, and under age 17 (whether or not disabled) for purposes of the child credit.

Children who support themselves

Under the Senate amendment, a child who provides over one half of his or her own support generally is not considered a qualifying child of another taxpayer. The Senate amendment retains the present-law rule, however, that a child who provides over one half of his or her own support may constitute a qualifying child of another taxpayer for purposes of the earned income credit.

Tie-breaking rules

If a child would be a qualifying child with respect to more than one individual (e.g., a child lives with his or her mother and grandmother in the same residence) and more than one person claims a benefit with respect to that child, then the following "tie-breaking" rules apply. First, if only one of the individuals claiming the child as a qualifying child is the child's parent, the child is deemed the qualifying child of the parent. Second, if both parents claim the child and the parents do not file a joint return, then the child is deemed a qualifying child first with respect to the parent with whom the child resides for the longest period of time, and second with respect to the parent with the highest adjusted gross income. Third, if the child's parents do not claim the child, then the child is deemed a qualifying child with respect to the claimant with the highest adjusted gross income.

---

[65] The provision eliminates the present-law rule requiring that if a child is the taxpayer's sibling or stepsibling or a descendant of any such individual, the taxpayer must care for the child as if the child were his or her own child.

[66] The provision retains the present-law definition of full-time student set forth in section 151(c)(4).

Interaction with present-law rules

Taxpayers generally may claim an individual who does not meet the uniform definition of qualifying child with respect to any taxpayer as a dependent if the present-law dependency requirements (including the gross income and support tests) are satisfied.[67] Thus, for example, as under present law, a taxpayer may claim a parent as a dependent if the taxpayer provides more than one half of the support of the parent and the parent's gross income is less than the exemption amount. As another example, under the Senate amendment a grandparent may claim a dependency exemption with respect to a grandson who does not reside with any taxpayer for over one half the year, if the grandparent provides more than one half of the support of the grandson and the grandson's gross income is less than the exemption amount.

Citizenship and residency

Children who are U.S. citizens living abroad or non-U.S. citizens living in Canada or Mexico may qualify as a qualifying child, as is the case under the present-law dependency tests. A legally adopted child who does not satisfy the residency or citizenship requirement may nevertheless qualify as a qualifying child (provided other applicable requirements are met) if (1) the child's principal place of abode is the taxpayer's home and (2) the taxpayer is a citizen or national of the United States.

Children of divorced or legally separated parents

The Senate amendment retains the present-law rule that allows a custodial parent to release the claim to a dependency exemption (and, therefore, the child credit) to a noncustodial parent. Thus, under the Senate amendment, custodial waivers that are in place and effective on the date of enactment will continue to be effective after the date of enactment if they continue to satisfy the waiver rule. In addition, the Senate amendment retains the custodial waiver rule for purposes of the dependency exemption (and, therefore, the child credit) for decrees of divorce or separate maintenance or written separation agreements that become effective after the date of enactment. Under the Senate amendment, as under present law, the custodial waiver rules do not affect eligibility with respect to children of divorced or legally separated parents for purposes of the earned income credit, the dependent care credit, and head of household filing status.

While retaining the substantive effect of the present-law waiver provisions, the Senate amendment modifies the mechanical structure of the rules. Under present law, a waiver may be made with respect to the dependency exemption. The waiver then automatically carries over to the child credit, because in order to claim the child credit, the taxpayer must be allowed the dependency exemption with respect to the child. Thus, if the dependency exemption is waived, the child credit applies to the taxpayer who is allowed the dependency exemption under the waiver.

The Senate amendment obtains the same result, but through a slightly modified statutory structure. Under the Senate amendment, if a waiver is made, the waiver applies for purposes of determining whether a child meets the definition of a qualifying child or a qualifying relative under section 152(c) or 152(d) as amended by the provision. While the definition of qualifying child is generally uniform, for purposes of the earned income credit, head of household status, and the dependent care credit, the definition of qualifying child is made without regard to the waiver provision.[68] Thus, as under present law, a waiver that applies for the dependency exemption will also apply for the child credit, and the waiver will not apply for purposes of the other provisions.

Other provisions

The Senate amendment retains the applicable present-law requirements that a taxpayer identification number for a child be provided on the taxpayer's return. * * *

Effect of Senate amendment on particular tax benefits

Dependency exemption

For purposes of the dependency exemption, the Senate amendment defines a dependent as a qualifying child or a qualifying relative. The qualifying child test eliminates the support test (other than in the case of a child who provides more than one half of his or her own support), and replaces it with the residency requirement described above. Further, the present-law gross income test does not apply to a qualifying child. The rules relating to multiple support agreements do not apply with respect to qualifying children because the support test does not apply to them. Special tie-breaking rules (described above) apply if more than one taxpayer claims a

---

[67] Individuals who satisfy the present-law dependency tests and who are not qualifying children are referred to as "qualifying relatives" under the provision.

[68] See secs. 2(b)(1)(A)(i) and 32(c)(3)(A) as amended by the provision, and sec. 21(e)(5).

qualifying child under the Senate amendment. These tie-breaking rules do not apply if a child constitutes a qualifying child with respect to multiple taxpayers, but only one eligible taxpayer actually claims the qualifying child.

The Senate amendment generally permits taxpayers to continue to apply the present-law dependency exemption rules to claim a dependency exemption for a qualifying relative who does not satisfy the qualifying child definition. In such cases, the present-law gross income and support tests, including the special rules for multiple support agreements, the special rules relating to income of handicapped dependents, and the special support test in case of students, continue to apply for purposes of the dependency exemption.

As is the case under present law, a child who provides over half of his or her own support is not considered a dependent of another taxpayer under the Senate amendment. Further, an individual shall not be treated as a dependent of any taxpayer if such individual has filed a joint return with the individual's spouse for the taxable year.

* * *

Effective Date

The provision is effective for taxable years beginning after December 31, 2003.

Conference Agreement

The conference agreement includes the Senate amendment provision with the following modifications. The conference agreement modifies the definition of adopted child, for purposes of determining whether an adopted child is treated as a child by blood, to mean an individual who is legally adopted by the taxpayer, or an individual who is lawfully placed with the taxpayer for legal adoption by the taxpayer.

Effective Date

The provision is effective for taxable years beginning after December 31, 2004.

[**Law at** ¶5010, ¶5015, ¶5025, ¶5055, ¶5075, ¶5105, ¶5110, ¶5115, ¶5120, ¶5125, ¶5130, ¶5140, ¶5145, ¶5150, ¶5165, ¶5185, ¶5190, ¶5195, ¶5250, ¶5355, ¶5360, ¶5400, ¶5405 and ¶5410. **CCH Explanation at** ¶145 **and** ¶170.]

[¶ 10,120] Act Sec. 202. Establish uniform definition of a qualifying child: Head of household filing status

Conference Committee Report (H.R. CONF. REP. NO. 108-696)

[Code Sec. 2(b)]

Present Law

In general

Present law contains five commonly used provisions that provide benefits to taxpayers with children: (1) the dependency exemption; (2) the child credit; (3) the earned income credit; (4) the dependent care credit; and (5) head of household filing status. Each provision has separate criteria for determining whether the taxpayer qualifies for the applicable tax benefit with respect to a particular child. The separate criteria include factors such as the relationship (if any) the child must bear to the taxpayer, the age of the child, and whether the child must live with the taxpayer. Thus, with respect to the same individual, a taxpayer is required to determine eligibility for each benefit separately, and an individual who qualifies a taxpayer for one provision does not automatically qualify the taxpayer for another provision.

* * *

Head of household filing status[63]

A taxpayer may claim head of household filing status if the taxpayer is unmarried (and not a surviving spouse) and pays more than one half of the cost of maintaining as his or her home a household which is the principal place of abode for more than one half of the year of (1) an unmarried son, daughter, stepson or stepdaughter of the taxpayer or an unmarried descendant of the taxpayer's son or daughter, (2) an individual described in (1) who is married, if the taxpayer may claim a dependency exemption with respect to the individual (or could claim the exemption if the taxpayer had not waived the exemption to the noncustodial parent), or (3) a relative with respect to whom the taxpayer may claim a dependency exemption.[64] If certain other requirements are satisfied, head of household filing status also may be claimed if the taxpayer is entitled to a dependency exemption with respect to one of the taxpayer's parents.

House Bill

No provision.

---

[63] Sec. 2(b).

[64] Sec. 2(b)(1)(A)(ii), as qualified by sec. 2(b)(3)(B). An individual for whom the taxpayer is entitled to claim a

dependency exemption by reason of a multiple support agreement does not qualify the taxpayer for head of household filing status.

Senate Amendment

In general

In general

The Senate amendment establishes a uniform definition of qualifying child for purposes of the dependency exemption, the child credit, the earned income credit, the dependent care credit, and head of household filing status. A taxpayer generally may claim an individual who does not meet the uniform definition of qualifying child (with respect to any taxpayer) as a dependent if the present-law dependency requirements are satisfied. The Senate amendment generally does not modify other parameters of each tax benefit (e.g., the earned income requirements of the earned income credit) or the rules for determining whether individuals other than children of the taxpayer qualify for each tax benefit.

Under the uniform definition, in general, a child is a qualifying child of a taxpayer if the child satisfies each of three tests: (1) the child has the same principal place of abode as the taxpayer for more than one half the taxable year; (2) the child has a specified relationship to the taxpayer; and (3) the child has not yet attained a specified age. A tie-breaking rule applies if more than one taxpayer claims a child as a qualifying child.

Under the Senate amendment, the present-law support and gross income tests for determining whether an individual is a dependent generally do not apply to a child who meets the requirements of the uniform definition of qualifying child.

Residency test

Under the uniform definition's residency test, a child must have the same principal place of abode as the taxpayer for more than one half of the taxable year. It is intended that, as is the case under present law, temporary absences due to special circumstances, including absences due to illness, education, business, vacation, or military service, are not treated as absences.

Relationship test

In order to be a qualifying child under the Senate amendment, the child must be the taxpayer's son, daughter, stepson, stepdaughter, brother, sister, stepbrother, stepsister, or a descendant of any such individual. An individual legally adopted by the taxpayer, or an individual who is placed with the taxpayer by an author-ized placement agency for adoption by the taxpayer, is treated as a child of such taxpayer by blood. A foster child who is placed with the taxpayer by an authorized placement agency or by judgment, decree, or other order of any court of competent jurisdiction is treated as the taxpayer's child.[65]

Age test

Under the Senate amendment, the age test varies depending upon the tax benefit involved. In general, a child must be under age 19 (or under age 24 in the case of a full-time student) in order to be a qualifying child.[66] In general, no age limit applies with respect to individuals who are totally and permanently disabled within the meaning of section 22(e)(3) at any time during the calendar year. The Senate amendment retains the present-law requirements that a child must be under age 13 (if he or she is not disabled) for purposes of the dependent care credit, and under age 17 (whether or not disabled) for purposes of the child credit.

Children who support themselves

Under the Senate amendment, a child who provides over one half of his or her own support generally is not considered a qualifying child of another taxpayer. The Senate amendment retains the present-law rule, however, that a child who provides over one half of his or her own support may constitute a qualifying child of another taxpayer for purposes of the earned income credit.

Tie-breaking rules

If a child would be a qualifying child with respect to more than one individual (e.g., a child lives with his or her mother and grandmother in the same residence) and more than one person claims a benefit with respect to that child, then the following "tie-breaking" rules apply. First, if only one of the individuals claiming the child as a qualifying child is the child's parent, the child is deemed the qualifying child of the parent. Second, if both parents claim the child and the parents do not file a joint return, then the child is deemed a qualifying child first with respect to the parent with whom the child resides for the longest period of time, and second with respect to the parent with the highest adjusted gross income. Third, if the child's parents do not claim the child, then the child is deemed a qualifying child with respect to the claimant with the highest adjusted gross income.

---

[65] The provision eliminates the present-law rule requiring that if a child is the taxpayer's sibling or stepsibling or a descendant of any such individual, the taxpayer must care for the child as if the child were his or her own child.

[66] The provision retains the present-law definition of full-time student set forth in section 151(c)(4).

Interaction with present-law rules

Taxpayers generally may claim an individual who does not meet the uniform definition of qualifying child with respect to any taxpayer as a dependent if the present-law dependency requirements (including the gross income and support tests) are satisfied.[67] Thus, for example, as under present law, a taxpayer may claim a parent as a dependent if the taxpayer provides more than one half of the support of the parent and the parent's gross income is less than the exemption amount. As another example, under the Senate amendment a grandparent may claim a dependency exemption with respect to a grandson who does not reside with any taxpayer for over one half the year, if the grandparent provides more than one half of the support of the grandson and the grandson's gross income is less than the exemption amount.

Citizenship and residency

Children who are U.S. citizens living abroad or non-U.S. citizens living in Canada or Mexico may qualify as a qualifying child, as is the case under the present-law dependency tests. A legally adopted child who does not satisfy the residency or citizenship requirement may nevertheless qualify as a qualifying child (provided other applicable requirements are met) if (1) the child's principal place of abode is the taxpayer's home and (2) the taxpayer is a citizen or national of the United States.

Children of divorced or legally separated parents

The Senate amendment retains the present-law rule that allows a custodial parent to release the claim to a dependency exemption (and, therefore, the child credit) to a noncustodial parent. Thus, under the Senate amendment, custodial waivers that are in place and effective on the date of enactment will continue to be effective after the date of enactment if they continue to satisfy the waiver rule. In addition, the Senate amendment retains the custodial waiver rule for purposes of the dependency exemption (and, therefore, the child credit) for decrees of divorce or separate maintenance or written separation agreements that become effective after the date of enactment. Under the Senate amendment, as under present law, the custodial waiver rules do not affect eligibility with respect to children of divorced or legally separated parents for purposes of the earned income credit, the dependent care credit, and head of household filing status.

While retaining the substantive effect of the present-law waiver provisions, the Senate amendment modifies the mechanical structure of the rules. Under present law, a waiver may be made with respect to the dependency exemption. The waiver then automatically carries over to the child credit, because in order to claim the child credit, the taxpayer must be allowed the dependency exemption with respect to the child. Thus, if the dependency exemption is waived, the child credit applies to the taxpayer who is allowed the dependency exemption under the waiver.

The Senate amendment obtains the same result, but through a slightly modified statutory structure. Under the Senate amendment, if a waiver is made, the waiver applies for purposes of determining whether a child meets the definition of a qualifying child or a qualifying relative under section 152(c) or 152(d) as amended by the provision. While the definition of qualifying child is generally uniform, for purposes of the earned income credit, head of household status, and the dependent care credit, the definition of qualifying child is made without regard to the waiver provision.[68] Thus, as under present law, a waiver that applies for the dependency exemption will also apply for the child credit, and the waiver will not apply for purposes of the other provisions.

Other provisions

The Senate amendment retains the applicable present-law requirements that a taxpayer identification number for a child be provided on the taxpayer's return. * * *

Effect of Senate amendment on particular tax benefits

* * *

Head of household filing status

Under the Senate amendment, a taxpayer is eligible for head of household filing status only with respect to a qualifying child or an individual for whom the taxpayer is entitled to a dependency exemption. Under the Senate amendment, a taxpayer may claim head of household filing status if the taxpayer is unmarried (and not a surviving spouse) and pays more than one half of the cost of maintaining as his or her home a household which is the principal place of abode for more than one half the year of (1) a qualifying child, or (2) an individual for whom the

---

[67] Individuals who satisfy the present-law dependency tests and who are not qualifying children are referred to as "qualifying relatives" under the provision.

[68] See secs. 2(b)(1)(A)(i) and 32(c)(3)(A) as amended by the provision, and sec. 21(e)(5).

taxpayer may claim a dependency exemption. As under present law, a taxpayer may claim head of household status with respect to a parent for whom the taxpayer may claim a dependency exemption and who does not live with the taxpayer, if certain requirements are satisfied.

Effective Date

The provision is effective for taxable years beginning after December 31, 2003.

Conference Agreement

The conference agreement includes the Senate amendment provision with the following modifications. The conference agreement modifies the definition of adopted child, for purposes of determining whether an adopted child is treated as a child by blood, to mean an individual who is legally adopted by the taxpayer, or an individual who is lawfully placed with the taxpayer for legal adoption by the taxpayer.

Effective Date

The provision is effective for taxable years beginning after December 31, 2004.

[Law at ¶5010. CCH Explanation at ¶150.]

[¶ 10,130] Act Sec. 203. Establish uniform definition of a qualifying child: Dependent care credit

Conference Committee Report (H.R. CONF. REP. NO. 108-696)

[Code Sec. 21]

Present Law

In general

Present law contains five commonly used provisions that provide benefits to taxpayers with children: (1) the dependency exemption; (2) the child credit; (3) the earned income credit; (4) the dependent care credit; and (5) head of household filing status. Each provision has separate criteria for determining whether the taxpayer qualifies for the applicable tax benefit with respect to a particular child. The separate criteria include factors such as the relationship (if any) the child must bear to the taxpayer, the age of the child, and whether the child must live with the taxpayer. Thus, with respect to the same individual, a taxpayer is required to determine eligibility for each benefit separately, and an individual who qualifies a taxpayer for one provision does not automatically qualify the taxpayer for another provision.

* * *

Dependent care credit[59]

The dependent care credit may be claimed by a taxpayer who maintains a household that includes one or more qualifying individuals and who has employment-related expenses. A qualifying individual means (1) a dependent of the taxpayer under age 13 for whom the taxpayer is entitled to a dependency exemption,[60] (2) a dependent of the taxpayer who is physically or mentally incapable of caring for himself or herself,[61] or (3) the spouse of the taxpayer, if the spouse is physically or mentally incapable of caring for himself or herself. In addition, a taxpayer identification number for the qualifying individual must be included on the return.

A taxpayer is considered to maintain a household for a period if over one half the cost of maintaining the household for the period is furnished by the taxpayer (or, if married, the taxpayer and his or her spouse). Costs of maintaining the household include expenses such as rent, mortgage interest (but not principal), real estate taxes, insurance on the home, repairs (but not home improvements), utilities, and food eaten in the home.

A special rule applies in the case of a child who is under age 13 or is physically or mentally incapable of caring for himself or herself if the custodial parent has waived his or her dependency exemption to the noncustodial parent.[62] For the dependent care credit, the child is treated as a qualifying individual with respect to the custodial parent, not the parent entitled to claim the dependency exemption.

* * *

---

[59] Sec. 21.

[60] The IRS has issued guidance stating that for purposes of the dependent care credit, an individual attains a specified age on the anniversary of the date that the child was born (e.g., a child born on January 1, 1987, attains the age of 17 on January 1, 2004). Rev. Rul. 2003-72, 2003-33 I.R.B. 346.

[61] Although such an individual must be a dependent of the taxpayer as defined in section 152, it is not required that the taxpayer be entitled to a dependency exemption with respect to the individual under section 151. Thus, such an individual may be a qualifying individual for purposes of the dependent care credit, even though the taxpayer is not entitled to a dependency exemption because the individual does not meet the gross income test.

[62] Sec. 21(e)(5).

Act Sec. 203 ¶10,130

House Bill

No provision.

Senate Amendment

In general

In general

The Senate amendment establishes a uniform definition of qualifying child for purposes of the dependency exemption, the child credit, the earned income credit, the dependent care credit, and head of household filing status. A taxpayer generally may claim an individual who does not meet the uniform definition of qualifying child (with respect to any taxpayer) as a dependent if the present-law dependency requirements are satisfied. The Senate amendment generally does not modify other parameters of each tax benefit (e.g., the earned income requirements of the earned income credit) or the rules for determining whether individuals other than children of the taxpayer qualify for each tax benefit.

Under the uniform definition, in general, a child is a qualifying child of a taxpayer if the child satisfies each of three tests: (1) the child has the same principal place of abode as the taxpayer for more than one half the taxable year; (2) the child has a specified relationship to the taxpayer; and (3) the child has not yet attained a specified age. A tie-breaking rule applies if more than one taxpayer claims a child as a qualifying child.

Under the Senate amendment, the present-law support and gross income tests for determining whether an individual is a dependent generally do not apply to a child who meets the requirements of the uniform definition of qualifying child.

Residency test

Under the uniform definition's residency test, a child must have the same principal place of abode as the taxpayer for more than one half of the taxable year. It is intended that, as is the case under present law, temporary absences due to special circumstances, including absences due to illness, education, business, vacation, or military service, are not treated as absences.

Relationship test

In order to be a qualifying child under the Senate amendment, the child must be the taxpayer's son, daughter, stepson, stepdaughter, brother, sister, stepbrother, stepsister, or a descendant of any such individual. An individual

legally adopted by the taxpayer, or an individual who is placed with the taxpayer by an authorized placement agency for adoption by the taxpayer, is treated as a child of such taxpayer by blood. A foster child who is placed with the taxpayer by an authorized placement agency or by judgment, decree, or other order of any court of competent jurisdiction is treated as the taxpayer's child.[65]

Age test

Under the Senate amendment, the age test varies depending upon the tax benefit involved. In general, a child must be under age 19 (or under age 24 in the case of a full-time student) in order to be a qualifying child.[66] In general, no age limit applies with respect to individuals who are totally and permanently disabled within the meaning of section 22(e)(3) at any time during the calendar year. The Senate amendment retains the present-law requirements that a child must be under age 13 (if he or she is not disabled) for purposes of the dependent care credit, and under age 17 (whether or not disabled) for purposes of the child credit.

Children who support themselves

Under the Senate amendment, a child who provides over one half of his or her own support generally is not considered a qualifying child of another taxpayer. The Senate amendment retains the present-law rule, however, that a child who provides over one half of his or her own support may constitute a qualifying child of another taxpayer for purposes of the earned income credit.

Tie-breaking rules

If a child would be a qualifying child with respect to more than one individual (e.g., a child lives with his or her mother and grandmother in the same residence) and more than one person claims a benefit with respect to that child, then the following "tie-breaking" rules apply. First, if only one of the individuals claiming the child as a qualifying child is the child's parent, the child is deemed the qualifying child of the parent. Second, if both parents claim the child and the parents do not file a joint return, then the child is deemed a qualifying child first with respect to the parent with whom the child resides for the longest period of time, and second with respect to the parent with the highest adjusted gross income. Third, if the child's parents do not claim the child, then the child is deemed a qualifying child with respect to the claimant with the highest adjusted gross income.

---

[65] The provision eliminates the present-law rule requiring that if a child is the taxpayer's sibling or stepsibling or a descendant of any such individual, the taxpayer must care for the child as if the child were his or her own child.

[66] The provision retains the present-law definition of full-time student set forth in section 151(c)(4).

Interaction with present-law rules

Taxpayers generally may claim an individual who does not meet the uniform definition of qualifying child with respect to any taxpayer as a dependent if the present-law dependency requirements (including the gross income and support tests) are satisfied.[67] Thus, for example, as under present law, a taxpayer may claim a parent as a dependent if the taxpayer provides more than one half of the support of the parent and the parent's gross income is less than the exemption amount. As another example, under the Senate amendment a grandparent may claim a dependency exemption with respect to a grandson who does not reside with any taxpayer for over one half the year, if the grandparent provides more than one half of the support of the grandson and the grandson's gross income is less than the exemption amount.

Citizenship and residency

Children who are U.S. citizens living abroad or non-U.S. citizens living in Canada or Mexico may qualify as a qualifying child, as is the case under the present-law dependency tests. A legally adopted child who does not satisfy the residency or citizenship requirement may nevertheless qualify as a qualifying child (provided other applicable requirements are met) if (1) the child's principal place of abode is the taxpayer's home and (2) the taxpayer is a citizen or national of the United States.

Children of divorced or legally separated parents

The Senate amendment retains the present-law rule that allows a custodial parent to release the claim to a dependency exemption (and, therefore, the child credit) to a noncustodial parent. Thus, under the Senate amendment, custodial waivers that are in place and effective on the date of enactment will continue to be effective after the date of enactment if they continue to satisfy the waiver rule. In addition, the Senate amendment retains the custodial waiver rule for purposes of the dependency exemption (and, therefore, the child credit) for decrees of divorce or separate maintenance or written separation agreements that become effective after the date of enactment. Under the Senate amendment, as under present law, the custodial waiver rules do not affect eligibility with respect to children of divorced or legally separated parents for purposes of the earned income credit, the dependent care credit, and head of household filing status.

While retaining the substantive effect of the present-law waiver provisions, the Senate amendment modifies the mechanical structure of the rules. Under present law, a waiver may be made with respect to the dependency exemption. The waiver then automatically carries over to the child credit, because in order to claim the child credit, the taxpayer must be allowed the dependency exemption with respect to the child. Thus, if the dependency exemption is waived, the child credit applies to the taxpayer who is allowed the dependency exemption under the waiver.

The Senate amendment obtains the same result, but through a slightly modified statutory structure. Under the Senate amendment, if a waiver is made, the waiver applies for purposes of determining whether a child meets the definition of a qualifying child or a qualifying relative under section 152(c) or 152(d) as amended by the provision. While the definition of qualifying child is generally uniform, for purposes of the earned income credit, head of household status, and the dependent care credit, the definition of qualifying child is made without regard to the waiver provision.[68] Thus, as under present law, a waiver that applies for the dependency exemption will also apply for the child credit, and the waiver will not apply for purposes of the other provisions.

Other provisions

The Senate amendment retains the applicable present-law requirements that a taxpayer identification number for a child be provided on the taxpayer's return. * * *

Effect of Senate amendment on particular tax benefits

* * *

Dependent care credit

The present-law requirement that a taxpayer maintain a household in order to claim the dependent care credit is eliminated. Thus, if other applicable requirements are satisfied, a taxpayer may claim the dependent care credit with respect to a child who lives with the taxpayer for more than one half the year, even if the taxpayer does not provide more than one half of the cost of maintaining the household.

The rules for determining eligibility for the credit with respect to an individual who is physically or mentally incapable of caring for himself

---

[67] Individuals who satisfy the present-law dependency tests and who are not qualifying children are referred to as "qualifying relatives" under the provision.

[68] See secs. 2(b)(1)(A)(i) and 32(c)(3)(A) as amended by the provision, and sec. 21(e)(5).

or herself are amended to include a requirement that the taxpayer and the dependent have the same principal place of abode for more than one half the taxable year.

* * *

Effective Date

The provision is effective for taxable years beginning after December 31, 2003.

Conference Agreement

The conference agreement includes the Senate amendment provision with the following

modifications. The conference agreement modifies the definition of adopted child, for purposes of determining whether an adopted child is treated as a child by blood, to mean an individual who is legally adopted by the taxpayer, or an individual who is lawfully placed with the taxpayer for legal adoption by the taxpayer.

Effective Date

The provision is effective for taxable years beginning after December 31, 2004.

[**Law at ¶ 5015. CCH Explanation at ¶ 155.**]

[¶ 10,140] Act Sec. 204. Establish uniform definition of a qualifying child: Child tax credit

Conference Committee Report (H.R. CONF. REP. NO. 108-696)

[Code Sec. 24(c)]

Present Law

In general

Present law contains five commonly used provisions that provide benefits to taxpayers with children: (1) the dependency exemption; (2) the child credit; (3) the earned income credit; (4) the dependent care credit; and (5) head of household filing status. Each provision has separate criteria for determining whether the taxpayer qualifies for the applicable tax benefit with respect to a particular child. The separate criteria include factors such as the relationship (if any) the child must bear to the taxpayer, the age of the child, and whether the child must live with the taxpayer. Thus, with respect to the same individual, a taxpayer is required to determine eligibility for each benefit separately, and an individual who qualifies a taxpayer for one provision does not automatically qualify the taxpayer for another provision.

* * *

Child credit[54]

Taxpayers with incomes below certain amounts are eligible for a child credit for each qualifying child of the taxpayer. The amount of the child credit is up to $1,000, in the case of

taxable years beginning in 2003 or 2004. The child credit reverts to $700 for taxable years beginning in 2005 through 2008, $800 for taxable years beginning in 2009, and $1,000 for taxable years beginning in 2010. The credit declines to $500 in taxable year 2011.[55] For purposes of this credit, a qualifying child is an individual: (1) with respect to whom the taxpayer is entitled to a dependency exemption for the year; (2) who satisfies the same relationship test applicable to the earned income credit; and (3) who has not attained age 17 as of the close of the calendar year.[56] In addition, the child must be a citizen or resident of the United States.[57] A portion of the child credit is refundable under certain circumstances.[58]

* * *

House Bill

No provision.

Senate Amendment

In general

In general

The Senate amendment establishes a uniform definition of qualifying child for purposes of the dependency exemption, the child credit, the earned income credit, the dependent care

---

[54] Sec. 24.

[55] EGTRRA, Pub. L. No. 107-16, sec. 901(a) (2001).

[56] The IRS has issued guidance stating that for purposes of the child credit, an individual attains a specified age on the anniversary of the date that the child was born (e.g., a child born on January 1, 1987, attains the age of 17 on January 1, 2004). Rev. Rul. 2003-72, 2003-33 I.R.B. 346.

[57] The child credit does not apply with respect to a child who is a resident of Canada or Mexico and is not a U.S.

citizen, even if a dependency exemption is available with respect to the child. Sec. 24(c)(2). The child credit is, however, available with respect to a child dependent who is not a resident or citizen of the United States if: (1) the child has been legally adopted by the taxpayer; (2) the child's principal place of abode is the taxpayer's home; and (3) the taxpayer is a U.S. citizen or national. See sec. 24(c)(2) and sec. 152(b)(3).

[58] Sec. 24(d).

credit, and head of household filing status. A taxpayer generally may claim an individual who does not meet the uniform definition of qualifying child (with respect to any taxpayer) as a dependent if the present-law dependency requirements are satisfied. The Senate amendment generally does not modify other parameters of each tax benefit (e.g., the earned income requirements of the earned income credit) or the rules for determining whether individuals other than children of the taxpayer qualify for each tax benefit.

Under the uniform definition, in general, a child is a qualifying child of a taxpayer if the child satisfies each of three tests: (1) the child has the same principal place of abode as the taxpayer for more than one half the taxable year; (2) the child has a specified relationship to the taxpayer; and (3) the child has not yet attained a specified age. A tie-breaking rule applies if more than one taxpayer claims a child as a qualifying child.

Under the Senate amendment, the present-law support and gross income tests for determining whether an individual is a dependent generally do not apply to a child who meets the requirements of the uniform definition of qualifying child.

Residency test

Under the uniform definition's residency test, a child must have the same principal place of abode as the taxpayer for more than one half of the taxable year. It is intended that, as is the case under present law, temporary absences due to special circumstances, including absences due to illness, education, business, vacation, or military service, are not treated as absences.

Relationship test

In order to be a qualifying child under the Senate amendment, the child must be the taxpayer's son, daughter, stepson, stepdaughter, brother, sister, stepbrother, stepsister, or a descendant of any such individual. An individual legally adopted by the taxpayer, or an individual who is placed with the taxpayer by an authorized placement agency for adoption by the taxpayer, is treated as a child of such taxpayer by blood. A foster child who is placed with the taxpayer by an authorized placement agency or by judgment, decree, or other order of any court of competent jurisdiction is treated as the taxpayer's child.[65]

Age test

Under the Senate amendment, the age test varies depending upon the tax benefit involved. In general, a child must be under age 19 (or under age 24 in the case of a full-time student) in order to be a qualifying child.[66] In general, no age limit applies with respect to individuals who are totally and permanently disabled within the meaning of section 22(e)(3) at any time during the calendar year. The Senate amendment retains the present-law requirements that a child must be under age 13 (if he or she is not disabled) for purposes of the dependent care credit, and under age 17 (whether or not disabled) for purposes of the child credit.

Children who support themselves

Under the Senate amendment, a child who provides over one half of his or her own support generally is not considered a qualifying child of another taxpayer. The Senate amendment retains the present-law rule, however, that a child who provides over one half of his or her own support may constitute a qualifying child of another taxpayer for purposes of the earned income credit.

Tie-breaking rules

If a child would be a qualifying child with respect to more than one individual (e.g., a child lives with his or her mother and grandmother in the same residence) and more than one person claims a benefit with respect to that child, then the following "tie-breaking" rules apply. First, if only one of the individuals claiming the child as a qualifying child is the child's parent, the child is deemed the qualifying child of the parent. Second, if both parents claim the child and the parents do not file a joint return, then the child is deemed a qualifying child first with respect to the parent with whom the child resides for the longest period of time, and second with respect to the parent with the highest adjusted gross income. Third, if the child's parents do not claim the child, then the child is deemed a qualifying child with respect to the claimant with the highest adjusted gross income.

Interaction with present-law rules

Taxpayers generally may claim an individual who does not meet the uniform definition of qualifying child with respect to any taxpayer as a dependent if the present-law dependency requirements (including the gross income and sup-

---

[65] The provision eliminates the present-law rule requiring that if a child is the taxpayer's sibling or stepsibling or a descendant of any such individual, the taxpayer must care for the child as if the child were his or her own child.

[66] The provision retains the present-law definition of full-time student set forth in section 151(c)(4).

port tests) are satisfied.[67] Thus, for example, as under present law, a taxpayer may claim a parent as a dependent if the taxpayer provides more than one half of the support of the parent and the parent's gross income is less than the exemption amount. As another example, under the Senate amendment a grandparent may claim a dependency exemption with respect to a grandson who does not reside with any taxpayer for over one half the year, if the grandparent provides more than one half of the support of the grandson and the grandson's gross income is less than the exemption amount.

Citizenship and residency

Children who are U.S. citizens living abroad or non-U.S. citizens living in Canada or Mexico may qualify as a qualifying child, as is the case under the present-law dependency tests. A legally adopted child who does not satisfy the residency or citizenship requirement may nevertheless qualify as a qualifying child (provided other applicable requirements are met) if (1) the child's principal place of abode is the taxpayer's home and (2) the taxpayer is a citizen or national of the United States.

Children of divorced or legally separated parents

The Senate amendment retains the present-law rule that allows a custodial parent to release the claim to a dependency exemption (and, therefore, the child credit) to a noncustodial parent. Thus, under the Senate amendment, custodial waivers that are in place and effective on the date of enactment will continue to be effective after the date of enactment if they continue to satisfy the waiver rule. In addition, the Senate amendment retains the custodial waiver rule for purposes of the dependency exemption (and, therefore, the child credit) for decrees of divorce or separate maintenance or written separation agreements that become effective after the date of enactment. Under the Senate amendment, as under present law, the custodial waiver rules do not affect eligibility with respect to children of divorced or legally separated parents for purposes of the earned income credit, the dependent care credit, and head of household filing status.

While retaining the substantive effect of the present-law waiver provisions, the Senate amendment modifies the mechanical structure of the rules. Under present law, a waiver may be made with respect to the dependency exemption. The waiver then automatically carries over to the child credit, because in order to claim the child credit, the taxpayer must be allowed the

dependency exemption with respect to the child. Thus, if the dependency exemption is waived, the child credit applies to the taxpayer who is allowed the dependency exemption under the waiver.

The Senate amendment obtains the same result, but through a slightly modified statutory structure. Under the Senate amendment, if a waiver is made, the waiver applies for purposes of determining whether a child meets the definition of a qualifying child or a qualifying relative under section 152(c) or 152(d) as amended by the provision. While the definition of qualifying child is generally uniform, for purposes of the earned income credit, head of household status, and the dependent care credit, the definition of qualifying child is made without regard to the waiver provision.[68] Thus, as under present law, a waiver that applies for the dependency exemption will also apply for the child credit, and the waiver will not apply for purposes of the other provisions.

Other provisions

The Senate amendment retains the applicable present-law requirements that a taxpayer identification number for a child be provided on the taxpayer's return. * * *

Effect of Senate amendment on particular tax benefits

* * *

Child credit

The present-law child credit generally uses the same relationships to define an eligible child as the uniform definition. The present-law requirement that a foster child and certain other children be cared for as the taxpayer's own child is eliminated. The age limitation under the Senate amendment retains the present-law requirement that the child must be under age 17, regardless of whether the child is disabled.

* * *

Effective Date

The provision is effective for taxable years beginning after December 31, 2003.

Conference Agreement

The conference agreement includes the Senate amendment provision with the following modifications. The conference agreement modifies the definition of adopted child, for purposes of determining whether an adopted child is

---

[67] Individuals who satisfy the present-law dependency tests and who are not qualifying children are referred to as "qualifying relatives" under the provision.

[68] See secs. 2(b)(1)(A)(i) and 32(c)(3)(A) as amended by the provision, and sec. 21(e)(5).

treated as a child by blood, to mean an individual who is legally adopted by the taxpayer, or an individual who is lawfully placed with the taxpayer for legal adoption by the taxpayer.

[Law at ¶ 5020. CCH Explanation at ¶ 160.]

Effective Date

The provision is effective for taxable years beginning after December 31, 2004.

[¶ 10,150] Act Sec. 205. Establish uniform definition of a qualifying child: Earned income credit

Conference Committee Report (H.R. CONF. REP. NO. 108-696)

[Code Sec. 32]

Present Law

In general

Present law contains five commonly used provisions that provide benefits to taxpayers with children: (1) the dependency exemption; (2) the child credit; (3) the earned income credit; (4) the dependent care credit; and (5) head of household filing status. Each provision has separate criteria for determining whether the taxpayer qualifies for the applicable tax benefit with respect to a particular child. The separate criteria include factors such as the relationship (if any) the child must bear to the taxpayer, the age of the child, and whether the child must live with the taxpayer. Thus, with respect to the same individual, a taxpayer is required to determine eligibility for each benefit separately, and an individual who qualifies a taxpayer for one provision does not automatically qualify the taxpayer for another provision.

* * *

Earned income credit[48]

In general

In general, the earned income credit is a refundable credit for low-income workers. The amount of the credit depends on the earned income of the taxpayer and whether the taxpayer has one, more than one, or no "qualifying children." In order to be a qualifying child for the earned income credit, an individual must satisfy a relationship test, a residency test, and an age test. In addition, the name, age, and taxpayer identification number of the qualifying child must be included on the return.

Relationship test

An individual satisfies the relationship test under the earned income credit if the individual is the taxpayer's: (1) son, daughter, stepson, or stepdaughter, or a descendant of any such individual;[49] (2) brother, sister, stepbrother, or stepsister, or a descendant of any such individual, who the taxpayer cares for as the taxpayer's own child; or (3) eligible foster child. An eligible foster child is an individual (1) who is placed with the taxpayer by an authorized placement agency, and (2) who the taxpayer cares for as her or his own child. A married child of the taxpayer is not treated as meeting the relationship test unless the taxpayer is entitled to a dependency exemption with respect to the married child (e.g., the support test is satisfied) or would be entitled to the exemption if the taxpayer had not waived the exemption to the noncustodial parent.[50]

Residency test

The residency test is satisfied if the individual has the same principal place of abode as the taxpayer for more than one half of the taxable year. The residence must be in the United States.[51] As under the dependency exemption (and head of household filing status), temporary absences due to special circumstances, including absences due to illness, education, business, vacation, and military service are not treated as absences for purposes of determining whether the residency test is satisfied.[52] Under the earned income credit, there is no requirement that the

---

[48] Sec. 32.

[49] A child who is legally adopted or placed with the taxpayer for adoption by an authorized adoption agency is treated as the taxpayer's own child. Sec. 32(c)(3)(B)(iv).

[50] Sec. 32(c)(3)(B)(ii).

[51] The principal place of abode of a member of the Armed Services is treated as in the United States during any period

during which the individual is stationed outside the United States on active duty. Sec. 32(c)(4).

[52] IRS Publication 596, *Earned Income Credit (EIC)*, at 14. H. Rep. 101-964 (October 27, 1990), at 1037.

taxpayer maintain the household in which the taxpayer and the qualifying individual reside.

Age test

In general, the age test is satisfied if the individual has not attained age 19 as of the close of the calendar year.[53] In the case of a full-time student, the age test is satisfied if the individual has not attained age 24 as of the close of the calendar year. In the case of an individual who is permanently and totally disabled, no age limit applies.

* * *

House Bill

No provision.

Senate Amendment

In general

In general

The Senate amendment establishes a uniform definition of qualifying child for purposes of the dependency exemption, the child credit, the earned income credit, the dependent care credit, and head of household filing status. A taxpayer generally may claim an individual who does not meet the uniform definition of qualifying child (with respect to any taxpayer) as a dependent if the present-law dependency requirements are satisfied. The Senate amendment generally does not modify other parameters of each tax benefit (e.g., the earned income requirements of the earned income credit) or the rules for determining whether individuals other than children of the taxpayer qualify for each tax benefit.

Under the uniform definition, in general, a child is a qualifying child of a taxpayer if the child satisfies each of three tests: (1) the child has the same principal place of abode as the taxpayer for more than one half the taxable year; (2) the child has a specified relationship to the taxpayer; and (3) the child has not yet attained a specified age. A tie-breaking rule applies if more than one taxpayer claims a child as a qualifying child.

Under the Senate amendment, the present-law support and gross income tests for determining whether an individual is a dependent generally do not apply to a child who meets the requirements of the uniform definition of qualifying child.

Residency test

Under the uniform definition's residency test, a child must have the same principal place of abode as the taxpayer for more than one half of the taxable year. It is intended that, as is the case under present law, temporary absences due to special circumstances, including absences due to illness, education, business, vacation, or military service, are not treated as absences.

Relationship test

In order to be a qualifying child under the Senate amendment, the child must be the taxpayer's son, daughter, stepson, stepdaughter, brother, sister, stepbrother, stepsister, or a descendant of any such individual. An individual legally adopted by the taxpayer, or an individual who is placed with the taxpayer by an authorized placement agency for adoption by the taxpayer, is treated as a child of such taxpayer by blood. A foster child who is placed with the taxpayer by an authorized placement agency or by judgment, decree, or other order of any court of competent jurisdiction is treated as the taxpayer's child.[65]

Age test

Under the Senate amendment, the age test varies depending upon the tax benefit involved. In general, a child must be under age 19 (or under age 24 in the case of a full-time student) in order to be a qualifying child.[66] In general, no age limit applies with respect to individuals who are totally and permanently disabled within the meaning of section 22(e)(3) at any time during the calendar year. The Senate amendment retains the present-law requirements that a child must be under age 13 (if he or she is not disabled) for purposes of the dependent care credit, and under age 17 (whether or not disabled) for purposes of the child credit.

Children who support themselves

Under the Senate amendment, a child who provides over one half of his or her own support generally is not considered a qualifying child of another taxpayer. The Senate amendment retains the present-law rule, however, that a child who provides over one half of his or her own support may constitute a qualifying child of another taxpayer for purposes of the earned income credit.

---

[53] The IRS has issued guidance stating that for purposes of the earned income credit, an individual attains a specified age on the anniversary of the date that the child was born (e.g., a child born on January 1, 1987, attains the age of 17 on January 1, 2004). Rev. Rul. 2003-72, 2003-33 I.R.B. 346.

[65] The provision eliminates the present-law rule requiring that if a child is the taxpayer's sibling or stepsibling or a

descendant of any such individual, the taxpayer must care for the child as if the child were his or her own child.

[66] The provision retains the present-law definition of full-time student set forth in section 151(c)(4).

Tie-breaking rules

If a child would be a qualifying child with respect to more than one individual (e.g., a child lives with his or her mother and grandmother in the same residence) and more than one person claims a benefit with respect to that child, then the following "tie-breaking" rules apply. First, if only one of the individuals claiming the child as a qualifying child is the child's parent, the child is deemed the qualifying child of the parent. Second, if both parents claim the child and the parents do not file a joint return, then the child is deemed a qualifying child first with respect to the parent with whom the child resides for the longest period of time, and second with respect to the parent with the highest adjusted gross income. Third, if the child's parents do not claim the child, then the child is deemed a qualifying child with respect to the claimant with the highest adjusted gross income.

Interaction with present-law rules

Taxpayers generally may claim an individual who does not meet the uniform definition of qualifying child with respect to any taxpayer as a dependent if the present-law dependency requirements (including the gross income and support tests) are satisfied.[67] Thus, for example, as under present law, a taxpayer may claim a parent as a dependent if the taxpayer provides more than one half of the support of the parent and the parent's gross income is less than the exemption amount. As another example, under the Senate amendment a grandparent may claim a dependency exemption with respect to a grandson who does not reside with any taxpayer for over one half the year, if the grandparent provides more than one half of the support of the grandson and the grandson's gross income is less than the exemption amount.

Citizenship and residency

Children who are U.S. citizens living abroad or non-U.S. citizens living in Canada or Mexico may qualify as a qualifying child, as is the case under the present-law dependency tests. A legally adopted child who does not satisfy the residency or citizenship requirement may nevertheless qualify as a qualifying child (provided other applicable requirements are met) if (1) the child's principal place of abode is the taxpayer's home and (2) the taxpayer is a citizen or national of the United States.

Children of divorced or legally separated parents

The Senate amendment retains the present-law rule that allows a custodial parent to release the claim to a dependency exemption (and, therefore, the child credit) to a noncustodial parent. Thus, under the Senate amendment, custodial waivers that are in place and effective on the date of enactment will continue to be effective after the date of enactment if they continue to satisfy the waiver rule. In addition, the Senate amendment retains the custodial waiver rule for purposes of the dependency exemption (and, therefore, the child credit) for decrees of divorce or separate maintenance or written separation agreements that become effective after the date of enactment. Under the Senate amendment, as under present law, the custodial waiver rules do not affect eligibility with respect to children of divorced or legally separated parents for purposes of the earned income credit, the dependent care credit, and head of household filing status.

While retaining the substantive effect of the present-law waiver provisions, the Senate amendment modifies the mechanical structure of the rules. Under present law, a waiver may be made with respect to the dependency exemption. The waiver then automatically carries over to the child credit, because in order to claim the child credit, the taxpayer must be allowed the dependency exemption with respect to the child. Thus, if the dependency exemption is waived, the child credit applies to the taxpayer who is allowed the dependency exemption under the waiver.

The Senate amendment obtains the same result, but through a slightly modified statutory structure. Under the Senate amendment, if a waiver is made, the waiver applies for purposes of determining whether a child meets the definition of a qualifying child or a qualifying relative under section 152(c) or 152(d) as amended by the provision. While the definition of qualifying child is generally uniform, for purposes of the earned income credit, head of household status, and the dependent care credit, the definition of qualifying child is made without regard to the waiver provision.[68] Thus, as under present law, a waiver that applies for the dependency exemption will also apply for the child credit, and the waiver will not apply for purposes of the other provisions.

---

[67] Individuals who satisfy the present-law dependency tests and who are not qualifying children are referred to as "qualifying relatives" under the provision.

[68] See secs. 2(b)(1)(A)(i) and 32(c)(3)(A) as amended by the provision, and sec. 21(e)(5).

Other provisions

The Senate amendment retains the applicable present-law requirements that a taxpayer identification number for a child be provided on the taxpayer's return. For purposes of the earned income credit, a qualifying child is required to have a social security number that is valid for employment in the United States (that is, the child must be a U.S. citizen, permanent resident, or have a certain type of temporary visa).

Effect of Senate amendment on particular tax benefits

* * *

Earned income credit

In general, the Senate amendment adopts a definition of qualifying child that is similar to the present-law definition under the earned income credit. The present-law requirement that a foster child and certain other children be cared for as the taxpayer's own child is eliminated. The present-law tie-breaker rule applicable to the earned income credit is used for purposes of the uniform definition of qualifying child. The Sen-

ate amendment retains the present-law requirement that the taxpayer's principal place of abode must be in the United States.

* * *

Effective Date

The provision is effective for taxable years beginning after December 31, 2003.

Conference Agreement

The conference agreement includes the Senate amendment provision with the following modifications. The conference agreement modifies the definition of adopted child, for purposes of determining whether an adopted child is treated as a child by blood, to mean an individual who is legally adopted by the taxpayer, or an individual who is lawfully placed with the taxpayer for legal adoption by the taxpayer.

Effective Date

The provision is effective for taxable years beginning after December 31, 2004.

[Law at ¶ 5040. CCH Explanation at ¶ 165.]

[¶ 10,200] Act Sec. 301. Extension of the research credit

Conference Committee Report (H.R. Conf. Rep. No. 108-696)

[Code Sec. 41]

Present Law

Section 41 provided a research tax credited equal to 20 percent of the amount by which a taxpayer's qualified research expenses for a taxable year exceeded its base amount for that year. Taxpayers were permitted to elect an alternative incremental research credit regime in which the taxpayer was assigned a three-tiered fixed-base percentage and the credit rate likewise is reduced. Under the alternative credit regime, a credit rate of 2.65 percent applied to the extent that a taxpayer's current-year research expenses exceed a base amount computed by using a fixed-base percentage of one percent but do not exceed a base amount computed by using a fixed-base percentage of 1.5 percent. A credit rate of 3.2 percent applied to the extent that a taxpayer's current-year research expenses exceeded a base amount computed by using a fixed-base percentage of 1.5 percent but did not exceed a base amount computed by using a fixed-base percentage of two percent. A credit rate of 3.75 percent applied to the extent that a taxpayer's current-year research expenses exceeded a base amount computed by using a fixed-base percentage of two percent.

A 20-percent research tax credit also applied to the excess of (1) 100 percent of corporate cash expenses (including grants or contributions) paid for basic research conducted by universities (and certain nonprofit scientific research organizations) over (2) the sum of (a) the greater of two minimum basic research floors plus (b) an amount reflecting any decrease in nonresearch giving to universities by the corporation as compared to such giving during a fixed-base period, as adjusted for inflation.

The research tax credit expired and generally does not apply to amounts paid or incurred after June 30, 2004.

House Bill

No provision.

Senate Amendment

No provision.

Conference Agreement

The conference agreement extends the present-law research credit to qualified amounts paid or incurred before January 1, 2006.

Effective Date   [Law at ¶5050. CCH Explanation at ¶205.]

Effective for amounts paid or incurred after June 30, 2004.

[¶ 10,210] Act Sec. 302. Extension of parity in the application of certain limits to mental health benefits

Conference Committee Report (H.R. Conf. Rep. No. 108-696)

[Code Sec. 9812]

Present Law

The Mental Health Parity Act of 1996 amended the Employee Retirement Income Security Act of 1974 ("ERISA") and the Public Health Service Act ("PHSA") to provide that group health plans that provide both medical and surgical benefits and mental health benefits cannot impose aggregate lifetime or annual dollar limits on mental health benefits that are not imposed on substantially all medical and surgical benefits. The provisions of the Mental Health Parity Act were initially effective with respect to plan years beginning on or after January 1, 1998, for a temporary period. Since enactment, the mental health parity requirements in ERISA and the PHSA have been extended on more than one occasion and currently are scheduled to expire with respect to benefits for services furnished on or after December 31, 2004.

The Taxpayer Relief Act of 1997 added to the Code the requirements imposed under the Mental Health Parity Act, and imposed an excise tax on group health plans that fail to meet the requirements. The excise tax is equal to $100 per day during the period of noncompliance and is generally imposed on the employer sponsoring the plan if the plan fails to meet the requirements. The maximum tax that can be imposed during a taxable year cannot exceed the lesser of 10 percent of the employer's group health plan expenses for the prior year or $500,000. No tax is imposed if the Secretary determines that the employer did not know, and exercising reasonable

diligence would not have known, that the failure existed.

The Code provisions were initially effective with respect to plan years beginning on or after January 1, 1998, for a temporary period.[70] The Code provisions have been extended on a number of occasions, and expired with respect to benefits for services furnished after December 31, 2003.

House Bill

No provision.

Senate Amendment

No provision.

Conference Agreement

The conference agreement extends the ERISA and PHSA provisions relating to mental health parity to benefits for services furnished before January 1, 2006. The conference agreement also extends the Code provisions relating to mental health parity to benefits for services furnished on or after the date of enactment and before January 1, 2006. Thus, the excise tax on failures to meet the requirements imposed by the Code provisions does not apply after December 31, 2003, and before the date of enactment.

Effective Date

The provision is effective on the date of enactment.

[Law at ¶5425 and ¶7015. CCH Explanation at ¶247.]

---

[70] The excise tax does not apply to benefits for services furnished on or after September 30, 2001, and before January 10, 2002.

[¶ 10,220] Act Sec. 303. Extension of the work opportunity tax credit

Conference Committee Report (H.R. CONF. REP. NO. 108-696)

[Code Sec. 51]

Present Law

Work opportunity tax credit

Targeted groups eligible for the credit

The work opportunity tax credit is available on an elective basis for employers hiring individuals from one or more of eight targeted groups. The eight targeted groups are: (1) certain families eligible to receive benefits under the Temporary Assistance for Needy Families Program; (2) high-risk youth; (3) qualified ex-felons; (4) vocational rehabilitation referrals; (5) qualified summer youth employees; (6) qualified veterans; (7) families receiving food stamps; and (8) persons receiving certain Supplemental Security Income (SSI) benefits.

A qualified ex-felon is an individual certified as: (1) having been convicted of a felony under State or Federal law; (2) being a member of an economically disadvantaged family; and (3) having a hiring date within one year of release from prison or conviction.

Qualified wages

Generally, qualified wages are defined as cash wages paid by the employer to a member of a targeted group. The employer's deduction for wages is reduced by the amount of the credit.

Calculation of the credit

The credit equals 40 percent (25 percent for employment of 400 hours or less) of qualified first-year wages. Generally, qualified first-year wages are qualified wages (not in excess of $6,000) attributable to service rendered by a member of a targeted group during the one-year period beginning with the day the individual began work for the employer. Therefore, the maximum credit per employee is $2,400 (40 percent of the first $6,000 of qualified first-year wages). With respect to qualified summer youth employees, the maximum credit is $1,200 (40 percent of the first $3,000 of qualified first-year wages).

Minimum employment period

No credit is allowed for qualified wages paid to employees who work less than 120 hours in the first year of employment.

Coordination of the work opportunity tax credit and the welfare-to-work tax credit

An employer cannot claim the work opportunity tax credit with respect to wages of any employee on which the employer claims the welfare-to-work tax credit.

Other rules

The work opportunity tax credit is not allowed for wages paid to a relative or dependent of the taxpayer. Similarly wages paid to replacement workers during a strike or lockout are not eligible for the work opportunity tax credit. Wages paid to any employee during any period for which the employer received on-the-job training program payments with respect to that employee are not eligible for the work opportunity tax credit. The work opportunity tax credit generally is not allowed for wages paid to individuals who had previously been employed by the employer. In addition, many other technical rules apply.

House Bill

No provision.

Senate Amendment

No provision.

Conference Agreement

The conference agreement extends the work opportunity tax credit for two years (through December 31, 2005).

Effective Date

The extension of the work opportunity tax credit is effective for wages paid or incurred for individuals beginning work after December 31, 2003.

[Law at ¶ 5075. CCH Explanation at ¶ 211.]

[¶ 10,230] Act Sec. 303. Extension of the welfare-to-work tax credit

Conference Committee Report (H.R. CONF. REP. NO. 108-696)

[Code Sec. 51A]

Present Law

Welfare-to-work tax credit

Targeted group eligible for the credit

The welfare-to-work tax credit is available on an elective basis to employers of qualified long-term family assistance recipients. Qualified long-term family assistance recipients are: (1) members of a family that has received family assistance for at least 18 consecutive months ending on the hiring date; (2) members of a family that has received such family assistance for a total of at least 18 months (whether or not consecutive) after August 5, 1997 (the date of enactment of the welfare-to-work tax credit) if they are hired within 2 years after the date that the 18-month total is reached; and (3) members of a family who are no longer eligible for family assistance because of either Federal or State time limits, if they are hired within 2 years after the Federal or State time limits made the family ineligible for family assistance.

Qualified wages

Qualified wages for purposes of the welfare-to-work tax credit are defined more broadly than the work opportunity tax credit. Unlike the definition of wages for the work opportunity tax credit which includes simply cash wages, the definition of wages for the welfare-to-work tax credit includes cash wages paid to an employee plus amounts paid by the employer for: (1) educational assistance excludable under a section 127 program (or that would be excludable but for the expiration of sec. 127); (2) health plan coverage for the employee, but not more than the applicable premium defined under section 4980B(f)(4); and (3) dependent care assistance excludable under section 129. The employer's deduction for wages is reduced by the amount of the credit.

Calculation of the credit

The welfare-to-work tax credit is available on an elective basis to employers of qualified long-term family assistance recipients during the first two years of employment. The maximum credit is 35 percent of the first $10,000 of qualified first-year wages and 50 percent of the first $10,000 of qualified second-year wages. Qualified first-year wages are defined as qualified wages (not in excess of $10,000) attributable to service rendered by a member of the targeted group during the one-year period beginning with the day the individual began work for the employer. Qualified second-year wages are defined as qualified wages (not in excess of $10,000) attributable to service rendered by a member of the targeted group during the one-year period beginning immediately after the first year of that individual's employment for the employer. The maximum credit is $8,500 per qualified employee.

Minimum employment period

No credit is allowed for qualified wages paid to a member of the targeted group unless they work at least 400 hours or 180 days in the first year of employment.

Coordination of the work opportunity tax credit and the welfare-to-work tax credit

An employer cannot claim the work opportunity tax credit with respect to wages of any employee on which the employer claims the welfare-to-work tax credit.

Other rules

The welfare-to-work tax credit incorporates directly or by reference many of these other rules contained on the work opportunity tax credit.

House Bill

No provision.

Senate Amendment

No provision.

Conference Agreement

The conference agreement extends the welfare-to-work tax credit for two years (through December 31, 2005).

Effective Date

The extension of the welfare-to-work tax credit is effective for wages paid or incurred for individuals beginning work after December 31, 2003.

[Law at ¶ 5080. CCH Explanation at ¶ 213.]

[¶ 10,240] Act Sec. 304. Qualified zone academy bonds

Conference Committee Report (H.R. CONF. REP. NO. 108-696)

[Code Sec. 1397E]

Present Law

Generally, "qualified zone academy bonds" are bonds issued by a State or local government, provided that at least 95 percent of the proceeds are used for one or more qualified purposes with respect to a "qualified zone academy" and private entities have promised to contribute to the qualified zone academy certain equipment, technical assistance or training, employee services, or other property or services with a value equal to at least 10 percent of the bond proceeds. Qualified purposes with respect to any qualified zone academy are (1) rehabilitating or repairing the public school facility in which the academy is established, (2) providing equipment for use at such academy, (3) developing course materials for education at such academy, and (4) training teachers and other school personnel. A total of $400 million of qualified zone academy bonds

was authorized to be issued annually in calendar years 1998 through 2003.

House Bill

No provision.

Senate Amendment

No provision.

Conference Agreement

The conference agreement extends the authority to issue qualified zone academy bonds through 2005.

Effective Date

The authority to issue qualified zone academy bonds is effective for obligations issued after December 31, 2003.

[Law at ¶ 5320. CCH Explanation at ¶ 239.]

[¶ 10,250] Act Sec. 305. Extension of cover over of excise tax on distilled spirits to Puerto Rico and Virgin Islands

Conference Committee Report (H.R. CONF. REP. NO. 108-696)

[Code Sec. 7652]

Present Law

A $13.50 per proof gallon (a proof gallon is a liquid gallon consisting of 50 percent alcohol) excise tax is imposed on distilled spirits produced in or imported into the United States.

The Code provides for cover over (payment) to Puerto Rico and the Virgin Islands of the excise tax imposed on rum imported into the United States, without regard to the country of origin. The amount of the cover over is limited under section 7652(f) to $10.50 per proof gallon ($13.25 per proof gallon during the period July 1, 1999 through December 31, 2003).

Thus, tax amounts attributable to rum produced in Puerto Rico are covered over to Puerto Rico. Tax amounts attributable to rum produced in the Virgin Islands are covered over to the Virgin Islands. Tax amounts attributable to rum produced in neither Puerto Rico nor the Virgin Islands are divided and covered over to the two possessions under a formula. All of the amounts covered over are subject to the limitation.

House Bill

No provision.

Senate Amendment

No provision.

Conference Agreement

The conference agreement temporarily suspends the $10.50 per proof gallon limitation on the amount of excise taxes on rum covered over to Puerto Rico and the Virgin Islands. Under the conference agreement, the cover over amount of $13.25 per proof gallon is extended for rum brought into the United States after December 31, 2003 and before January 1, 2006. After December 31, 2005, the cover over amount reverts to $10.50 per proof gallon.

Effective Date

The provision is effective for articles brought into the United States after December 31, 2003.

[Law at ¶ 5395. CCH Explanation at ¶ 265.]

[¶ 10,260] Act Sec. 306. Charitable contributions of computer technology and equipment used for educational purposes

Conference Committee Report (H.R. CONF. REP. NO. 108-696)

[Code Sec. 170]

Present Law

A deduction by a corporation for charitable contributions of computer technology and equipment generally is limited to the corporation's basis in the property. However, certain corporations may claim a deduction in excess of basis for a qualified computer contribution. Such enhanced deduction for qualified computer contributions expired for contributions made during any taxable year beginning after December 31, 2003.

House Bill

No provision.

Senate Amendment

No provision.

Conference Agreement

The conference agreement extends the enhanced deduction for qualified computer contributions to contributions made during any taxable year beginning before January 1, 2006.

Effective Date

Taxable years beginning after December 31, 2003.

[Law at ¶ 5165. CCH Explanation at ¶ 207.]

[¶ 10,270] Act Sec. 307. Certain expenses of elementary and secondary school teachers

Conference Committee Report (H.R. CONF. REP. NO. 108-696)

[Code Sec. 62]

Present Law

In general, ordinary and necessary business expenses are deductible (sec. 162). However, in general, unreimbursed employee business expenses are deductible only as an itemized deduction and only to the extent that the individual's total miscellaneous deductions (including employee business expenses) exceed two percent of adjusted gross income. An individual's otherwise allowable itemized deductions may be further limited by the overall limitation on itemized deductions, which reduces itemized deductions for taxpayers with adjusted gross income in excess of $142,700 (for 2004). In addition, miscellaneous itemized deductions are not allowable under the alternative minimum tax.

Certain expenses of eligible educators are allowed an above-the-line deduction. Specifically, for taxable years beginning in 2002 and 2003, an above-the-line deduction is allowed for up to $250 annually of expenses paid or incurred by an eligible educator for books, supplies (other than nonathletic supplies for courses of instruction in health or physical education), computer equipment (including related software and services) and other equipment, and supplementary materials used by the eligible educator in the classroom. To be eligible for this deduction, the expenses must be otherwise deductible under 162 as a trade or business expense. A deduction is allowed only to the extent the amount of ex-

penses exceeds the amount excludable from income under section 135 (relating to education savings bonds), 529(c)(1) (relating to qualified tuition programs), and section 530(d)(2) (relating to Coverdell education savings accounts).

An eligible educator is a kindergarten through grade 12 teacher, instructor, counselor, principal, or aide in a school for at least 900 hours during a school year. A school means any school which provides elementary education or secondary education, as determined under State law.

The above-the-line deduction for eligible educators is not allowed for taxable years beginning after December 31, 2003.

House Bill

No provision.

Senate Amendment

No provision.

Conference Agreement

The conference agreement extends the above-the-line deduction for two years, i.e., for taxable years beginning in 2004 and 2005.

Effective Date

The conference agreement is effective for taxable years beginning in 2004 and 2005.

[Law at ¶ 5095. CCH Explanation at ¶ 185.]

[¶ 10,280] Act Sec. 308. Expensing of environmental remediation costs

Conference Committee Report (H.R. CONF. REP. NO. 108-696)

[Code Sec. 198]

Present Law

Taxpayers can elect to treat certain environmental remediation expenditures that would otherwise be chargeable to capital account as deductible in the year paid or incurred (sec. 198). The deduction applies for both regular and alternative minimum tax purposes. The expenditure must be incurred in connection with the abatement or control of hazardous substances at a qualified contaminated site.

A "qualified contaminated site" generally is any property that (1) is held for use in a trade or business, for the production of income, or as inventory and (2) is at a site on which there has been a release (or threat of release) or disposal of certain hazardous substances as certified by the appropriate State environmental agency (so called "brownfields"). However, sites that are identified on the national priorities list under the Comprehensive Environmental Response, Com-

pensation, and Liability Act of 1980 cannot qualify as targeted areas.

Eligible expenditures were those paid or incurred before January 1, 2004.

House Bill

No provision.

Senate Amendment

No provision.

Conference Agreement

The conference agreement extends the present law expensing provision for two years (through December 31, 2005).

Effective Date

Effective for expenses paid or incurred after December 31, 2003.

[Law at ¶ 5180. CCH Explanation at ¶ 209.]

[¶ 10,290] Act Sec. 309. New York Liberty Zone provisions

Conference Committee Report (H.R. CONF. REP. NO. 108-696)

[Code Sec. 1400L]

Present Law

An aggregate of $8 billion in tax-exempt private activity bonds is authorized for the purpose of financing the construction and repair of infrastructure in New York City ("Liberty Zone bonds"). The bonds must be issued before January 1, 2005.

Certain bonds used to fund facilities located in New York City are permitted one additional advance refunding before January 1, 2005 ("advance refunding bonds"). In addition to satisfying other requirements, the bond refunded must be (1) a State or local bond that is a general obligation of New York City, (2) a State or local bond issued by the New York Municipal Water Finance Authority or Metropolitan Transportation Authority of the City of New York, or (3) a qualified 501(c)(3) bond which is a qualified hospital bond issued by or on behalf of the State of New York or the City of New York. The maximum amount of advance refunding bonds is $9 billion.

House Bill

No provision.

Senate Amendment

No provision.

Conference Agreement

The conference agreement extends authority to issue Liberty Zone bonds through December 31, 2009. The conference agreement also extends the additional advance refunding authority through December 31, 2005. In addition, the conference agreement provides that bonds of the Municipal Assistance Corporation are eligible for advance refunding.

The purpose in extending the New York Liberty Bond program through December 31, 2009, is to facilitate the full designation of New York Liberty Bond authority. Congress could consider a further extension of the New York Liberty Bond program beyond 2009 if circumstances justify such an extension.

Effective Date

The Liberty Zone bonds and general additional advance refunding provisions are effective on the date of enactment. The provision relating to the advance refunding of bonds of the Municipal Assistance Corporation is effective as if included in the amendments made by section 301 of the Job Creation and Worker Assistance Act of 2002.

[Law at ¶ 5350. CCH Explanation at ¶ 235.]

[¶ 10,300] Act Sec. 310. Tax incentives for investment in the District of Columbia

Conference Committee Report (H.R. Conf. Rep. No. 108-696)

[Code Secs. 1400, 1400A, 1400B, 1400C and 1400F]

Present Law

Certain economically depressed census tracts within the District of Columbia are designated as the District of Columbia Enterprise Zone (the "D.C. Zone") within which businesses and individual residents are eligible for special tax incentives. The designation expired on December 31, 2003.

First-time homebuyers of a principal residence in the District of Columbia are eligible for a nonrefundable tax credit of up to $5,000 of the amount of the purchase price. The credit expired for property purchased after December 31, 2003.

House Bill

No provision.

Senate Amendment

No provision.

Conference Agreement

The conference agreement extends the D.C. Zone designation and related tax incentives for two years. The conference agreement extends the first-time homebuyer credit for two years.

Effective Date

The extension of the D.C. Zone designation and related tax incentives is generally effective on January 1, 2004, except that the provision relating to tax-exempt financing incentives applies to obligations issued after the date of enactment.

[Law at ¶5330, ¶5335, ¶5340 and ¶5345. CCH Explanation at ¶237.]

[¶ 10,310] Act Sec. 311. Combined employment tax reporting

Conference Committee Report (H.R. Conf. Rep. No. 108-696)

[Code Sec. 6103]

Present Law

Traditionally, Federal tax forms are filed with the Federal government and State tax forms are filed with individual States. This necessitates duplication of items common to both returns.

The Taxpayer Relief Act of 1997 permitted implementation of a limited demonstration project to assess the feasibility and desirability of expanding combined Federal and State reporting. First, it was limited to the sharing of information between the State of Montana and the IRS. Second, it was limited to employment tax reporting. Third, it was limited to disclosure of the name, address, TIN, and signature of the taxpayer, which is information common to both the Montana and Federal portions of the combined form. Fourth, it was limited to a period of five years (expiring August 5, 2002).

House Bill

No provision.

Senate Amendment

No provision.

Conference Agreement

The conference agreement provides authority through December 31, 2005, for any State to participate in a combined Federal and State employment tax reporting program, provided that the program has been approved by the Secretary.

Effective Date

The provision takes effect on the date of enactment.

[Law at ¶5390. CCH Explanation at ¶253.]

Act Sec. 311 ¶10,310

[¶ 10,320] Act Sec. 312. Nonrefundable personal credits allowed against the alternative minimum tax

Conference Committee Report (H.R. CONF. REP. NO. 108-696)

[Code Sec. 26]

Present Law

Present law provides for certain nonrefundable personal tax credits (i.e., the dependent care credit, the credit for the elderly and disabled, the adoption credit, the child tax credit,[71] the credit for interest on certain home mortgages, the HOPE Scholarship and Lifetime Learning credits, the credit for savers, and the D.C. first-time homebuyer credit).

For taxable years beginning in 2003, all the nonrefundable personal credits are allowed to the extent of the full amount of the individual's regular tax and alternative minimum tax.

For taxable years beginning after 2003, the credits (other than the adoption credit, child credit and credit for savers) are allowed only to the extent that the individual's regular income tax liability exceeds the individual's tentative minimum tax, determined without regard to the minimum tax foreign tax credit. The adoption credit, child credit, and IRA credit are allowed to the full extent of the individual's regular tax and alternative minimum tax.

House Bill

No provision.

Senate Amendment

No provision.

Conference Agreement

The conference agreement extends the provision allowing the nonrefundable personal credits to the full extent of the regular tax and the alternative minimum tax for taxable years beginning in 2004 and 2005.

Effective Date

Taxable years beginning after December 31, 2003.

[Law at ¶ 5030, ¶ 5285 and ¶ 7020. CCH Explanation at ¶ 135.]

[¶ 10,330] Act Sec. 313. Extension of credit for electricity produced from certain renewable resources

Conference Committee Report (H.R. CONF. REP. NO. 108-696)

[Code Sec. 45]

Present Law

An income tax credit is allowed for the production of electricity from either qualified wind energy, qualified "closed-loop" biomass, or qualified poultry waste facilities. The amount of the credit is 1.8 cents per kilowatt hour for 2004. The credit amount is indexed for inflation.

The credit applies to electricity produced by a wind energy facility placed in service after December 31, 1993, and before January 1, 2004, to electricity produced by a closed-loop biomass facility placed in service after December 31, 1992, and before January 1, 2004, and to a poultry waste facility placed in service after December 31, 1999, and before January 1, 2004. The credit is allowable for production during the 10-year period after a facility is originally placed in service.

House Bill

No provision.

Senate Amendment

No provision.

Conference Agreement

The conference agreement extends the placed in service date for wind energy facilities, "closed-loop" biomass facilities, and poultry waste facilities to include facilities placed in service prior to January 1, 2006.

Effective Date

Effective for facilities placed in service after December 31, 2003.

[Law at ¶ 5060. CCH Explanation at ¶ 227.]

---

[71] A portion of the child credit may be refundable.

[¶ 10,340] Act Sec. 314. Suspension of 100-percent-of-net-income limitation on percentage depletion for oil and gas from marginal wells

Conference Committee Report (H.R. Conf. Rep. No. 108-696)

[Code Sec. 613A]

Present Law

Percentage depletion method for oil and gas properties applies to independent producers and royalty owners. Generally, under the percentage depletion method, 15 percent of the taxpayer's gross income from an oil- or gas-producing property is allowed as a deduction in each taxable year. The amount deducted generally may not exceed 100 percent of the net income from the property in any year (the "net-income limitation"). The 100-percent net-income limitation for marginal wells is suspended for taxable years beginning after December 31, 1997, and before January 1, 2004.

House Bill

No provision.

Senate Amendment

No provision.

Conference Agreement

The conference agreement extends the suspension of the net-income limitation for marginal wells for taxable years beginning before January 1, 2006.

Effective Date

The provision is effective for taxable years beginning after December 31, 2003.

[Law at ¶ 5260. CCH Explanation at ¶ 229.]

[¶ 10,350] Act Sec. 315. Indian employment tax credit

Conference Committee Report (H.R. Conf. Rep. No. 108-696)

[Code Sec. 45A]

Present Law

In general, a credit against income tax liability is allowed to employers for the first $20,000 of qualified wages and qualified employee health insurance costs paid or incurred by the employer with respect to certain employees (sec. 45A). The credit is equal to 20 percent of the excess of eligible employee qualified wages and health insurance costs during the current year over the amount of such wages and costs incurred by the employer during 1993. The credit is an incremental credit, such that an employer's current-year qualified wages and qualified employee health insurance costs (up to $20,000 per employee) are eligible for the credit only to the extent that the sum of such costs exceeds the sum of comparable costs paid during 1993. No deduction is allowed for the portion of the wages equal to the amount of the credit.

The wage credit is available for wages paid or incurred on or after January 1, 1994, in taxable years that begin before January 1, 2005.

House Bill

No provision.

Senate Amendment

No provision.

Conference Agreement

The conference agreement extends the Indian employment credit incentive for one year (to taxable years beginning before January 1, 2006).

Effective Date

The provision is effective on the date of enactment.

[Law at ¶ 5065. CCH Explanation at ¶ 215.]

[¶ 10,360] Act Sec. 316. Accelerated depreciation for business property on Indian reservations

Conference Committee Report (H.R. CONF. REP. NO. 108-696)

[Code Sec. 168(j)]

Present Law

With respect to certain property used in connection with the conduct of a trade or business within an Indian reservation, depreciation deductions under section 168(j) will be determined using the following recovery periods:

	Years
3-year property	2
5-year property	3
7-year property	4
10-year property	6
15-year property	9
20-year property	12
Nonresidential real property	22

"Qualified Indian reservation property" eligible for accelerated depreciation includes property which is (1) used by the taxpayer predominantly in the active conduct of a trade or business within an Indian reservation, (2) not used or located outside the reservation on a regular basis, (3) not acquired (directly or indirectly) by the taxpayer from a person who is related to the taxpayer (within the meaning of section 465(b)(3)(C)), and (4) described in the recovery-period table above. In addition, property is not "qualified Indian reservation property" if it is placed in service for purposes of conducting gaming activities. Certain "qualified infrastruc-ture property" may be eligible for the accelerated depreciation even if located outside an Indian reservation, provided that the purpose of such property is to connect with qualified infrastructure property located within the reservation (e.g., roads, power lines, water systems, railroad spurs, and communications facilities).

The depreciation deduction allowed for regular tax purposes is also allowed for purposes of the alternative minimum tax. The accelerated depreciation for Indian reservations is available with respect to property placed in service on or after January 1, 1994, and before January 1, 2005.

House Bill

No provision.

Senate Amendment

No provision.

Conference Agreement

The conference agreement extends eligibility for the special depreciation periods to property placed in service before January 1, 2006.

Effective Date

The provision is effective on the date of enactment.

[Law at ¶ 5160. CCH Explanation at ¶ 217.]

[¶ 10,370] Act Sec. 317. Disclosure of return information relating to student loans

Conference Committee Report (H.R. CONF. REP. NO. 108-696)

[Code Sec. 6103(l)(13)]

Present Law

An exception to the general rule prohibiting disclosure is provided for disclosure to the Department of Education (but not to contractors thereof) to establish an appropriate repayment amount for an applicable student loan. The Department of Education disclosure authority is scheduled to expire after December 31, 2004.

House Bill

No provision.

Senate Amendment

No provision.

Conference Agreement

The conference agreement extends the disclosure authority relating to the disclosure of return information to carry out income-contingent repayment of student loans. Under the conference agreement, no disclosures can be made after December 31, 2005.

Effective Date

The provision is effective on the date of enactment.

[Law at ¶ 5390. CCH Explanation at ¶ 255.]

[¶ 10,380] Act Sec. 318. Credit for qualified electric vehicles

Conference Committee Report (H.R. CONF. REP. NO. 108-696)

[Code Sec. 30]

Present Law

A 10-percent tax credit is provided for the cost of a qualified electric vehicle, up to a maximum credit of $4,000. A qualified electric vehicle generally is a motor vehicle that is powered primarily by an electric motor drawing current from rechargeable batteries, fuel cells, or other portable sources of electrical current. The full amount of the credit is available for purchases prior to 2004. The credit phases down in the years 2004 through 2006, and is unavailable for purchases after December 31, 2006. Under the phase down, the credit for 2004 is 75 percent of the otherwise allowable credit.

House Bill

No provision.

Senate Amendment

No provision.

Conference Agreement

Repeals the phase down of the allowable tax credit for electric vehicles in 2004 and 2005. Thus, a taxpayer who purchases a qualifying vehicle may claim 100 percent of the otherwise allowable credit for vehicles purchased in 2004 and 2005. For vehicles purchased in 2006 the credit remains at 25 percent of the otherwise allowable amount as under present law.

Effective Date

Effective for vehicles placed in service after December 31, 2003.

[Law at ¶ 5035. CCH Explanation at ¶ 223.]

[¶ 10,390] Act Sec. 319. Deduction for qualified clean-fuel vehicle property

Conference Committee Report (H.R. CONF. REP. NO. 108-696)

[Code Sec. 179A]

Present Law

Certain costs of qualified clean-fuel vehicle may be expensed and deducted when such property is placed in service. Qualified clean-fuel vehicle property includes motor vehicles that use certain clean-burning fuels (natural gas, liquefied natural gas, liquefied petroleum gas, hydrogen, electricity and any other fuel at least 85 percent of which is methanol, ethanol, any other alcohol or ether). The maximum amount of the deduction is $50,000 for a truck or van with a gross vehicle weight over 26,000 pounds or a bus with seating capacities of at least 20 adults; $5,000 in the case of a truck or van with a gross vehicle weight between 10,000 and 26,000 pounds; and $2,000 in the case of any other motor vehicle. The deduction phases down in the years 2004 through 2006, and is unavailable for purchases after December 31, 2006. Under the phase down, the deduction permitted for 2004 is 75 percent of the otherwise allowable amount.

House Bill

No provision.

Senate Amendment

No provision.

Conference Agreement

Repeals the phase down of the allowable deduction for clean-fuel vehicles in 2004 and 2005. Thus, a taxpayer who purchases a qualifying vehicle may claim 100 percent of the otherwise allowable deduction for vehicles purchased in 2004 and 2005. For vehicles purchased in 2006 the deduction remains at 25 percent of the otherwise allowable amount as under present law.

Effective Date

Effective for vehicles placed in service after December 31, 2003.

[Law at ¶ 5175. CCH Explanation at ¶ 225.]

[¶ 10,400] Act Sec. 320. Disclosures relating to terrorist activities

Conference Committee Report (H.R. CONF. REP. NO. 108-696)

[Code Sec. 6103]

Present Law

In connection with terrorist activities, the IRS was permitted to disclose return information, other than taxpayer return information, to officers and employees of Federal law enforcement upon a written request. The Code required the request to be made by the head of the Federal law enforcement agency (or his delegate) involved in the response to or investigation of terrorist incidents, threats, or activities, and set forth the specific reason or reasons why such disclosure may be relevant to a terrorist incident, threat, or activity. Disclosure of the information was permitted to officers and employees of the Federal law enforcement agency who were personally and directly involved in the response to or investigation of terrorist incidents, threats, or activities. The information was to be used by such officers and employees solely for such response or investigation.[72]

The Code permitted the head of the Federal law enforcement agency to redisclose the information to officers and employees of State and local law enforcement personally and directly engaged in the response to or investigation of the terrorist incident, threat, or activity. The State or local law enforcement agency was required to be part of an investigative or response team with the Federal law enforcement agency for these disclosures to be made.[73]

Return information includes a taxpayer's identity.[74] If a taxpayer's identity is taken from a return or other information filed with or furnished to the IRS by or on behalf of the taxpayer, it is taxpayer return information. Since taxpayer return information was not covered by this disclosure authorization, taxpayer identity so obtained could not be disclosed under this authority and thus associated with the other information being provided.

The Code also allowed the IRS to disclose return information (other than taxpayer return information) upon the written request of an officer or employee of the Department of Justice or Treasury who is appointed by the President with the advice and consent of the Senate, or who is the Director of the U.S. Secret Service, if such individual is responsible for the collection and analysis of intelligence and counterintelligence concerning any terrorist incident, threat, or activity.[75] Taxpayer identity information for this purpose was not considered taxpayer return information. Such written request was required to set forth the specific reason or reasons why such disclosure may be relevant to a terrorist incident, threat, or activity. Disclosures under this authority were permitted to be made to those officers and employees of the Department of Justice, Treasury, and Federal intelligence agencies who were personally and directly engaged in the collection or analysis of intelligence and counterintelligence information or investigation concerning any terrorist incident, threat, or activity. Such disclosures were permitted solely for the use of such officers and employees in such investigation, collection, or analysis.

The IRS, on its own initiative, was permitted to disclose in writing return information (other than taxpayer return information) that may be related to a terrorist incident, threat, or activity to the extent necessary to apprise the head of the appropriate investigating Federal law enforcement agency.[76] Taxpayer identity information for this purpose was not considered taxpayer return information. The head of the agency was permitted to redisclose such information to officers and employees of such agency to the extent necessary to investigate or respond to the terrorist incident, threat, or activity.

If taxpayer return information was sought, the disclosure was required to be made pursuant to the ex parte order of a Federal district court judge or magistrate.

No disclosures may be made under these provisions after December 31, 2003.

House Bill

No provision.

Senate Amendment

No provision.

Conference Agreement

The conference agreement extends the disclosure authority relating to terrorist activities. Under the conference agreement, no disclosures can be made after December 31, 2005.

The conference agreement also makes a technical change to clarify that a taxpayer's iden-

---

[72] Sec. 6103(i)(7)(A).
[73] Sec. 6103(i)(7)(A)(ii).
[74] Sec. 6103(b)(2)(A).

[75] Sec. 6103(i)(7)(B).
[76] Sec. 6103(i)(3)(C).

tity is not treated as taxpayer return information for purposes of disclosures to law enforcement agencies regarding terrorist activities.

Effective Date

The provision extending authority is effective for disclosures made on or after the date of enactment. The technical change is effective as if included in section 201 of the Victims of Terrorism Tax Relief Act of 2001.

[Law at ¶5390. CCH Explanation at ¶257.]

[¶ 10,410] Act Sec. 321. Extension of joint review of strategic plans and budget for the Internal Revenue Service

Conference Committee Report (H.R. CONF. REP. NO. 108-696)

[Code Secs. 8021 and 8022]

Present Law

The Code required the Joint Committee on Taxation to conduct a joint review[79] of the strategic plans and budget of the IRS from 1999 through 2003.[80] The Code also required the Joint Committee to provide an annual report[81] from 1999 through 2003 with respect to:

Strategic and business plans for the IRS;

Progress of the IRS in meeting its objectives;

The budget for the IRS and whether it supports its objectives;

Progress of the IRS in improving taxpayer service and compliance;

Progress of the IRS on technology modernization; and

The annual filing season.

House Bill

No provision.

Senate Amendment

No provision.

Conference Agreement

The conference agreement requires that the Joint Committee conduct a joint review before June 1, 2005. The conference agreement also requires that the Joint Committee provide an annual report with respect to such joint review, and specifies that the content of the annual report is the matters addressed in the joint review.[82]

Effective Date

The conference agreement is effective on the date of enactment.

[Law at ¶5415, ¶5420 and ¶7022. CCH Explanation at ¶259.]

[¶ 10,420] Act Sec. 322. Extension of Archer Medical Savings Accounts ("MSAs")

Conference Committee Report (H.R. CONF. REP. NO. 108-696)

[Code Sec. 220]

Present Law

In general

Within limits, contributions to an Archer MSA are deductible in determining adjusted gross income if made by an eligible individual and are excludable from gross income and wages for employment tax purposes if made by the employer of an eligible individual. Earnings on amounts in an Archer MSA are not currently taxable. Distributions from an Archer MSA for medical expenses are not includible in gross income. Distributions not used for medical expenses are includible in gross income. In addition, distributions not used for medical expenses are subject to an additional 15-percent tax unless the distribution is made after age 65, death, or disability.

---

[79] The joint review was required to include two members of the majority and one member of the minority of the Senate Committees on Finance, Appropriations, and Governmental Affairs, and of the House Committees on Ways and Means, Appropriations, and Government Reform and Oversight.

[80] Sec. 8021(f).

[81] Sec. 8022(3)(C).

[82] Accordingly, the provision deletes the specific list of matters required to be covered in the annual report.

Eligible individuals

Archer MSAs are available to employees covered under an employer-sponsored high deductible plan of a small employer and self-employed individuals covered under a high deductible health plan.[77] An employer is a small employer if it employed, on average, no more than 50 employees on business days during either the preceding or the second preceding year. An individual is not eligible for an Archer MSA if he or she is covered under any other health plan in addition to the high deductible plan.

Tax treatment of and limits on contributions

Individual contributions to an Archer MSA are deductible (within limits) in determining adjusted gross income (i.e., "above-the-line"). In addition, employer contributions are excludable from gross income and wages for employment tax purposes (within the same limits), except that this exclusion does not apply to contributions made through a cafeteria plan. In the case of an employee, contributions can be made to an Archer MSA either by the individual or by the individual's employer.

The maximum annual contribution that can be made to an Archer MSA for a year is 65 percent of the deductible under the high deductible plan in the case of individual coverage and 75 percent of the deductible in the case of family coverage.

Definition of high deductible plan

A high deductible plan is a health plan with an annual deductible of at least $1,700 and no more than $2,600 in the case of individual coverage and at least $3,450 and no more than $5,150 in the case of family coverage. In addition, the maximum out-of-pocket expenses with respect to allowed costs (including the deductible) must be no more than $3,450 in the case of individual coverage and no more than $6,300 in the case of family coverage.[78] A plan does not fail to qualify as a high deductible plan merely because it does not have a deductible for preventive care as required by State law. A plan does not qualify as a high deductible health plan if substantially all of the coverage under the plan is for permitted coverage (as described above). In the case of a self-insured plan, the plan must in fact be insurance (e.g., there must be appropriate risk shifting) and not merely a reimbursement arrangement.

Cap on taxpayers utilizing Archer MSAs and expiration of pilot program

The number of taxpayers benefiting annually from an Archer MSA contribution is limited to a threshold level (generally 750,000 taxpayers). The number of Archer MSAs established has not exceeded the threshold level.

After 2003, no new contributions may be made to Archer MSAs except by or on behalf of individuals who previously had Archer MSA contributions and employees who are employed by a participating employer.

Trustees of Archer MSAs are generally required to make reports to the Treasury by August 1 regarding Archer MSAs established by July 1 of that year. If any year is a cut-off year, the Secretary is required to make and publish such determination by October 1 of such year.

House Bill

No provision.

Senate Amendment

No provision.

Conference Agreement

The conference agreement extends Archer MSAs through December 31, 2005. The conference agreement also provides that the reports required by MSA trustees for 2004 are treated as timely if made within 90 days after the date of enactment. In addition, the determination of whether 2004 is a cut-off year and the publication of such determination is to be made within 120 days of the date of enactment. If 2004 is a cut-off year, the cut-off date will be the last day of such 120-day period.

Effective Date

The provision is generally effective on January 1, 2004. The provisions relating to reports and the determination by the Secretary are effective on the date of enactment.

[Law at ¶5190 and ¶7023. CCH Explanation at ¶245.]

---

[77] Self-employed individuals include more than two-percent shareholders of S corporations who are treated as partners for purposes of fringe benefit rules pursuant to section 1372.

[78] These dollar amounts are for 2004. These amounts are indexed for inflation, rounded to the nearest $50.

[¶ 10,500] Act Sec. 401. Tax technical corrections: Medicare Prescription Drug, Improvement, and Modernization Act of 2003

Conference Committee Report (H.R. CONF. REP. NO. 108-696)

[Act Sec. 401]

Present Law

Certain recently enacted tax legislation needs technical, conforming, and clerical amendments in order to properly carry out the intention of the Congress.[83]

House Bill

No provision.

Senate Amendment

No provision.

Conference Agreement

The conference agreement includes technical corrections to recently enacted tax legislation. Except as otherwise provided, the amendments made by the technical corrections contained in the conference agreement take effect as if included in the original legislation to which each amendment relates. The following is a description of the provisions contained in the technical corrections title:

Amendments related to the Medicare Prescription Drug, Improvement, and Modernization Act of 2003

Additional tax relating to health savings accounts.—Under present law, section 26(b) pro-

vides that "regular tax liability" does not include certain "additional taxes" and similar amounts. Under present law, regular tax liability does not include the additional tax on Archer MSA distributions not used for qualified medical expenses (sec. 220(f)(4)). The provision adds to the list of such amounts the additional tax on distributions not used for qualified medical expenses (sec. 223(f)(4)) under the rules relating to health savings accounts.

Health coverage tax credit.—Under present law, section 35(g)(3) provides that any amount distributed from an Archer MSA will not be taken into account for purposes of determining the amount of health coverage tax credit ("HCTC") an individual is eligible to receive. Under the provision, section 35(g)(3) is amended to provide that amounts distributed from health savings accounts are not to be taken into account for purposes of determining the amount of HCTC an individual is entitled to receive.

* * *

[Law at ¶5030 and ¶5045. CCH Explanation at ¶357.]

[¶ 10,510] Act Sec. 402. Tax technical corrections: Jobs and Growth Tax Relief Reconciliation Act of 2003

Conference Committee Report (H.R. CONF. REP. NO. 108-696)

[Act Sec. 402]

Present Law

Certain recently enacted tax legislation needs technical, conforming, and clerical amendments in order to properly carry out the intention of the Congress.[83]

House Bill

No provision.

Senate Amendment

No provision.

Conference Agreement

The conference agreement includes technical corrections to recently enacted tax legislation. Except as otherwise provided, the amendments made by the technical corrections contained in the conference agreement take effect as if in-

---

[83] Tax technical corrections legislation, the "Tax Technical Corrections Act of 2003," was introduced in the House of Representatives (H.R. 3654) on December 8, 2003, and in the Senate (S. 1984) on December 9, 2003.

[83] Tax technical corrections legislation, the "Tax Technical Corrections Act of 2003," was introduced in the House of Representatives (H.R. 3654) on December 8, 2003, and in the Senate (S. 1984) on December 9, 2003.

cluded in the original legislation to which each amendment relates. The following is a description of the provisions contained in the technical corrections title:

* * *

Amendments related to the Jobs and Growth Tax Relief Reconciliation Act of 2003

Dividends taxed at capital gain rates.—Section 302 of the Jobs and Growth Tax Relief Reconciliation Act of 2003 ("JGTRRA") generally provides that qualified dividend income of taxpayers other than corporations is taxed at the same tax rates as the net capital gain. The conference agreement makes the following amendments to the provisions adopted by that section:[84]

The provision clarifies that the determination of net capital gain, for purposes of determining the amount taxed at the 25-percent rate (section 1(h)(1)(D)(i)), is made without regard to qualified dividend income.

Under present law, the deduction for estate taxes paid on gain that is income in respect of a decedent reduces the amount of gain otherwise taken into account in computing the amount eligible for the lower tax rates on net capital gain (sec. 691(c)(4)). Since it is not entirely clear under present law whether this provision also applies to qualified dividends eligible for the lower tax rates on net capital gain, the conference agreement clarifies that the provision does so apply.

The provision clarifies that the extraordinary dividend rule applies to trusts and estates as well as individuals.

The provision rewrites portions of the provisions relating to the treatment of dividends received from a regulated investment company ("RIC") or a real estate investment trust ("REIT") to set forth the rules directly rather than be reference to rules applicable to dividends received by corporate shareholders.

The provision provides that all distributions by a RIC or REIT of the earnings and profits from C corporation years can be treated as qualifying dividends eligible for the lower rate.

The provision extends the 60-day period for notifying shareholders of the amount of the qualified dividend income distributed by a RIC or REIT for taxable years ending on or before November 30, 2003, to the date the 1099-DIV for 2003 is required.

The provision provides that, in the case of partnerships, S corporations, common trust funds, trusts, and estates, section 302 of JGTRRA applies to taxable years ending after December 31, 2002, except that dividends received by the entity prior to January 1, 2003, are not treated as qualified dividend income. JGTRRA provided a similar rule in the case of RICs and REITs.

Satisfaction of certain holding period requirements if stock is acquired on the day before ex-dividend date.—Under several similar holding period requirements relating to the tax consequences of receiving dividends, a taxpayer who acquires stock the day before the ex-dividend date cannot satisfy these holding period requirements with respect to the dividend. The conference agreement modifies the stock holding period requirements to permit taxpayers to satisfy the requirements when they acquire stock on the day before the ex-dividend date of the stock. Specifically, the conference agreement modifies the holding period requirement for the dividends-received deduction under section 246(c) (as modified by section 1015 of the Taxpayer Relief Act of 1997) by changing from 90 days to 91 days (and from 180 days to 181 days in the case of certain dividends on preferred stock) the period within which a taxpayer may satisfy the requirement. In addition, the conference agreement modifies the holding period requirement for foreign tax credits with respect to dividends under section 901(k) (enacted in section 1053 of the Taxpayer Relief Act of 1997) by changing from 30 days to 31 days (and from 90 days to 91 days in the case of certain dividends on preferred stock) the period within which a taxpayer may satisfy the requirement. The conference agreement modifies the holding period requirement for dividends to be taxed at the tax rates applicable to net capital gain under section 1(h)(11) (enacted in section 302 of JGTRRA) by changing from 120 days to 121 days (and from 180 days to 181 days in the case of certain dividends on preferred stock) the period within which a taxpayer may satisfy the requirement.

* * *

[Law at ¶5005, ¶5265, ¶5270, ¶5275 and ¶7025. CCH Explanation at ¶305, ¶307 and ¶309.]

---

[84] IR-2004-22 (Feb. 19, 2004) announced that the IRS agreed to make the technical correction provisions relating to dividends contained in the Technical Corrections Act of 2003, as introduced, available to taxpayers in advance of their passage.

[¶ 10,520] Act Sec. 403. Tax technical corrections: Job Creation and Worker Assistance Act of 2002

Conference Committee Report (H.R. CONF. REP. NO. 108-696)

[Act Sec. 403]

Present Law

Certain recently enacted tax legislation needs technical, conforming, and clerical amendments in order to properly carry out the intention of the Congress.[83]

House Bill

No provision.

Senate Amendment

No provision.

Conference Agreement

The conference agreement includes technical corrections to recently enacted tax legislation. Except as otherwise provided, the amendments made by the technical corrections contained in the conference agreement take effect as if included in the original legislation to which each amendment relates. The following is a description of the provisions contained in the technical corrections title:

* * *

Amendments related to the Job Creation and Worker Assistance Act of 2002

Bonus depreciation.—Section 101 of the Job Creation and Worker Assistance Act of 2002 ("JCWA") provides generally for 30-percent additional first-year depreciation for qualifying property. Qualifying property is defined to include certain property subject to the capitalization rules of section 263A by reason of having an estimated production period exceeding 2 years or an estimated production period exceeding 1 year and a cost exceeding $1 million (secs. 168(k)(2)(B)(i)(III) and 263A(f)(1)(B)(ii) or (iii)). An unintended interpretation of this rule could preclude property from qualifying for bonus depreciation if it meets this description but is subject to the capitalization rules of section 263A by reason of section 263A(f)(1)(B)(i) (having a long useful life). The provision clarifies that qualifying property includes such property that is subject to the capitalization rules of section 263A and is described in the provisions requiring an estimated production period exceeding 2 years or an estimated production period exceeding 1 year and a cost exceeding $1 million.

Section 101 of JCWA provides a binding contract rule in determining property that qualifies for it. The requirements that must be satisfied in order for property to qualify include that (1) the original use of the property must commence with the taxpayer on or after September 11, 2001, (2) the taxpayer must purchase the property after September 10, 2001, and before September 11, 2004, and (3) no binding written contract for the acquisition of the property is in effect before September 11, 2001 (or, in the case of self-constructed property, manufacture, construction, or production of the property does not begin before September 11, 2001). In addition, JCWA provides a special rule in the case of certain leased property. In the case of any property that is originally placed in service by a person and that is sold to the taxpayer and leased back to such person by the taxpayer within three months after the date that the property was placed in service, the property is treated as originally placed in service by the taxpayer not earlier than the date that the property is used under the leaseback. JCWA did not specifically address the syndication of a lease by the lessor.

The provision clarifies that property qualifying for additional first-year depreciation does not include any property if the user or a related party to the user or owner of such property had a written binding contract in effect for the acquisition of the property at any time on or before September 10, 2001 (or, in the case of self-constructed property, the manufacture, construction, or production of the property began on or before September 10, 2001). For example, if a taxpayer sells to a related party property that was under construction on or prior to September 10, 2001, the property does not qualify for the additional first-year depreciation deduction. Similarly, if a taxpayer sells to a related party property that was subject to a binding written contract on or prior to September 10, 2001, the property does not qualify for the additional first-year depreciation deduction. As a further example, if a taxpayer sells property and leases the property back in a sale-leaseback arrangement, and the lessee had a binding written contract in effect for the acquisition of such property on or prior to September 10, 2001, then the lessor is not entitled to the additional first-year depreciation deduction.

---

[83] Tax technical corrections legislation, the "Tax Technical Corrections Act of 2003," was introduced in the House of Representatives (H.R. 3654) on December 8, 2003, and in the Senate (S. 1984) on December 9, 2003.

In addition, the provision provides that if property is originally placed in service by a lessor (including by operation of section Code 168(k)(2)(D)(i)), such property is sold within three months after the date that the property was placed in service, and the user of such property does not change, then the property is treated as originally placed in service by the taxpayer not earlier than the date of such sale.

Five-year carryback of net operating losses ("NOLs").—Section 102 of JCWA temporarily extends the NOL carryback period to five years (from two years, or three years in certain cases) for NOLs arising in taxable years ending in 2001 and 2002. The Act was enacted in March 2002, after some taxpayers had filed returns for 2001.

The provision (1) clarifies that only the NOLs arising in taxable years ending in 2001 and 2002 qualify for the 5-year period, and (2) provides that any election to forego any carrybacks of NOLs arising in 2001 or 2002 can be revoked prior to November 1, 2002. The provision also allows taxpayers until November 1, 2002, to use the tentative carryback adjustment procedures of section 6411 for NOLs arising in 2001 and 2002 (without regard to the 12-month limitation in section 6411). In addition, the provision clarifies that an election to disregard the 5-year carryback for certain NOLs is treated as timely made if made before November 1, 2002 (notwithstanding that section 172(j) requires the election to be made by the due date (including extensions) for filing the taxpayer's return for the year of the loss).[85]

The provision also makes several clerical changes to the NOL provisions relating to the alternative minimum tax.

New York Liberty Zone bonus depreciation.— Section 301 of JCWA provides tax benefits for the area of New York City damaged in terrorist attacks on September 11, 2001 (an area defined in the provision and named the New York Liberty Zone). Under these rules, an additional first-year depreciation deduction is allowed equal to 30 percent of the adjusted basis of qualified New York Liberty Zone ("Liberty Zone") property. A taxpayer is allowed to elect out of the additional first-year depreciation for any class of property for any taxable year. In addition, the Act provides a special rule in the case of certain leased property. In the case of any property that is originally placed in service by a person and that is sold to the taxpayer and leased back to such person by the taxpayer within three months after the date that the property was placed in service, the property would be treated as originally placed in service by the taxpayer not earlier than

the date that the property is used under the leaseback. JCWA did not specifically address the syndication of a lease by the lessor.

The provision clarifies that property qualifying for additional first-year depreciation does not include any property if the user or a related party to the user or owner of such property had a written binding contract in effect for the acquisition of the property at any time before September 11, 2001 (or in the case of self constructed property the manufacture, construction, or production of the property began before September 11, 2001). In addition, the provision provides that if property is originally placed in service by a lessor (including by operation of section 168(k)(2)(D)(i)), such property is sold within three months after the date that the property was placed in service, and the user of such property does not change, then the property is treated as originally placed in service by the taxpayer not earlier than the date of such sale.

New York Liberty Zone expensing.—Section 301 of JCWA increases the amount a taxpayer may expense under section 179 to the lesser of $35,000 or the amount of Liberty Zone property placed in service for the year. In addition, section 301(a) of the Act states that if property qualifies for both the general additional first-year depreciation and Liberty Zone additional first-year depreciation, it is deemed to be eligible for the general additional first-year depreciation and is not considered Liberty Zone property (i.e., only one 30-percent additional first-year depreciation deduction is allowed). Because only Liberty Zone property is eligible for the increased section 179 expensing amount, this rule has the unintended consequence of denying the increased section 179 expensing to Liberty Zone property. The provision corrects this unintended result (such that qualifying Liberty Zone property qualifies for both the 30-percent additional first-year depreciation and the additional section 179 expensing).

Provide election out of Liberty Zone five-year depreciation for leasehold improvements.—Section 1400L(c), as added by section 301 of JCWA, provides for a 5-year recovery period for depreciation of qualified New York Liberty Zone leasehold improvement property that is placed in service after September 10, 2001, and before January 1, 2007 (and meets certain other requirements). Unlike the rules relating to bonus depreciation and to Liberty Zone bonus depreciation property (see Code sections 168(k)(2)(C)(iii) and 1400L(b)(2)(C)(iv)), which permit a taxpayer to elect out, this 5-year depreciation rule is not elective. The provision adds a rule permitting

---

[85] The corrections are consistent with the guidance issued by the IRS (Rev. Proc. 2002-40, 2002-1 C. B. 1096).

taxpayers to elect out of the 5-year recovery period.

Interest rate for defined benefit plan funding requirements.—Section 405(c) of JCWA increases the interest rate used in determining the amount of unfunded vested benefits for PBGC variable rate premium purposes for plan years beginning in 2002 or 2003 from 85 percent to 100 percent of the interest rate on 30-year Treasury securities for the month preceding the month in which the applicable plan year begins. The provision makes conforming changes so that this rule applies for purposes of notices and reporting re-

quired under Title IV of ERISA with respect to underfunded plans.

Exclusion for employer-provided adoption assistance.—The provision corrects an incorrect reference in a technical correction to a provision relating to the exclusion for employer-provided adoption assistance.

* * *

[Law at ¶5090, ¶5160, ¶5170, ¶5350 and ¶7030. CCH Explanation at ¶321, ¶327, ¶329, ¶331, ¶333, ¶335, ¶337, ¶339 and ¶341.]

[¶ 10,530] Act Sec. 404. Tax technical corrections: Economic Growth and Tax Relief Reconciliation Act of 2001

Conference Committee Report (H.R. CONF. REP. NO. 108-696)

[Act Sec. 404]

Present Law

Certain recently enacted tax legislation needs technical, conforming, and clerical amendments in order to properly carry out the intention of the Congress.[83]

House Bill

No provision.

Senate Amendment

No provision.

Conference Agreement

The conference agreement includes technical corrections to recently enacted tax legislation. Except as otherwise provided, the amendments made by the technical corrections contained in the conference agreement take effect as if included in the original legislation to which each amendment relates. The following is a description of the provisions contained in the technical corrections title:

* * *

Amendments related to the Economic Growth and Tax Relief Reconciliation Act of 2001

Coverdell education savings accounts.—The provision corrects the application of a conforming change to the rule coordinating Coverdell education savings accounts with Hope and Lifetime Learning credits and qualified tuition programs. The conforming change was made in connection with the expansion of Coverdell edu-

cation savings accounts to elementary and secondary education expenses in section 401 of the Economic Growth and Tax Relief Reconciliation Act of 2001 "(EGTRRA").

Base period for cost-of-living adjustments to Indian employment credit rule.—The Indian employment credit is not available with respect to an employee whose wages exceed $30,000 (sec. 45A). For years after 1994, this $30,000 amount is adjusted for cost-of-living increases at the same time, and in the same manner, as cost-of-living adjustments to the dollar limits on qualified retirement plan benefits and contributions under section 415. Section 611 of EGTRAA increases the dollar limits under section 415 and adds a new base period for making cost-of-living adjustments. The provision clarifies that the pre-existing base period applies for purposes of the Indian employment credit.

Rounding rule for retirement plan benefit and contribution limits.—Section 611 of EGTRRA increases the dollar limits on qualified retirement plan benefits and contributions under Code section 415, and adds a new rounding rule for cost-of-living adjustments to the dollar limit on annual additions to defined contribution plans. This new rounding rule is in addition to a pre-existing rounding rule that applies to benefits payable under defined benefit plans. The provision clarifies that the pre-existing rounding rule applies for purposes of other Code provisions that refer to Code section 415 and do not contain a specific rounding rule.

Excise tax on nondeductible contributions.—Under section 614 of EGTRRA, the limits on deductions for employer contributions to quali-

---

[83] Tax technical corrections legislation, the "Tax Technical Corrections Act of 2003," was introduced in the House of Representatives (H.R. 3654) on December 8, 2003, and in the Senate (S. 1984) on December 9, 2003.

fied retirement plans do not apply to elective deferrals, and elective deferrals are not taken into account in applying the deduction limits to other contributions. The provision makes a conforming change to the Code provision that applies an excise tax to nondeductible contributions.

SIMPLE plan contributions for domestic or similar workers.—Section 637 of EGTRRA provides an exception to the application of the excise tax on nondeductible retirement plan contributions in the case of contributions to a SIMPLE IRA or SIMPLE section 401(k) plan that are nondeductible solely because they are not made in connection with a trade or business of the employer (e.g., contributions on behalf of a domestic worker). Section 637 of EGTRRA did not specifically modify the present-law requirement that compensation for purposes of determining contributions to a SIMPLE plan must be wages subject to income tax withholding, even though

wages paid to domestic workers are not subject to income tax withholding. The provision revises the definition of compensation for purposes of determining contributions to a SIMPLE plan to include wages paid to domestic workers, even though such amounts are not subject to income tax withholding.

Rollovers among various types of retirement plans.—Section 641 of EGTRRA expanded the rollover rules to allow rollovers among various types of tax-favored retirement plans. The provision makes a conforming change to the cross-reference to the rollovers rules in the Code provision relating to qualified retirement annuities.

* * *

[Law at ¶5065, ¶5220, ¶5225, ¶5240, ¶5255 and ¶5365. CCH Explanation at ¶343, ¶345, ¶347, ¶349 and ¶365.]

[¶10,540] Act Sec. 405. Tax technical corrections: Community Renewal Tax Relief Act of 2000

Conference Committee Report (H.R. Conf. Rep. No. 108-696)

[Act Sec. 405]

Present Law

Certain recently enacted tax legislation needs technical, conforming, and clerical amendments in order to properly carry out the intention of the Congress.[83]

House Bill

No provision.

Senate Amendment

No provision.

Conference Agreement

The conference agreement includes technical corrections to recently enacted tax legislation. Except as otherwise provided, the amendments made by the technical corrections contained in the conference agreement take effect as if included in the original legislation to which each amendment relates. The following is a description of the provisions contained in the technical corrections title:

* * *

Amendment related to the Community Renewal Tax Relief Act of 2000

Tax treatment of options and securities futures contracts.—The provision clarifies that the Secretary of the Treasury has the authority to prescribe regulations regarding the status of an option or a contract the value of which is determined directly or indirectly by reference to an index which becomes (or ceases to be) a narrow-based security index (as defined in section 1256(g)(6)). This authority includes, but is not limited to, regulations that provide for preserving the status of such an option or contract as appropriate.

* * *

[Law at ¶5295 and ¶5300. CCH Explanation at ¶311.]

---

[83] Tax technical corrections legislation, the "Tax Technical Corrections Act of 2003," was introduced in the House of Representatives (H.R. 3654) on December 8, 2003, and in the Senate (S. 1984) on December 9, 2003.

[¶ 10,550] Act Sec. 406. Tax technical corrections: Taxpayer Relief Act of 1997

Conference Committee Report (H.R. CONF. REP. NO. 108-696)

[Act Sec. 406]

Present Law

Certain recently enacted tax legislation needs technical, conforming, and clerical amendments in order to properly carry out the intention of the Congress.[83]

House Bill

No provision.

Senate Amendment

No provision.

Conference Agreement

The conference agreement includes technical corrections to recently enacted tax legislation. Except as otherwise provided, the amendments made by the technical corrections contained in the conference agreement take effect as if included in the original legislation to which each amendment relates. The following is a description of the provisions contained in the technical corrections title:

* * *

Amendments related to the Taxpayer Relief Act of 1997

Qualified tuition programs.—Section 211 of the Taxpayer Relief Act of 1997 modified section 529(c)(5), relating to gift tax rules for qualified tuition programs, but did not include in the statutory language the requirement that, upon a change in the designated beneficiary of the program, the new beneficiary must be a member of the family of the old beneficiary for gift taxes not to apply. The legislative history for the provision stated that the new beneficiary had to be of the same generation as the old beneficiary and a member of the family of the old beneficiary for gift taxes not to apply. The provision clarifies that the gift taxes apply unless the new beneficiary is of the same (or higher) generation than the old beneficiary and is a member of the family of the old beneficiary.

Coverdell education savings accounts.—The provision corrects section 530(d)(4)(B)(iii), relating to Coverdell education savings accounts, by substituting for the undefined term "account holder" the defined term "designated beneficiary."

Constructive sale exception.—Section 1001(a) of the Taxpayer Relief Act of 1997 provides an exception from constructive sale treatment for any transaction that is closed before the end of the thirtieth day after the close of the taxable year in which the transaction was entered into, provided certain requirements are met after closing the transaction (section 1259(c)(3)). In the case of positions that are reestablished following a closed transaction but prior to satisfying the requirements for the exception from constructive sale treatment, the exception applies in a similar manner if the reestablished position itself is closed and similar requirements are met after closing the reestablished position. The provision clarifies that the exception applies in the same manner to all closed transactions, including reestablished positions that are closed.

Basis adjustments for QZAB held by S corporation.—Under present law, a shareholder of an S corporation that is an eligible financial institution may claim a credit with respect to a qualified zone academy bond ("QZAB") held by the S corporation. The amount of the credit is included in gross income of the shareholder. An unintended interpretation of these rules would be that the shareholder's basis in the stock of the S corporation is increased by the amount of the income inclusion, notwithstanding that the benefit of the credit flows directly to the shareholder rather than to the corporation, and the corporation has no additional assets to support the basis increase. The provision clarifies that the basis of stock in an S corporation is not affected by the QZAB credit.

Capital gains and AMT.—The provision provides that the maximum amount of adjusted net capital gain eligible for the five-percent rate under the alternative minimum tax is the excess of the maximum amount of taxable income that may be taxed at a rate of less than 25 percent under the regular tax (for example, $56,800 for a joint return in 2003)) over the taxable income reduced by the adjusted net capital gain.

The provision may be illustrated by the following example:

---

[83] Tax technical corrections legislation, the "Tax Technical Corrections Act of 2003," was introduced in the House of Representatives (H.R. 3654) on December 8, 2003, and in the Senate (S. 1984) on December 9, 2003.

For example, assume that a married couple with no dependents in 2003 has $32,100 of salary, $82,000 of long-term capital gain from the sale of stock, $73,000 of itemized deductions consisting entirely of state and local taxes and allowable miscellaneous itemized deductions. For purposes of the regular tax, the taxable income is $35,000 ($32,100 plus $82,000 minus $73,000 minus $6,100 deduction for personal exemptions). For purposes of the alternative minimum tax, the taxable excess is $56,100 ($32,100 plus $82,000 less the $58,000 exemption amount).

Under present law, the amount taxed under the regular tax at five percent is $35,000 (the lesser of (i) taxable income ($35,000), (ii) adjusted net capital gain ($82,000), or (iii) the excess of the maximum amount taxed at the 10- and 15-percent rates ($56,800 in 2003) over the ordinary taxable income (zero)). Thus, the regular tax is $1,750.

Under present law, $35,000 is taxed at five percent in computing the alternative minimum tax (the lesser of (i) amount of the adjusted net capital gain which is taxed at the five percent under the regular tax ($35,000), or (ii) the taxable excess ($56,100)). The remaining $21,100 of taxable excess is taxed at 15 percent, for a total tentative minimum tax of $4,915.

Under the provision, in computing the alternative minimum tax, $56,100 is taxed at five percent (the lesser of (i) the taxable excess ($56,100), (ii) the adjusted net capital gain ($82,000), or (iii) the excess of the maximum amount taxed at the 10- and 15-percent rates under the regular tax ($56,800) over the ordinary taxable income (zero)). The tentative minimum tax is $2,805.

* * *

[**Law at ¶5085, ¶5200, ¶5250, ¶5255, ¶5280, ¶5305 and ¶5320. CCH Explanation at ¶305, ¶313, ¶315, ¶367, ¶369 and ¶375.**]

[¶ 10,560] Act Sec. 407. Tax technical corrections: Small Business Job Protection Act of 1996

Conference Committee Report (H.R. CONF. REP. NO. 108-696)

[Act Sec. 407]

Present Law

Certain recently enacted tax legislation needs technical, conforming, and clerical amendments in order to properly carry out the intention of the Congress.[83]

House Bill

No provision.

Senate Amendment

No provision.

Conference Agreement

The conference agreement includes technical corrections to recently enacted tax legislation. Except as otherwise provided, the amendments made by the technical corrections contained in the conference agreement take effect as if included in the original legislation to which each amendment relates. The following is a description of the provisions contained in the technical corrections title:

* * *

Amendment related to the Small Business Job Protection Act of 1996

S corporation post-termination transition period.—Shareholders of an S corporation whose status as an S corporation terminates are allowed a period of time after the termination (the post-termination transition period ("PTTP")) to utilize certain of the benefits of S corporation status. The shareholders may claim losses and deductions previously suspended due to lack of stock or debt basis up to the amount of the stock basis as of the last day of the PTTP (sec. 1366(d)). Also, shareholders may receive cash distributions from the corporation during the PTTP that are treated as returns of capital to the extent of any balance in the S corporation's accumulated adjustments account ("AAA") (sec. 1371(e)).

The PTTP generally begins on the day after the last day of the corporation's last tax year as an S corporation and ends on the later of the day which is one year after such last day or the due date for filing the return for such last year as an S corporation (including extensions). Section 1307 of the Small Business Job Protection Act of 1996 added a new 120-day PTTP following an

---

[83] Tax technical corrections legislation, the "Tax Technical Corrections Act of 2003," was introduced in the House of Representatives (H.R. 3654) on December 8, 2003, and in the Senate (S. 1984) on December 9, 2003.

audit of the corporation that adjusts an S corporation item of income, loss, or deduction arising during the most recent period while the corporation was an S corporation. This provision was enacted to allow the tax-free distribution of any additional income determined in the audit.

As a result of the 1996 legislation, an S corporation shareholder might take the position that an audit adjustment allows the shareholder to utilize suspended losses and deductions in excess of the amount of the audit deficiency. For example, assume that, at the end of the one-year PTTP following the termination of a corporation's S corporation status, a shareholder has $1 million of suspended losses in the corporation. Later, the shareholder purchases additional stock in the corporation for $1 million. The corporation's audit determines a $25,000 increase in the S corporation's income. Although the $25,000 increase in income would allow $25,000 of suspended losses to be allowed, the shareholder might take the position that the entire $1,000,000 of suspended losses could be utilized during the 120-day PTTP following the end of the audit. Similarly, an S corporation that had failed to distribute the entire amount in its AAA during the one-year PTTP following the loss of S corporation status might argue that it could distribute that amount, in addition to the amount determined in the audit, during the 120-day period following the audit.

The provision provides that the 120-day PTTP added by the 1996 Act does not apply for purposes of allowing suspended losses to be deducted (since the increased income determined in the audit can be offset with the losses), and allows tax-free distributions of money by the corporation during the 120-day period only to the extent of any increase in the AAA by reason of adjustments from the audit.

Defined contribution plans.—The Small Business Job Protection Act of 1996 amended section 401(a)(26) (generally requiring that a qualified retirement plan benefit the lesser of 50 employees or 40 percent of the employer's workforce) so that it no longer applies to defined contribution plans. Section 401(a)(26)(C) (which treats employees as benefiting in certain circumstances) was not repealed even though it relates only to defined contribution plans. The provision repeals section 401(a)(26)(C).

* * *

[Law at ¶5215 and ¶5315. CCH Explanation at ¶351 and ¶377.]

[¶10,570] Act Sec. 408. Tax technical corrections: Clerical amendments

Conference Committee Report (H.R. Conf. Rep. No. 108-696)

[Act Sec. 408]

Present Law

Certain recently enacted tax legislation needs technical, conforming, and clerical amendments in order to properly carry out the intention of the Congress.[83]

House Bill

No provision.

Senate Amendment

No provision.

Conference Agreement

The conference agreement includes technical corrections to recently enacted tax legislation. Except as otherwise provided, the amendments made by the technical corrections contained in the conference agreement take effect as if included in the original legislation to which each amendment relates. The following is a description of the provisions contained in the technical corrections title:

* * *

Clerical amendments

The conference agreement makes a number of clerical and typographical amendments.

[Law at ¶5005, ¶5030, ¶5055, ¶5105, ¶5135, ¶5155, ¶5160, ¶5205, ¶5210, ¶5220, ¶5225, ¶5230, ¶5235, ¶5240, ¶5245, ¶5290,¶5310, ¶5370, ¶5375, ¶5380, ¶5385, ¶5390 and ¶7035. CCH Explanation at ¶359 and ¶30,050]

---

[83] Tax technical corrections legislation, the "Tax Technical Corrections Act of 2003," was introduced in the House of Representatives (H.R. 3654) on December 8, 2003, and in the Senate (S. 1984) on December 9, 2003.

¶ 20,001

Effective Dates

Working Families Tax Relief Act of 2004

This CCH-prepared table presents the general effective dates for major law provisions added, amended or repealed by the Working Families Tax Relief Act of 2004. Entries are listed in Code Section order.

Code Sec.	Act Sec.	Act Provision Subject	Effective Date
1(f)(8)	101(c)	Repeal of scheduled reductions in child tax credit, marriage penalty relief, and 10-percent rate bracket—Marriage penalty relief in 15-percent income tax bracket	Tax years beginning after December 31, 2003
1(g)(7)(B)	408(a)(1)	Clerical amendments	Date of enactment
1(h)(1)(D)	402(a)(1)	Amendments related to Jobs and Growth Tax Relief Reconciliation Act of 2003	Tax years beginning after December 31, 2002, generally
1(h)(6)(A)	408(a)(2)	Clerical amendments	Date of enactment
1(h)(11)	402(a)(2)-(3)	Amendments related to Jobs and Growth Tax Relief Reconciliation Act of 2003	Tax years beginning after December 31, 2002, generally
1(i)(1)(B)	101(d)(1)	Repeal of scheduled reductions in child tax credit, marriage penalty relief, and 10-percent rate bracket—10-percent rate bracket	Tax years beginning after December 31, 2003
1(i)(1)(C)	101(d)(2)	Repeal of scheduled reductions in child tax credit, marriage penalty relief, and 10-percent rate bracket—10-percent rate bracket—Inflation adjustment	Tax years beginning after December 31, 2003
2(a)(1)(B)	207(1)	Technical and conforming amendments	Tax years beginning after December 31, 2004
2(b)(1)(A)	202(a)	Modifications of definition of head of household—Head of household	Tax years beginning after December 31, 2004
2(b)(2)-(3)	202(b)	Modifications of definition of head of household—Head of household—conforming amendment	Tax years beginning after December 31, 2004
21(a)(1)	203(a)	Modifications of dependent care credit	Tax years beginning after December 31, 2004
21(b)(1)	203(b)	Modifications of dependent care credit—Qualifying individual	Tax years beginning after December 31, 2004
21(e)(1)	203(c)	Modifications of dependent care credit—Qualifying individual—conforming amendment	Tax years beginning after December 31, 2004
21(e)(5)	207(2)	Technical and conforming amendments	Tax years beginning after December 31, 2004
21(e)(6)	207(3)	Technical and conforming amendments	Tax years beginning after December 31, 2004
24(a)	101(a)	Repeal of scheduled reductions in child tax credit, marriage penalty relief, and 10-percent rate bracket—Child tax credit	Tax years beginning after December 31, 2003

Code Sec.	Act Sec.	Act Provision Subject	Effective Date
24(c)(1)	204(a)	Modifications of child tax credit	Tax years beginning after December 31, 2004
24(c)(2)	204(b)	Modifications of child tax credit—conforming amendment	Tax years beginning after December 31, 2004
24(d)(1)	104(a)	Earned income includes combat pay—Child tax credit	Tax years beginning after December 31, 2003
24(d)(1)(B)	102(a)	Acceleration of increase in refundability of the child tax credit	Tax years beginning after December 31, 2003
25B(c)(2)(B)	207(4)	Technical and conforming amendments	Tax years beginning after December 31, 2004
26(a)(2)	312(a)	Allowance of nonrefundable personal credits against regular and minimum tax liability	Tax years beginning after December 31, 2003
26(b)(2)	408(a)(5)	Clerical amendments	Date of enactment
26(b)(2)(Q)-(S)	401(a)(1)	Amendments related to Medicare Prescription Drug, Improvement, and Modernization Act of 2003	Tax years beginning after December 31, 2003
30(b)(2)	318(a)	Elimination of phaseout of credit for qualifited electric vehicles for 2004 and 2005	Property placed in service after December 31, 2003
32(c)(1)(C)-(G)	205(b)(1)	Modifications of earned income credit—Qualifying child—conforming amendments	Tax years beginning after December 31, 2004
32(c)(2)(B)	104(b)	Earned income includes combat pay—Earned income credit	Tax years ending after date of enactment
32(c)(3)	205(a)	Modifications of earned income credit—Qualifying child	Tax years beginning after December 31, 2004
32(c)(4)	205(b)(2)	Modifications of earned income credit—Qualifying child—conforming amendments	Tax years beginning after December 31, 2004
32(m)	205(b)(3)	Modifications of earned income credit—Qualifying child—conforming amendments	Tax years beginning after December 31, 2004
35(g)(3)	401(a)(2)	Amendments related to Medicare Prescription Drug, Improvement, and Modernization Act of 2003	Tax years beginning after December 31, 2003
41(h)(1)(B)	301(a)(1)	Research credit—Extension	Amounts paid or incurred after June 30, 2004
42(d)(2)(D)	408(a)(3)	Clerical amendments	Date of enactment
42(i)(3)(D)	207(8)	Technical and conforming amendments	Tax years beginning after December 31, 2004
45(c)(3)(A)-(C)	313(a)	Credit for electricity produced from certain renewable resources	Facilities placed in service after December 31, 2003
45A(c)(3)	404(b)(1)	Amendments related to Economic growth and Tax Relief Reconciliation Act of 2001	Years beginning after December 31, 2001
45A(f)	315	Indian employment tax credit	Date of enactment
45C(b)(1)(D)	301(a)(2)	Researc credit—Extension—conforming amendment	Amounts paid or incurred after June 30, 2004

Code Sec.	Act Sec.	Act Provision Subject	Effective Date
51(c)(4)	303(a)(1)	Work opportunity credit and welfare-to-work credit—Extension of credit	Individuals who begin work for the employer after December 31, 2003
51(i)(1)(A)-(C)	207(5)	Technical and conforming amendments	Tax years beginning after December 31, 2004
51A(f)	303(a)(2)	Work opportunity credit and welfare-to-work credit—Extension of credit—Long-term family assistance recipients	Individuals who begin work for the employer after December 31, 2003
55(b)(3)(B)	406(d)	Amendments related to Taxpayer Relief Act of 1997	Tax years ending after May 6, 1997
55(d)(1)(A)-(B)	103(a)	Extension of minimum tax relief to individuals	Tax years beginning after December 31, 2004
56(d)(1)(A)	403(b)(4)	Amendments related to Job Creation and Worker Assistance Act of 2002	Tax years after December 31, 1990
62(a)(2)(D)	307(a)	Deduction for certain expenses of school teachers	Expenses paid or incurred in tax years beginning after December 31, 2003
63(c)(2)	101(b)(1)	Repeal of scheduled reductions in child tax credit, marriage penalty relief, and 10-percent rate bracket—Marriage penalty relief in standard deduction	Tax years beginning after December 31, 2003
63(c)(4)	101(b)(2)(A)	Repeal of scheduled reductions in child tax credit, marriage penalty relief, and 10-percent rate bracket—Marriage penalty relief in standard deduction—conforming amendment	Tax years beginning after December 31, 2003
63(c)(7)	101(b)(2)(B)	Repeal of scheduled reductions in child tax credit, marriage penalty relief, and 10-percent rate bracket—Marriage penalty relief in standard deduction—conforming amendment	Tax years beginning after December 31, 2003
72(f)	408(a)(4)	Clerical amendments	Date of enactment
72(t)(2)(D)	207(6)	Technical and conforming amendments	Tax years beginning after December 31, 2004
72(t)(7)(A)	207(7)	Technical and conforming amendments	Tax years beginning after December 31, 2004
105(b)-(c)	207(9)	Technical and conforming amendments	Tax years beginning after December 31, 2004
120(d)(4)	207(10)	Technical and conforming amendments	Tax years beginning after December 31, 2004
125(e)(1)(D)	207(11)	Technical and conforming amendments	Tax years beginning after December 31, 2004
129(c)(2)	207(12)	Technical and conforming amendments	Tax years beginning after December 31, 2004
132(h)(2)(B)	207(13)	Technical and conforming amendments	Tax years beginning after December 31, 2004
138(a)-(f)	408(a)(5)	Clerical amendments	Date of enactment
151(c)	206	Modifications of deduction for personal exemption for dependents	Tax years beginning after December 31, 2004
152(a)-(f)	201	Uniform definition of child, etc.	Tax years beginning after December 31, 2004

Code Sec.	Act Sec.	Act Provision Subject	Effective Date
153(1)-(4)	207(14)	Technical and conforming amendments	Tax years beginning after December 31, 2004
165(i)(1)	408(a)(7)	Clerical amendments	Date of enactment
165(k)	408(a)(7)	Clerical amendments	Date of enactment
168(j)(8)	316	Accelerated depreciation for business property on Indian reservation	Date of enactment
168(k)(2)	403(a)	Amendments related to Job Creation and Worker Assistance Act of 2002	Property placed in service after September 10, 2001, in tax years ending after that date
168(k)(2)	408(a)(8)	Clerical amendments	Date of enactment
168(k)(2)(D)	408(a)(6)	Clerical amendments	Date of enactment
170(e)(6)(G)	306(a)	Deduction for corporate donations of scientific property and computer technology	Contributions made in tax years beginning after December 31, 2003
170(g)(1)	207(15)	Technical and conforming amendments	Tax years beginning after December 31, 2004
170(g)(3)	207(16)	Technical and conforming amendments	Tax years beginning after December 31, 2004
172(b)(1)(H)	403(b)(1)	Amendments related to Job Creation and Worker Assistance Act of 2002	Net operating losses for tax years ending after December 31, 2000
179A(b)(1)(B)	319(a)	Elimination of phaseout for deduction for clean-fuel vehicle property for 2004 and 2005	Property placed in service after December 31, 2003
198(h)	308(a)	Expensing of environmental remediation costs	Expenditures paid or incurred after December 31, 2003
213(a)	207(17)	Technical and conforming amendments	Tax years beginning after December 31, 2004
213(d)(11)	207(18)	Technical and conforming amendments	Tax years beginning after December 31, 2004
220(d)(2)(A)	207(19)	Technical and conforming amendments	Tax years beginning after December 31, 2004
220(i)(2)-(3)	322(a)	Availability of Medical Savings Accounts	January 1, 2004
220(j)	322(b)	Availability of Medical Savings Accounts—conforming amendments	January 1, 2004
221(d)(4)	207(20)	Technical and conforming amendments	Tax years beginning after December 31, 2004
246(c)	406(f)	Amendments related to Taxpayer Relief Act of 1997	Dividends received or accrued after September 4, 1997, generally
246A(b)(1)	408(a)(9)	Clerical amendments	Date of enactment
263(g)(2)(B)	408(a)(10)	Clerical amendments	Date of enactment
401(a)(26)	407(b)	Amendments related to Small Business Job Protection Act of 1996	Years beginning after December 31, 1996
403(a)(4)(B)	404(e)	Amendments related to Economic growth and Tax Relief Reconciliation Act of 2001	Distributions after December 31, 2001
403(b)(7)(A)	408(a)(11)	Clerical amendments	Date of enactment
408(a)(1)	408(a)(12)	Clerical amendments	Date of enactment
408(n)(2)	408(a)(13)	Clerical amendments	Date of enactment

¶20,001

Code Sec.	Act Sec.	Act Provision Subject	Effective Date
408(p)(6)(A)	404(d)	Amendments related to Economic growth and Tax Relief Reconciliation Act of 2001	Tax years beginning after December 31, 2001
411(a)(12)(B)	408(a)(14)	Clerical amendments	Date of enactment
414(q)(7)	408(a)(15)	Clerical amendments	Date of enactment
415(c)(7)(C)	408(a)(17)	Clerical amendments	Date of enactment
415(d)(4)(A)	404(b)(2)	Amendments related to Economic growth and Tax Relief Reconciliation Act of 2001	Tax years beginning after December 31, 2001
416(i)(1)(A)	408(a)(16)	Clerical amendments	Date of enactment
529(c)(5)(B)	406(a)	Amendments related to Taxpayer Relief Act of 1997	Transfers made after August 5, 1997
529(e)(2)(B)	207(21)	Technical and conforming amendments	Tax years beginning after December 31, 2004
530(d)(2)(C)	404(a)	Amendments related to Economic growth and Tax Relief Reconciliation Act of 2001	Tax years beginning after December 31, 2001
530(d)(4)(B)	406(b)	Amendments related to Taxpayer Relief Act of 1997	Tax years beginning after December 31, 1997
613A(c)(6)(H)	314(a)	Taxable income limit on percentage depletion for oil and natural gas produced from marginal properties	Tax years beginning after December 31, 2003
691(c)(4)	402(a)(4)	Amendments related to Jobs and Growth Tax Relief Reconciliation Act of 2003	Tax years beginning after December 31, 2002, generally
854(b)(1)	402(a)(5)(A)-(B)	Amendments related to Jobs and Growth Tax Relief Reconciliation Act of 2003	Tax years ending after December 31, 2002, generally
854(b)(2)	402(a)(5)	Amendments related to Jobs and Growth Tax Relief Reconciliation Act of 2003	Tax years ending after December 31, 2002, generally
854(b)(5)	402(a)(5)(D)	Amendments related to Jobs and Growth Tax Relief Reconciliation Act of 2003	Tax years ending after December 31, 2002, generally
857(c)(2)	402(a)(5)(E)-(F)	Amendments related to Jobs and Growth Tax Relief Reconciliation Act of 2003	Tax years ending after December 31, 2002, generally
901(k)	406(g)	Amendments related to Taxpayer Relief Act of 1997	Dividends paid or accrued after September 4, 1997
904(h)	312(b)(1)	Allowance of nonrefundable personal credits against regular and minimum tax liability—conforming provisions	Tax years beginning after December 31, 2003
1033(h)(3)	408(a)(7)	Clerical amendments	Date of enactment
1234B(c)	405(a)(1)	Amendments related to Community Renewal Tax Relief Act of 2000	December 21, 2000
1256(g)(6)	405(a)(2)	Amendments related to Community Renewal Tax Relief Act of 2000	December 21, 2000
1259(c)(2)-(3)	406(e)	Amendments related to Taxpayer Relief Act of 1997	Constructive sales after June 8, 1997, generally
1296(h)	408(a)(19)	Clerical amendments	Date of enactment
1377(b)	407(a)	Amendments related to Small Business Job Protection Act of 1996	Determinations after December 31, 1996

Code Sec.	Act Sec.	Act Provision Subject	Effective Date
1397E(e)(1)	304(a)	Qualified zone academy bonds	Obligations issued after December 31, 2003
1397E(i)	406(c)	Amendments related to Taxpayer Relief Act of 1997	Obligations issued after December 31, 1997
1400(f)	310(a)	Tax incentives for investment in the District of Columbia—Designation of zone	January 1, 2004
1400A(b)	310(b)	Tax incentives for investment in the District of Columbia—Tax-exempt economic development bonds	Obligations issued after date of enactment
1400B(b)	310(c)(1)	Tax incentives for investment in the District of Columbia—Zero percent capital gains rate	January 1, 2004
1400B(e)(2)	310(c)(2)(A)	Tax incentives for investment in the District of Columbia—Zero percent capital gains rate—conforming amendments	January 1, 2004
1400B(g)(2)	310(c)(2)(B)	Tax incentives for investment in the District of Columbia—Zero percent capital gains rate—conforming amendments	January 1, 2004
1400C(i)	310(d)	Tax incentives for investment in the District of Columbia—First-time homebuyer credit	January 1, 2004
1400F(d)	310(c)(2)(C)	Tax incentives for investment in the District of Columbia—Zero percent capital gains rate—conforming amendments	January 1, 2004
1400L(a)-(c)	403(c)(1)-(3)	Amendments related to Job Creation and Worker Assistance Act of 2002	March 9, 2002
1400L(d)-(e)(1)	309(a)-(b)	Certain New York Liberty Zone benefits	Date of enactment
1400L(e)(2)	309(c)	Certain New York Liberty Zone benefits	March 9, 2002
1400L(f)(2)	403(c)(4)	Amendments related to Job Creation and Worker Assistance Act of 2002	March 9, 2002
2032A(c)(7)(D)	207(22)	Technical and conforming amendments	Tax years beginning after December 31, 2004
2057(d)(2)(B)	207(23)	Technical and conforming amendments	Tax years beginning after December 31, 2004
4972(c)(6)(A)	404(c)	Amendments related to Economic growth and Tax Relief Reconciliation Act of 2001	Years beginning after December 31, 2001
4973(c)	408(a)(22)	Clerical amendments	Date of enactment
4978(a)(2)	408(a)(23)	Clerical amendments	Date of enactment
5064(b)(3)	408(a)(7)	Clerical amendments	Date of enactment
5708(a)	408(a)(7)	Clerical amendments	Date of enactment
6103(d)(5)	311(a)	Disclosure of tax information to facilitate combined employment tax reporting	Date of enactment
6103(i)(3)(C)	320(a)	Disclosures relating to terrorist activities	Disclosures on or after date of enactment
6103(i)(7)(A)	320(b)	Disclosures relating to terrorist activities—Disclosure of taxpayer identity to law enforcement agencies investigating terrorism	Disclosures on or after January 23, 2002
6103(i)(7)(E)	320(a)	Disclosures relating to terrorist activities	Disclosures on or after date of enactment

Code Sec.	Act Sec.	Act Provision Subject	Effective Date
6103(l)(13)(D)	317	Disclosure of return information relating to student loans	Date of enactment
6103(p)(4)	408(a)(24)	Clerical amendments	Date of enactment
7652(f)(1)	305(a)	Cover over of tax on distilled spirits	Articles brought into the United States after December 31, 2003
7701(a)(17)	207(24)	Technical and conforming amendments	Tax years beginning after December 31, 2004
7702B(f)(2)(C)	207(25)	Technical and conforming amendments	Tax years beginning after December 31, 2004
7703(b)(1)	207(26)	Technical and conforming amendments	Tax years beginning after December 31, 2004
8021(f)(2)	321(a)	Joint review of strategic plans and budget for the Internal Revenue Service	Date of enactment
8022(3)(C)	321(b)	Joint review of strategic plans and budget for the Internal Revenue Service—Report	Date of enactment
9812(f)	302(a)	Parity in the application of certain limits to mental health benefits	Date of enactment
...	105	Application of EGTRRA sunset to this title	Date of enactment
...	302(b)	Parity in the application of certain limits to mental health benefits—ERISA	Date of enactment
...	302(c)	Parity in the application of certain limits to mental health benefits—PHSA	Date of enactment
...	321(c)	Joint review of strategic plans and budget for the Internal Revenue Service—Time for joint review	Date of enactment
...	402(a)(6)	Amendments related to Jobs and Growth Tax Relief Reconciliation Act of 2003	May 28, 2003
...	403(b)(3)	Amendments related to Job Creation and Worker Assistance Act of 2002	March 9, 2002
...	403(d)	Amendments related to Job Creation and Worker Assistance Act of 2002	March 9, 2002
...	403(e)	Amendments related to Job Creation and Worker Assistance Act of 2002	March 9, 2002
...	408(a)(18)	Clerical amendments	Date of enactment
...	408(a)(20)	Clerical amendments	Date of enactment
...	408(a)(21)	Clerical amendments	Date of enactment
...	408(b)(1)	Clerical amendments	Date of enactment
...	408(b)(2)	Clerical amendments	Date of enactment
...	408(b)(3)	Clerical amendments	Date of enactment
...	408(b)(4)	Clerical amendments	Date of enactment
...	408(b)(5)	Clerical amendments	Date of enactment
...	408(b)(6)	Clerical amendments	Date of enactment
...	408(b)(7)	Clerical amendments	Date of enactment
...	408(b)(8)	Clerical amendments	Date of enactment
...	408(b)(9)	Clerical amendments	Date of enactment

¶20,001

¶ 25,001

Code Section to Explanation Table

¶ 25,005
# Code Sections Added, Amended or Repealed

The list below notes all the Code Sections or subsections of the Internal Revenue Code that were added, amended or repealed by the Working Families Tax Relief Act of 2004 (H.R. 1308). The first column indicates the Code Section added, amended or repealed and the second column indicates the Act Section.

Working Families Tax Relief Act of 2004

Code Sec.	Act Sec.	Code Sec.	Act Sec.
1(f)(8)	101(c)	45A(c)(3)	404(b)(1)
1(g)(7)(B)(ii)(II)	408(a)(1)	45A(f)	315
1(h)(1)(D)(i)	402(a)(1)	45C(b)(1)(D)	301(a)(2)
1(h)(6)(A)(ii)(I)-(II)	408(a)(2)(A)-(B)	51(c)(4)	303(a)(1)
1(h)(11)(B)(iii)(I)	402(a)(2)(A)-(C)	51(i)(1)(A)-(B)	207(5)(A)
1(h)(11)(D)(ii)	402(a)(3)	51(i)(1)(C)	207(5)(B)
1(i)(1)(B)(i)	101(d)(1)	51A(f)	303(a)(2)
1(i)(1)(C)	101(d)(2)	55(b)(3)(B)	406(d)
2(a)(1)(B)(i)	207(1)	55(d)(1)(A)-(B)	103(a)
2(b)(1)(A)(i)	202(a)	56(d)(1)(A)(i)(I)	403(b)(4)(A)
2(b)(2)(A)-(D)	202(b)(1)	56(d)(1)(A)(ii)(I)	403(b)(4)(B)(i)-(ii)
2(b)(3)(B)(i)-(ii)	202(b)(2)	62(a)(2)(D)	307(a)
21(a)(1)	203(a)	63(c)(2)	101(b)(1)
21(b)(1)	203(b)	63(c)(4)	101(b)(2)(A)
21(e)(1)	203(c)	63(c)(7)	101(b)(2)(B)
21(e)(5)	207(2)(B)	72(f)	408(a)(4)
21(e)(5)(A)	207(2)(A)	72(t)(2)(D)(i)(III)	207(6)
21(e)(6)(B)	207(3)	72(t)(7)(A)(iii)	207(7)
24(a)	101(a)	105(b)	207(9)
24(c)(1)	204(a)	105(c)(1)	207(9)
24(c)(2)	204(b)	120(d)(4)	207(10)
24(d)(1)	104(a)	125(e)(1)(D)	207(11)
24(d)(1)(B)(i)	102(a)	129(c)(2)	207(12)
25B(c)(2)(B)	207(4)	132(h)(2)(B)	207(13)
26(a)(2)	312(a)(1)-(2)	138(b)	408(a)(5)(C)
26(b)(2)	408(a)(5)(A)	138(c)(2)	408(a)(5)(D)
26(b)(2)(Q)-(S)	401(a)(1)	138(c)(2)(C)(i)	408(a)(5)(E)
30(b)(2)	318(a)	138(f)	408(a)(5)(F)
32(c)(1)(C)-(G)	205(b)(1)	138	408(a)(5)(A)
32(c)(2)(B)(iv)-(vi)	104(b)(1)-(3)	138	408(a)(5)(B)
32(c)(3)	205(a)	151(c)	206
32(c)(4)	205(b)(2)	152	201
32(m)	205(b)(3)	153(1)-(4)	207(14)
35(g)(3)	401(a)(2)	165(i)(1)	408(a)(7)(A)
41(h)(1)(B)	301(a)(1)	165(k)	408(a)(7)(B)
42(d)(2)(D)(iii)(I)	408(a)(3)	168(j)(8)	316
42(i)(3)(D)(ii)(I)	207(8)	168(k)(2)(B)(i)	403(a)(1)
45(c)(3)(A)-(C)	313(a)	168(k)(2)(D)(ii)	403(a)(2)(B)

¶25,005

¶ 25,010

Table of Amendments to Other Acts

Working Families Tax Relief Act of 2004

Amended Act Sec.	H.R. 1308 Sec.	Par. (¶)	Amended Act Sec.	H.R. 1308 Sec.	Par. (¶)
Jobs and Growth Tax Relief Reconciliation Act of 2003 (JGTRRA) (P.L. 108-27)			531(b)	408(b)(6)	7035
			619(c)(3)	408(b)(7)	7035
302(f)(2)	402(a)(6)	7025	652(b)(3)	408(b)(9)	7035
Job Creation and Worker Assistance Act of 2002 (P.L. 107-147)			**Community Renewal Tax Relief Act of 2000 (P.L. 106-554)**		
102(c)(2)	403(b)(3)	7030	156(c)	408(b)(1)	7035
411(c)(2)(B)	403(e)	7030	**Employee Retirement Income Security Act of 1974 (P.L. 93-406)**		
Railroad Retirement and Survivors' Improvement Act of 2001 (P.L. 107-90)			203(a)(4)(B)	408(b)(8)	7035
			712(f)	302(b)	7015
204(e)(1)	408(b)(4)	7035	4006(a)(3)(E)(iii)(IV)	403(d)	7030
Public Law 107-22			**Public Health Service Act (P.L. 78-410)**		
1(a)(6)	408(b)(2)	7035	2705(f)	302(c)	7015
1(b)(3)(A)	408(b)(3)	7035			
Economic Growth and Tax Relief Reconciliation Act of 2001 (EGTRRA) (P.L. 107-16)					
412(b)(2)	408(b)(5)	7035			

¶ 25,015

Table of Act Sections Not Amending Internal Revenue Code Sections

Working Families Tax Relief Act of 2004

¶ 25,020

Act Sections Amending Code Sections

Working Families Tax Relief Act of 2004

Act Sec.	Code Sec.	Act Sec.	Code Sec.
101(a)	24(a)	207(17)	213(a)
101(b)(1)	63(c)(2)	207(18)	213(d)(11)
101(b)(2)(A)	63(c)(4)	207(19)	220(d)(2)(A)
101(b)(2)(B)	63(c)(7)	207(20)	221(d)(4)
101(c)	1(f)(8)	207(21)	529(e)(2)(B)
101(d)(1)	1(i)(1)(B)(i)	207(22)	2032A(c)(7)(D)
101(d)(2)	1(i)(1)(C)	207(23)	2057(d)(2)(B)
102(a)	24(d)(1)(B)(i)	207(24)	7701(a)(17)
103(a)	55(d)(1)(A)-(B)	207(25)	7702B(f)(2)(C)(iii)
104(a)	24(d)(1)	207(26)(A)-(B)	7703(b)(1)
104(b)(1)-(3)	32(c)(2)(B)(iv)-(vi)	301(a)(1)	41(h)(1)(B)
201	152	301(a)(2)	45C(b)(1)(D)
202(a)	2(b)(1)(A)(i)	302(a)(1)-(2)	9812(f)(1)-(3)
202(b)(1)	2(b)(2)(A)-(D)	303(a)(1)	51(c)(4)
202(b)(2)	2(b)(3)(B)(i)-(ii)	303(a)(2)	51A(f)
203(a)	21(a)(1)	304(a)	1397E(e)(1)
203(b)	21(b)(1)	305(a)	7652(f)(1)
203(c)	21(e)(1)	306(a)	170(e)(6)(G)
204(a)	24(c)(1)	307(a)	62(a)(2)(D)
204(b)	24(c)(2)	308(a)	198(h)
205(a)	32(c)(3)	309(a)	1400L(d)(2)(D)
205(b)(1)	32(c)(1)(C)-(G)	309(b)	1400L(e)(1)
205(b)(2)	32(c)(4)	309(c)	1400L(e)(2)(B)
205(b)(3)	32(m)	310(a)	1400(f)
206	151(c)	310(b)	1400A(b)
207(1)	2(a)(1)(B)(i)	310(c)(1)	1400B(b)
207(2)(A)	21(e)(5)(A)	310(c)(2)(A)(i)-(ii)	1400B(e)(2)
207(2)(B)	21(e)(5)	310(c)(2)(B)	1400B(g)(2)
207(3)	21(e)(6)(B)	310(c)(2)(C)	1400F(d)
207(4)	25B(c)(2)(B)	310(d)	1400C(i)
207(5)(A)	51(i)(1)(A)-(B)	311(a)	6103(d)(5)
207(5)(B)	51(i)(1)(C)	312(a)(1)-(2)	26(a)(2)
207(6)	72(t)(2)(D)(i)(III)	312(b)(1)	904(h)
207(7)	72(t)(7)(A)(iii)	313(a)	45(c)(3)(A)-(C)
207(8)	42(i)(3)(D)(ii)(I)	314(a)	613A(c)(6)(H)
207(9)	105(b)	315	45A(f)
207(9)	105(c)(1)	316	168(j)(8)
207(10)	120(d)(4)	317	6103(l)(13)(D)
207(11)	125(e)(1)(D)	318(a)	30(b)(2)
207(12)	129(c)(2)	319(a)	179A(b)(1)(B)
207(13)	132(h)(2)(B)	320(a)	6103(i)(3)(C)(iv)
207(14)	153(1)-(4)	320(a)	6103(i)(7)(E)
207(15)	170(g)(1)	320(b)	6103(i)(7)(A)(v)
207(16)	170(g)(3)	321(a)	8021(f)(2)

¶25,020

¶ 29,001

Sunset Provisions

The Working Families Tax Relief Act of 2004 contains one provision that sunsets some of the changes made by the new law. Provisions in Title I of the 2004 Act that have been made subject to the sunset in the Economic Growth and Tax Relief Reconciliation Act of 2001 (EGTRRA) (P.L. 107-16) will not apply to tax years beginning after December 31, 2010. The inclusion of the sunset language means that Congress will eventually need to pass legislation that restores the provisions before the scheduled expiration date. If Congress takes no action, the expiration of the provisions will take effect.

Specifically, Act Section 105 of the Working Families Tax Relief Act of 2004 provides:

SEC. 105. APPLICATION OF EGTRRA SUNSET TO THIS TITLE

Each amendment by this title [Title I of the 2004 Act] shall be subject to title IX of the Economic Growth and Tax Relief Reconciliation Act of 2001 to the same extent and in the same manner as the provision of such Act to which such amendment relates.

Act Section 109 of the Economic Growth and Tax Relief Reconciliation Act of 2001 (P.L. 107-16), as amended by P.L. 107-358, §2, provides:

SEC. 901. SUNSET OF PROVISIONS OF ACT

(a) IN GENERAL.—All provisions of, and amendments made by, this Act shall not apply—

(1) to taxable, plan, or limitation years beginning after December 31, 2010, or

(2) in the case of title V, to estates of decedents dying, gifts made, or generation skipping transfers, after December 31, 2010.

(b) APPLICATION OF CERTAIN LAWS.—The Internal Revenue Code of 1986 and the Employee Retirement Income Security Act of 1974 shall be applied and administered to years, estates, gifts, and transfers described in subsection (a) as if the provisions and amendments described in subsection (a) had never been enacted.

(c) EXCEPTION.—Subsection (a) shall not apply to section 803 (relating to no federal income tax on restitution received by victims of the Nazi regime or their heirs or estates).

¶ 30,050
Clerical Amendments

The Working Families Tax Relief Act of 2004 makes numerous clerical amendments to the Internal Revenue Code and various non-Code provisions of previous tax acts (Act Sec. 408 of the 2004 Act).

The following Code Sections are amended to reflect these changes:

(1) Code Sec. 1(g)(7)(B)(ii)(II), relating to the election to claim certain unearned income of a child on the parent's return;

(2) Code Sec. 1(h)(6)(A)(ii), relating to the amount of unrecaptured Code Sec. 1250 gain subject to the capital gains tax rate;

(3) Code Sec. 42(d)(2)(D)(iii)(I), relating to eligible basis for existing buildings for purposes of determining the low-income housing credit amount;

(4) Code Sec. 72(f), relating to special rules for computing the amount of employees' contributions to annuities;

(5) Code Secs. 26(b)(2), and 138, providing a new name for Medicare+Choice MSAs (see further details at ¶359);

(6) Code Secs. 165(i)(1), 165(k), 1033(h)(3), 5064(b)(3) and 5708(a), relating to disaster losses and disaster areas;

(7) Code Sec. 168(k)(2), relating to the special depreciation allowance for property acquired before January 1, 2005;

(8) Code Sec. 246A(b)(1), relating to the reduction of the dividend received deduction where a dividend is paid on debt-financed portfolio stock;

(9) Code Sec. 263(g)(2)(B)(ii), relating to interest and carrying costs allocated to personal property that is part of a straddle;

(10) Code Sec. 403(b)(7)(A)(ii), relating to custodial accounts for regulated investment company stock;

(11) Code Sec. 408(a)(1), relating to contributions to individual retirement accounts (IRAs);

(12) Code Sec. 408(n)(2), relating to the definition of a "bank" as used in the IRA rules;

(13) Code Sec. 411(a)(12)(B), relating to vesting rules for matching contributions to retirement plans;

(14) Code Sec. 414(q)(7), relating to the definition of a "highly compensated employee;"

(15) Code Sec. 415(c)(7)(C), relating to the limit on contributions to retirement plans on behalf of foreign missionaries;

(16) Code Sec. 416(i)(1)(A), relating to the definition of a "key employee;"

(17) Code Sec. 1296(h), relating to the impact of the mark-to-market election for marketable securities on the qualification of a corporation as a regulated investment company;

(18) Code Sec. 4973(c), relating to the tax on excess contributions to Code Sec. 403(b) plans;

(19) Code Sec. 4978(a)(2), relating to the tax on dispositions by ESOPs and cooperatives; and

(20) Code Sec. 6103(p)(4), relating to the statutory safeguards concerning the disclosure of returns and return information.

Clerical amendments were also made by Act Sec. 408 of the 2004 Act to the following non-Code provisions contained in prior legislation:

(1) Act Sec. 156(c) of the Community Renewal Tax Relief Act of 2000 (P.L. 106-554), relating to the final report to be issued by the Community Renewal Advisory Council;

(2) Act Secs. 1(a)(6) and 1(b)(3)(A) of P.L. 107-22, relating to the renaming of education individual retirement accounts as Coverdell education savings accounts;

(3) Act Sec. 204(e)(1) of the Railroad Retirement and Survivors' Improvement Act of 2001 (P.L. 107-90), relating to the tier 2 railroad retirement tax rate adjustments;

(4) Act Sec. 412(b)(2) of the Economic Growth and Tax Relief Reconciliation Act of 2001 (P.L. 107-16), relating to the income limitation for the student loan interest deduction;

(5) Act Sec. 531(b) of the Economic Growth and Tax Relief Reconciliation Act of 2001 (P.L. 107-16), relating to the reduction of the credit for state death taxes;

(6) Act Sec. 619(c)(3) of the Economic Growth and Tax Relief Reconciliation Act of 2001 (P.L. 107-16), relating to the credit for pension plan startup costs of small employers;

(7) Act Sec. 652(b)(3) of the Economic Growth and Tax Relief Reconciliation Act of 2001 (P.L. 107-16), relating to the maximum contribution deduction rules for defined benefit plans; and

(8) Section 203(a)(4)(B) of the Employee Retirement Income Security Act of 1974 (P.L. 93-406), relating to vesting rules for matching contributions to retirement plans.

★ *Effective date.* No specific effective date is provided by the 2004 Act. These provisions are, therefore, considered effective on the date of the enactment of the Act.

INDEX

References are to explanation paragraph (¶) numbers.